THE NORTHERN
MAGUS

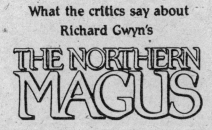

THE NORTHERN MAGUS

Pierre Trudeau and Canadians

by Richard Gwyn

edited by Sandra Gwyn

PaperJacks LTD.

Markham, Ontario, Canada

A CANADIAN

One of a series of Canadian books
published by PaperJacks Ltd.

The photograph of Trudeau and Hébert which appears in the insert
of this book is from *Two Innocents in Red China* and is used by
permission of Oxford University Press.

McClelland and Stewart edition published in 1980
PaperJacks edition published in October, 1981

ISBN 0-7701-0201-8

To my father
Philip Jermy-Gwyn, 1899-1976

Contents

*These chapters, which deal with themes such as bilingualism, foreign affairs, and Trudeau's marriage, encompass the period 1968-80.

Author's Note

I started work on this book late in November 1979, soon after Pierre Trudeau's resignation as Liberal leader, to be interrupted by circumstances over which I had no control–but then, neither did the Prime Minister of the day. I resumed writing and interviewing in mid-March, and finished in mid-July.

Subconsciously, at least, I began work much earlier, gathering material and insights from three different perspectives: from 1968 to 1970, as executive assistant to the Hon. Eric Kierans; from 1970 to 1973, as a civil servant with a long-winded title; and from 1973, as a columnist for the *Toronto Star*.

The book is neither a definitive biography nor a work of historical scholarship. As a further limitation, Trudeau is still around, which makes him a moving target. I considered waiting until he had finally and irrevocably retired, but concluded that aside from the risk of having to wait for one year at a minimum, and for a decade at a tentative maximum, the difference between writing about a politician in power and one out of it is the difference between doing a live and a taped television show: when live on TV, sheer terror produces a surge of adrenalin; being recorded on tape, you know that if you goof, no one cares but the cost accountants.

The book's objectives are two-fold: to describe the kind of person Trudeau is; to describe the kind of Prime Minister he has been. The first objective is the more ambitious; for Trudeau has devoted a lifetime to evading being defined. As an encouragement, though, a friend of his responded to my describing how I saw him by saying, "I think you have caught part of him." The second objective is more conventional. My judgements about the rightness or wrongness of Trudeau's policy decisions are no better than the next person's. However, because a recurring theme here is the nature of the relationship between Trudeau and Canadians, I have tried to present my opinions in stereoscopic perspective: before looking back at events with the sickly glare of hindsight, I have made a deliberate effort to set these events into the context and mood of the times in which they happened.

The book contains a fair amount of new information, from the identity of the persons who actually convinced Trudeau to run for the Liberal leadership in 1968, to the circumstances of Trudeau's return as leader in 1979. To anticipate potential criticism, I stand ready to plead guilty to a reporter's temptation to give such new information more prominence in chronicling events than future historians are likely to do. The events following the February 1980 election are described only in summary, partly because more time will be needed to cast them into perspective, but also because while they were happening I was functioning like a mole with its forepaws glued to a typewriter.

In the course of research, I interviewed approximately one hundred people: cabinet ministers, M.P.s, Prime Ministerial and ministerial aides, party officials, civil servants, and personal friends of Trudeau. All were exceedingly co-operative; several surprised me by their candour. Only one individual declined to be interviewed: Pierre Trudeau.

The author's note in my two earlier books contained the sentence, "This book could not, and would not, have been written but for my wife, Sandra." So now, does this one. The difference is that this time, the title page, as I believe is unusual, identifies her contribution properly. Every word that you are about to read, other than those contained in this paragraph, has passed on from my typewriter to hers; some passages have emerged reborn, others have been enriched, others have been consigned to an ever-growing pile of drafts in our basement. We have laboured together, in love.

Leaving aside those persons whose prospects for successful careers will be enhanced by my not mentioning them, I would like to single out four individuals for thanks. Alrick Huebener, my researcher, has been diligent in digging out facts, scrupulous in checking them, and a zealot at the xerox machine. Denis Harvey, Editor-in-Chief of the *Toronto Star* encouraged me to undertake the project, and made it possible for me to do so by arranging a salaried sabbatical. Erik Spicer, Librarian of Parliament, extended to me the quite exceptional facilities of his institution; the efficiency and enthusiasm of his staff of researchers have never failed to awe me. I am grateful also to Jack McClelland for bullying me until I stopped inventing excuses and got down to a long-delayed project.

'A last note. Apart from interviews, the material for this book has been culled from conventional sources: books, newspaper and magazine articles, speeches, transcripts of interviews and press conferences, government reports, and studies by various public and private agencies. To avoid cluttering up the text with numerals, I have not identified the source of all quotations, only the major ones. In the same reportorial style, I have not provided a bibliography. The motherlode, though, can be found in my basement.

R.G.
Ottawa, July 1980

Prologue

"What do you call a great magician?"
"A man who can stand stark naked in the midst of a crowd and keep it gaping while he manipulates a few cards, or coins or billiard balls. I can do that, and I can do it better than anybody today, or anybody who has ever lived."

Robertson Davies
World of Wonders

Pierre Elliott Trudeau often seems more like the hero of a novel about the occult than a Canadian Prime Minister. He looks distant, pagan, ageless, like the photographs of Nijinsky: the aquiline nose and high Slavic cheekbones, the taut, sculptured face, the ambiguous grace. His countenance, chilly and cerebral, flared nostrils hinting at a sneer, gives him a natural, aristocratic quality of dominion over others. Above all, there are the pale and predatory eyes, that tell at once of skepticism, inquiry, ferocity. "Eyes very blue, very bright," as a Sudanese child once said of General Gordon of Khartoum, "and I frighted when I see eyes." Not to mention the voice: languid and sing-song, like a monk chanting the responses to a Latin mass, yet encompassing within its cadences the bullhorn of a parade square. A man smaller than you expect, and slighter, but with the presence and bearing of a pro-consul.

Trudeau is central to the Canadian imagination as no other Prime Minister has been before him. Indeed, among all the democratically elected leaders in all countries in all the years since World War Two, he has commanded the attention of the crowd for longer than all but five.* Indelible images of Trudeau, over the dozen years of his stewardship, are part of our collective memory. He slides down the banisters at Lancaster House; he yo-yo's to the cameras in Sweden. He stands alone and

*The top five: Tage Erlander of Sweden (twenty-three years); Einar Gerhardsen of Norway (twenty); Jawarharlal Nehru of India (eighteen); Robert Menzies of Australia (seventeen); Konrad Adenauer of West Germany (fourteen). By winning again in 1980, Trudeau ensured that he would out-distance the twelve years of both Charles de Gaulle of France and B.J. Vorster of South Africa.

unflinching on the reviewing stand at Montreal's 1968 St. Jean Baptiste Day parade as the Coke bottles shatter round him. He snarls "Just watch me" at the television cameras, at the height of the 1970 October Crisis. He elopes with a flower child, who bears him the first two of their three sons on Christmas Day.

Who else, without losing a shred of dignity, could endure the public humiliation of a marriage unravelling in the pages of *People* and *Playgirl*? Who else, without losing credibility, could announce his resignation and a month later, tear it up and then go on to win the easiest victory of his career? One incident in that 1980 campaign conveys the essence of Trudeau's mystique. "I felt I was pulled along," wrote Carole Treiser, a twenty-four-year-old cub reporter for the *Sherbrooke Record*, after Trudeau had persuaded her to follow him into a motel sauna, wearing only a towel. "He was the elusive jester who dared us to catch him and laughed as we tried."

Four years ago, trying to come to terms with Trudeau's mystique in a 1976 magazine piece, at a time when he had fallen further in the polls than any Prime Minister before him, so that the notion of his ever being re-elected Prime Minister seemed impossible, I built an escape hatch in the last paragraph. "There is a quality in the man that persists," I wrote. I couldn't define the quality then. Now I understand: he is a great magician.

* * *

Magicians, by nature of their trade, deal mostly in ephemera. So often, do rulers. Between the esteem in which they are held and their actual accomplishments, no certain relationship exists. The Americans loved John F. Kennedy as perhaps no other president since Lincoln, yet hindsight has reduced his record to the insignificant. The English idolized Richard the Lionhearted; he in return detested them and their damp little island, and wasted its substance in vainglorious crusades. In the Middle Ages, no monarch was more revered than Prester John; to his great benefit, he didn't exist, so that accounts of his victories and virtues could never be contradicted.

Up to 1980, when he won his miraculous second chance, Trudeau's accomplishments were scanty. Bilingualism. Petro-Canada. Some initiatives in foreign policy. A daring energy policy, in 1973-74, which he later emasculated. Certain overdue reforms to the structure of government, although these turned out to be prelude to "losing financial control" in the words of the auditor general. Even a supportive biographer, George Radwanski, writing in 1978, could accord him no higher ranking than that of "unfulfilled" as opposed to "failed" Prime Minister. In half the time, Lester Pearson had done more, and John Diefenbaker had done almost as much.

The riddles run on and on. Repeatedly, Trudeau has denounced Quebec nationalism as "tribalism"; yet this tribalism alone has kept him in power. He was first elected and then consistently re-elected, to "save Canada"; yet the country has come closer to fracturing during his term than it has ever done before. The record book will show Trudeau as having been Canada's most popular politician in this century; yet, in fact, most of his own time he was less popular than his heir-apparent, John Turner, whom circumstances, and Trudeau, prevented from ever reaching for the crown. Trudeau's international reputation dates from October 1970 when, in an act of daring other leaders applauded and envied, he became the first western leader, except for David Ben-Gurion, to refuse to yield to the blackmail of terrorists; yet in the minds of many Canadians the memory of that same act remains an incurable, shameful wound.

This book is an attempt to describe some of these riddles and to suggest ways in which some may begin to be unravelled. Many riddles, though, can never be resolved, except through the opaque and tentative processes of psychoanalysis and of mass psychology. For instance, in trying to come to terms with Trudeau's conduct during the October Crisis, it is as important to know that once engaged in a fight, *any* fight, he refuses to yield an inch in his determination to win it (and to wonder why this is so) as it is to know about and sympathize with his very real administrative difficulties at that time, such as the lack of knowledge of the police forces, about what often was really happening on the streets. Similarly, by his almost obsessive rhetorical overkill, Trudeau has manufactured quite unnecessary difficulties for himself. His "Zap, you're frozen" ridicule of wage and price controls in the 1974 election, for one example; his cheap oil promise of 1980 for another. Once over-committed, Trudeau will never retract. Inability to admit error is usually the mark of a leader with shaky self-esteem – a Richard Nixon, for instance – not at all the behaviour a psychologist would expect from so self-contained and self-motivated a person as Trudeau.

All the Trudeau riddles, solvable or not, are inseparable from the texture of his and our times. The Canada that elected him in 1968 seems nearly as remote, a dozen years later, as World War One, say, seemed in 1968. Nothing has turned out as either he or we expected. Trudeau, in the beginning, had to contend with what then seemed a series of transformational social changes—each interacting on all the others: the Rebellion of Youth, which for a while made all other forms of rebellion, including urban terrorism, seem glamorous; the defensive-aggressive nationalism of all cultural minorities, from Québécois to Inuit and Indians; the confused, agonized search for some counterpoise to technocratic materialism—a search that made dropouts of some, cultists of others, and in its final betrayal produced the Me Generation. From roughly the mid-point of his term to now, the issues facing Trudeau have been of an entirely different order: social narcissism and its political concomitant, single-issue politics and, overarching these, a ''siege economy'' in which Canada, like most other western countries, has been caught in the quadruple vice-grip of inflation, slackened productivity, de-industrialization, and debt accumulated on the outdated premise that our income would expand exponentially, for ever. Trying to comprehend Trudeau's astonishing staying power in the teeth of events, all roads lead back to magicianship, to the mythic bond between him and Canadians.

* * *

Max Weber, the German sociologist, was the first to use the word, ''charisma.'' Since the Oxford English Dictionary defines charisma as ''a special gift or favour vouchsafed by God,'' this amounts to employing the inexplicable to explain the inexplicable. Tom Wolfe's phrase, ''The Right Stuff,'' from the title of his book about the U.S. astronauts is plainer, simpler, and closer to the truth. The Right Stuff, as Wolfe defines it, is a macho cool, an Appalachian drawl, grace under pressure. With a brilliant insight, Wolfe goes on to explain why the astronauts were treated, in their hey-day, as demigods by the American public. In their contest with Soviet cosmonauts for victory in the Cold War, these laconic pilots "brought back to life one of the ancient superstitions of warfare: Single Combat."

For the sake of his army, or of his tribe, the single combatant goes out alone against the opposing champion. Achilles against Hector. David against Goliath. Richard Coeur de Lion against Saladin. Arthur against Mordred.

Trudeau is *our* Single Combat warrior. He spent much of his boyhood and early manhood training for this kind of battle, first with his fists, later with his tongue and his brain. As Prime Minister, like all solitary champions, Trudeau has assumed a role in which he either wins all for his people or loses all for himself. We, like all followers, have transferred to him our collective burden; indeed, the reason Joe Clark fell so fast may well be that, as a smaller-than-life leader, Clark lacked the credibility to be a scapegoat for our hostilities. Like voyeurs, we have watched Trudeau sally out on our behalf. Against René Lévesque. Against, part of the time, Claude Ryan during his "special status" phase. Against FLQ terrorists. Against, his heir-presumptuous, John Turner. Against provincial premiers, who "want to reduce Confederation to ten self-governing entities." Against Alberta. Against abstract opponents like inflation, which he personalized by promising to "wrestle it to the ground." Against Margaret, the most painful battle of all, and yet the one Canadians found easiest to identify with.

Since boyhood, when he scrapped on the streets of Outremont, Trudeau has never lost a single fight nor, to anyone's recollection, has he lost an argument. Always, for him, winning has been the only thing; each victory another triumphal demonstration of his virility. Only one opponent, while the crowd gaped, has held Trudeau at least to a draw. Margaret.

Along with the lure of the lone hero, Trudeau bewitches by the uncanny appeal – those two Christmas day sons, for the most dramatic manifestation – of the sorcerer.

James Frazer has written in *The Golden Bough* that among the ancients the rise of the sorcerer "place[d] the control of affairs in the hands of the ablest man; it shifted the balance of power from the many to the one; it substituted a monarchy for a democracy."

Television has retribalized us. Amid anomie and urban rootlessness and free-floating liberation, the screen alone speaks to our collective unconscious nowadays. From the day we first spotted him, winning in Single Combat against Quebec Premier Daniel Johnson at the 1968 Federal-Provincial Conference and vaulting from there straight into the Liberal leadership, Trudeau has used television to command our allegiance. Among those most attuned to television, the young, this allegiance has been, as Trudeau moves into his sixties, the most fervent of all.

For television's masque, Trudeau's own mask is precisely right. The right voice, the right gestures, the right eyes. Dr. Marshall McLuhan, who made the phrase "the medium is the message" part of the language, has called Trudeau "the first Post-Renaissance Man"; he projects precisely the Right Stuff.

"Avoid their wish to define you." In her one-person tour de force, *Maggie and Pierre*, the actress Linda Griffiths has Trudeau explain how, all these years, he has successfully evaded each and every journalist who has tried to pin him down. Some look at him and see arrogance; others say he is shy. Some see him as cold and rude; others as courteous and considerate. Most people who meet him are awed by his mind; yet some dismiss him as an intellectual dilettante who toys with the fashionable notion of the moment, whether Participatory Democracy or Galbraithian economics.

Out of all these contradictions, eventually, a common thread begins to emerge. Trudeau is *aware* of the contradictions; he *enjoys* them; he *perpetuates* them. They are devices for attracting attention to himself, just as, long ago as a bachelor-intellectual in Montreal, he would sometimes slip away from the chattering crowd and very quietly, so quietly that everyone would notice, stand on his head in a corner. They are devices also for diverting attention toward himself as an entertainer, away from his real self.

A performer who can keep a crowd gaping year after year must also have an extra dimension. He must be able to provide it with something that he and the crowd know it lacks. Thomas Carlyle proclaimed (his capitals) that "Society is founded on Hero-Worship." Canadians, at first blush, seem to be an unlikely people to take to worshipping heroes. We are, as we all tell each other constantly, a cautious, conservative people, God-fearing, tax-paying, weighed down by insurance policies.

Yet our historical record suggests that we have an instinct for hero-worship. For almost half the years since Confederation, we have elected leaders who possessed charisma, or the Right Stuff, or magic: John A. Macdonald, Wilfrid Laurier; John Diefenbaker; Trudeau.

Perhaps we use heroes to fill our political centre because, otherwise, the centre is soft. Many of the issues which most affect us – economics, defence, mass culture – are decided outside our borders. Because we have sublimated the class struggle into regional rivalries which redirect to an enemy without the competition between economic and social groups within each region, our domestic political drama lacks resonance. Except for French-English relations, the one, home-grown issue which can alter decisively the way we live our lives, our politics, if it is not about personality, is about almost nothing at all.

Trudeau is a personality, a performer, an actor who needs an audience through which to fulfil himself and who in exchange provides his audience with something it lacks. Martin Goldfarb, the Liberal pollster, believes that Canadians are attracted to Trudeau because we see in him "a man who has lived his dream, and ours."

One last link between Trudeau and Canadians can be suggested. Like most conservative people, we admire people like Trudeau, who are prepared to dare greatly. We also like to think that if we tried, we could do it ourselves. The last time, perhaps the only time we dared to dare greatly together was at Expo '67. For once, a people of whom two-thirds aspire to "survival," in Margaret Atwood's word, and of whom the other third aspire, in their phrase, to "*la survivance*," set off, while the world watched, to fly to the sun.

Trudeau is an icon of that summer of excellence. How much that is excellent that he has accomplished, bilingualism apart, as Prime Minister is beside the point. By keeping him around we keep alive the collective memory of the time of brave hopes when we reached beyond our limits; we also keep alive the hope that someday, somehow, the magician will fly us back to the sun.

1

"A Character That Does Not Scan"

"Man invents himself through exercising his freedom of choices."

Jean Paul Sartre

The instant Pierre Trudeau comes into a room the atmosphere changes. He slips in quietly, almost deferentially, yet everyone knows immediately that he is there, and subtly, willingly, they behave differently. "He sucks in all the oxygen," says one of his oldest friends. Trudeau has always been able to do this. His favourite teacher at Collège Jean de Brébeuf, Père Robert Bernier, has remarked on his ability "to command, even at his age, the total attention without raising his voice."

Trudeau didn't set out to become Prime Minister. Yet from his earliest days he trained himself to dominate others and himself. He did this by constructing a personality, a public persona, a mask to present to the world and to keep it at bay. He used this outer layer to keep others at their distance and to control them, while his inner self slipped away to do whatever he chose. "His creativity is all in his personality," says an old and close friend. "He guards his ambiguity jealously. His character, deliberately, does not scan."

* * *

Trudeau was born into two cultures, and born rich. He grew up as a Victorian, *haut-bourgeois* Outremont between the wars being decades behind the times. Put the question – who in character and mindset is Trudeau most like? – and the analogies that come most readily to mind are not Canadian or even North American, but those extraordinary late nineteenth century philosopher-activists: George Curzon, scholar-viceroy of India, or Richard Burton, traveller-poet, or, somewhat later, Teilhard de Chardin, soldier-mystic.

The first Canadian Trudeau, a carpenter named Etienne Tru-

21

teau, arrived from La Rochelle, in 1659. He settled as a farmer, and sired fourteen children. His descendants stayed on the land for nearly three centuries, until Charles-Emile Trudeau, father of the future Prime Minister, capitalized on the post-World War One boom and sold his automotive service business to Imperial Oil for $1.4 million at the height of the Depression, and then merrily and daringly, through investments in mines, real estate, amusement parks, and part-ownership of a baseball club, pyramided this into well over $2 million before he died in 1935. Each of his three children, in seniority, Suzette, Pierre Elliott, and Charles (a first son died at birth, in 1916), are multi-millionaires.

"My father taught me order and discipline," Trudeau has said. "And my mother freedom and fantasy."

Charlie, as everyone called him, was short and slight, with a tooth-brush moustache, quick and profane in his speech, a bold, boisterous man who loved gambling and the company of athletes, outgoing, energetic, and authoritarian. Trudeau occasionally plays poker and plays a cool hand. But except for the occasional, mild, *shit*, he eschews profanity. In the manner of a Victorian papa, Charlie saw his children each day at 5.00 p.m., for an hour during which he gave them total and undivided attention, then vanished for another twenty-three hours. With his own sons, Trudeau follows much the same regime.

Trudeau talks about his father enthusiastically, and without inhibition. "He taught me boxing, to shoot a rifle, he taught me to talk, to read." From Charlie, on trips into the Laurentians, trips that Trudeau recalls as "an idyllic time passed in the discovery of nature and its creatures," he learned about nature. Through Charlie's own father, Joseph, a farmer who had lasted just long enough in school to learn to write his name, Trudeau learned about Quebec. At the family farm in the Richelieu Valley, Trudeau met rural cousins who introduced him to *joual*, and to local characters, the village drunk and the village idiot.

The one lesson Charlie left his son to learn alone was the most crucial one of all: how to turn from boy into man. When Charlie died suddenly in Florida, from influenza that turned to pneumonia, Trudeau was only fifteen. He cries now at funerals, because each one brings back the memory of his father's.

Trudeau's life-long ambivalence about authority, tweaking its nose in others, insisting on his own, can only be the legacy of the father-son competitiveness that he was denied the chance to resolve. Indirectly, Trudeau has said this much himself. 'He wielded some authority, that made me respect him and, during the last years of his life, probably also challenge him from time to time, as adolescents do. But he died before I ever got into any open conflict with him,'' he confided to Radwanski.

Part of the son Charlie left behind has always remained a boy. Behind the mask of the statesman, so often serious and self-important, a *farouche* Peter Pan peeps out every now and then, to make a saucy pirouette behind the Queen, or an obscene gesture to the press of the world, assembled at the 1978 Bonn Economic Summit. Peter Pan has another aspect: for years, Trudeau let it be known that he was two years younger than he really was; only in 1968 did an enterprising *Time Canada* researcher discover, from the baptismal records at St-Viateur d'Outremont, that the year of his birth was 1919, not 1921. Some observers, watching him boogie at sixty, at parties where the oldest guest is thirty, find the spectacle faintly bizarre: the incongruity never strikes Trudeau. "He has a horror of aging," says a friend. "Margaret was his elixir of perpetual youth."

* * *

"Formidable" is the word Trudeau sometimes uses to describe his father. Everyone else applies it to his mother, Grace Elliott. She and Charlie were total opposites and although proprieties naturally were maintained, it is difficult to believe that their marriage was close. Physically, Trudeau resembles his mother much more than his father. He has her almond-shaped eyes. What is known of Grace Trudeau's character – she died in 1973 aged eighty-two – is, like her son's, full of question marks.

Grace Elliott was a product of that other dominant strain in the Canadian mosaic: United Empire Loyalist with Scottish overtones; she was the daughter of a wealthy businessman. Her mother, though, had been French Canadian and as was often the case in such marriages, while her two brothers were brought up Protestant, Grace, as the daughter and thereby less important, was Catholic. She was handsome rather than pretty judging from her photographs, tallish, with bright blue eyes and prominent teeth, soft-voiced, delicate in her comportment, refined, and above all, reserved. Yet Grace brimmed with spunk. She was a whiz at Scottish country dancing, an avid cross-country skier. At sixty-one, she drove across Paris on the back of Pierre's motorbike. At sixty-six, in the company of Thérèse Casgrain, the firebrand Quebec socialist and feminist, she travelled through Asia. In the late 1940's, when Montreal suddenly sprouted a lively group of avant-garde painters and sculptors, she became their patron; through a brother who had settled in France, she became a friend of Georges Braque.

The Braques on the wall apart, the atmosphere Grace created at 84 McCulloch Avenue in Outremont, the squat, unprepossessing brick house she and Charlie bought in 1930, in which she lived till she died, was by all accounts, dull, oppressive, intimidating. "Full of browns and laces," is Margaret's description, "with a mahogany grand piano and petit point upholstered chairs." "People talked in low voices," recalls an old Montreal friend. "No one laughed much. Madame Trudeau was very much the grande dame, sitting ramrod straight behind the tea table, looking very English. Somehow, it was always a relief when it was time to go." Perhaps, like mother, like son, it helps to know that Grace Trudeau's own childhood had been traumatic: her mother had died when Grace was nine.

Trudeau's relationship with his mother was, as friends recall, intense. "I couldn't help but feel," says one, "she was a heavy burden for him to carry around." Yet Trudeau's own reminiscences are surprisingly cursory. "She was a good mother, spent a lot of time with us." His single extended conversation about her was with Edith Iglauer of the *New Yorker*. "She never gave me the impression of an overly protective mother . . . If I was going off to James Bay, for example, she would say, 'So long. Have a nice trip and don't get drowned.' She never said, 'Why don't you work or study instead?' . . . She left her children free."

Consistently, when talking about his mother, Trudeau attributes his own passion for freedom to her. Yet bonds never articulated are often the strongest bonds of all. A mother who demands nothing can also demand everything. Trudeau lived with his mother until he was over forty. As Prime Minister, even during election campaigns, he telephoned her almost every day. Shortly after his father died, Trudeau made Elliott part of his first name. (He'd been christened Joseph Philippe Pierre Yves Elliott Trudeau.)

24

Grace's tangible legacy to Trudeau is his knowledge of culture, or the knowledge at least that he *ought* to appreciate it. As Prime Minister, in fact, he seldom bothered with the politics of culture; as an aide has said, "To him, culture is something his mother did, not of the same order as foreign policy or regional economic expansion." Today the art he appreciates most, demonstrating an empathetic understanding of the mastery of the body that it demands, is ballet. And though music to him is marginal – the Sunday evening classical record concerts he and his brother Charles used to organize in the basement family room never really took hold – he has a feel for the visual arts: the muted, abstract but disciplined landscapes of the British Columbia painter Toni Onley are among his favourites.

As for Trudeau's responses to architecture, his friend Arthur Erickson, who is Canada's most renowned architect, says: "He has an exceptional understanding of space and of the relationship of forms," but adds, "he can abstract himself so totally from his physical surroundings that he becomes totally oblivious to them." The only house he has ever chosen for himself – in 1979, at the age of sixty – embodies both extremes. To the critic Adele Freedman, Trudeau's Art Deco palace on Pine Avenue in Montreal, designed in 1930 by the Quebec architect Ernest Cormier, who also designed Ottawa's Supreme Court, is both a fantasy of "grace and refined eccentricity" and an "Egyptian tomb." To Margaret, it's an impossible house to bring up children in, with just cubicles in the basement for bedrooms, into which the children would have to squeeze. For Trudeau, surely, the house combines simultaneously the pleasures of absolute withdrawal (the study has no windows) with being a cynosure of attention. (The place is listed as an official historic monument.)

From Grace, Trudeau also learned to be frugal. His parsimony, except to those to whom he is emotionally attached, is legendary. In Montreal; in mid-winter, he would run coatless to restaurants, to save the checkroom tip. He seldom pays for someone's meal, nor carries enough money to cover the bill. At the state funeral for Pierre Laporte, an aide had to slip him a $10 bill when the collection plate was passed: Trudeau looked at the amount, and frowned. In 1975, as Prime Minister, he disputed in public an $8 tax increase on his Laurentian estate imposed by the municipality of St. Adolph D'Howard. Yet when his close friend Jacques

Hébert faced a jail term for his book, *J'Accuse les Assassins de Coffin*, Trudeau took on the full legal burden of defending Hébert, for free; he funded the literary projects of friends, and once sent $3,000 to a penniless friend in Paris.

Of all the legacies Grace Elliott passed on to her son, the most important was reserve. The inner life at 84 McCulloch will never be known for certain; what *is* certain is that each of the three children who grew up there grew up withdrawn almost to the point of neuroticism. Suzette, until she married an outgoing, ebullient Montreal dentist, Pierre Rouleau, was, a friend remembers, "shy, almost mute." Charles in his early forties abandoned a brilliant architectural career to live as a near recluse in the Laurentians.* One old friend remembers them as "an extraordinarily close family, which made a very sharp distinction between itself and the rest of the world" – so close that they never needed to give each other Christmas presents. Trudeau's own most dominant characteristic is an intense *noli me tangere* remove from others, a ferocious, intensely English reserve that hovers on the brink of superciliousness to freeze the blood of an intruder.

Grace Elliott never entirely mastered French. So, Trudeau spoke English to her and French to his father and got as far as fourth grade never really knowing which he was. Often, as a child, he treated the two languages as one, as in, for instance, "We must go down to the *bord de l'eau*." But beyond a doubt, as Charlie Trudeau's ultimate triumph, Trudeau's spirit is Gallic. His heart is in Quebec. He has said that if Quebec separates, he will go back there. Except for a brief flirtation with British Columbia in the early years with Margaret, he has never considered living anywhere but Quebec. He writes better in French; when tired, he occasionally has to grope for the right English word. All his intimate friends – Gérard Pelletier, Jacques Hébert, Jean Marchand, Jean LeMoyne – are Québécois. With them, he becomes a person even close anglophone friends never see: relaxed, colloquial, animated without being aggressive, jokey.

Yet Trudeau, when he finally came to marry, married an unilingual anglophone. His sons, as he must have known would hap-

---

*In 1968, Trudeau's mother, sister, and brother sat in his box at the leadership convention. Their experiences so bruised them that they have never again appeared with him in public.

26

pen, are more English than French. *His character, deliberately, does
not scan.*

* * *

When Trudeau was twelve, he left childish things behind and
entered Collège Jean de Brébeuf, flagship of the Jesuit teaching
order in Quebec. He remained there until he was twenty. September to June, he was at school six days a week, often in the
evenings for debates or special activities, and on Sundays for
mass. Almost as much as by his parents, Trudeau's character
was defined by Brébeuf, by the Jesuit mystique.

That mystique, like most mysteries, rests on a simple premise:
the pursuit of excellence. Gentler, more humanistic Catholic
teaching orders, the Benedictines, for example, educate the boy;
the Jesuits train the future man. Will is the dynamo; guilt, omnipresent in most boys, is the catalyst. In the Jesuit system, will and
guilt, interacting upon each other, fuse mind, body, and character
into more than the sum of their parts. Jesuit products, all their
lives, tend to manifest this sense of standing apart from the common herd: California Governor Jerry Brown, for example, as
much as Trudeau. It isn't arrogance, exactly; more an inner certitude of being special.

The Brébeuf Jesuits, in Trudeau's time, had much in common
with those eminent Victorians who invented British public
schools. Just the *mise en scène* alone, a group of imposing, neoclassic brick buildings set back off Côte Ste Catherine, resembled
one of those schools for young English gentlemen where the
dormitories were drafty and the rod stung. Upward striving,
mind over matter, cold showers. (Trudeau still sleeps with his
windows wide open in mid-winter, a practice Margaret found
unromantic.) No cheating, no tale-telling, no crying. Like the
Victorians, the Brébeuf Jesuits trained the sons of one generation of rulers to become themselves the next generation.
Neither was the least bit squeamish about using words like
"elite" and "power."

The Victorians, at least in outward appearances, were more
puritanical. To grasp the prickliest nettle straightaway, Trudeau
emerged from Brébeuf anything but a sexual prude. He had
many affairs, and during his long bachelorhood, used to inform

27

his married friends that to demand fidelity of their spouses was to infringe upon their freedom—predictably, when theory became a personal reality, he saw things differently. He felt no shame about his body. Even as Prime Minister, he has sunbathed nude in mixed company.

What really mattered to the Jesuits, in contrast to the Victorians, was the mind. To them, *mens sana in corpore sano*, meant not just a healthy mind but an excellent one. *Cogito ergo sum*, Descartes had informed the Jesuits. Thought as the *omega* of existence. Will could transform a sluggish brain into an instrument of perfection, just as it could a sickly body.

The Victorians, in their turn, cared passionately about fair play. Be a good loser. Don't hit a man when he's down. On the playing fields of Brébeuf, Trudeau never learned these conditioned reflexes of Anglo-Saxons. Always, he detested team sports. His opponents, down the years, have been repeatedly taken by surprise, ambushed even, by discovering too late that Trudeau does not play fair, that he has no sympathy whatever for the underdog.

The boy at Brébeuf, nearly half a century ago, foreshadowed the man today. Classmates remember Trudeau as bright, quick, and retentive; as courageous and at times, totally captivating. They also remember him as aloof, conceited, arrogant, and much of the time, as thoroughly disagreeable. Out of the eight years he spent there, only one contemporary, Roger Rolland, later his speechwriter, became a life-long friend.

Trudeau was a smart-ass, or since that term had not yet been invented, a pain in the neck. "I had to have the last word," he admits. At the very least, Trudeau always had to be different. In history class, after everyone else had cheered French successes, he applauded Wolfe's victory on the Plains of Abraham. Trudeau was also—a harbinger of some of his later behaviour such as telling unemployed postal drivers to "eat shit"—a bit of a bully.

Bullying in boyhood can be a sign of unhappiness, an unresolved inner conflict, projected onto others. Trudeau, once he learned to box, provoked scores of fist fights. More often, the content of his bullying was psychological. "He always kept his distance from others," recalls Jean de Grandpré, a classmate, later Chairman of Bell Canada. "It was really a temperamental preference, and perhaps also a certain arrogance, which even then led him to

28

ridicule people who were not bright." His sister Suzette told Radwanski, "He'd like to tease, to see how far we [she and Charles] could stand being teased before we broke out." Maturity has modified these traits but they remain. More than one aide has found himself sent suddenly to Coventry – memos unread, advice ignored – for no other reason than that as he eventually comes to recognize, Trudeau has had a sudden whim to put him down. At cabinet meetings, Trudeau sometimes suddenly will escalate a routine exchange of opinions into a ferocious contest of intellects. He invariably wins, but then wonders, at the next meeting, why last week's opponent keeps quiet "If someone is not performing he's as likely to tell them out loud in front of others as to draw them aside to tell them alone," says one cabinet minister, Francis Fox

Trudeau often bruises other people's self-esteem without really intending to, or having any idea he has done it. He grew up convinced he was weak and unbright. "I don't know if it's true of all competitiveness," he has said, "but mine was probably born of a fear of being left behind rather than from a desire to succeed." Even today, he isn't entirely convinced of his strength. Although he is the single most successful contemporary politician in the world today, he still defers to those who carry the title "professional pol."

To the boys at Brébeuf, he was as much a puzzle as he is to us. He adored plays on words and practical jokes. Typically, later in life, he once sublet his apartment and hid in the closet to watch an unsuspecting prospective tenant's behaviour when he came to look over the place. But the notion of sending *himself* up never occurred to him. Gérard Pelletier remembers that when Trudeau was a young man, "you could never tell how far you could go in teasing him before his face would turn red and he'd blow up." Ask one of his present associates about his sense of humour and the answer comes out protectively, "Not a sense of humour, exactly, but a sense of delight." Senator Keith Davey, a master of one-liners, recalls that at the start of their relationship, each time he came out with a quip, Trudeau would look puzzled, and then say, "that was a joke, wasn't it?" Because he lacks a sense of the ridiculous, Trudeau keeps his aides continually on edge. "There is just no way," says one, "you can get yourself out of a bad situation by producing the line that will break him up"

To a few at Brébeuf Trudeau showed another dimension: an exceptional capacity for sensitivity. One classmate, there as a poor scholarship boy, remembers being "touched by his simplicity" because when they went together to a provincial meeting of students, Trudeau deliberately dressed in his shabbiest clothes so as not to embarrass his friend. As he grew older and more in control of his mask, he showed this sweeter side of his nature more readily. Almost always with children, his own or other people's, or in encounters with students, he will let his guard down totally; even when still in his own teens he knew instinctively how to make little children respond to his magic, gathering them round him on a beach or on a streetcorner like a Pied Piper, spinning tall tales in adult language, never talking down.

Ambiguity is the only consistency. On the one hand, the boy in disguise, uncertain of his own worth, tender and utterly loyal toward those to whom he has committed himself. On the other, the single combatant who fights to win, by any method at hand. Trudeau has a talent—one he shares with world-class fencers and boxers—for "white hatred," focused intransigent fury that unlike ordinary red anger, does not impair the faculties. Once engaged in combat—a schoolyard scrap; an election campaign; a joust with reporters—nothing will induce Trudeau to let up until he has won.

He has no talent for acquaintanceship, projecting around him a chilly, austere ambience, yet he has a true gift for friendship. Close friends like Pelletier and Hébert and Jean LeMoyne talk about him with a rare tenderness. "He would never, could never, let a friend down," says Pelletier.

When Jean Marchand, in mid-term, became an embarrassment to the government, Trudeau stood by him; in 1980, he ignored the wishes of almost all the Liberal Senators to make Marchand Senate Speaker because, by then lonely and lost, Marchand needed the prestige, and the money. When a young minister, Francis Fox, had to resign from the cabinet after admitting he had forged abortion papers for a mistress, Trudeau (who perhaps saw in Fox something of himself) had him round to dinner at 24 Sussex twice, for gentle, evening-long discussions.

Margaret, as one would expect, spotted this vulnerable side early on. "Behind the silky, charming manner and the absolute confidence that had given him such a reputation for arrogance, was a curiously solitary figure," she has written. Trudeau himself told Radwanski, with great candour, "The least word of blame, or indeed the least word of praise moved me to tears, and I guess it was a basic insecurity as a child." He cried when a Brébeuf teacher praised him for trouncing the school tough. Years later, he came to the brink of tears when Senator Eugene Forsey praised him for a speech.

* * *

The organizing principle of Trudeau's carefully wrought personality is self-discipline, harsh almost to the point of self-flagellation. At Brébeuf, he learned how to overcome his weaknesses – although he never could invest himself with stamina: he tires easily, and quickly wears out if he doesn't get eight hours of sleep. He exercised daily. He boxed, hiked, swam, canoed, skied, scorned junk foods, except for an incurable yen for chocolates, as he now scorns cigarettes and hard liquor. Later he learned judo and scuba diving. Once, when a student in Paris, he set out on a skiing vacation barely two weeks after an appendectomy. As Prime Minister, as aides nervously looked on, he shot down the brutal Cresta bobsled run at St. Moritz, twice. At sixty, his body, while not precisely that of a twenty-five-year-old, is superbly conditioned: a trim 160 pounds on a five-foot-nine-inch frame; heavily muscled in neck and shoulders, with a slight tendency to paunch which compels him to watch what he eats.

Trudeau described his philosophy of asceticism in quasi-mystical terms, in his first published essay, "Exhaustion and Fulfilment: The Ascetic in a Canoe." This may be his single finest piece of writing:

What is essential at beginning is the resolve to reach the saturation point. Ideally, the trip should end only when the members are making no further progress within themselves ... It is a condition of such a trip that you entrust yourself, stripped of worldly goods, to nature. Canoe and paddle, blanket and knife, salt pork and flour, fishing rod and rifle, that is about the extent of your wealth. To remove all the useless material baggage from a man's heritage is, at the same time, to free his mind from petty preoccupations, calculations and memories.

Later, in a television interview, he restated this philosophy: "I want to be as little as possible a slave to material things. To be able to appreciate a meal, a good book, a holiday, is marvellous. But to suffer, if one is deprived of them, is to be a slave to material things. I hope that my own children will not need distractions, whether of candy or of television." When it comes to material possessions, Trudeau likes the best. Yet the otter coat, the superbly cut suits, the Mercedes 300sl have always been deceptive. For all that a dozen years at 24 Sussex have given him imperial tastes, his worldly goods even now amount to only a few paintings and a great many books.

Even more than his body, Trudeau disciplined his mind. Blessed with an exceptional memory, he read omnivorously and with a ferocious, head-down tenacity. "I was never satisfied with reading eight chapters of a book, I had to read twelve." Even when teachers recommended it, he never skipped. He has never altered this linear approach. Early in 1979, when members of the Task Force on National Unity gave Trudeau an advance copy of their report and met with him privately to discuss it, he asked them questions only about the first three chapters – all he'd had time to read. By contrast, Marc Lalonde at the same meeting hopped all over the map because, as most of us would when pushed for time, he had read only the summary of recommendations.

At times, his concentration comes close to being obsessive. He will allow no one, nor anything, to interrupt him. When he became Prime Minister, dinner guests, once even his close friend Jean Marchand, were informed they must leave by 9.45 p.m. so that he could spend an hour alone with his documents boning up for the next day's round of committee meetings. Passengers in his official car were instructed to stay silent while he worked on his papers in the back; once, near the end of a two-hour drive to Montreal, his press secretary, Pat Gossage, exclaimed in delight at the autumn colours. "Pat, you *promised*," came the reprimand from the bowed head in the back.*

Trudeau owes the catholicity of his intellectual interests primarily to one teacher at Brébeuf: Père Robert Bernier. In an interview with Edith Iglauer, Bernier described his curriculum. "Literature, philosophy, music, painting – all went together . . I also gave a history course. I insisted not only on facts and dates

---

*Trudeau's chauffeur, forbidden also from turning on the radio, at last secured permission to install a tape deck with an ear plug.

but on thought; the importance of the democratic spirit; a pluralistic society with a sense of the universal and a love of differences for themselves, where outside all the differences of nation, religion, sex, colour and so on, a man is a man and is respected as such. In addition, I taught them French, Greek and Latin literature ... outside of class we would read and discuss, in English, Hemingway, Faulkner, Henry James, Hawthorne and Thoreau ... We could enter easily the mind of Locke, de Tocqueville, Acton, Jefferson ... I insisted on a respect for manmade beauty."

The mouth waters. Trudeau sucked it all in. Thanks to Bernier's curriculum, he developed an appetite for the kind of knowledge that most political leaders are too pragmatic, too one-dimensional to be bothered with. "I have probably read more of Dostoevsky, Stendhal and Tolstoy than the average statesman," Trudeau has said. "And less of Keynes, Mill and Marx." He's also said that, except at Harvard and the London School of Economics, "most of my reading was in French or Latin."

But there was one lesson Trudeau never learned at Brébeuf – nor anywhere else. He never came to recognize how extraordinarily lucky he was. By chance, he was brilliant, athletic, good-looking, commanding in his presence, and filthy rich. Most people are none of these things. He never understood this. Instilling a social conscience isn't central to Jesuit training. Indeed, most of it presumes the direct opposite: anyone, by will alone, can aspire to anything. Failure is sin. The day-to-day Brébeuf regimen prevented the boys, almost consciously, from acquiring any understanding of the human consequences – the humiliation, the indignities, the crushed pride – of failure. Outside the school walls, the Depression raged and unemployed men shuffled the streets of Montreal. Inside, in Bernier's words, was "a little world of ourselves ... an atmosphere of elation where everything was beautiful." Nothing in Trudeau's political career has been so marked as his inability to comprehend the feelings of ordinary Canadians who in their personal lives have failed: the young who have failed to find jobs; the middle class who have failed to make inflationary ends meet; the middle-age civil servants who failed to become bilingual.

* * *

Two final legacies from Trudeau's schooldays remain to be counted. Brébeuf anchored him for life to the Catholic Church. He isn't entirely a conventional Catholic and doesn't accept all the dogmas. "I believe in the Protestant rule of conscience, and that you must not deliberately hurt others. That's the only really basic sin, to hurt others." (Actually, Cardinal Newman authored this doctrine.) But the church as an institution he accepts totally. He rarely misses Sunday mass; through his twenties he went to mass daily with his mother. (Twice, as Prime Minister, when Margaret demurred, he went to Christmas Eve midnight mass with John and Geills Turner.) After his audience with the Pope in 1969, an aide remembers that on the overnight flight home, "he stayed wide awake all night; his eyes open, and shining."

The last legacy from Brébeuf is the most obvious: Trudeau *argues* like a Jesuit. The merits of a case aside, he can out-argue almost anybody. His dialectic tricks have become familiar to the point of tedium, yet, reinforced by his intimidating presence and his gift of memory, they still nearly always work. The trick of answering a question with a question. The trick of reducing an opponent's argument to a syllogistic absurdity; if you believe Proposition A, then you must also believe Proposition B and on from there to some idiotic Z. Last, the trick of timing. Trudeau is a counter-puncher who never releases his best shot until his opponent has lowered his guard. Out of hundreds of verbal jousts as Prime Minister, the one that perhaps reveals his style best is a 1974 interview with Peter Gzowski, then the host of CBC's "This Country in the Morning." Gzowski was boring in on Trudeau's refusal to concede to Quebec nationalism any positive aspect. Then Trudeau, in an apparently bland reply, dropped the phrase, "Toronto separatists." Reading the transcript of the interview it is fascinating to watch Gzowski losing momentum as he struggles from this point on to defend himself against the implied accusation that he was one of those sentimental, English-Canadian intellectuals who wanted to be "fair" to Quebec and allow it special status.

* * *

When Trudeau left Brébeuf in the spring of 1940, only the details of his constructed persona remained to be added. Already, he was starred for achievement. He hadn't come top of his class; he'd missed out on becoming school president. Père Bernier,

even in hindsight, remembered him only as "one of the best."
But he was tough. He had style and panache. In the school paper,
as editor, he wrote: "This paper has a well-defined attitude; it
consists of having no well-defined attitude." He was athletic,
self-confident, and beyond all of these, utterly bound and determined to be the best

It took him the next quarter century to find out what, exactly,
he would be *best·at*

2

Citizen of the World

"In Melville's *Moby-Dick*, I believe it was Ishmael who said that when he feels that desire to go out and knock men's hats off, he realizes it's time to go to sea."

Pierre Trudeau
Interview in the *United Church Observer*, 1971

If Outremont, Brébeuf, his family, and his own will-power shaped Trudeau's character, it was an individual, Gérard Pelletier, who helped shape him toward a purpose. Pelletier influenced Trudeau to become a political activist in Quebec. "We were the first generation to say, 'God damn it, we'll stay home and change the place,'" Pelletier has said.

Later, inside Trudeau's cabinet, Pelletier was described most often as an *éminence grise*. In fact, though the description would mortify Pelletier, he was a spiritual mentor. Physically and temperamentally he resembles an abbot: domed bald head, inquisitive eyes, soft voice; shy, bookish, earnest, and courteous. Pelletier's surpassing quality is integrity. He supported the War Measures Act with "death in my soul." The same Péquistes who liked nothing better than skirmishing with Trudeau were faintly embarrassed about scoring points off Pelletier. And Pelletier has guts. In 1975, breaching the convention that federal ministers should stay out of provincial politics, he wrote a long essay in *Le Devoir* about Quebec's "crisis of leadership"; well ahead of most observers, he sensed the ground crumbling under Robert Bourassa's feet. When Pelletier left Ottawa in 1975 to become Ambassador to France, Trudeau saluted him as pupil to master. "A moral authority of the highest importance, and my friend."

The words carry emotional freight. Trudeau mostly keeps his friendships in self-contained compartments: Dr. Joe MacInnis, the underwater explorer, for scuba diving; old *Cité Libre* hands to visit for occasional casual nostalgic suppers; Jacques Hébert and Arthur Erickson for foreign travel; Peter Stollery, the Toronto

M.P. among others, for wilderness canoeing; Jean Marchand for politics and so on. Erickson, a close friend for a decade, says, "When he's with someone he can be totally, and marvellously, responsive. When they're not there, he's on another plane entirely. He doesn't carry other people's burdens." Pelletier and his wife Alex are perhaps the only friends Trudeau has for all seasons; the kind he would put his hand in the fire for. Trudeau spends every Bastille Day at their cottage in the Laurentians. In the autumn of 1979, when he was contemplating stepping down as Opposition Leader, he spent several days in Paris with the Pelletiers, talking things over. A month later, when deciding whether to come back, he telephoned Pelletier twice.

The two were born the same year. Like Trudeau, Pelletier lost his father young. Beyond that, their circumstances were a world apart. Pelletier was the youngest of ten children of an Eastern Townships railway agent who had taught himself to read. After his father died, only an archetypal Quebec *maman* kept Pelletier moving forward through abject poverty, to classical college (an unfashionable one). After the war, like another young man of similar background and mindset, Claude Ryan, he went to work for the Catholic Youth Movement, a syndicalist movement of student collectives and worker organizations. He met and married Alexandrine Leduc, a journalist and screenwriter, a woman of talent and insight. Through much of the 1950's, their combined salary was $80 weekly.

Pelletier and Trudeau met first in the late 1930's, when both were student editors. "I liked him," says Pelletier, "though his flippancy disconcerted me a little. . . . He was more petulant then, and quicker to lose his temper." Their true friendship dates from the winter of 1946-47 Pelletier was in Europe, working for a student relief agency. Trudeau came there, in search of great thoughts. They met, usually in Paris, saw each other often, discovered a soul-mate intelligence and common attachment to civil liberties. "I can remember us having endless discussions about the need for reforms, and how Trudeau always would say 'Okay, but where do we start?'" They had to start, they agreed, in Quebec by becoming *hommes engagés*. "I think he envied me a certain gift for action," Pelletier has said. "I was more involved, because I had to earn a living." Then Pelletier went home, to join *Le Devoir*. Two years later, Trudeau followed.

The quickest way to bring Trudeau's famous temper to the boil is to suggest that during the years between Brébeuf and Ottawa he behaved like a dilettante. If he condescends to answer at all, Trudeau will insist that he worked *all* the time, very hard. The truth is that he worked hard intermittently, always on projects he chose for himself.

The first four years after he left Brébeuf are a chapter of Trudeau's life that quite clearly, he would like to forget, or at least not talk about. He was a rebel without a cause, a decade ahead of James Dean. He was also a bully and a troublemaker. He studied law at the University of Montreal, and was bored. He articled with a Montreal firm, and was bored. He stayed out of the war, and was bored. More for something to do than out of conviction—"I think it was sort of to bug the government," he has said himself—he campaigned in a 1942 by-election for Jean Drapeau, the anti-conscriptionist *Bloc Populaire* candidate. Other activities fringed on delinquency. Trudeau and other cockalorums crashed around the countryside on motorbikes, wearing World War One Prussian helmets.

Time and again, Trudeau's lack of a war record has come back to haunt him, and he hates explaining why he didn't enlist. When pressed, he will say: "I scarcely paid any attention to the news." Other reasons can be suggested: he loathed the regimentation of army life and quickly got himself kicked out of the University of Montreal officer training corps. He's also squeamish. "Such a pacifist," as Margaret has observed, "that he won't kill anything, not even insects."

In 1945, Trudeau's instinct for self-discipline conquered the pattern of drift. He went off to Harvard, for a master's degree in political economy. Suddenly he realized, "How far behind we [in Quebec] were." In his two years there, he met most of the Cambridge luminaries: Joseph Schumpeter, Wassily Leontief, Adam Ulam, and Louis Hartz. He hung a sign on his door that read, "Pierre Trudeau, Citizen of the World."

Then to Paris for more study—though, in fact, in 1946-47, Trudeau spent less time attending lectures at the Sorbonne—"In all modesty, I knew more about these subjects than most of my professors"—than on soaking up the ambience of Paris and talking about Quebec with Pelletier in left-bank cafés. Through his expatriate uncle, Gordon Elliott, he got to meet Braque, the American sculptor Alexander Calder, the surrealist painter-photographer Man Ray. The next year he crossed the Channel to study hard once more, this time under Harold Laski at the London School of Economics. "A super teacher" he has said, "with a very organized mind." He found time as well to dig into the Archives of the Public Records Office for material on Canadian economic history and told Pelletier there was incomparably more there than back in Ottawa.

Trudeau by now was nearly thirty. The salons of London and Paris were milieux into which a brilliant, good-looking, flawlessly bilingual Montrealer could fit as snugly as a Stendhal hero – just a bit too snugly. But the time to go home was not quite yet. In the spring of 1948, he set out on the last, best phase of his education: a solitary pilgrimage through the world. The trip took a year; all he took with him was a knapsack.

* * *

Even by the standards of the 1980's – easy air connections, universal credit cards, the sight of young Canadian hitch-hikers with beards and maple leaves on their jean jackets commonplace from Tibet to Patagonia – the scope of Trudeau's trip is out of the ordinary. Germany to Eastern Europe to the Balkans to Turkey; the Middle East to India, Burma, Indo-China, China. By the standards of 1948 – the world teeming with revolution and civil war, the Iron Curtain clanking shut – it was extraordinary. Partly, Trudeau set out in the spirit of a Single Combat warrior. "Having missed the big war," he said, "I wanted to see other battles." Even more, he set out in the spirit of those mythic Victorian travellers, Curzon, Burton, Robert Louis Stevenson, on a harrowing, quasi-mystical journey in search of himself. "I tempted fate. I used to deliberately put myself into some pretty tricky situations just to see how I would handle them."

Like Burton and Stevenson he took on the colour of each country. In India, he wore a turban, in Jordan, a burnoose. In Afghanistan, he lived on goat's milk and wild honey. At times, he was all earnest academic, taking copious notes everywhere, lecturing on political science in Istanbul and Lucknow. Other times he was a missionary: at the mouth of the Ganges and Brahmaputra rivers, he worked on a rice boat helping the Holy Cross fathers resupply their mission with rice. At all times he tempted fate. In Belgrade, where he arrived without a visa, he spent three days in jail. In Jerusalem, he was arrested as a spy. At Ur of the Chaldees, when brigands attacked, he faked a fit of madness to ward them off. He pushed on into Indo-China, and despite the Civil War, crossed the border into China.

From that journey, and the many that followed – Russia in 1952; China in 1960; sojourns in Europe too numerous to count – Trudeau emerged, like Ulysses, as part of all he'd met. Few modern statesmen have come to office knowing so much about the world. Trudeau hadn't just been nearly everywhere; he understood how societies worked. Once, at a cabinet meeting, he warned that a Canadian International Development Agency plan to ship food by barge to an offshore island in Bangladesh was impossible: at that time of year – Trudeau knew because he'd been there in 1949 – the winds blew offshore and the barges would be beached. (CIDA went ahead anyway; the barges were beached.) In 1979, after his defeat, Trudeau travelled to Tibet with Arthur Erickson and an architect colleague: the two were astonished by Trudeau's detailed knowledge to the point that he could engage Tibetan monks in lengthy, historical and cultural discussions. Nor is Trudeau's insatiable curiosity about how the world works limited to the arcane. Once, for half-an-hour, he grilled a chimney-sweep who'd come to clean his chimney; likewise a tree surgeon.

The world is so full of a number of things, wrote Stevenson, I'm sure we should all be as happy as kings. When Trudeau talks about his travels, often round a campfire at the end of a day's canoeing, a kind of Stevenson figure takes over. "You get a glimpse of a quite different kind of person," says a journalist who listened in the summer of 1979. "He doesn't brag. He doesn't posture. What comes across is a marvellous sense of curiosity, a child-like sense of wonder." It may be that Trudeau was born too late for his true calling. A hundred years earlier, he might have been a brilliant explorer-journalist in the manner of Stevenson. Instead, he became a politician in the manner of Curzon.

* * *

When Trudeau came home to Montreal in the spring of 1949, he had been away five years. The serenities of 84 McCulloch were constant; outside, as he quickly found out from Pelletier, Quebec was in turmoil; the word, Asbestos, on everyone's lips. At this grubby mining town in the Eastern Townships, 5,000 miners had been on strike for three months. Early on, Quebec Premier Maurice Duplessis, in one of the most obscene of his authoritarian gestures, had sent the Quebec Provincial Police into Asbestos as strikebreakers. To idealists like Pelletier, Asbestos served as a symbol, not just of wages and working conditions, but of human dignity; of democracy versus autocracy; of social justice. If the Quiet Revolution had its beginnings at Asbestos, so also did Pierre Elliott Trudeau, future Prime Minister.

Pelletier, covering the strike for *Le Devoir*, was in the thick of the fight. On April 22, he collected Trudeau – sandals, tattered raincoat, a scruffy blond beard – and the pair drove to Asbestos in Pelletier's battered right-hand drive Singer. Their first encounter was straight out of Marx Brothers: a policeman who'd never seen a right-hand drive car arrested them because Trudeau, sitting in what the officer assumed was the driver's seat, couldn't produce a licence. That sorted out, Pelletier introduced Trudeau to Jean Marchand, the fiery young labour leader masterminding the strike. Marchand asked Trudeau to talk to the miners about their legal rights. Instead, that night in St. Aimé church hall, Trudeau talked to them so passionately about *human* rights, the right of the oppressed to resist the oppressor, that Marchand by the end – "miners are not schoolchildren, you know" – was on the edge of his seat. Trudeau didn't linger long in Asbestos. Although he turned down Marchand's proposal to join the union as legal counsel, he negotiated for them, provided free legal advice, and later wrote a brilliant long introduction to a book about the strike, *La Grève de l'Amiante*, which he also edited.*

Although the Abestos strike ended in failure, out of it was born an idea. The idea was *Cité Libre*. For a decade, *Cité Libre* Magazine became Trudeau's intellectual and spiritual home: a proving ground for his ideas, a pulpit from which to hurl anathemas against Duplessis.

*   *   *

When the first issue of *Cité Libre* rolled off the press in 1950,

---

*In 1975, as Prime Minister, Trudeau, for auld lang syne, sent a telegram of support to the Asbestos workers, again on strike.

Quebec existed in utter darkness. It was a fear-ridden banana republic, oppressive, obscurantist, and primitive. This austere, pocket-sized quarterly, unillustrated and printed on rough paper, was the torch that lit the way out the dark. So, at any rate, runs the mythology of *Cité Libre*. Trudeau himself has fed it. *Cité Libre*, runs his official biographical note in the *Canadian Parliamentary Guide*, was "the mainspring of reform in Quebec during the 1950's and the 1960's."

Like all myths, the halo around *Cité Libre* contains a core of truth and a good deal of embroidery. For one thing, the magazine's political influence was minimal; its audience never more than a few thousand. For another, as revisionist historians have begun to point out, there was more to Duplessis than Cité Librists cared to admit.

Conrad Black, in his epic biography, *Duplessis*, has put the case for the defence: Black describes Duplessis as "a great helmsman, defending the nation from threats from without, exorcising rotten elements within, helping the little, collaborating with the big." Instead of holding Quebec back, Duplessis accomplished "incomparable material and social advancement," more university students and, proportionately more teachers at all levels, than Ontario, and as high a rate of growth in manufacturing and of wage increases.

Black overstates his case. The wage statistics concealed the disparities between anglophones and francophones and the fact that during the Duplessis era, Montreal slipped irredeemably behind Toronto as a commercial centre. Yet much of Black's thesis holds up: Duplessis, in fact, no more crushed his peoples' spirit than his contemporary among provincial autocrats, Joey Smallwood, crushed the spirit of Newfoundlanders. And Black is dead on when he notes that ordinary Québécois, under Duplessis, were relatively well off. The beneficiaries of the Quiet Revolution and of its noisier successors, scarcely by coincidence, have been the same liberal intellectuals and professionals who attacked Duplessis.*

*Trudeau spotted this irony early on and has made it the foundation of his case against nationalism. In 1965, in a paper later published in *Federalism and the French Canadians*, he wrote: "A sound economic policy must never be based on the assumption that workers would be ready to accept a drastic lowering of standards of living for the mere pleasure of seeing a nationalist middle class replace a foreign one at the helm of various enterprises."

Duplessis's dark side, as Black doesn't deny, was that he "dulled some of the democratic instincts of his people." The Cité Librists – and this is their true glory – kept those instincts alive. Besides Trudeau and Pelletier, the group included Pierre Juneau, later a top federal civil servant, Jacques Hébert, and Roger Rolland, both journalists, and Charles Lussier, later director of the Canada Council.* Like Ionian monks holding fast amid the barbarians, the Cité Librists kept alive certain intellectual and moral ideals: judicial justice, democracy, truth, and freedom. Much like Soviet dissidents today, they enriched the collective memory of Québécois by demonstrating courage in a hopeless cause. Québécois, as Black has written, were "profoundly seduced" by Duplessis. They became his sycophants, and, in the way of all sell-outs, turned ferociously upon any who dared to dissent. The University of Montreal refused Trudeau a professorship: almost the instant Duplessis died, he was offered two. "Very few would talk to us," Alex Pelletier has recalled. "We had to be concerned for our children. They would come home from school and ask if Dad was a Communist."

Cité Librists were internationalists; even more, they were liberal idealists. Understandably, they thought of themselves as forerunners of the future. In hindsight they emerge as a transitional generation; a human bridge between the arid clericalism of pre-war Quebec, personified by the closed-in characters in Marie Claire Blais's novels, and the Cité Librists' nationalist successors of the mid-1960's onward; harsher, narrower, more in touch with political practicalities. A transitional generation, though, is different from a dead-end generation, as the Bright Young Things of the 1920's proved to be or as the Me Generation of the 1970's promises to be. The beliefs of the Cité Librists – pluralism, the supremacy of reason over passion, the belief, at core, that all men are alike – are still alive in Quebec today; the self-confident generation of Québécois now emerging to succeed the nationalists, can indeed look to the Cité Librists as spiritual godfathers.

Anyway, they were young and they all had a wonderful time. They met once a month, most often in Charles Lussier's basement, to read articles aloud to one another, delighting in their

*Also, later, Pierre Laporte and Pierre Vallières.

43

verbal skills and in their courage to say the unsayable, and then to print it. All Cité Librists, it goes without saying, were male. One wife recalls: "Endless talk, with pregnant wives falling asleep, waiting for our bright boys to be done so we could go home."

* * *

For the first two years of his involvement with *Cité Libre*, Trudeau commuted. He'd gone to Ottawa in 1949, to work at the Privy Council Office, a bureaucratic perch then used often by Quebec intellectuals (Maurice Lamontagne as an example) as a refuge from Duplessis. Trudeau wrote memos on how the constitution might be amended; in the dull stretches, he walked down the halls on his hands. Back in Montreal, he practised law off and on. He tended the family business interests. He was a dashing elusive bachelor, with, as a friend Charles Taylor remembers, a "rather carefully chosen flamboyance, the clothes he wears, and the kind of blondes he dates." He travelled compulsively. "You'd write him a letter in Montreal," says Ramsay Cook of York University, another friend, "and back the answer would come from Sardinia." All the way up to 1965 Trudeau's only lasting commitment was to *Cité Libre*

The ideas Trudeau put forward in *Cité Libre* are discussed in the next chapter. The point to consider here, for what it reveals of the man, is the style and tone of his articles. He was a master polemicist. His prose was lucid, knowledgeable, consistently fresh and provocative, not in any way dense or obscure. He was refreshingly free of cant, but at times insufferably self-righteous. He could be merciless. An attack on Prime Minister Pearson for changing his mind about nuclear warheads was titled, "Pearson, the Defrocked Priest of Peace." Federal Liberal M.P.s were "trained donkeys." As for the French Fact in Ottawa,

with the sole exception of Laurier I fail to see a single French Canadian in more than three-quarters of a century whose presence in the federal cabinet might be considered indispensable to the history of Canada as written – except at election time, of course, when the tribe always invokes the aid of its witch-doctors.

Some of this was overkill. When André Laurendeau of *Le Devoir* reviewed Trudeau's book on the Asbestos strike, he tempered his praise: "The author pronounces judgement, he demands heads, and we have seen that his guillotine functions a little too arbitrarily."

But since no one around could match Trudeau for intellectual acuity, still less dialectical adroitness, there was no one to tone him down. "He was intimidating and demoralizing," recalls one member of a group of seven lawyers and academics who began to meet in 1963 to develop an anti-nationalist manifesto. "He'd come to meetings late, look over drafts that others had slaved over, rip them to shreds. The trouble was, he was usually right."

* * *

After the Quiet Revolution election of 1960, Cité Librists began to fall out of step with the times. For quite different reasons Trudeau and the others began to be subjected to the same kind of social ostracism they'd suffered under Duplessis. Or perhaps the reasons weren't that different. Quebec had secularized itself, but nationalism had become the new religion. No longer "Communists" and "Atheists," Cité Librists were now "vendus" and "traîtres." As always, when attacked Trudeau counter-attacked, harder. In 1961, in Cité Libre, "Let's open the borders. This people is dying of asphyxiation." In 1962, his best-known essay: "The New Treason of the Intellectuals."

Trudeau, by now a professor of law at the University of Montreal, a stylish figure round the campus in a flowing green opera cape, was beginning to show signs of restiveness. He was beginning to sense, perhaps, that history was passing him by. While he composed angry essays, others were changing society: in Ottawa a "New Guard" of Quebec Liberals – Maurice Lamontagne, Maurice Sauvé, Guy Favreau; and at Quebec City, a noisy crowd of Quiet Revolutionaries – Jean Lesage, René Lévesque, Eric Kierans; and passing up memos from the wings – technocrats like Jacques Parizeau and Claude Morin.

In the fall of 1963, a rising CBC producer-performer, Patrick Watson, travelled to Montreal to search for a co-host for a new national public affairs program, Inquiry. He went to the University of Montreal to interview a law professor, little known in English Canada but who, Watson knew, possessed the mental agility and physical presence to become an instant television star. Their conversation came to nothing because Trudeau insisted on full control of his own material. But Watson remembers Trudeau explaining why he had considered the proposition seriously: "I've been thinking it's time to get back into the mêlée."*

---

*Later that day, Watson went on to another Montreal campus and by evening had signed up another professor, Laurier LaPierre, from McGill.

3

Philosopher King

She: "Do you think in French words or in English words?"
He: "I don't think in words, Margaret. I think in the abstract."

Margaret Trudeau
Beyond Reason

No doubt she felt like heaving a frying pan at him. But Trudeau was telling Margaret the exact truth. Whenever he can, he thinks in the abstract, the general: from there, he proceeds to the particular, the pragmatic, the immediate. As one would expect of a Jesuit-trained Québécois.

All Prime Ministers come to office with opinions, thoughts, instincts, ideals, self-interests, dreams, hopes, plans. Trudeau alone among Canadian Prime Ministers came to office with ideas. In essence, he came with two defining ideas: rational man as the highest order of human evolution; federalism as the highest form of political organization.

Quite apart from defining him as a particular kind of person, Trudeau's ideas mattered because they defined him as a particular kind of politician. He became one, he told a BBC interviewer, "to apply my ideas in practice." To guess what he would try to do once political power became his, all anyone needed to do was to read what he had written.

Participatory Democracy is the best example. During his 1968-72 term, Trudeau attempted to engage the mass of Canadians in their own governance. He'd prefigured this in a 1958 article he wrote for *Vrai* Magazine:

Democracy is the only form of government that fully respects the dignity of man, because it alone is based on the belief that all men can be made fit to participate, directly or indirectly, in the guidance of the society of which they are members.

Constitutional revision is another case in point. The kind of equipoise between the two orders of government, and between governments and all citizens that Trudeau sought to achieve by the rule of law, are all set down in the essay, *Quebec and the Constitutional Problem*, written in 1965.

> A Bill of Rights ... to limit the powers that legal authorities have over human rights ... (to) put the French and English languages on an equal basis before the law ... the central government could be revised to give it a more authentically federal character ... (and) get rid of some of the constitution's imperial phraseology ... The Senate could also be reformed so that it represented the provinces more directly.

Third, planning and the application of modern management techniques to improve the government's problem-solving efficiency. In a 1964 essay, Trudeau had written:

> In the world of tomorrow, the expression 'banana republic' will not refer to independent, fruit-growing nations but to countries where formal independence has been given priority over the cybernetic revolution ... of advanced technology and scientific investigation, as applied to the fields of law, economics, social psychology, international affairs and other areas of human relations.

Trudeau's ideas were unique, not in themselves but in their context. Few countries have been ruled by Philosopher Kings; most muddle along with the shadows on Plato's wall. The last country in which anyone would expect to find a Philosopher King actually in power is Canada. Our intellectual history is almost barren of original ideas. In politics, the closest we've come to a consistent ideology is a mild form of social democracy. We sublimate the class struggle – that breeding ground for ideologies – by regional rivalries. Our consistent political philosophy is muddling through.

We're also too cold a country, and much too fragmented geographically, to have produced, until quite recently, the critical mass of leisured intellectuals necessary to germinate political ideas. In the nineteenth century, there was Goldwin Smith, lamenting, "In this country, what is there for Conservatives to conserve, or for Reformers to reform?" Early in this century, there was Mackenzie King, labouring over *Industry and Humanity*, and then forgetting about it. In the 1940's, there was Harold Innis, a thinker whom only a few understood, postulating that Canada was indeed an organic economic unit from east to west, and beginning the exploration of the transformational power of communications technology that Marshall McLuhan later extrapolated from and popularized.

By the late 1950's, and into the early 1960's, as Canada became increasingly urbanized and affluent, ideas at last began to become negotiable currency – if only on the margins of the political system. Donald Creighton wrote of the empire of the St. Lawrence; Gad Horowitz defined his theory of Red Toryism. Most thinkers, in this period, belonged to one of two main groups. Within Quebec, a succession of activist thinkers – André Laurendeau, Claude Ryan, Maurice Lamontagne, Jean-Marc Léger, Trudeau, and Pelletier; (to be followed later by Claude Morin, René Lévesque, Pierre Vallières) – considered the condition of French Canadians and proposed ways, however much these contradicted one another, in which the relations between this threatened minority and the dominant majority could be re-ordered. In English Canada, Walter Gordon became spiritual godfather to a comparable succession of activist thinkers: Eric Kierans, Abraham Rotstein, Mel Watkins, later James Laxer, Allan Blakeney, Ed Broadbent, who addressed themselves to the threat that Canada's majority faced from the incomparably larger majority south of the border.

All these thinkers responded to a concrete situation: French Canadians as a people colonized politically: English Canadians as a people colonized economically. They proposed concrete remedies. They wrote, or spoke, for the moment.

The list of contemporary Canadians who have developed their political ideas from a basis of first principles is brief: Trudeau; George Grant, the Dalhousie philosopher; and, as Grant's successor, espousing not conservatism but, its refined logical extension, gentle anarchism, George Woodcock. Of the three, the contrasts between Grant and Trudeau, each in the mainstream, the one conservative, the other liberal, are particularly revealing.* In *Lament for a Nation* (1965), and more clearly so in *Technology and Empire* (1969), Grant used circumstances that happened to apply in Canada as a convenient point of entry into an inquiry into the human condition threatened, as he saw it, by the homogenizing onslaught of technological liberal materialism. Just as Trudeau used Duplessis's Quebec as a proving ground for his ideas about

*For this perception, I am indebted to Ramsay Cook. For a scholarly analysis of contemporary Canadian political ideas, see Cook's *The Maple Leaf Forever*, Macmillan, 1971.

federalism, so Grant used Canada in the 1960's as a cautionary example of social dehumanization. Federalism in Canada, Trudeau wrote, could be "a brilliant prototype for the moulding of tomorrow's civilization." In counterpoint, Grant wrote, "What lies behind the small practical question of Canadian nationalism is the larger context of the fate of western civilization ... in advanced, technological societies."

Trudeau differed from Grant, obviously, in that he won the chance to put his ideas into practice. Less obviously, but more significantly, while Grant is a pessimist, Trudeau is (or was) an optimist. Grant, early in the 1960's, already saw English Canada as doomed. (One of Grant's unstated assumptions, unstated also by most other Canadian nationalists like him, is that "English Canada" is peopled exclusively by English Canadians.)

Trudeau's unstated assumption, as the logical and inevitable consequence of a belief in rationalism, is human perfectibility. Rationalists have to be optimists. They have to believe that individuals will automatically seek excellence, which is the rational thing to do; have to believe, further, that political problems can be solved, or at least ameliorated, by applying the solvent of rationalism. Crucial to the story of Trudeau in power is his transition from optimist to pessimist, as he discovered that most people are *not* rational, that most can't be bothered to pursue excellence, and that many political problems cannot be solved by *any* means.

* * *

To grasp Trudeau's ideas, it's necessary first to grasp the mind that conceived them. As important as *what* Trudeau thinks, is the *way* he thinks.

In sheer power and range, Trudeau's mind is the finest of all our Prime Ministers. (Some claim, though this is probably just nostalgia, that Arthur Meighen was his intellectual equal.) By his mind alone, Trudeau dominates almost everyone who meets him. "Pearson was merely one of us," Mitchell Sharp has said, "whereas Trudeau was not – he was someone extraordinary." A former aide, himself uncommonly intelligent says, "I loved him for that marvellous, marvellous mind."

Memory is the single most impressive component. Almost everyone likens Trudeau's mind to a computer: capacious, inexhaustible, and precise. He could (and frequently did) quote back

50

passages of a memorandum six months after receiving it. An aide remembers him giving a political speech that reproduced, word for word, a text he'd read only twice before (once in the car en route to the rally). In argument, he can use his memory to devastating effect, recalling statements an opponent made months before which contradict whatever he happens now to be saying.

Next, *ability to concentrate*. Trudeau devotes the same total attention to analyzing each successive problem as he does to any task, whether this is polishing up his scuba diving technique, or boning up on Tibetan culture in advance of his trip there. At cabinet meetings, Trudeau invariably knew as much or more about the issue at hand as the minister responsible – although as the years passed, this phenomenon became less marked. To prepare himself, Trudeau performed like a workoholic mandarin. Night after night, at home, he ploughed his way through the "damned brown boxes" as Margaret called them. Predictably, the real mandarins took advantage of Trudeau's single-mindedness and piled more and more briefing notes and memoranda into the boxes; to their delight all this paper burden would come back to their desks, underlinings and annotations in Trudeau's bold, declarative handwriting on every page.

Clarity is the third defining quality. Trudeau's mind is ordered, sequential, linear. When he's reading, he never skips. When he's analyzing a problem, he never slides past a part of the problem that seem unresolvable, nor fails to pursue to the uttermost limit all the consequences, political and intellectual, of any solution that comes to his own or to anyone else's mind. The observation he makes most frequently in cabinet discussions is, "But if we do X, surely Y will happen." An aide recalls, "Those pitiless, pitiless questions. He was not interested in showing you to be wrong, but in making certain that you were right." One of Trudeau's ministers, Francis Fox, says: "His ability to think things right through, to foresee the implications of proposals, was uncanny and unnerving."

Because he impressed almost everyone by the quality of his mind, Trudeau misled many about its nature. "A sharp mind, but not a deep one," says an associate of many years. "He has trained it as he has trained his body, he stretches it to the limit." To a degree, his gift of memory makes the power behind it seem more incandescent than it really is. Canadians were dazzled by his ability to drop aphorisms from Georges Buffon—"*le style c'est l'homme même*"—and to rattle off passages from Baudelaire. Such pyrotechnics aren't showing off, so much as the outward manifestation of a life-long love of reading and a photographic recall.

But Trudeau's mind is *analytical*, not *creative*. In his youth, unlike most nascent intellectuals, he never attempted poetry or fiction; his analogies, in essays, rarely soar off the page. Pelletier says that he found writing hard: "He used to compare it to having a tooth pulled." Perhaps the only time he demonstrated imaginative powers was in his 1944 essay, "Exhaustion and Fulfilment: The Ascetic in a Canoe." In contrast to Grant, who has attempted to advance the analysis of technological society beyond the point reached by Jacques Ellul in the mid-1950's, Trudeau's political thought contains no element of originality. When first discovered in 1967-68, his ideas seemed to be original because there were then so few political ideas extant in Canada, and because he expressed them in such evocative, epigrammatic prose—as in, "the glue of nationalism will become as obsolete as the divine right of kings." Instead of being original, Trudeau's ideas are rather the product of his schooling, his reading, and the times in which he came of intellectual age, all of these refined through the prism of his original personality.

* * *

The sources of Trudeau's ideas are easy to trace. They are derived from nineteenth century Liberalism, derived in turn from eighteenth century Rationalism, and brought up to date to take account of advances in science and the new phenomenon of the nation-state. The second source is the Jesuit doctrine of "sufficient grace."

The two sources have much in common. Each takes as its starting point the sovereignty of the individual. This sovereignty is supreme or sacred, and overarches political systems, which exist to serve the individual rather than a collectivity. Trudeau's ideas follow directly. Because the individual is rational, the state must be rational. Of all the political systems, federalism is the most rational, because it best protects the sovereignty of the individual.

At Harvard, Trudeau met Louis Hartz, who was then beginning the seminal study of the nature of liberalism in American society that profoundly influenced Grant; at the London School of Economics, thanks to Laski, he absorbed Lord Acton's theories of federalism. Perhaps, as decisively as by any teacher, Trudeau was influenced by the temper of the two intellectual climates in which he grew up: the astringent, Jesuitical atmosphere of Brébeuf; the heady, expansive atmosphere of post-war liberal idealism.

The prevailing Catholic dogma in Quebec during the years Trudeau attended Brébeuf was Jansenism. This profoundly pessimistic philosophy – perfectly suited to a society that aspired to nothing more than *la survivance* – holds that man can never recover from his fall from grace, from his original sin. In contrast, the Jesuits who taught Trudeau were, in the way of all Jesuits, *optimists*. They believed in the perfectibility of man. Through God's "sufficient grace," man could rise above his fall. "There is no soul so feeble that it cannot, if well-directed, acquire an absolute power over its passions," Descartes, greatest of all Jesuit students, wrote. Will, in other words, could enable rational man to conquer his passions and free himself to pursue excellence.

The sign "Pierre Trudeau, Citizen of the World" that Trudeau hung on his door at Harvard in 1945 mirrored the mood of the times. The war had proven that liberal democracy was the best of all systems. Having triumphed over irrational racism, the best and the brightest of that era set out to establish a new, rational, democratic order in which men, no matter their colour, creed, or language, would count for more than race, religion, or what George Orwell called "the nasty little isms" of ideology. World student movements, movements to promote world federalism, institutions dedicated to espousing the rule of law all exemplified the new, rational utopianism. Nothing exemplified it more eloquently than the 1948 Universal Declaration of Human Rights enshrined in the United Nations' Charter. "Recognition of the inherent dignity and of the equal and inalienable rights of all members of the human family is the foundation of freedom, justice and peace in the world." Between that brave espousal of the conviction that out of legal equalities all other equalities would flow, and Trudeau's decade-long attempt to incorporate a Bill of Rights into the Canadian constitution, the line is unbroken.

* * *

The sovereignty of the individual is the *alpha* and *omega* of Trudeau's political thinking. All men are brothers, that is to say equals, Bernier had taught him. Everything in between is just a means to promote this end.

An individual, although sovereign, cannot live in isolation. He must live in communion with others so that, as Trudeau has written, "we can tackle collectively the problems that we cannot solve individually." Yet by living with others, the individual surrenders a part of his sovereignty. To resolve this age-old dilemma of politics and of philosophy about the proper balance between freedom and order, Trudeau coined the phrase "the servant state." This concept – its evident antecedent is Rousseau's "social contract" – is the closest Trudeau has come to intellectual originality.

In his series *Approaches to Politics*, in the Montreal magazine, *Vrai*, Trudeau developed this idea. In living together in communities, men acted like bees. But unlike bees, "men are always free to decide what form of authority they will adopt, and who will exercise it. And it really is men who have the responsibility of taking these decisions, not God, Providence or Nature. In the last analysis, any given political authority exists only because men consent to obey it. In this sense, what exists is not so much the authority as the obedience."

In exchange for a surrender by individuals of part of their sovereignty, the state has also to surrender a part of its authority to its citizens. It has to allow them to participate. "A true political conscience will be born only at the instigation of a vast political education movement which will make the people conscious of their powers, and put them in a well-established position to exercise them."

Trudeau (in an aspect of his thinking that Canadians only really woke up to when he mused out loud in 1975 about a "New Society" in which the role of the state would constantly expand) harboured almost no doubts about the essential benignity of the servant state, particularly when he was at the head of it. After his defeat in 1979, he was as depressed by his conviction that years would pass before citizens, in their then prevailing neo-conservative mood, would again trust the state to do things for them, as he was by the defeat itself.

Much earlier, much of his quarrel with Duplessis had been with Duplessis's failure to *use* the state: "As long as the Quebec state is not equipped with a civil service that is really up to the job, it cannot be hoped that the state will protect the public good ... Everywhere in the world, strong states and competent administrations are required." Nor, as harbinger of the War Measures Act, did he deny to the state the right to use force, for the good of the citizens. "The truly democratic state should rather court obedience ... [it] must use force only to the extent that individuals or organizations try to use it themselves against the common good."

* * *

Democracy, civil liberties, rationalism. For Trudeau, these were the essentials. Once they were achieved, the particular political system that a particular state adopted mattered incomparably less. Contrary to Trudeau's reputation for being a fanatic of federalism – a "rigid centralist" in the parlance of his critics – federalism is almost an accidental by-product of his political thought. He only really wrote extensively about federalism from about 1960 on, when, fulfilling his concept of "counterweights," he defended federalism against what he considered to be irrational, and potentially racist, nationalism.

Federalism attracted Trudeau because it was inherently rational. Authority was delegated to junior governments, which were closer to the people, thus making participation easier to attain. Federalism allowed people of different cultures to live together and to enrich one another without crushing one another.

In support of federalism, Trudeau quoted Acton:

The co-existence of several nations under the same State is a test, as well as the best security of its freedom ... Where political and national boundaries coincide, society ceases to advance, and nations relapse into a condition corresponding to that of men who renounce intercourse with their fellow-men.

About the nature of his opposition to nationalism, Trudeau – in striking contrast to those who shouted " *Vendu*" at him – was clear and specific. He didn't oppose the cultural manifestations of nationalism at all. Rather, he espoused cultural distinctiveness – "pluralism" – as holding the promise of being "a brilliant prototype for the moulding of tomorrow's civilization." Cultural pluralism had to be preserved, enhanced, set free to seek its own limits. English Canadians could not, must not, assimilate the French-speaking minority. The two languages and cultures should be made equal. "In Canada, there are two main ethnic and

55

linguistic groups; each is too strongly and too deeply-rooted in the past, too firmly-bound to a mother culture, to be able to engulf the other." If only each group would embrace the other or, at least, accept the other, "Canada could become the envied seat of a form of federalism that belongs to tomorrow's world."

All Trudeau's opposition to nationalism centred on its political aspects. "It is not the concept of nation that is retrograde," runs the opening passage of the most famous of his essays, "The New Treason of the Intellectuals," in 1962, "It is the idea that the nation must necessarily be sovereign. The nation-state which has managed to cripple the advance of civilization," he wrote in the body of that piece. Political nationalism was retrograde because it turned people away from the pursuit of social, economic, political, and juridical advancements, and turned them in upon themselves. "We remain stewing steadily in our own juice without daring even once to peek over the edge of the pot . . . [Separatists] want to make the whole tribe return to the wigwams."

After 1976, the Parti Québécois demonstrated that Quebec could have both nationalism and "good government" at once. But in the 1950's, under Duplessis, and with memories of Nazism so recent, Trudeau was almost writing the obvious when he described Quebec as a "charnel-house" and wrote: "A nationalistic government is by nature intolerant, discriminatory and when all is said and done, totalitarian."

* * *

"Consistency," John Saywell writes in his introduction to *Federalism and the French Canadians*, "is the most remarkable quality of Mr. Trudeau's thoughts and actions over the past two decades." The riposte, made many times, is that Trudeau thereby demonstrates rigidity and inflexibility. More important to the story of Trudeau as a man and as a politician is that for all the power, lucidity, style of his writings, he emerges out of them as a one-dimensional thinker.

Considering how much Trudeau has read, it is striking how much he failed to absorb. He studied Schumpeter at Harvard, yet either missed or ignored Schumpeter's 1950 analysis of how the benign state can turn into a malignant bureaucracy that "grows everywhere, whatever the political method a nation may adopt. Its expansion is the one certain thing over our future." Milovan

Djilas, in *The New Class*, said the same thing in more vivid, personal terms. Trudeau read all the political classics, yet overlooked Edmund Burke's dictum about the limits to rational problem-solving: "Know how much of an evil ought to be tolerated, lest by attempting a degree of purity impractical, one succeeds only in producing new corruptions." He was steeped in the literature of the Jesuits, down to the writings of Juan de Mariana on the legitimacy of overthrowing a tyrant, yet somehow missed the warning by Jacques Maritain, the post-war Jesuit scholar, that to believe too literally in human perfectibility leads to "angelism" – the belief that man could become an angel.

Looked at closely, some of the lacunae in Trudeau's writing become almost as noticeable as his sweeping, erudite analyses. To cover them up, he enunciated his theory of "counterweights," or of counter-punching the conventional wisdom. Playing devil's advocate in a faculty room debate is one thing; having no idea what to do about most of the things a Prime Minister has to do something about is quite another.

Economics, for instance, is hardly touched on at all. It enters only as an afterthought, as an extension of the notion of the sovereignty of the individual. "A sound economic policy must never be based on the assumption, for example, that workers would be ready to accept a drastic lowering of standards of living for the mere pleasure of seeing a national middle-class replacing a foreign one at the helm of various enterprises." In contradiction to the view of many Canadian businessmen that Trudeau is some kind of closet socialist,* in contradiction also to his own concept of the benign state, Trudeau in his writings (no doubt influenced by the memory of his father) appears as a private enterpriser. He will accept that "the state must occasionally intervene in the play of economic forces to better ensure the pursuit of social objectives." But not too often. "The role of politics is even more delicate regarding technology than it is regarding population or capital"; "The economy of Quebec must not be isolated, but open to the whole world, for then it will find new markets as well as the competition it has to expect."

When it comes to social policy, Trudeau has even less to say. It

*In 1976, following Trudeau's "New Society" musing on television, some out-of-context citations of his, all taken from his 1964 essay for the book, *Social Purpose for Canadians*, were circulated among corporate boardrooms.

consists "in so organizing a political community that all its members have the essentials before a few are allowed to enjoy the superfluous." By the standards of those times – Trudeau was writing in 1965 – his thinking about social matters would scarcely have qualified him for the label social democrat. Rather, he was a juridical democrat. "In a constitutional society, it is not men but rather laws that control us." Given equality before the law, and a certain minimal economic equality, all would be free, equally, to pursue excellence, and thus to solve their own problems. When it came to human frailties which inhibited so many from seeking excellence – the inferiority complex of French Canadians, of native peoples, of women – Trudeau evidenced not the slightest awareness.

There are other blind spots. Trudeau never discusses the role of leadership – as if Quebec would have been the same without Duplessis. He ignored the role of institutions, whether in promoting pluralistic federalism, as in the case of the Canada Council, or in retarding it, as the St. Jean Baptiste Society. He ignores, it hardly needs to be said, the human condition.

A final example of something else Trudeau overlooked demonstrates an instance where he fails conspicuously to follow the logical consequences of his own analysis. Participatory democracy, taken to its natural conclusions, amounts to government by plebiscite. People deal directly with the state, and it with them. No role remains to Parliament. Trudeau has always found it hard to take Parliament seriously. He finds it boring, silly, time-wasting, a kind of club for overgrown schoolboys in which M.P.s rag one another and adopt positions they don't believe in, just to embarrass the other side. "It's a place where men are shouting . . . and I find that vulgar, it offends me," he has said. Those who accused Trudeau of seeking to establish an imperial presidency were on target. The president, who just so happened to be him, would rule, not by divine right but by participatory right, and by virtue of his being rational, wise, and benign.

*　*　*

For all his shortcomings, Trudeau is without intellectual equal among Canadian politicians, today or in the past, and there are few in the world who can challenge him. (Of all the leaders Trudeau met, the one who most impressed him, left him awed, was Chou En-lai.)

In power, Trudeau tried to practise his beliefs; whether or not this was sensible, or practical, it was courageous and consistent. He also, though this was never his intention, symbolized in his person a role model of intellectual excellence that many thousands of Canadians have attempted, perhaps unconsciously, to emulate in their private lives.

About what he truly believes in, Trudeau refuses to compromise—even an iota. Several times, for instance, his Quebec ministers pleaded with him to compromise on bilingualism, so that the program could be sold more easily. Each time Trudeau was adamant. The principle was right and just; English Canadians would have to accept it—pushed down their throats if necessary. "Bilingualism, for him, was far more than just something that was essential to the survival of French Canadians," one of Trudeau's senior francophone ministers has said. "For him, it was a *human right*, no different from freedom of speech, or freedom of religion. He would no more have compromised on it than he would have compromised on any basic human right."

4

The Morning of
the Magician

"There was a sense during that remarkable summer that, as a people, we might never be the same again."

Robert Fulford
This was Expo

Later, Trudeau teasingly told reporters they'd "invented him." Reporters hadn't though, at the time, almost all of them were his adoring acolytes. Canadians invented Trudeau. We invented him because after that long magical summer, we wanted to re-invent ourselves.

Without Expo, Trudeau could never have become Prime Minister. He was too unconventional, too uncommon, too fey. Once Expo had happened, he, or someone like him, was inevitable. We knew we needed a leader with magical qualities. When the historian John Saywell described Trudeau as "an experiment in Canadian public life," when the columnist Peter C. Newman wrote that he could lead us to "an unknown, exciting future," they were commenting as much upon a collective happening as upon the person who happened to be on the scene at the same time. Newman called Expo "one of those rare moments that change the direction of a nation's history." Dalton Camp called it a "national liberation of creative talent." But the best insight into how Expo had disconnected us from our accustomed selves so that we fell over one another to embrace Trudeau was made by an Ottawa woman, Norma Summers, in a letter to the editor in *Maclean's*.

What could we sober, Canadian squares possibly be thinking of, wanting this strange little customer for Prime Minister? It's madness. The whole country needs a cold shower. Yet I, like the rest, will vote for him anyway.

* * *

We suspended disbelief to believe in Trudeau because Expo, for the first time, had made us believe in ourselves. Until then, we'd had little enough to believe in. Our history was bland, despite the best efforts of a Donald Creighton, a Pierre Berton, to make it seem heroic. Our roles in two World Wars had been minor, though honourable. No civil wars or revolutions. No being best in the world at anything except – in those days – hockey. We had the Royal Canadian Mounted Police. We grew a lot of wheat. We prospered. That, plus the ethic of survival/*la survivance* was about it. The only metaphor that had ever cast us romantically was Douglas LePan's wonderful phrase, "frockcoat and moccasins," and that era was long gone. Mostly, we dealt in British or French hand-me-downs, or carbon copies passed up from south of the border. "A Canadian," William Kilbourn wrote, "has been defined as someone who does not play for keeps."

At Expo, we went for broke. We put forward our very best, invited the world – 50 million visitors in six months – to come and judge. The world cheered. "Canada has attained adulthood," declared *Le Figaro*. "What's got into our good, grey neighbours?" read the caption on the cover of *Look*. "Canada Discovers Itself" pronounced *Time*. We risked national humiliation, and we brought off an international sensation.

At Expo, the mood was wondrous, innocent, and joyful. Strangers would meet each other on St. Helen's Island, try out each other's languages, wind up holding each other's hands. Hardly anyone got drunk; hardly anyone fought; hardly anyone was robbed. Again and again, we visited Expo to gawk at the hostesses in mini-skirts, to tumble merrily down the flume ride at *La Ronde*, to marvel at the sly self-mockery of the British pavilion, the insouciant gaiety of the U.S. dome, the frivolity of the Czechs, who dared so bravely to show the human face of socialism. Above all, we marvelled at ourselves. Much of the fairest at the fair was all our own. The incandescent, multi-image movies, like *Labyrinth* and *A Place to Stand*, the delicate, humanist architecture of Man and the Community, and the gravity-defying daring of the inverted ziggurat, *Katimavik*. As we watched an Atlantic schooner being lovingly crafted together, listened to *chansonniers* at the Quebec *boîte*, we learned about our regional differences, and we began to treasure them.

Because this was Centennial year, the spirit of Expo went on all year long. During 1967, 700,000 small-sized Maple Leaf flags were sold, and 85,000 large ones. Spontaneously, in Europe and South America, young Canadian wanderers stitched maple leafs to their knapsacks, or stuck them on the bumpers of their Volkswagen bugs. In the official celebrations, we all participated democratically. On July 1, pomp, circumstance, and the Queen were all in Ottawa. But the party was everywhere. In Yellowknife, the town turned out to watch a twenty-four-hour midnight sun; in Halifax, a picnic in the Public Gardens attracted 20,000, the largest gathering in the city since VE Day. We wanted the party to go on forever. On New Year's Eve, the citizens of Bowsman, Ontario, lit a ceremonial bonfire and burned thirty-three outhouses made obsolete by a new sewage system paid for by a Centennial grant.

Here and there, those days of wine and roses, there were worms in the bud. Charles De Gaulle had come, had said, "Vive le Québec Libre" from the balcony of Montreal's City Hall, and then left in a huff when Prime Minister Pearson said he was no longer welcome. Montreal's St. Jean Baptiste Society boycotted Centennial celebrations on July 1. In *Le Devoir*, Claude Ryan wrote opaque, discursive editorials which, when they finally arrived at their point, declared that Quebec had to have "special status." In November, René Lévesque formed *Le Mouvement Souveraineté Association* and explained, "We are attached to this one corner of the earth where we can be completely ourselves."

Even so, as a collective pursuit of excellence, it had been as close to flawless as any nation could hope to accomplish. In the end, as Fulford noted in his book, the defining image of Canada created by Expo and the Centennial was a cartoon in the November 18, 1967 issue of the *New Yorker*. Two men sit in a Manhattan bar. One says to the other. "But you don't *look* like a Canadian."

* * *

Trudeau didn't look like a Canadian. This was the beginning from which all the rest would flow. Trudeau might just stop us from drifting back into being the kind of Canadians we had been before.

We first began to notice him toward the end of 1967. He had been in Parliament for two years, and except for once having outraged Diefenbaker by coming into the Commons in ascot and sandals, had made no mark whatsoever. Even though he arrived in 1965 in a flurry of publicity as one of Pearson's Three Wise Men recruits from Quebec, almost all the attention had been paid to Jean Marchand.

If not for Trudeau's urgings, Marchand and Pelletier might never have come to Ottawa. Back in 1963, when Pearson made his first attempt to recruit the trio, Marchand had wanted to go to Quebec City, where the Quiet Revolution was in full flight, while Pelletier hadn't wanted to go anywhere.

Pearson's reversal on nuclear weapons ended the 1963 initiative. In *Cité Libre*, Trudeau denounced Pearson's "hypocrisy" and called him the "defrocked Priest of Peace." By 1965, though, the Liberals' need for new Quebec strength had become acute: a series of squalid scandals had destroyed all of Pearson's earlier recruits: Guy Favreau, Maurice Lamontagne, Lucien Cardin, René Tremblay. Liberal organizers offered Marchand the Quebec leadership if only he would come in. Marchand agreed, but only if Pelletier and Trudeau came in beside him. When Liberals demurred that Trudeau had said too many unforgivable things, Marchand stood firm, and did so on the best of all possible advice. Telephoning long distance from Newfoundland, where he'd gone to attend a "Thinkers' Conference" organized by Joey Smallwood, René Lévesque urged that the three must go together as a reform-minded "bloc," not all alone and vulnerable, as he had gone to Quebec City. In the end, everyone agreed to let bygones be bygones. All three ran. All three, in the general election of November 8, 1965, were elected easily.

In contrast to Marchand, the group leader, and much more so to Pelletier, retiring by nature, Trudeau was at home in Ottawa from the start. He had friends who remembered him from his Privy Council Office days in the early 1950's. He was flawlessly bilingual. Best of all, his freedom was scarcely impaired. In his riding of Mount Royal he could count on being re-elected forever without needing to set foot in the place. He could take off for a wilderness river, or London, New York, or Paris, at the drop of a hat.

Trudeau, in fact, had no desire to do more. When Marchand, in January 1966, convinced Pearson to promote Trudeau to the prestige post as his Parliamentary Secretary, he had to spend three days convincing Trudeau to accept. "He said he didn't want to give up his lifestyle," Marchand recalls. "He said he didn't want to be locked up in a room all day writing texts for the Prime Minister." In April 1967, when Marchand persuaded Pearson to name Trudeau Justice Minister, Trudeau again played reluctant debutant. Then, once he'd been named minister, Trudeau dropped promptly from sight.

On December 5, 1967, Trudeau leapt into the spotlight. In the Commons, he spoke for forty minutes on Bill C-187, "An Act Respecting Divorce." Grounds for divorce would be expanded from old-fashioned adultery to include perversions such as bestiality and rape, "physical and mental cruelty of a kind to render intolerable continued cohabitation," and, the broadest category of all, "marriage breakdown." As compelling as the policy was the person who became an instant star by the way he argued his brief; eloquent, cool, cerebral yet impassioned, fluent in both languages, and above all, so modern and so daring—a Catholic widening the grounds for dissolving a sacrament that his church held to be indissoluble.

Abruptly, the press began to write about Trudeau. They wrote more two weeks later, when he brought down the Omnibus Bill to reform the Criminal Code—legalizing lotteries and therapeutic abortions, and decriminalizing a variety of acts, the most contentious being homosexuality when "performed in private between consenting adults." To justify this, Trudeau tossed off the most resonant of all his phrases: "The state has no place in the bedrooms of the nation."* The entire nation sat up and took notice.

* * *

The race for the Liberal leadership began officially on December 14, 1967, when Pearson announced his retirement and set April 4-6, 1968, as the dates for the leadership convention. Quickly, the Liberal luminaries and lesser lights began to rally their troops: Paul Martin, Mitchell Sharp, Paul Hellyer, John Turner, Allan MacEachen, Joe Greene, Eric Kierans. Absent from the list, markedly, was a single French Canadian.

Marchand, Minister of Manpower and Immigration, was the obvious candidate. He was Quebec leader. He was the senior French-speaking minister. Pearson wanted him as successor. So did a group of influential English Canadians led by Walter Gordon.

---

*This is the way the phrase always is quoted, although Trudeau actually said, in an interview on December 22, 1967, "The state has no place in the nation's bedroom." The original author of the phrase was *Globe and Mail* editorial writer Martin O'Malley

Yet by the fall of 1967 Marchand had already decided he would not seek the prize. His reasons for doing so define the man: emotional, impulsive, generous.

* * *

Of the Three Wise Men in 1965, Marchand had been the "catch." Yet from first to last, he fared the least well. In 1980, he ended up in the undemanding role of Senate Speaker, a position which removed him from the Liberal caucus, and from direct involvement in the Quebec referendum.

In December 1967, though, Marchand was still flying high. He was incomparably better known than Trudeau, and incomparably better liked by M.P.s. He was rumpled, plainspoken, down to earth. He'd grown up the youngest of six, in a Montreal slum, worked his way through Laval University, then battled to the top of the Confederation of National Trade Unions (CNTU). As a union leader, he was fearless, tough, autocratic, and ruthless.

But in Ottawa, except when he was banging heads within the Quebec Liberal federation or passing convivial evenings with backbenchers, Marchand found the going tough. He lacked the administrative ability to run a department (though between 1972-75, he did creditably enough as Minister of Transport). Because he lacked verbal self-control, he was always in hot water. He called English Canadians "bigots" for voting against Trudeau in 1972; in 1975, he admitted his Transport Department was "a mess."

Despite the urgings of Gordon, Marchand foresaw all these inadequacies. As well, his health was uncertain (he suffers from high blood pressure which produces dizzy spells) and his English was indifferent. Still, had he run, Marchand would have run well, even though he probably would not have won. Instead, in a rare act of political self-sacrifice, Marchand thrust the glittering prize away from himself, and thrust it directly into Trudeau's hands.

* * *

Once Marchand was out, Trudeau had to come in. Otherwise there would have been no French Canadian in the race. The story of how Trudeau won, once he entered, has been recounted many times, most vividly and fully in Martin Sullivan's *Mandate '68*. In essence, he could not lose. He had everything. Style: the rose in the lapel and the silver Mercedes. Wit: asked about the Mercedes, he replied, "Do you mean the car – or the girl?" Presence: a "skull-formed face," wrote Newman, "which might have been carved in alabaster to commemorate some distant war of the crusades." A top-flight organization: bareknuckle Québécois and brainy, trendy, English-speaking small l Liberals in roughly equal parts. Above all, Trudeau had luck. In January, though not yet a declared candidate, he toured the provincial capitals in a dashing leather coat as Pearson's constitutional emissary and thus managed to appear on television almost every night; early in February, at Pearson's side, he slugged it out in Single Combat with Quebec Premier Daniel Johnson, winning on all cards, in the conference chamber and on the television screens. Most of all, he won because if Expo had been a person, that person would have been Trudeau.

The story that remains to be told about Trudeau's accession to the leadership is when, exactly, he decided to run, and who, in the last analysis, persuaded him. "I was pushed," he has said, and left it at that. The truth is that he was pushed decisively on two separate occasions, and changed his mind in between. Three people were involved.

* * *

The first operative was Roy Faibish, then a CBC producer, now a Canadian Radio-Television and Telecommunications Commission commissioner. A romantic from Saskatchewan, Faibish had been one of the most important figures in the Diefenbaker government's back rooms; he lived more or less constantly in a state of feverish intensity. For Faibish, Trudeau's ideas now had become seminal. On December 14, 1967, at a small private dinner party in Rockcliffe, Faibish manoeuvred Trudeau into the library and for fifteen minutes explained feverishly that for the sake of the country, and as the only conceivable political response to the new mood of the times, he had to run. Later, Trudeau wrote to Faibish, thanking him for "talking me into it."

But Trudeau, in the style he was to repeat a dozen years later while trying to decide whether to return as Liberal leader, continued to pretend he hadn't made up his mind. He dropped hints, but didn't commit himself. Over the holidays, he flew to Tahiti to think things through while staring up at the sun; instead, he found himself staring into the lavender-blue eyes of one of the daughters of a former Liberal minister (and dedicated Turner supporter), James Sinclair. He came back, dined with Marchand and Pelletier, and let on, privately, that he was in the race. His supporters plunged quickly into the business of organizing "spontaneous events." Then, a few weeks later, Trudeau changed his mind.

On February 13, Trudeau phoned his two closest advisers: Marc Lalonde and Michael Pitfield, then both rising stars at the Prime Minister's Office and Privy Council Office respectively. For nearly six months, these two close friends — they met in 1959 when both were aides to Conservative Justice Minister Davie Fulton —had been pressing Trudeau to contest the leadership, because they were convinced only he could save Canada. For weeks, the two had been euphoric; abruptly, their upbeat mood dissolved. He'd made up his mind definitely at last, Trudeau told them. He would not run and nothing would convince him to change his mind. In despair, the two asked Trudeau to give them one last chance to state their case. Trudeau agreed. That evening, he met Lalonde and Pitfield in his House of Commons office.

Their problem, then as earlier, wasn't convincing Trudeau that he could do the job. "He never had any doubts he could do it," Lalonde recalls. The sticking point instead was to convince Trudeau that the job would suit *him*. He was adamant he wouldn't accept a job that would deny him his freedom.*

However the arguments went, when Lalonde and Pitfield left two hours later, they had Trudeau's promise to be a candidate. "Michael was brilliant," Lalonde later told associates. "He picked apart every single one of Trudeau's objections." In return, Trudeau extracted from the pair the promise – given eagerly – that they'd stay on and work for him. Then he put on his coat and walked alone around Parliament Hill, in the snow.

Some of this hesitation may have been play-acting, the ingrained desire of an intellectual to be seduced into doing something as grubby as becoming a politician. In 1975, in an interview with the BBC, Trudeau had a straight-forward explanation of his decision: after so many years as a critic telling governments what to do, he said, "if you have the chance of doing them yourself,

---

*Earlier, another aide, Ivan Head, had answered Trudeau's protests that he would be overworked by concocting the argument he would have to work less hard than he had had to as Justice Minister, because as Prime Minister, he wouldn't be responsible for any department.

you seize it, and I did." Three days later, at any rate, he wrote a formal note to John Nichol, the Liberal Party president. "After much thought, I have decided to offer my candidature for the position of leader of the Liberal Party of Canada."

* * *

The April convention was less a leadership contest than a love-in. A pre-convention poll showed public support for Trudeau at 32 per cent, against 14 per cent for Martin, 10 per cent for Winters, and with the rest nowhere. There were a few bad moments. The Quebec caucus whom Trudeau had described once as "donkeys" mutinied, and had to be bludgeoned into line by Marchand. Trudeau's convention speech was flat and uninspired.

None of this mattered. He had everything. The prettiest hostesses, in persimmon-coloured shifts from Montreal's *Poupée Rouge* boutique. Again, all the luck. Sharp withdrew on the first day and joined Trudeau in his box, a bony-faced model of WASP fiscal rectitude.

As well, Trudeau turned out to have qualities no one had counted on: the instincts of a consummate actor. He would wave to the crowds looking endearingly bashful, an impish little-boy half grin on his face, as a signal to the audience that he knew, and they knew, and each knew the other knew, that he wasn't all that bashful. It was a delicious matinée-idol bit of teasing, that made the adoring crowds work all the harder to evoke from him a full smile, in public confession of how much he was enjoying himself. It was Trudeau, and not any of his razor-keen advisers, who concocted the idea of the solitary Christ-like walk to the platform to give his speech, while in the auditorium the audience suddenly bloomed with white and orange placards, Birnam Wood come to Dunsinane. A few days earlier, preparing for his famous television interview with Patrick Watson (replayed on closed-circuit television to delegates in their hotel rooms) Faibish had advised Trudeau to make a special point of his newness and freshness. Trudeau waited until almost the end of the half-hour interview, then seized on Watson's last question to produce his resonant line: "New guys with new ideas."

All of Canada, glued to its television sets, wanted a new guy with new ideas to perpetuate Expo. The Liberal delegates, in fact, were more recalcitrant. They didn't know Trudeau; worse, in terms of their prospects for patronage, he didn't know them. Yet the public, the press, the spirit of the times, could not be denied. The count on the last ballot was: Trudeau, 1,203; Winters, 954; Turner 195 (among these to the end, James Sinclair's vote). When the result was announced, Trudeau plucked the carnation from his buttonhole and tossed it over the edge of his box.

*　*　*

The love-in continued. Within two weeks, Trudeau had taken a holiday in Florida (while photographers clicked, he executed backflips into the hotel pool), had shuffled his cabinet (Winters quit), had brought the Commons together, and on the same day dissolved it for an election on June 25.

The outcome was certain. He had, as McLuhan pronounced, "The perfect mask – a charismatic mask. He has the face of a North American Indian." The only point of doubt was the magnitude of the victory, and its extent across the country. In the west, the crowds were the largest since Diefenbaker; more than 1,000 in Yellowknife, 5,000 in Kamloops; 2,000 in Penticton for a flapjack picnic where the organizers quickly ran out of pancake mix; a tumultuous rally in Edmonton; a rapturous one in Regina, where the crowd held up hand-painted signs, "Vive le Canada; Merci Pierre"; and on to Toronto (60,000); and Montreal (45,000).

Once again, he could do nothing wrong. When a heckler, angry about the "permissiveness" of the Criminal Code amendments shouted, "What about masturbation?" Trudeau retorted, "I suppose everyone has his problems." When a pretty, nineteen-year-old co-ed declined his invitation to join him in a hotel pool because she lacked a bathing suit, Trudeau replied, "Marilyn Monroe did it." At the campaign's end, as if Trudeau needed any more luck, thugs broke up the St. Jean Baptiste Day parade in Montreal and the entire country watched on their screens as Trudeau, alone among the dignitaries on the reviewing stand, sat unflinching while Coke bottles whizzed past his head. Next day, a nun said to Trudeau, "I am so glad you weren't killed last night." "But my goodness," said Trudeau, "I was sitting beside the Archbishop."

Yet it had been a nearer run thing than the country realized at the time. Trudeau, for all he was so fit and lithe and graceful, lacked stamina. Though he adored being adored, he also found it a

69

bit of a bore. Toward the end of the campaign, he nearly quit. Not his job as Prime Minister. Just the campaign.

He was scheduled, during the second last week, to hop-skip through the west once again, from Vancouver to Victoria to Calgary to Winnipeg, then on to Toronto. He wouldn't do it, he told his organizers. He was tired and the trip wasn't necessary to win votes. For three days anxious messages flew back and forth between Trudeau's staff ("That's what he wants, and that's what he'll get") and Liberal headquarters. ("He can't do it. The program has been announced. Not to go is disaster.")

On Saturday, June 15, Trudeau flew into Ottawa. Party president Nichol and Marc Lalonde met him at the airport. They climbed into Trudeau's car and headed for 24 Sussex. During the drive, the conversation between Nichol and Trudeau went roughly as follows: "You have to go." "I'm not going." "You *are* going." "I'm bloody well *not* going." "*I'm* not going to phone the [western] organizers to cancel the program." "*You'll* damn well *have* to phone them." The contretemps continued in front of the canopied doorway at 24 Sussex, the driver sitting stolidly in front with Lalonde, Nichol and Trudeau in the back shouting at each other. An RCMP officer, alarmed, walked over, tapped on the car window, and asked Trudeau if everything was all right. He reassured the constable, and went back to shouting at Nichol. Then Trudeau stormed out of the car. As he reached the door, he turned. "God damn you," he said to Nichol. "I'll go."

Probably, if Trudeau had not gone west, Canadians would have cheered him for being so "unconventional," just as they cheered him throughout the campaign for making no promises – "Ottawa is not Santa Claus," he said – although in fact the reason for the absence of promises was that Trudeau had called the election so abruptly that he had no time to hammer together a platform. Yet the incident backstage contained a portent for the future. Trudeau revelled in being worshipped, but on his own terms. And no one around him doubted that it would never have entered Trudeau's mind to cancel a series of major public rallies if these had been scheduled for Quebec, rather than in the west.

On election night, June 25, 1968, Trudeau won 155 seats. The Conservatives held on to just 72, their worst performance since 1953. The New Democratic Party squeaked through with 22 and the Créditistes, confounding the pundits, actually increased their vote and returned 14 M.P.s. Trudeau had won 45.3 per cent of the total vote, a fifteen year high-water mark for the Liberals. More important than the size of his majority was its scope: 27 in the four western provinces, four, even in Alberta, and a clear majority in British Columbia (where NDP leader Tommy Douglas lost his seat).

*　*　*

More than simply the formal beginning of Trudeau's career as Prime Minister in his own right, the election of June 1968 is a benchmark of everything that has happened to him and us since.

The 1968 election was our last joyous collective experience together – except for the last minute of the eighth game of the first Canada-USSR hockey series of 1972, when Paul Henderson flipped the puck home and made us again, briefly, the best in the world. Otherwise, the 1968 election and the Centennial and Expo were together the last time we were wholly confident of ourselves as a country. We'd dreamed the impossible dream, in the words of the song from *Man from La Mancha* everyone was humming that year. And we'd fulfilled our dream, in Centennial and in Expo, and now in electing a Prime Minister whom almost everyone envied us for.

A friend of Trudeau attributes his unparallelled political longevity to his ability to remain "co-terminous with each new generation." In 1968, when the kissing was at its zenith, Trudeau won 53 per cent of votes of Canadians under thirty. In 1980, by then a sexagenarian, he won almost the same proportion – 50 per cent. The source of Trudeau's undimmed appeal is that he has become keeper of the magic flame: talisman of the last time all of us were young. In 1968, we invested a part of our national psyche in Trudeau. Although many times he has disappointed us, offended us, enraged us, we've never really wanted to take back our investment. We can't think of anyone else who might, one day, bring back the magical flame. We called it, in 1968, Trudeau-mania. Really, it was Canada-mania.

5

Sorcerer's Apprentices

"I first tried to learn the bent of his mind and then acted accordingly."

> J.W. Pickersgill, *éminence grise*
> to Prime Ministers Mackenzie King
> and Louis St. Laurent

The kissing stopped almost as soon as the ballots were counted. In its place, "the routinization of charisma" in Weber's phrase, set in. As early as August, reporters were complaining about the lack of news; Trudeau had told his ministers that anyone who "leaked" would be fired. His first Throne Speech in September was disappointing. Instead of bold phrases and promises of new departures, it was written in unassertive administrative prose and spelled out no new initiatives. Louis Giguère, a party drudge, turned up as Trudeau's first Senate appointment. Later Giguère turned up as central figure in the Sky Shops scandal.

Trudeau had foreseen the post-election letdown. "The trick will be to do enough fast enough before people like you are disappointed," he told writer Merle Shain shortly after the leadership convention. He didn't intend "to deliver a brand new Canada in six months," he told reporters.

If Trudeau had come to office with no precise idea of *what* he would do, he knew precisely *how* he would do it. Rational planning, made possible by the "cybernetic revolution," as he had called it; a "parallel power" to the bureaucracy of "new guys with new ideas."

Journalist Walter Stewart, a couple of years later, called this new cadre "The Supergroup." Getting a bit carried away, Stewart went on to describe it as "a positive evil . . . an administrative machine of awesome power." Supergroup, then as now, encompassed both Trudeau's political aides in the Prime Minister's Office, which doubled to 85, and the civil servants who served him in the Privy Council Office, which doubled also to just under 300. Most worked in the East Block (later, across Wellington Street in the Langevin

Building); all fervently denied they were members of Super-group.*

In 1968 (also in 1980) Supergroup contained three groups; the Insiders, who mattered; the In-Betweeners, who sometimes mattered; the Outsiders, who came, did their jobs, and then left, seldom with a thank you from Trudeau, but almost always convinced the experience of having worked with him was thanks enough, and more.

In 1968, the Insiders numbered seven. (An eighth, Jim Coutts, came later, and so will be described later.) Of the original septet, two – Pelletier and Marchand – were cabinet ministers; the only ministers who could drop into 24 Sussex uninvited and who, once inside, dared address Trudeau as "*tu*." After 1972, their influence on policy waned, and both were eclipsed by Lalonde. Pelletier continued to be Trudeau's closest friend; Marchand, though, became increasingly bitter about his exclusion from the centre. Three others were political aides: Marc Lalonde, who served as chief of staff from 1968 to 1972, and then became a senior minister; Ivan Head, adviser on foreign affairs until 1978; Jim Davey, who served as program secretary for four years but who was moved after the debacle of the 1972 election of which he was the strategist. The remaining two were civil servants: Michael Pitfield, Gordon Robertson.

Pitfield and Lalonde mattered the most by far. They made Trudeau Prime Minister: they have been at his side ever since. Of the pair, the most interesting, and by any standard the most important, is Pitfield. To write about Trudeau without writing about Pitfield would be like writing about Louis XIII without writing about Richelieu, or about Napoleon without Talleyrand or, a more benign analogy, about Franklin Roosevelt without Harry Hopkins. The careers of the two are symbiotic. They created each other. But for Pitfield, Trudeau never would have run for the Liberal leadership; but for Trudeau, Pitfield never would have become Clerk of the Privy Council, and come to wield more power than anyone in Canadian bureaucratic history since the mythic progenitors of the

*Supergroup, of course, was and is a myth, in the same way that the Establishment is a myth. Just as no businessman or society matron dares ignore the standards of behaviour laid down by the mythical Establishment, no Liberal politician or upwardly mobile civil servant dared to ignore the political codes laid down by the non-existent Supergroup.

modern bureaucracy, O.D. Skelton and Clifford Clark.

* * *

Once Pitfield reached the top, he assiduously covered all traces of his ties to Trudeau. These stretched back much further than the encounter of February 13, 1968, in which he personally convinced Trudeau to contest the leadership, as recounted in the previous chapter.

On a fine day in the spring of 1966, Marchand, Pelletier, and Trudeau gathered at Marchand's house at Cap Rouge just outside Quebec City to debate their post-Pearson political strategy. Once their meeting was done, they gathered outside on the lawn so that Georgette Marchand could capture the historic moment with her camera. This snap shows five people: the Three Wise Men as they had come to be known; Marc Lalonde, who as a political aide to Pearson had every right to be there; and Pitfield, who as an assistant secretary at PCO had no right to be there at all. Pitfield had come along at Lalonde's invitation: the two had been close friends since 1959 when they both worked in Davie Fulton's office. But Pitfield already had marked Trudeau as a comer: as early as 1962, he urged fellow public servants to hire "this bright Montreal law professor" on contract. In 1964, Pitfield translated the anti-nationalist Canadian manifesto of which Trudeau and Lalonde were the principal authors.

Although Pitfield was almost two decades younger than Trudeau, the two had a lot in common. Like Trudeau, Pitfield was a Montrealer, born to wealth. His father had died when he was a child. He grew up bilingual. His mother had the reputation for being a grande dame and her name by chance happened to be Grace. He was parsimonious, if possible even more so than Trudeau.* His intellectual biases ran toward the abstract, the federalist and the centralist.

Trudeau's pedigree though, wasn't nearly as classy. He was

---

*When Pitfield left the Civil Service in 1979, after turning down an offer from the new Conservative government to become ambassador to the Organization for Economic Cooperation and Development (OECD), he wangled for himself an unprecedented termination settlement, of $107,800. When he returned to his old job he repaid just $10,000, and when reporters questioned him about the propriety of this, said, "It's god-damn unfair."

haut-bourgeois Outremont, just a generation away from the land; Pitfield was a Square Mile aristocrat, as close as a colonial can get to Debrett, his father a brilliant financier originally from New Brunswick, who'd been an associate of Izaak Walton Killam; his mother a shipping heiress, with links to every important family in Montreal. In contrast to the daredevil Trudeau at Brébeuf, Pitfield at Lower Canada College, later at West Point, had been miserable. He was precocious and hopelessly unathletic, so that other boys didn't want to play with him. A contemporary remembers him as "a pathetic, sad stringy little boy with buck teeth and no friends."

Though he adored his mother she ignored him. He was the youngest of seven children, and after his father died, his brother Ward, now president of Pitfield Mackay Ross in Toronto, became head of the family. Acquaintances remember Michael saying, when he became Privy Council Clerk, "This'll show Ward who's the better man."

Pitfield's intelligence grew and grew and grew. At fourteen he went to St. Lawrence University in Canton New York because no other college would accept him so young. Later, after the spell at West Point, he collected two more degrees and briefly practised law. When he was twenty-four, Pitfield set out to find the youth he'd never known. He enrolled in the Naval Reserve as a sub-lieutenant and for a couple of summers tried to gear himself down to the intellectual pace and up to the knockabout lifestyle of the gunroom. He won a footnote in Naval folklore for his curious habit of marching, as one brother officer put it, "like a penguin." The physical awkwardness lingered, but he grew into a towering presence, with the narrow intellectual head, and pouty, sensual lips of Aldous Huxley in early portraits.

Idealism and self-interest propelling him in equal measure, Pitfield raced up the ladder. In 1959, at twenty-two, he came to Ottawa as Fulton's aide. The next year, he was appointed executive director to the Royal Commission on Publications chaired by the Conservative Senator Grattan O'Leary. Ever afterwards, Pitfield has attached himself to the coat-tails of a patron, the classic route upward, but in Pitfield's case, surely, also, the classic search for a father-figure. O'Leary, a romantic, racy Irishman perhaps came closest to filling that role. Pitfield idolized him, and through O'Leary's last, long, lingering illness, was a tireless visitor and bringer of news, gossip, and presents.

Next came Governor General Georges Vanier, for whom Pitfield wrote speeches and with whom he lived at Rideau Hall, in an apartment converted from the billiards room. Then Robert Bryce, Privy Council Clerk, who recruited Pitfield to that office in 1965. Then Trudeau.

Pitfield now was just past thirty. He was admired and feared in equal parts. Brains, connections, ambition, application, and an adroit choice of mentors had carried him this far. Trudeau pulled him right to the top, and indeed, in 1970, when Pitfield was just thirty-two, offered him the crown of the Privy Council Clerkship, which Pitfield, realizing he wasn't ready for, sagaciously declined until 1974. Yet Pitfield, because of two other aspects of his character, probably would have gone all the way anyway, his brilliance and his dedication quite apart.

The first aspect derives from a flaw. In contrast to Trudeau's almost superhuman self-sufficiency, Pitfield, as perhaps the legacy of an unhappy childhood, is curiously vulnerable. There is a sheen of sang-froid, but with everyone he meets he is wary. He has no real friends. A close acquaintance puts it this way: "Michael has, I think, a streak of paranoia. In the competitive jungle of Ottawa, that's enormously to his advantage. It makes him super-sensitive to plots and conspiracies that might threaten him and allows him, self-righteously, to strike rivals down, even if they aren't really rivals." Beyond a doubt Pitfield is the most adept, and most ferocious, bureaucratic infighter in Ottawa.

The other aspect is charm. Pitfield's charm is studied, but potent. He's a born courtier, an astute flatterer, and an artful self-promoter. In conversation he drops erudite quotes and famous names. Visitors who matter are shown his prizes: antique oriental rugs, a collection of Krieghoff's. Journalists considered important enough to talk to always are asked what *they* think.

Many in Ottawa think they have seen through Pitfield. His enemies, including cabinet ministers, call him "a big black spider." Almost alone among the key mandarins, Pitfield has never been invited to join the Five Lakes Fishing Club, the retreat in the Gatineau Hills where deputy ministers gather off duty to fish, canoe, hike, and trade gossip.

Not even his worst enemies question Pitfield's brains. Some

think his mind is superior to Trudeau's. His memory, for instance, is as capacious and he's as omnivorous a reader, although over a narrower range: history and political science. The key to their partnership, some suggest, is that their intellects complement each other. Trudeau is the analyst. Pitfield is the synthesizer. He can weave masses of disparate data into an integrated whole and, at the same time, relate gritty facts to lofty abstractions. Pitfield also has more political savvy: he identified Trudeau as a comer before Trudeau had identified himself as one; in 1972 he spotted another comer, a Toronto management consultant called Jim Coutts.

Nor do Pitfield's enemies question his idealism. His view of the civil service is that of a romantic: it exists to provide advice, disinterested and excellent, to the politicians whose duty it is to make the decisions. He's as much a romantic about Canada, and in the early 1960's, far ahead of all but a handful, concluded that fundamental changes had to be made if the country were to be kept as one.

Ottawa has gossiped incessantly about the relationship between Pitfield and Trudeau — they holidayed together as bachelors, married within a few months of each other, after which Nancy Pitfield became one of Margaret's closest friends. One Canadian novelist set out to write a *roman à clef* about the pair and then abandoned the attempt as beyond his powers of imagination. One close observer suggests that the relationship may be the inverse of what everyone assumes, that perhaps Pitfield is the sorcerer and Trudeau his apprentice. It is true that it took Pitfield to persuade Trudeau to run; true that Trudeau called Pitfield before making up his mind to run again in 1979 and got from him a commitment to return as Privy Council Clerk before making up his own mind; true that many times at cabinet meetings the arguments Trudeau has made have been replications, line for line, of briefing notes.

Yet Pitfield remains dependent on Trudeau. Trudeau can do so much that Pitfield cannot: be an athlete; be an object of desire to women; be a writer (Pitfield's prose is leaden); be popular; be elected Prime Minister. "Michael is scared of Pierre" says someone who knows both well. For all Pitfield's power and intimidating presence, there clings to him a faint aura of Widmerpool, the dogged, seeker after power in Anthony Powell's series of novels, *A Dance to the Music of Time*. Despite his extraordinary success,

Pitfield remains curiously solitary, uncertain, vulnerable. Only after about 1977, by then confident of his position, did Pitfield begin to act, as one minister describes it, "not as Trudeau's representative to the civil service, but as he should have all along, the representative of the civil service to the Prime Minister."

By then it was too late. His dismissal – the first ever of a Privy Council Clerk for partisanship – was inevitable once Joe Clark came to power in 1979. Pitfield, the self-aggrandizing romantic, had convinced himself it could not happen. After Clark had asked for his resignation, Pitfield assembled his Privy Council staff: his voice broke, and tears streamed down his face. Within two days of Trudeau's 1980 victory, deputy-ministers heard the familiar voice again; a fortnight later, Pitfield was formally re-appointed. The Pitfield who re-emerged was different: at Harvard, where he'd gone into exile, he learned that he really could function outside the womb of the civil service, and learned self-confidence for the first time in his life.

The irony in Pitfield's career—he is still only forty-four—is that although he truly loves the public service he has done it real harm. His organizational changes during 1968-72 – new superfluous ministries such as Urban Affairs, and Science and Technology – were uniformly disastrous. During his term as Privy Council Clerk, government "lost control" of its spending, in the phrase of the auditor general; the civil service became infected with a deep "malaise" in the phrase of a public service commissioner, and the public lost confidence that anyone in Ottawa knew what on earth they were doing.

Pitfield's more damaging legacy is to have politicized the public service as did, at least by passive consent, his predecessor Gordon Robertson who when he moved on to become Secretary for Federal-Provincial Relations retained responsibility for senior appointments. During the Pitfield-Robertson era, the top ranks of the civil service became indistinguishable, for all practical purposes, from the Liberal Party. Trudeau's political aides moved into top civil service positions, and vice versa; a deputy minister, Jack Austin, became Trudeau's chief of staff. Liberals were allowed to parachute themselves into almost any public service post they wanted – ex-minister Bryce Mackasey's appointment as Chairman of Air Canada being the most blatant example – and did so to a degree unequalled since the establishment of the civil service merit principle in 1918.

Pitfield set the pattern. His personal friendship with Trudeau was one thing. His partisanship was quite another. Robert Andras, a senior minister, remembers Pitfield giving him drafts for the Liberal election platform in 1972, of which Andras was the campaign chairman. Keith Davey remembers Pitfield arguing against the appointment of Martin Goldfarb as Liberal pollster in 1973, on the grounds that Goldfarb had written a magazine article describing how Trudeau could be beaten. Down the line, civil servants took their cues from Pitfield: it was all right to bend the rules, provided you didn't get caught. Liberal cabinet ministers, meanwhile, took their cues from Trudeau: it was all right to fill civil service posts with Liberals (Bill Teron at the Central Mortgage and Housing Corporation; Pierre Juneau at the National Capital Commission and, later, Secretary of State) provided the election was sufficiently far away for voters to have time to forget.

Just as in Powell's novels Widmerpool emerges in the end as the most memorable of the characters, Pitfield, in his way, is as memorable a figure as Trudeau. As complicated, less-controlled, more human* for all his ruthlessness, and essentially more creative. Pitfield's shining accomplishment has been to create the modern Privy Council Office, and to structure it, superbly efficient despite its flaws, as the central nervous system for the entire government. "PCO," says a colleague, "is Michael's Sistine Chapel."

* * *

Marc Lalonde was best man at Pitfield's wedding. But he is an entirely different breed of cat. A peasant, for one thing, and proud of the fact. His family has farmed on Ile Perrot on Montreal's western approaches for nine generations: he's the first Lalonde to go to university (first Montreal, then Oxford). In manner and in dress (sports jackets more often than suits) Lalonde is utterly unpretentious. He's also a bit puritanical: a friend reckons that

---

*In a Widmerpoolish way, Pitfield is a fanatic about secrecy in government, but gauchely so: he once sent a postcard to a colleague to thank him for sending him some documents, and marked it prominently, "CONFIDENTIAL."

Lalonde at one and the same time disapproves of Trudeau's lifestyle and envies it. This censoriousness, and the gap of class may be the reason why Lalonde, unlike Pitfield, unlike Pelletier, is not personally close to Trudeau. He rarely went to Harrington Lake or 24 Sussex during four years as Trudeau's chief political adviser. One of their rare, out-of-office get-togethers turned into a disaster. At Banff for a conference, Lalonde and his wife Claire, who is frail and whom he idolizes, went riding with Trudeau. Claire Lalonde tired quickly, and dismounted. So did Lalonde. Trudeau, who'd been showing off his horsemanship, waited impatiently for a few minutes, then cantered off, accompanied by his worried Mountie. The Lalondes walked their horses back to the lodge.

Unlike Pitfield, unlike almost every other aide, Lalonde was not afraid of Trudeau—and this widened the gap between them. Quite often, he and Trudeau slugged it out verbally. They could do this and still work closely together because they are ideological clones, about federalism, about Quebec as a province like the others, about bilingualism, about rationality. In 1969, in language Trudeau could have used, Lalonde defined the government's goal: "to apply reason to broad social and economic problems."

Lalonde is also "the dimension that Trudeau doesn't like to be," as the Quebec M.P. Serge Joyal once put it. He is Trudeau's hatchetman. He has the mien of a Robespierre: a hooked nose, high-domed forehead, a look of implacable severity except when he breaks into a sweet, boyish smile. As Trudeau's chief of staff, Lalonde hired and fired for Trudeau, rigidly controlled access to him, despatched orders to bureaucrats, told off cabinet ministers. Later, as Quebec leader, he kept the backbenchers in line for his leader, at least until 1979 when, freed from his discipline by being in Opposition, the Quebec M.P.s rebelled and asserted their independence.

Lalonde is Trudeau's equal in intellect, his superior in stamina. The puzzle has always been: how someone so bright could so often act so stupidly? He's a humanitarian who as Minister of Health and Welfare engineered the only major increase in social spending of the Trudeau era. Few ministers have a more compassionate appreciation of the problems of the underprivileged: once, he startled a senior official by musing that the trouble with militant Indian groups was that they weren't militant enough, and so failed to embarrass the government into addressing their concerns. Yet he could also be brutally insensitive. As Minister of Federal-Provincial Relations, he told "Newfie jokes" to reporters; informed, as Health Minister, that some hamburger meat contained animal dung, he retorted, "Fry it."

One side, the listening side, of Lalonde's brain seems to be under-developed. Mostly he is courteous and is candid to the point that, almost uniquely in official Ottawa, he will always talk on the record with journalists. But the instant someone confronts Lalonde with an opinion he believes is unfounded, he becomes closed, unyielding as a rock, hostile as a badger. He refused to listen to party types who warned him that he was cutting Trudeau off from the public in 1968-72. He refused to listen to aides who pleaded with him not to take a free flight to Israel aboard a Seagram jet, sure that because he was so high-minded his motives were above suspicion. He refused to listen to younger Quebec M.P.s who pleaded with him to recognize that by the mid-1970's Quebec nationalism had evolved into social democratic nationalism.

For Lalonde, everything that Quebec nationalists said was unfounded. "Nostalgia for tribal security," is the phrase he liked to use. So he turned hostile. Even more than Trudeau, he declared holy war upon the separatists. He was outraged, for instance, when Kierans included among economists he'd gathered to debate communications policy, Jacques Parizeau, then a Quebec civil servant and widely suspected as a separatist. Lalonde tore a strip off Kierans, who retorted that of the economists, "Parizeau was by far the best." The incident cut the last link between Parizeau and Ottawa.

Mistakes like these aside, Lalonde served Trudeau as no one else could have; totally loyal, tireless, fearless, so self-secure that he never felt the need to make his own mark, to become his own man rather than just Trudeau's. He intended to follow Trudeau out of politics in 1979; not until after the 1980 election did Lalonde, by his National Energy Program, set out to carve his own niche in history, separate from Trudeau's.

* * *

No other Supergroup insiders were as super as Pitfield and Lalonde. Pelletier and Marchand, of the other members of the original seven, have been described in earlier chapters. In rough order of influence, here are the remaining three:

GORDON ROBERTSON: Tall, angular, greying, imposing. He looked like the quintessential Ottawa mandarin. He behaved like one, down to the old-fashioned fountain pen and distinctive aquamarine ink he used to annotate memos.* Robertson *was* the quintessential mandarin. He'd joined External Affairs in 1941, became Deputy Minister of Northern Affairs at thirty-six; had been named Clerk of the Privy Council in 1963; became Secretary for Federal-Provincial Relations in 1975. When he left the public service on December 31, 1979, there was no one left in government who could still remember that most legendary of all the mandarins, O.D. Skelton.

Much of Robertson's influence with Trudeau derived directly from this wealth of experience. Just as Trudeau looked up to, almost deferred to, "Old Guard" Pearsonian ministers like Bud Drury and Mitchell Sharp, he looked up to Robertson. A rather unimaginative conservative in policy matters, Robertson's strength was as a brilliant bureaucratic fire-fighter who, when any crisis struck could instantly delve into a mental file of precedents to produce a range of practical responses. Robertson was also an intensely competitive bureaucratic infighter, skilled enough to know when he was licked. To retain his position, he allowed, as no predecessor would have, a subordinate, Pitfield, to have direct access to the Prime Minister. In 1975, Robertson made way for Pitfield to succeed him as Privy Council Clerk at Trudeau's request, but stayed nearly as powerful in his new post as Secretary for Federal-Provincial Relations.

Robertson's mindset was identical to Trudeau's. Much of Trudeau's so-called "rigid federalism" flowed directly from Robertson's pen. He quit soon after Trudeau's defeat in 1979, giving as his reason that he was too closely identified with Trudeau. (After Trudeau returned in 1980, Robertson returned, as a consultant.) He also magnified Trudeau's own instinct to control the flow of information. When a PCO official submitted a report recommending that more information be made public, Robertson disposed of it by stamping it SECRET. In the style of an old-school mandarin Robertson kept his profile low so that few on the outside

---

*Pitfield, who was always canny enough to mimic his superiors, invariably worked in his office on Saturday mornings, like Robertson. Pitfield also used an old-fashioned fountain pen, with *brown* ink.

recognized his importance to Trudeau. But on the day in December 1979 that Trudeau made up his mind to return as Liberal leader, the two lunched together in the Chateau Grill.

IVAN HEAD: Peter Newman has said it best. From 1968 to 1978, he performed "like a sub-Arctic Henry Kissinger, flying about the world on the Prime Minister's behalf, by-passing apoplectic officials." Head – a University of Alberta law professor who met Trudeau in 1967 as a member of his constitutional advisory group at Justice and stayed on to become international affairs adviser – did occasionally chat with Kissinger, and made certain everyone knew. He was good-looking, bouncy, athletic enough to beat Trudeau bobsledding on the Cresta run. He was also ambitious. Margaret, as she makes plain in her book, detested him.

But Head had a way with words. Though most of the speeches he churned out for Trudeau were high-minded and pretentious – "monographs for a foreign affairs quarterly" in the words of another aide – a few, notably Trudeau's 1975 address at London's Mansion House, were superb. And Head possessed two other qualities. Like Lalonde, he was unafraid of Trudeau: once, at a Commonwealth Conference, when a session was dragging on into infinity, he restrained Trudeau, physically, from leaving his chair to stalk out of the room. (No one else, in anyone's memory, has ever dared to breach Trudeau's Touch Me Not aura.) Head had an original mind with an idealistic cast to it: he was the inspiration for Trudeau's decision to develop a network of personal friendships with Third World leaders, and to become an authority on north-south relations. In 1978, Head left to become President of the International Development Research Centre.

JIM DAVEY: Intense, idealistic, gentle, and self-effacing; the only member of Supergroup not born in Canada. An Oxford-trained physicist, Davey had emigrated in the late 1950's to work on the Avro Arrow program, then joined a Montreal consulting firm. From there, he set out to learn French and to get involved in politics, first through a group of reform-minded Liberals centred round Maurice Sauvé, later as leader of the Montreal group for Trudeau. In 1968, he became program chief, or number two, to Lalonde.

Davey's consuming passion wasn't so much programs as the *programming* of programs; and all that stuff. Davey was fond of phrases like "multi-model conceptual framework"; in an East

Block attic known as the "war-room," he covered the walls with flow charts of Trudeau's schedule for a year ahead; to his chagrin, secretaries kept forgetting to move the drawing pins. Between 1968 and 1972, Davey was the architect both of Trudeau's ill-fated attempt to govern by reason, and by computers: he was also the architect of Trudeau's disastrous 1972 campaign strategy. He later became an aide to Marchand, as Minister of Transport, and died tragically in 1975, from a fall while repairing his house.

* * *

In-Betweeners next. There were, in the beginning, about a dozen. Unlike the Insiders, none played crucial roles. Yet some individual In-Betweeners, and their wives, were closer to Trudeau personally than some Insiders. These four, in the early years, mattered most.

TIM PORTEOUS: A lawyer from McGill, co-author of the smash-hit college show of the 1950's, *My Fur Lady,* he'd first met Trudeau on a World University Service jaunt to Nigeria in 1957, where they discovered a mutual predilection for adventuresome travel.* Porteous and his wife, Wendy, an ascendant mandarin in her own right, often accompanied Trudeau on wilderness vacations. As a speechwriter, later as executive assistant, Porteous made a slight impression in Trudeau's office, but later emerged as a person in his own right as Canada Council Associate Director.

GORDON GIBSON: One of the first, late in 1967 to boost Trudeau for Prime Minister, Gibson, in 1971, was one of the first to leave his staff—for British Columbia—to enter provincial politics. Later he ran unsuccessfully, federally, in 1979 and 1980. Gibson was the PMO's small l Liberal idealist, a writer of lengthy memos and, more importantly, one of the few who could actually get Trudeau to listen to what he had to say about the west. In the early, Camelot-North period, Gibson and his wife, Valerie, gave Ottawa's best parties.

FERNAND CADIEU: No one, Trudeau included, knew what Cadieu's role was, exactly. But everyone, including Trudeau, was in awe of him. Cadieu, who died in 1976, was a gloomy sepulchral figure: Quebec's unpublished McLuhan, whom almost nobody could understand but whom everyone was certain was profound.

*On the same trip Trudeau also formed a friendship with Don Johnston, now President of the Treasury Board, who became his tax lawyer and who played a key part in convincing Trudeau to return as Liberal leader in December 1979.

He wrote many of Trudeau's statements during the 1970 October Crisis.

JEAN LeMOYNE: Relatively little known in English Canada, LeMoyne, a profoundly civilized man of letters, is perhaps the most distinguished essayist Quebec has produced. During LeMoyne's term as speechwriter (1969-78) Trudeau often accepted his drafts without changing a comma. Trudeau's first crucial speech in Quebec, after the November 15, 1976, Parti Québécois victory, was in fact undiluted LeMoyne.

* * *

Outsiders, last. They simply worked for Trudeau, either in Trudeau's own office, or in PCO down the hall. All of Trudeau's press secretaries were Outsiders: not one exercised the least influence on policy. Frequently the most grandiose titles meant the least. In 1972, a defeated minister from Toronto, Martin O'Connell, succeeded Lalonde as principal secretary. But O'Connell was so intimidated by Trudeau that he communicated with him mostly by memo. O'Connell's successor Jack Austin was also an outsider, though for diametrically opposite reasons. Trudeau found Austin's hustle-bustle style so exhausting that in 1975 he moved him sideways, to the Senate, and brought in instead the next, and the last, real insider: Jim Coutts. About whom, more later.

* * *

The real point about Trudeau's personal staff is this: collectively, they mattered far more to him than his cabinet. Several key aides changed the course of Trudeau's political career. Cabinet ministers who played roles as important can be counted on the fingers of one hand: Pelletier, Marchand, and Lalonde, who in fact all played double roles; John Turner, the heir-apparent, and Allan MacEachen, who as House Leader ensured Trudeau's survival through the minority government of 1973-74, and who later made it possible for him to become Prime Minister again by stage-managing the defeat of the Clark government in December 1979. All the other ministers performed like Supergroup Outsiders: they came, did their jobs, and went. Never have so many politicians mattered so little, for so long.

Some individual ministers left an imprint inside their own bailiwick. Donald Macdonald at Energy, 1972-75; Otto Lang at the

Wheat Board rather than at his actual portfolios of Justice or Transport; Roméo LeBlanc at Fisheries; Jean Chrétien at Indian and Northern Affairs, where he created ten new national parks, including the first ever in Quebec, and later as head of Ottawa's campaign during the 1980 Quebec referendum; Bryce Mackasey, with his reform of unemployment insurance; Bob Andras with his reforms of Mackasey's reforms; Barney Danson, for his Katimavik program rather than his portfolio of Defence. Also, among Supergroup types while wearing their ministerial hats, Lalonde at Health and Welfare during his early, free-spending years, and Pelletier at Secretary of State, for his policies on youth, bilingualism, and "democratization and decentralization" of the arts.

That is just about it. For the rest, after they left, the machinery of government ground on precisely as it had before they arrived. With the crucial exception of Turner, ministers who quit – Hellyer and Kierans in the 1968-72 period; Mackasey, James Richardson; Macdonald later – promptly disappeared down a political black hole. Later, when they talked about their term in office and why they'd ended it, these men always sounded melancholy. They were sad about having somehow failed, about having somehow been bested by Trudeau; sadder still about not being missed.

Kierans has given the most graphic description of how it felt to be a minister dealing with Supergroup: "It was like a procession," he has said. "When the Pope gets down off the altar at St. Peter's and walks down the aisle, then the one thing you know is that he's going to get to the other end of the aisle. You can argue, and argue, and in the end, the procession goes on its way."

Supergroup members act hurt by such accusations. Gordon Robertson, who has served five Prime Ministers, back to Mackenzie King, has said, "Trudeau probably was the most likely to be guided by consensus, and the least likely to assert his own views." It is true that Trudeau sometimes allowed ministers to get away with policies he disagreed with – Turner's income tax give-aways – for instance. Yet no one can cite one example when cabinet collectively asserted its views in opposition to Trudeau. He was a master of the Jesuit technique of persuasion, which is not to sell opinions but to present them cloaked in rationality so that others reach the same conclusions by themselves, rationally of course. Almost all Trudeau's ministers were intimidated by him and tailored their arguments to suit his style.

"We were mesmerized," Robert Andras recalls, of the early years. "He was so extraordinarily intelligent, and such a hot political property." Often ministers felt like students facing a particularly stern principal. In 1971, for instance, when John Munro brought before cabinet his proposal for a Family Income Support Programme (FISP), Trudeau interrupted Munro's explanation to point out that the document – as usual, he'd studied this in detail himself – contained here a false premise, there an illogicality, there a misused statistic. Trudeau ended the discussion by telling Munro, "You'd better take this back and do your homework properly." Munro's colleagues restored his spirits by pointing out, quite correctly, that Trudeau's criticisms were quite impersonal: he was as likely to criticize before full cabinet an Insider like Pelletier, say, as a foot-soldier like Munro.

No matter how well-briefed, only a handful of ministers could manage to hold their own: Drury, Kierans, and Sharp in the early years; Lang, who could match Trudeau's intellectual pace all the way through; later, Lalonde and LeBlanc, also Jeanne Sauvé, who could match Trudeau's Outremont credentials, and Veterans Affairs Minister Dan MacDonald, a badly-maimed war hero and Prince Edward Island farmer for whom Trudeau had a particular soft spot.

* * *

The truth was, ministers either fitted into the pattern Trudeau imposed, or were hobbled by it. Partly, the pattern was set by the consensus system Robertson referred to. Instead of being responsible only for their own departments, "collegiality" required ministers to be collectively responsible for everything the government did and so to debate one another's proposals in detail. The system resulted in endless discussions and a great deal of log-rolling among ministers to win favour for each other's proposals. "It reinforced the weak," says Turner, "and frustrated the strong." Either way, ministers lost their individuality. They became replaceable and, therefore, disposable cogs in a machine. "Cabinet meetings went on for hours and hours, and after a while I went to as few as I could," remembers Hugh Faulkner.

Turner was the one minister who retained his independence. On the outside, he had his own quasi-charismatic personality and his famous card file of Liberal workers, Club 195. On the inside, he refused to play by Trudeau's rules. Turner attended meetings of cabinet committees only when he had an item on the agenda, and as soon as this had been disposed of, he would claim some urgent appointment and leave. Trudeau, in fact, rather admired Turner for this. "I often suspect the only appointment John has to keep is a tennis game, but he gets away with it," he told another minister.

The other part of the pattern was set by Trudeau's own personality. He came to office determined to be what he was, a rationalist. Through 1968-72, and intermittently afterwards, rationality was the context and the straight jacket inside which cabinet conducted its debates. The solution to be sought for each problem was not the practical one, but the *right* one.

Some ministers – Lang, Sharp, Lalonde, Faulkner – were cerebral, and enjoyed testing their intellectual and verbal skills. But most ministers were politicians first and intellectuals – if at all – a long way afterwards. Their strength was their ability to gauge the mood of the public, Parliament, press, and to be right a respectable number of times when they said, "I just feel in my gut, this solution will work." Without realizing he was doing it, Trudeau emasculated most of his ministers.

If ministers are hardly ever intellectuals, mandarins almost always are. Again, without realizing he was doing it, Trudeau bureaucratized the cabinet. As part of the machinery of consensus, he instituted a system of eight cabinet committees, at which ministers could scrutinize the fine print of each other's policy proposals.* As support, each minister brought along his senior civil servants as experts. (Robertson forbade ministers to bring their political aides to cabinet committee meetings.) Bureaucrats thus entered the mainstream of political decision-making and were all the more influential because – "Minister, might I suggest . . ." – they were so adroitly deferential.

Some ministers, Hellyer and Kierans during the early years, tried to buck the system, and were ejected by it. The others became part of the system and lost their identity. In the last couple of years before Trudeau's defeat in 1979, more and more ministers complained about the disproportionate influence of his personal staff, particularly of Pitfield and Coutts. By then, it was too

*Pearson actually introduced this system, early in 1968, as almost his last act as Prime Minister.

late. Cabinet, for all practical purposes had ceased to exist, as Trudeau had demonstrated in 1978 when he changed the government's entire spending policy without bothering to consult his ministers. In Opposition, Trudeau "repented" and his M.P.s became more visible in their own right. Even so, he made the continuation of Coutts as chief of staff a condition of his returning as leader in December 1979; right afterwards, Pitfield reappeared.

* * *

"Nothing propinques like propinquity," George Ball, the former U.S. Undersecretary of State once said. In the East Block, later the Langevin Building, Supergroupers propinqued from offices down the hall from Trudeau, or, like Pitfield, from an office directly above him. (The top four staffers saw him each morning at 9.00.) They wrote him memos and briefing notes and treasured his approving annotations (usually just a tick, or a passage underlined, or a question mark). The political aides travelled with him on election campaigns, which is where all leaders forge their closest links with those around them. In contrast to the roles played by Walter Gordon, say, during Pearson's campaigns, or by Gordon Churchill during Diefenbaker's, no minister, until 1980, had anything remotely to do with what Trudeau said or did on the hustings. Turner, for instance, found out about Trudeau's 1974 string of spending proposals from the newspapers, even though, as Finance Minister, he would have to be responsible for them.

During 1968-72, the aides' particular source of power was that so many of them were so like Trudeau. Most were brainy; all were fluently bilingual. Many were wealthy; disproportionately, they came from Montreal. Like Trudeau, none had ever known failure. Their cast of mind was the same. All the Insiders – Lalonde, Davey, Pitfield, Robertson, Head – were cerebral rationalists. They were acolytes, clustered around a high priest: in his presence, no one dared even smoke.*

In mid-1969, the political scientist Denis Smith wrote a paper in which he declared that Trudeau "seem[s] to have created in Canada a presidential system without any of its congressional advan-

---

*This inflexible, unwritten rule was broken at last in 1979, by Arnie Patterson, a gregarious radio station owner from Dartmouth, Nova Scotia, who throughout his three-month stint as temporary communications adviser, chainsmoked unabashedly.

tages." Transmuted into "Imperial Prime-Ministership," Smith's phrase took hold. Repeatedly thereafter Trudeau had to refute – more accurately, to brush aside – accusations he had displaced Parliament, and the Monarchy, with a presidential system.

In fact, Trudeau did just this – parliamentary power all but vanished – not as part of some devious plot, but by the sheer power of his own personality, and as the logical outcome of his political philosophy. (Until the introduction of TV in the Commons in 1978, Trudeau made almost all of his major speeches outside of the Chamber.)

The notion of a "plebiscitary leader" implicit in his writings hardened into reality once he acquired power. The Liberal Party, for example, ceased to function from 1968 to 1972. Trudeau never spoke to party president John Nichol; the traditional intelligence-gathering function of the party and of backbench M.P.s was usurped by the new "regional desks" in his own office. As his ex-aide Tom D'Aquino has written in *Canadian Public Administration*, "Norms and value-oriented politics was fostered in an environment in which brokerage politics had always been acceptable." Rational politics instead of political, and human, politics, in other words. Last, like all charismatic leaders, even rational ones, Trudeau believed he possessed a personal, direct relationship with the people. "He can go over your heads by going on T.V. any time he wants to," a Trudeau aide told a group of Press Gallery reporters. They were outraged, because they knew the aide was right.

Some of the change was inevitable. John F. Kennedy had glamorized the role of leader, and television, which has space on the screen for only one person, had magnified it. Trudeau escalated the pace of change. The *Toronto Star* cartoonist Duncan Macpherson, who'd had trouble getting a fix on Trudeau as a sub-arctic, Gallic, president, got it right at last when by sketching him as Louis XIV and once, after he'd told unemployed postal drivers to "eat shit," as Marie Antoinette.

* * *

The aphorism, "the office makes the man," has a double meaning. The office can magnify the incumbent, or it can diminish him. Early on, Trudeau demonstrated that he understood how to use his office to make himself seem larger than life. One astute observer of the Ottawa scene believes that the reason Trudeau always placed more confidence in his senior staff than his cabinet ministers was that "he knew they were dependent upon him." All ministers, even the meekest and most inconspicuous, commanded a certain constituency, and so to some degree were in competition with Trudeau. His staff, by contrast, all had one master – him – and no followers. Thus, Pitfield and Coutts ceased to exist the instant Trudeau stopped being Prime Minister; when he returned, they were re-invented.

What Trudeau understood much less was how his office was also diminishing him, how the remote men around him reinforced his predilection to be remote. They all told him exactly what he wanted to hear: about the effectiveness of rationality in political problem-solving, about the certainty that a "dialogue with Canadians" would win the 1972 election. They wrote the kinds of speeches he wanted to give: suitable, at best, for an audience of intellectual peers; at worst windy and pretentious, as in "Material affluence is not essential to human dignity. But self respect is. And self respect is a product of hope and faith in the future."

They isolated him, and only partly so because he wanted things that way. Trudeau's inability to ask people to help him, whether to work for him or to take on a particular assignment, has become as much part of his mystique as his *farouche* manner. Yet before he became Prime Minister, Trudeau asked for help on several occasions. He asked Head to stay on with him; as Justice Minister, he put the same proposition to Jerry Grafstein, who was leaving Turner's office to practise law in Toronto. But after 1968, some members of Trudeau's staff, particularly Pitfield, set out to exploit Trudeau's delight in avoiding failures in personnel management by taking on all hiring and firing responsibility for themselves. In the process, not by coincidence, they made sure that only they got to see him. Several times between 1968 and 1972, en route between office and 24 Sussex, Trudeau's limousine passed a prominent public figure who was also a friend of his. Each time, Trudeau would ask his driver to stop, would talk eagerly for a few minutes and then say, "This has been so good. We must get together properly. I'll call you as soon as I know when I'll have free time." Trudeau, who doesn't go in for meaningless social niceties, never called. Next time the two met, he would explain, almost sadly, how his engagement calendar had somehow been filled. As a more dramatic example, all the initial tensions between Trudeau and

Turner were produced, not by Trudeau himself, but by his staff, Lalonde in particular, who was furious about what he considered to be Turner's "softness" on bilingualism. Later on, staffers of Turner as well as of Trudeau widened the gap between the principals.

The men around Trudeau, a dictatorship of good intentions, were probably the ablest to serve any Canadian Prime Minister. They could manage crises brilliantly – as the October Crisis proved. They could conduct problem-solving exercises of a high intellectual order – identifying the inadequacies in our military contribution to NATO, for one example. First to last, they were efficient technically: Trudeau's mail was answered quickly; he never lost his luggage.

Yet ultimately, Trudeau's staff, first between 1968 and 1972, and then for different reasons, during his second majority term, 1974-79, was as destructive politically as any group of advisers who ever surrounded a Prime Minister. They isolated him from Canadians. None of his top aides, except perhaps Coutts, although he viewed human nature through a glass darkly, had more than a marginal comprehension of the country, or of the people in it. They themselves were technocrats, which most Canadians are not. They were smart, successful, self-confident, as few Canadians are. They viewed Canada as the hinterland of Ottawa; most Canadians view Ottawa as a black hole. In their own self-interest, they served a Sun King, instead of telling the King, which would have been truly to serve him well, that he was just a Prime Minister.

The real flaw to an Imperial Prime-Ministership is that it is un-Canadian. The concept is alien, not because it threatens the Queen, or threatens Parliament, but because it is out of keeping with the character of the country. The quintessence of Canada, the source of its strength as well as a good deal of the prevailing confusion, is that it is a regionalized, pluralistic federation. In such a country, power by definition must be dispersed and decentralized. Centralizing power in the office of a particular leader cuts against the very grain of the country. Trudeau tried. As soon as Canadians realized what he was doing, they threw him out – *almost*.

6

"Athens on the Rideau"

"And thus, in the four-years of Trudeau majority government, Parliament Hill was converted into a miniature Athens. As for the Privy Council Office, and the Prime Ministers Office, why that was the very Lyceum itself."

Larry Zolf
Dance of the Dialectic

One of the few changes Trudeau made when he first moved into 24 Sussex was to hang in the stairwell, where he would see it first thing in the morning and last thing at night, a banner with a strange device: a quilt, made for him by the artist Joyce Wieland, on which she patch-worked the phrase: *"La Raison avant La Passion."*

Trudeau's personal motto is Reason over Passion. Between 1968 and 1972, he made it the motto of his government. Not so much a motto, really, as a cry from the heart: years of solitary study and thought compressed into a single epigrammatic and idealistic phrase. The idea failed. To be rational about something as irrational as politics, Trudeau discovered, is to be irrational. "My faith in politics, my faith in the democratic process, has changed a bit," he said later, after Canadians had rejected both him and rationalism in the 1972 election. His share of the vote in that election, relative to that of the Conservatives, was actually smaller than in the 1979 election, when he lost power. Only electoral flukes and the tribal instincts of his own Quebecers, which he so deplored, saved him from being reduced to an historical footnote, a one-term Prime Minister.

Yet Trudeau's obsession with reason, 1968-72, was a magnificent obsession. "It was the *real* Trudeau," an aide of that era, Porteous, says. "It was the type of politics he felt ought to be possible in a democracy, and if it wasn't possible, it was a great shame."

The Athens, in Zolf's phrase, that Trudeau sought to build was to be constructed on three pillars: pluralistic federalism, to be described in a later chapter; rational planning and Participatory Democracy, to be dealt with here. Planning, to start out.

* * *

For all his air of absolute self-reliance, Trudeau had come to office well aware of his limitations.

There were, as his first Throne Speech in September 1968 declared, "great expectations of what this Parliament will produce." Yet Trudeau knew he knew nothing about practical politics, almost nothing about administration. Beyond Quebec, he knew only a handful of Ottawa civil servants and Toronto academics. "You know so many people you can phone," he said enviously to Sharp, shortly before he became Prime Minister. He was more than a little intimidated by the mandarins, so smooth, so supple, so experienced. Of Robertson and Pitfield he said in awe: "When I come in in the mornings, they've prepared answers to questions I haven't even thought of." To compound the unease, the federalist francophones around Trudeau were acutely aware of how few in number they were, and how vulnerable. "We always wondered for how long, and how far, English Canada would let us go," one member of the group recalls.

Once in a while, Trudeau allowed his sense of uncertainty to show. In the autumn of 1968, a dancing partner was daring enough to ask him what, exactly, he did as Prime Minister. After a pause, Trudeau answered almost sadly. "I don't really do anything. I tell others what to do, and they have the fun of doing it."

Trudeau knew what he wanted to do about only a handful of things. Bilingualism, of course, and the advancement of francophones to positions of prominence in the public service. He had said he wanted to ameliorate regional disparities, although Marchand the minister responsible has since said that Trudeau always argued with him that it made more sense to move people out of depressed regions to centres where jobs existed. Lastly, he wanted to redirect foreign policy, away from international helpful-fixing, toward "Canada first."

If he was unsure about ends, Trudeau was crystal clear about means. Problems would be solved by reason rather than "mere emotionalism," and by the techniques of "advanced technology and scientific investigation." Participatory Democracy was the mandatory, rational corollary to rational planning within. Combined, these forces would create "the servant state," efficient yet responsive, scientific yet humanist.

Planning of course would require planners. "New guys with new ideas."

* * *

The new guys with new ideas who flocked into Ottawa in festive camaraderie – "Altruistic Technocrats," in a phrase coined around that time in the U.S. – had read all the right guys with the right ideas: Toffler, Kahn, Roszak, Drucker, Marcuse, McLuhan, Bell, Reich. Like Trudeau, they knew that for every problem there was a rational solution. The future was no longer arduous and uncertain, but defined and programmatic. In Trudeau's Ottawa the future would be seen to work.

People took government seriously in those days. The city crackled with energy. Soon it bristled with policy analysts and program analysts; sociologists, ecologists, economists, and socio-economists; experts on communications; experts on natives; experts on native communications and native women. They manned task forces, worked as consultants, peopled the shiny new departments – Urban Affairs, Environment, Communications – the Citizenship Branch at Secretary of State, and the Policy Planning Branches that every department sprouted. They churned out earnest reports, attended endless seminars, dished out grants for community development projects, experiments in communications, experiments in political revolution. Foreign visitors were astounded: any and every policy idea seemed to be acceptable and everyone seemed to be so self-confident. By around 1970, Ottawa resembled neither Camelot nor Athens so much as a cross between the Harvard Business School, Berkeley in the free speech era, and a utopian commune.

The new guys didn't simply swell the civil service – a proliferation of high-sounding, high-salaried titles – they changed its nature utterly. Christina Newman's "Ottawa Man" – that Skeltonian mandarin with his Presbyterian predilection for frugality and low profile – gave way to what Sandra Gwyn described in *Saturday Night*, as "the New Ottawa Person." New Ottawa Persons (male) wore bushy moustaches and open-necked shirts, often with chains around the neck. New Ottawa Persons (female) defied all 1968-72 conventions by wearing pantsuits to work.

New Ottawa Persons imposed their style on the city itself. All over Ottawa, and across the river in Hull, twenty-storey steel-and-glass boxes decked with forests of philodendrons replaced green-walled cubicles in grimy brick buildings. In winter, they skated to work along the Rideau Canal; in summer they rode bikes to work, or jogged. Since Trudeau refused to join the Rideau Club, no one else applied; instead they lunched in the new sidewalk cafés outside the National Arts Centre and the spruced-up Chateau Laurier. They fixed up crumbling late Victorian townhouses in New Edinburgh, shopped in the new boutiques in Byward Market, sent their offspring to *Cours Claudel*. They were, they liked to tell one another, the most interesting, most creative bunch of civil servants ever assembled, anywhere.

They were right—up to a point. Ottawa, 1968-72, was also a city devoid of irony and with only a precarious hold on common sense. The New Ottawa Persons, for all their racy lifestyle, were more self-important than even the stodgiest member of the old mandarinate had ever dreamed of being. Those few who spotted the industrious game of self-delusion being played all around noticed the contradiction, that is, between having come to do good and having stayed on to do well, kept it to themselves: they too were players, doing very well. Certainly the last people capable of spotting the warning signals of a situation soon to spin out of control were Trudeau and those around him. Their eyes were fixed on the far horizon, on what Trudeau had called, "the Cybernetic Revolution."

* * *

Rational planning seemed, in 1968, like an idea whose time was long overdue. Back in 1962, the Glassco Commission had concluded: "Many tens of millions of dollars would be yielded annually by modern, scientific, highly-developed management techniques." Expo had been built, on time and magnificently (if over budget), to a computerized critical path. At the Ford Motor Company, Robert McNamara had applied the "Systems Method" with great success, if with less success in Vietnam. The Harvard Business School was big on systems.

Hand in hand with the idea went all the shiny new tools, artefacts for rational managers: computers, data banks, and high-speed communications systems; flow charts, flip charts, PERT charts, decision trees; new problem-crunching theologies, like PPBS (Programme, Planning and Budgeting Systems) and MBO (Management by Objectives). Plus the awesome new jargon: "interface"; "feedback"; "optimize"; "priorize"; "input"; "output."

It amounted to a new religion, complete with new prophets. Ellul had called technology "the metaphysics of the twentieth century." The "post industrial society" said Bell, would be fundamentally different, (if in ways not quite specified) from all earlier, more primitive, more emotional societies. For this new society, Drucker had called for "an ideal type of professional manager, who has technical knowledge and moral excellence, who can do and think." And the social sciences had become a secular religion.

Trudeau himself elevated the ethical and moral stakes. If rationalism failed, demagoguery and totalitarianism would triumph, he kept saying. "If Parliament does not answer the questions, does not settle the issues fast enough ... That is my fear, that the judgement of the people will be, Parliament is not good enough. Let us look for a strong man." Again, almost morbidly, "Legislative institutions which fail to reform themselves do so at peril of their own destruction."

For four years, rational planning swept through Ottawa much as St. Vitus's dance used to sweep mediaeval villages, and as with that mania, everyone in Ottawa dancing the dialectic knew for certain that everyone *not* dancing was mad. Trudeau aside, the chief choreographers were Jim Davey in Trudeau's office, and Al Johnson, the Treasury Board Secretary, a refugee from socialist Saskatchewan who pushed and pulled all departments upon the Procrustean bed of PPBS and MBO. (No department had any real objectives by which to manage itself, other than vague ones like "to do good" or "to try to do better." All departments, nevertheless, solemnly invented properly scientific objectives for themselves.)*

Ottawa meanwhile became a paper world. Out poured an interminable number of studies, White, Orange, and Green Papers,

*In its April 1979 report, the Lambert Royal Commission on Government Management chided that "virtually no effort has been made to establish clearly defined objectives against which the performance of a department or agency can be measured."

interim reports and "conceptual evaluations" evaluating every-thing anything, from taxation to urban affairs to Indian affairs to information itself. Each study treated its subject as if nothing had ever been said about it, or done about it, before. All studies reached the same conclusion: a new agency, or branch, or unit should be created to deal with the subject, mostly by studying it more.

The prototype for all of this, the one which Trudeau, personally, cared most about, was the review of foreign policy published in 1970. External Affairs turned out draft after draft, each rejected by Trudeau as unscientific. At last, an inspired departmental officer sat down with a bottle of scotch, the entire back file of *Cité Libre*, several texts on scientific management and redrafted the report to cast its main recommendations in the form of a hexagon and then stuffed into the text, like raisins in a rice pudding, every buzzword he could think of, from "conceptual framework" to "coherent" and "co-ordinated." Approved instantly, the review was pub-lished as a set of multi-coloured booklets in a nifty little box. Critics promptly pointed out that it said nothing at all about the only aspect of foreign policy that really mattered: Canada-U.S. relations. Trudeau explained that this subject was still being studied.

Out of sight of the public, mercifully, the studies grew wilder and wilder. For one entire afternoon the Planning and Priorities Committee of Cabinet hunkered down to debate a PCO paper delineating the differences between "public expectations" and "public aspirations." It reached no conclusion. Nor did an En-vironment Canada study into "the need for clear and adequate perception of our social and cultural situation as a basis for action within our confusing and problematic environment."

For days, top-ranking civil servants sat around playing Synectics. This involved sticking big sheets of paper around the walls and writing down every bright remark that anyone came up with. At the PMO, Jim Davey created an audio-visual briefing room; here, Trudeau would sit Buddha-like and certainly inscrutable, facing half a dozen screens on which rear projectors cast slides itemizing the "constraints" of problems (i.e., no money), then "alternative options," then finally "the optimum solution."

It all produced, in the end, very little. Mitchell Sharp, who at the time enormously enjoyed the intellectual high-flying, admits now, "I'd have to say that the system didn't produce any better legisla-

tion than Pearson's." Even in the matter of systems themselves—reforms to the government's decision-making apparatus
to make it more efficient—Joe Clark arguably executed more
ambitious reforms in his scant seven months than Trudeau in the
previous decade.*

Trudeau established a new system of cabinet committees, and
topped these with a small "quasi-inner" Cabinet Committee on
Priorities and Planning, which derived its authority from the presence of Trudeau, Pitfield, and Lalonde. He tried to make Parliamentary debate more rational by tightening the closure rules, by
transferring some debates from the Chamber to Committee, and
by instituting a new "roster" system that freed ministers from
attending Question Period every day. These changes left Parliament no more efficient than before but more fractious—Trudeau's
reforms were greeted by Opposition shouts of "Heil Hitler"—and
if anything, even slower in its despatch of the public's business.

In his own office, he established the "regional desks," expanded his staff, and created the Supergroup. Lastly, in keeping
with the ethic of Altruistic Technocrats, authority was shifted from
departments, headed by grubby-fingered politicians, to regulatory
agencies such as the CRTC and the National Energy Board, staffed
by disinterested, meritorious public servants. (Ottawa has spent
the last half decade trying to wrestle back this jurisdiction.)

* * *

The dance of the dialectic ended abruptly on October 30, 1972. Except for a brief reprise in 1974-75, it never resumed. In 1978, in a
study for the Institute for Research in Public Policy, two of Trudeau's former top level planners, Mike Kirby and Hal Kroeker
(who both returned to Ottawa in 1980) put the question, "Did it
work?" They answered jointly, "No." In their paper, they quoted,
almost mournfully, a 1967 edition of *Public Interest Quarterly* in
which political scientist James Wilson had remarked: "Some problems cannot be solved and some government functions cannot, in
principle, be done well. The rule of reason should be to try to do as
few undo-able things as possible."

Even if Trudeau, Lalonde, Davey, and the rest had read Wilson

---

*Clark reorganized fundamentally the structure of cabinet committees, and
implemented a system of expenditure control by "spending envelopes" that
Trudeau, back in power in 1980, retained.

at the time, they wouldn't have believed him. Common sense, while the planning mania raged, was the quality they conspicuously lacked. Just as conspicuously they also lacked a sense of humour, which, as someone has written, is only common sense, dancing. As any good manager knows, laughter is the best problem-solver of all.

This madness mattered relatively little in lost dollars and time, but a great deal in lost opportunity. Trudeau squandered his best chance, the chance that always exists when a leader is fresh and doesn't have to defend his mistakes, to make his mark as a creative Prime Minister. By trumpeting that the rational systems approach could solve all problems, he created exaggerated expectations – the same exaggerated expectations that Trudeau apologists accuse Canadians of having created themselves. It was a mark of Trudeau's innocence during his first term – not so much a "dilettante in power" in James Eayrs's phrase, as a high-minded *naif* – that he really thought all the shuffling of bureaucratic boxes, all the paper burden was accomplishing something. "We're setting up the machinery that will permit us to deal with the important and not only with the urgent," he said on one occasion, and on another, "I have the feeling of a mechanic who's retuning a car or something, and getting the thing ready to go." The car hummed all right. But it moved only in fits and starts, and not because of rationalism but in spite of it, as a function of Trudeau's own extraordinary intelligence and dedication, and of the quality of the cabinet and civil service that, almost entirely, he'd inherited from Pearson.

* * *

Participation next, which also failed. But this failure was of a quite different order. We failed Trudeau as much as he did us. And participation, unlike planning, did not fade away. Trudeau's dream of mass participation, on the Athens' model, turned out to be a grand illusion. Canada was just too large for everyone to walk to the Agora to take part in their own governance. Yet part of the dream survived. More citizens than ever before have got under the skin of government and into the system itself.

The dream at the outset was called Participatory Democracy. Trudeau's 1968 election manifesto spelled it out: "To make government more accessible to people, to give our citizens a sense

100

of full participation in the affairs of government." His prime available instrument for doing this was the Liberal Party.

The party did its bewildered best. Headquarters distributed a pamphlet which called for "More Power to Everyone." A committee of Liberal M.P.s compiled a high-minded report: "We must imbue in ourselves and in our fellow-citizens the spirit of participation, and most important of all create the necessary tools so that participation will become real, relevant, and the basis of peaceful social change." For all practical purposes, though, the participation program was run by Jim Davey. At a two-day conference in British Columbia, at Harrison Hot Springs hotel in November 1969, 300 Liberals listened as a succession of speakers – post-industrial gurus to the editor of the *Georgia Straight* – harangued them about everything from genetic engineering to the social consequences of electronic newspapers. They heard Trudeau describe the party as "society's radar," its gaze fixed upon the brave new world ahead rather than upon day-to-day trivia like unemployment and inflation.

Next, all constituency associations were requested to stage public debates: out of 262, 25 complied. Lastly, in November 1970, 2,400 Liberals gathered in Ottawa for a three-day policy conference, to grill ministers, and to pass resolutions.

Afterwards, a delegate asked Trudeau what would happen to the resolutions. "It may be that in respect of some, the government will not be able to proceed in accordance with the delegates' wishes," Trudeau replied. "Such cases will be rare I hope." They turned out to be the rule. Resolutions to decriminalize marijuana, to introduce a guaranteed annual income, to impose tighter controls on foreign investment, were all ignored. Asked to recommend the most effective anti-inflation policy, delegates overwhelmingly replied, "wage and price controls." That too was ignored. Asked why, Lalonde replied with disinguous candour: "People in riding associations don't have the sophisticated knowledge required. They're uninformed."

Mass participation had died. Yet the idea survived. Next, Trudeau applied it to youth.

* * *

On March 16, 1971, less than a fortnight after he'd married a flower child, Trudeau rose in the Commons to announce the most

101

adventurous of all his policies, before or since. It was called Opportunities for Youth: young people would be given money to do just about everything – provided it was socially useful – they wanted to do.

Youth, in Athens-on-the-Rideau, was the biggest idea of all. Half the population, as everyone kept saying, was under twenty-five, while forgetting that half of these were under twelve. Youth was vocal, energetic, self-confident, and often so angry. Trudeau worried about them. In 1969, in a magazine interview he said, "It is extremely important that those in authority keep up a dialogue with young people so that the values they are developing for themselves do not develop in isolation but are constantly being tested against the values in which we believe." The reason for Trudeau's concern was that youth were, and are, special to him: they are his tender core. With children, his iciness dissolves; talking to students, his impatience and verbal competitiveness vanish. He married youth.

Trudeau's plenipotentiary to youth was Pelletier, youngest in spirit of all his ministers. "He's fifty, going on twenty-five," Pelletier's eager young assistants liked to say. It took Pelletier three years to figure out what to do, threading his way through the cat's cradle of decision-making committees that Trudeau had spun around himself. Meanwhile, Pelletier established a Committee on Youth; he revamped his Citizenship Branch into "a consciousness raiser within government," as one report put it, staffed with young people in jeans who liked to stand on their heads in the corridors, and to call themselves "guerrilla bureaucrats." For "transient youth," the thousands of knapsacked kids with guitars hitch-hiking from coast to coast like a new breed of troubadors, Pelletier set up massive tepee tents. When these blew down, he chivied the Defence Department into opening up its armouries.

In the winter of 1971 Pelletier reached his goal. In the Commons, Trudeau explained OFY's purpose. "The government believes that youth is sincere in its efforts to improve society. We intend to challenge them to see if they have the stamina and self-discipline to follow through on their criticism and advice."

This idea, unlike Participatory Democracy, soared. Within a year, OFY's budget had doubled to $35 million; added to it were two other do-thine-own-thing programs: New Horizons for old people, and the Local Initiatives Programme for everyone in high-unemployment communities. OFY attracted by far the most attention – more than 2,500 separate stories in the first year: headlines ranged from "The future, it works," to "larceny perpetrated with Canadian tax dollars." It kept a lot of kids occupied and mostly they did a lot of good: from garbage pick-ups to cemetery clean-ups, to blazing trails, to staffing day care centres, and reading to the blind. A few, inevitably, took the money and planted pot. Provinces complained that the short-term projects raised expectations which they then had to fulfil. But later, provinces implemented the same kinds of projects themselves with their lottery slush funds. More perceptive critics pointed out that overwhelmingly it was middle-class youth who benefited. "It's the program I'm proudest of," Trudeau said of OFY. Yet in 1975, when he needed headlines to get across the message that he was practising restraint, he killed it, along with the Company of Young Canadians and Information Canada. By then, the golden days were over anyway; youth had become less interested in doing its own thing than in getting things out of the system. Conventional wisdom had shifted, and through programs such as Community Employment Service the government tried, with mixed success, to fund projects that could take off to the nirvana of "commercial viability." New programs, such as Canada Works, although more conventional, were aimed away from the middle class. The 1977 youth program, Katimavik, was specifically designed to provide not just the fun of doing your own thing, but the discipline of hard work out of doors and – a swear word in the 1960's – "structure."

· And yet, OFY left its mark. In the wake of the kids came wave after wave of "public interest groups," each funded by government to *oppose* government: native groups to demand land claims; women's groups to make their case for equality; environmental groups to point out everything government was doing wrong to the environment; consumer groups to harass government agencies, such as the National Energy Board and the Canadian Transport Commission. Between them, Pelletier and Trudeau redefined one of the fundamental concepts of the British and thus the Canadian Parliamentary system: the concept that the Opposition is both "Loyal" and "Official." By extension, those terms applied and still apply today to a new type of extra-Parliamentary Opposition. Though we bitch a lot about government, we have never, in contrast to what has happened in the U.S., denied government's basic legitimacy; one reason has to be that we know that in part, our government is us.

* * *

For most Canadians, as they watched unemployment and cost of living statistics soar, OFY and all the rest were fringe attractions. Trudeau's dream had been grander: he'd expected more from us. After the debacle of the 1972 election, he never again quite trusted the public. To mobilize it, he no longer relied on the force of reason, but more and more on the power of charisma, that "infantilizing" force in democratic politics, as Irvine Schiffer, in *Charisma: A Psychoanalytic Look at Mass Society* has described it.

Trudeau, though, once trusted Canadians. From 1968-72, he made a genuine attempt to open wide the doors of government; mostly, we hung about in the entrances, shuffling our feet. When things didn't go the way we wanted, we heaved rocks.

From his experiment with mass participation, Trudeau learned a painful lesson. The public, as such, doesn't exist; only *particular* publics exist, and these become engaged in politics only when their self-interests are at stake: bankers and businessmen in opposition to the 1969 White Paper on Taxation as a major example.

Several times, Trudeau had tried to explain what he meant — more important, what he *did not* mean – by participation. "There is a distinction between consultation and participation and decision-making," he said at a "teach-in" in Canberra in 1970. "The decision must always be taken by representatives of the people." Many had imagined that by participation he'd meant consensual decision-making and were let down by their own exaggerated expectations.

Trudeau provoked a good deal of the confusion himself. Participation without information amounts to manipulation. Trudeau, first to last, was as parsimonious with information as he was with his money. At the very beginning, he warned that ministers who "leaked" would be fired. Up to his defeat in 1979, he resisted pressure to create a Freedom of Information Act. Though he created Information Canada in 1970, after a Task Force had made all the right noises about "Reaching the Unreached," it soon became clear that the agency's purpose was to reach out with good news about the government. Mocked by the press, impotent because it lacked authority over departmental information programs, Infor-

104

mation Canada died unmourned in the austerity cuts of 1975.

All along, Trudeau had been more in love with the *idea* of participation than with a reality. He loved the idea of public debate about the big issues. But when the public, as it inevitably does, asked for things it ought not to have, Trudeau invoked closure.*

* * *

For all that the big ideas hadn't worked out as planned, Trudeau, between 1968-72, had provided scandal-free, reasonably competent administration. In strict terms of crisis management, his handling of the 1970 October Crisis had been brilliant. His foreign policy had been innovative, and after some early indiscretions – sliding down the banisters at Lancaster House, calling the Commonwealth an "anachronism" – he'd come to cut the kind of international dash that buttressed our self-esteem back home. Though the body economic manifested some aches and pains, it suffered no severe diseases. Further, in contrast to the ragged blue line around Stanfield, Trudeau's cabinet constituted an impressive management team: sturdy veterans, such as Sharp, Drury, MacEachen, Pépin, Chrétien; feisty newcomers like Macdonald, Lang, Munro, Mackasey; and – in a category all his own – Turner.

Portents suggested that maybe all of this would not be enough. Canadians by now had also heard Trudeau call Opposition M.P.s "nobodies"; ask western grain farmers "Why should I sell your wheat?"; say "fuck off" in the Commons (he claimed he said only "fuddle-duddle"); tell unemployed postal drivers to "eat shit." As early as mid-1970, a Gallup Poll found that by a margin of 43 to 37 per cent, the public believed that Trudeau was "out of touch with Canadians." More specifically, he had lost the support of key opinion-makers. Economic nationalists had been outraged when a deputation, headed by Walter Gordon, had called on Trudeau, to be told to keep up the good work, and then had realized that by this he had meant that they should do all the work of saving the economy from foreigners. Cultural nationalists were outraged that Expo's momentum had been allowed to dribble away

*By contrast, the 1979 Clark government practised what Trudeau once had preached: it brought down a Freedom of Information Act, published "Tax Expenditures," or hidden tax subsidies for the first time, while Clark himself wrote a personal letter to civil servants to tell them to talk freely to reporters.

without being used as springboard for the arts, publishing, magazines, and films. As for the press, the stern humourlessness of rational government had deprived reporters of the daily ration of gossip, anecdote, and melodrama they needed to feed what Norman Mailer calls "the Goat." By mid-term, reporters turned sullen and sniped at Trudeau at every turn.

Even so, late in August 1972, the Gallup put the Liberals ahead by a comfortable 10 percentage points. As a leader, he out-polled Stanfield two to one, and in case anyone actually believed reason matters more in politics than charisma, a 1972 Gallup Poll showed that Canadians picked leadership over issues almost three to one (56 per cent to 22 per cent). The only point at issue, patently, was whether Trudeau would win a large or narrow majority.

On September 1, 1972, at 6.00 p.m., Trudeau, a yellow rose in his lapel, strode into the ground-floor theatre of the National Press Building to announce that the election would be held on October 30. In an interview the next day he explained that he considered the election an opportunity for "settling all the piddling little questions of whether this little thing was right or wrong." He would take "the high road," Trudeau added, from which he would conduct a "dialogue" with Canadians.

Trudeau began his campaign a fortnight later, to the tune of a song: "Take Care, Take Time/The Land is Strong." He hopped aboard a plane, into a forward compartment sealed off from reporters, and flew in leisurely circles from coast to coast. Intermittently, he emerged to say things like: "Look about you at the numbers of new cars, at the activity of the stock markets, and the vacation trips."

However lackadaisical, it seemed to work. NDP Leader David Lewis made headlines with his attacks on "Corporate Welfare Bums," but Lewis, although Trudeau's equal in brains and debating skills, was just too harsh, too strident, too, well, *socialist*, to turn on any but his own faithful. As for Stanfield, he was, well, Stanfield. Decent, reliable, radiating integrity, but lacking Trudeau's magic allure and vital energy. Stanfield wasn't the issue, as he had been in 1968, when Trudeau had hung the "two nations" albatross round his neck, and his campaign was remarkably well organized. Yet instead of the crisp 30-second clips that television consumes, he spoke, as one reporter quipped, "in 30-second pauses."

While Trudeau talked about "four goals" – national integrity, economic growth, social justice, and "fulfilment of the individual – Stanfield talked about unemployment, unemployment insurance rip-offs, high taxes.

Suddenly, in the campaign's last week, the malaise some political pros and some reporters had sensed was all around them, but unfocused, found its target. Gallup cut Trudeau's lead to just 6 percentage points on October 28 (39-33). In his last campaign speech in Toronto, Trudeau seemed at last to recognize, that the land, rather than strong, was strongly hostile to him. "It's too bad it's been a dull campaign," he told a gathering of party workers. "We haven't made headlines."

A late campaign editorial in the *Calgary Herald* mirrored the public's attitude best:

More than any other leader in federal politics, Mr. Trudeau is guided by a clearly-stated, personal, social and cultural philosophy. No man better understands Quebec . . . Yet not a past Canadian leader has been so openly indifferent to the problems of individual citizens as human beings . . . The Prime Minister can demonstrate superb qualities of personal leadership. His handling of the October 1970 crisis will long remain an historical high-water mark. And yet, he is capable of demeaning himself and the whole process of public service by mouthing obscenities in public.

* * *

His personality, his forbidding presence, his Supergroup had combined to cut Trudeau off from reality. Perhaps more than all of these his obsession with rationalism had isolated him. Or rather, his fascination with the intellectual pretensions of rationalism. For four years Trudeau talked about the big ideas he wanted to talk about. He never once had listened to what the public was trying to say to him, about its problems, its fears, its dreams. Above all, in those years, he ignored rationalism's essential flaw. To be systematic is sensible. To be systematic without common sense, without humour, is to treat systems as more important than people. And politics is only people.

7

"Just Watch Me"

"Extremism in the defence of liberty is no vice."

Barry Goldwater

At 9.10 a.m. on Monday, October 5, 1970, British trade commissioner James Cross was abducted from his home in Montreal by four young men who identified themselves as members of the Liberation Cell of the *Front de Libération du Québec*. The cell declared that Cross would be executed unless seven demands were met, including $500,000 in gold bullion and the release of 23 so-called "political" prisoners – all FLQ members in jail for planting bombs.

For a week not much happened. The police quickly released the name of one kidnapper, Jacques Lanctôt, but were unable to find the cell's hiding place. While the Quebec and federal governments rejected the kidnapper's demands, they did initiate discussions and as a gesture of good intent arranged for the FLQ Manifesto to be read over the national television networks. The manifesto said rude things about financiers and big businessmen, and called Québécois, "a society of terrorized slaves." To the surprise of the authorities, a number of Québécois seemed to agree with these sentiments. The affair took on something of the air of a lark; press and public began to treat the kidnappers as Robin Hoods robbing Steinbergs and Molsons to give to the poor.

Then just before dusk on Saturday, October 10, Pierre Laporte, the Quebec Minister of Labour, was kidnapped while playing touch-football with his nephew, outside his house in the Montreal suburb of St. Lambert. His kidnappers identified themselves as members of the FLQ's Chenier Cell.

Abruptly, the nature of the crisis changed. Government attitudes hardened, despite pressures from some prominent Quebec citizens, notably Parti Québécois leader René Lévesque and *Le Devoir* editor Claude Ryan, for some prisoners to be released so as to secure the lives of the two captives. Troops moved into Ottawa, and later into Montreal, to protect VIPs. Meanwhile, political support for the FLQ grew, culminating, on Thursday, October 15 with a mass rally of 3,000 students and unionists at Montreal's Paul Sauvé Arena.

Right after Laporte's kidnap, key advisers around Trudeau and Bourassa concluded that the crisis could be dealt with only by invoking, for the first time in peacetime, the War Measures Act. The decision was approved unanimously by the federal cabinet on Thursday, October 15; the Act was promulgated at 4.00 a.m. on Friday. The Montreal and Quebec governments, Trudeau explained, had asked Ottawa to intervene "to apprehend an insurrection." The Act made membership in the FLQ a criminal offence and banned political rallies. It also suspended *habeas corpus*, and allowed the police to arrest, interrogate, and detain suspects without charge for up to twenty-one days. Eventually, almost 500 suspects were arrested.

The FLQ responded immediately. Late on Saturday, October 17, on instructions from the FLQ, Montreal police went to St. Hubert air base and found Laporte's body stuffed into the trunk of a Chevrolet. He had been strangled with his own gold neck chain.

Laporte's death was announced on Sunday, October 18. "The FLQ has sown the seeds of its own destruction," Trudeau declared on television. Laporte was buried three days later, after a state funeral in Montreal's Notre-Dame cathedral. Instantly, the FLQ lost all public sympathy; Canadians were outraged and revulsed.

Except for the round-up of the kidnappers and the release of Cross, the crisis was over. Within a week, most of those detained under the War Measures Act had been released. Only sixty-two were ever charged; fewer than a dozen were sentenced.

On December 2, 1970, the police moved in on a house on Rue des Recollets in north Montreal and after negotiations agreed to provide safe conduct out of the country for the Liberation Cell members. Next day, Cross was released on the old Expo site in Montreal; the kidnappers and their wives and children were flown to Cuba where they remained, unhappily, for four years before moving on to France.*

---

*Jacques and Louise Cossette Trudel returned to Canada in December 1978. In

On December 28, the last three members of the Chenier Cell still at large, Paul and Jacques Rose and Francis Simard, were arrested in a farmhouse south of Montreal. (The other member, Bernard Lortie, had been arrested earlier.) Paul Rose and Simard were sentenced to life imprisonment, Bernard Lortie to twenty years, and Jacques Rose, who was acquitted on the murder charge, to eight years.*

During the subsequent decade, not one terrorist bomb has exploded anywhere in the country: Canada probably has been the most peaceable industrial democracy in the world.

* * *

Exhuming the skeleton of the October Crisis is easy. Putting flesh on it is almost impossible. The story, at once the most sombre and most dramatic in Canadian history, is full of might-have-beens, and twists and turns of fate. Of all the separate psychodramas that make up the story the most compelling and most difficult to comprehend concerns Trudeau himself, the attitudes and instincts that sustained and motivated him, as he dealt with the most excruciating ordeal any Canadian Prime Minister has been put to in peacetime since Macdonald had to decide whether Louis Riel should hang.

The political consequences, at least, are easy to record. Because of his handling of the October Crisis, Trudeau achieved a singularity among Canadian Prime Ministers. He made himself into a War Leader, the first we've ever had, because Robert Borden and Mackenzie King, who governed during the two World Wars, were no more than managers of wartime administrations. By taking charge personally, Trudeau imprinted himself indelibly on the national consciousness as the compleat, Single Combat champion; fearless, decisive, above all, victorious. Ever since, Canadians have judged "toughness" an essential quality in a leader and have judged harshly those, such as Stanfield and Clark, whom

---

August 1979, both were sentenced to two years less a day. Both were released on parole in April 1980. Jacques Lanctôt, Louise's brother, came home in February 1979, and was sentenced to three years. He becomes eligible for parole in November 1980. The last two members of the cell, Marc Carbonneau and Yves Langlois remain in France. On July 10, 1980, police arrested and charged a long-suspected "sixth" alleged member of the Liberation Cell, British-born teacher, Nigel Hamer.

*Jacques Rose was paroled in July 1978.

they believed lacked toughness. Many of the reasons for Trudeau's staying power as Prime Minister derive directly from his status as War Leader – an accolade granted to him, as to De Gaulle, Churchill, Castro, Franco, Tito, Nehru, in gratitude for having brought his people through a collective ordeal, whether of war, civil war, national liberation or of "apprehended insurrection."

Trudeau's international reputation also derives from the October Crisis. No matter whether his true motive was idealism or vengefulness, Trudeau's refusal to pay Danegeld inspired the respect and envy of world leaders of every stripe, democratic or totalitarian, and has been followed since in almost every western country.

But there was another political consequence. During the October Crisis, Trudeau smeared irredeemably his reputation as a champion of civil liberties. No other Prime Minister has been so severely criticized for crushing civil liberties; both in the case of those Canadians wrongfully arrested under the War Measures Act, and later, in the case of those Canadians subjected to harassment by the RCMP in the force's blatant series of transgressions of the law during 1971-79. In his book, *Bleeding Hearts, Bleeding Country*, Denis Smith has put the case against Trudeau eloquently, in language almost identical to the condemnations Trudeau once hurled against Duplessis – with the difference that Smith wasn't afraid to let his anguish show:

> The democratic system, in all its disorder and confusion, in all its openness to abuse, must be sustained while Quebec and Canada, in the next few years, work out their destinies in freedom. The use of private terror in the name of a prophetic view, the limitation of civil liberty through emergency legislation, the unscrupulous manipulation or intimidation of the electorate, the use of fear or blackmail as political weapons from whatever source, all these must be condemned and rejected.

Anthony Westell, in the title of his 1972 study of Trudeau, defined him as a paradox. Nothing in Trudeau's career has been so paradoxical as his behaviour during the October Crisis. He had championed civil rights all his life, and he has tried, all his years in power, to add a Bill of Rights to our constitution. He crushed civil liberties in 1970 to protect, as he saw it, civil liberties. One last paradox: although our civil liberties indeed were crushed, we are

111

today, probably the freest, most tolerant society on earth.

There is no final resolution to any of these paradoxes. About the crisis itself, in the manner of John Kennedy's assassination, a sense of mystery lingers on, an endless string of "ifs" and "buts." "Who won?" Cross was asked in a retrospective interview. "I did," he replied and then added, unasked: "Who lost? Pierre Laporte and his family."

Trudeau, ultimately, won and lost. He proved himself to be a hero. He also showed himself to be a bully. In literature, Single Combat heroes have no faults. They take no pleasure in victory for its own sake; after winning they are humble, but as a human hero, Trudeau is flawed. By his famous "bleeding hearts" outburst, he laid bare a vein of nastiness, a quality of vengeful, predatory contempt. Once engaged in any competition, Trudeau's "white anger" takes hold until victory is long won. Fair play becomes to him a foolish sentimentality that bleeding hearts indulge in. Soon after the War Measures Act had been invoked, for example, it became evident that hundreds of people had been arrested wrongfully; neither then, nor after passions had cooled, did it occur to Trudeau to apologize, to admit that in the defence of civil liberties, he had been extreme.

Few Canadians, at the time, realized just how far Trudeau was prepared to go. Even now, the full story of his far-sighted courage on the one hand, his stubborn intransigence on the other, has yet to be told. Our recollections of the October Crisis are influenced profoundly by the images we retain: Laporte's mutilated body glimpsed on television, and the squalid blood-stained pillows in the trunk of the battered Chevrolet. We remember the troops in the streets, their very presence engendering an atmosphere of crisis, and the frightening mindlessness of the students and unionists as they chanted the FLQ slogan, "*Nous vaincrons*" at the Paul Sauvé Arena. We forget that when the crisis began, it was all quite different.

* * *

The first response to Cross's kidnapping was almost languid. The whole thing seemed absurd, all the more when the Liberation Cell, so obviously adolescent rebels in search of a cause, described Cross in a *communiqué* as a member of "the old, racist and colonialist system." When a group of senior PCO officials were told the news, they went right on with their meeting. When Sharp, on Monday evening, tried to make an official statement (as Minister of External Affairs, he was the minister responsible) he had to wait several minutes for enough laughing, chattering M.P.s to assemble in the Chamber to constitute a quorum. Quebec Premier Robert Bourassa announced he would go ahead with his planned mid-week visit to New York to talk to bankers, and told a companion as he boarded his plane, "Isn't it alarming that the people aren't concerned?" Trudeau announced he would go ahead with his official visit to Soviet Russia, scheduled to begin the following week-end.

About the only thing that Ottawa and Quebec really worried about was the positive response of some Québécois to the grandiloquent rhetoric – "the French-speaking majority of Quebec is jeered at and repressed on her own territory" – of the FLQ Manifesto. Still, the kidnappers quickly demonstrated their relative moderation. They secured a supply of the Serpasil that Cross needed for his high blood pressure. On Thursday, October 8, their *communiqué* announced that the threat to execute Cross had been "temporarily suspended" and that he would be released, "alive and well" if two out of the original seven demands were met: an end to police searches and raids; the release of twenty-three "political prisoners."

The kidnappers seemed to be no more than, as Cross put it later, "six kids trying to make a revolution." Clearly they were amateurs; they had even forgotten to put on their masks while abducting Cross. Their single skill was their understanding of how to manipulate the media. Brilliantly, they played upon journalists' collective self-indulgent sympathy for any underdog, and exploited what they later called the "competitive contradictions" of the media by sending *communiqués* first to one radio station and then to another, so that each would play its scoop to the hilt. These tactics forced the governments, to their anger and dismay, to negotiate in public with the Liberation Cell, on an equal footing.

The affair, it seemed certain that first week, would end in some kind of negotiated compromise. In his book, *The October Crisis*, Pelletier describes these negotiations as following a "conventional pattern" so that, "after a few weeks of shifting back and forth" a compromise "could be worked out." Just when this was about to happen, writes Pelletier, "Negotiations were short-circuited by the intervention of a new [FLQ] cell." What Pelletier doesn't mention is that this new cell, which kidnapped Laporte, intervened after Trudeau himself had short-circuited the negotiations.

* * *

The Liberation Cell set a 6.00 p.m., Saturday, October 10, deadline for a "final" official response to its demands. Responsibility for making that response rested with Jérôme Choquette, the Quebec Justice Minister, because his department was responsible for the issues (cessation of police raids, release of prisoners) raised by the cell, and because Bourassa was away in New York. Choquette announced he would give his reply on television at 5.30 p.m.

Early Saturday morning, Choquette phoned Sharp in Ottawa and read to him the text of the statement he intended to make. He would offer the FLQ a compromise, he told Sharp. In return for the release of Cross, five of the prisoners would be set free. Beyond this, taking account of the public's response to the FLQ manifesto, something called the Ministry of Social Peace would be established.

Choquette's call disturbed Sharp deeply. Trudeau all along had angrily rejected any description of the prisoners as "political"; he'd also been adamant that none should be released.

Sharp asked Choquette to telex him the text of his statement. When it had arrived in Ottawa, Sharp conferred with other key ministers, such as Turner, and with key aides, such as Lalonde. Together, they drafted an alternative text. Omitted from it was a pledge to release any of the prisoners.

Early Saturday afternoon, Sharp phoned Choquette and read him the revised version. Choquette said he could not accept it. He would stick to his original statement, he said. Sharp asked Choquette if he'd had word from the FLQ that his compromise offer would in fact secure the release of Cross. Choquette said that he had had no dealings with the FLQ, but that he "had reason to believe" that the terrorists would respond favourably. So he would deliver his original statement.

Sharp took a deep breath. If Choquette did this, Sharp told him, Ottawa would "disassociate itself" from the Quebec government. Choquette refused to back down and their conversation ended.

The four telephone calls that followed turned history around:

Lalonde to Trudeau; Trudeau to Bourassa, who was by now in Boston; Bourassa to Choquette; lastly, Choquette to Sharp once more, this time to say that he had changed his mind and would now read out the federal version of the text.

At 5.30, Choquette did precisely this, speaking directly to the FLQ. "Without giving into undue pressure, the 'ruling authorities' as you like to say, are not unaware that there are areas of discontent and injustice." No prisoners would be released, because to give in to blackmail "signifies the end of social order," but paroles would proceed uninterrupted for the five already eligible for it.

In a squalid bungalow on Armstrong Street in the Montreal suburb of St. Hubert, four men, coarse in speech and manner, watched the television program and jeered at Choquette. When his image disappeared, they clambered into a battered green Chevrolet. Fifteen minutes later, Pierre Laporte was kidnapped.

* * *

The might-have-beens of history are a fool's game. Arguably, if Choquette had released the five prisoners, the Liberation Cell might have freed Cross and Laporte might be alive today. Just as arguably, the FLQ, emboldened, might have hung onto Cross until all the other "political" prisoners had been released and Laporte might still have been kidnapped.

Only two things are certain. The instant Laporte was kidnapped, everything that happened afterwards was foreordained. One kidnap by one cell might have been a lucky fluke. Two kidnaps by two separate cells had to be conspiracy. From this moment on, the War Measures Act was inevitable; the wrongful arrests of hundreds of innocent people were inevitable; the extinction of civil liberties for a time was inevitable; even Laporte's death was inevitable. "*Laporte est mort*," Cross recalled his captors saying when they realized Laporte was being held by the murderous members of the Chenier Cell.

What's certain also is that Trudeau, even if he had known the consequences, would have done exactly what he did. He never considered, for an instant, even the slightest of concessions. The day before Choquette's statement, in his only extended speech about the crisis during its first moderate week, he had said: "The experience of man demonstrates with blinding clarity that in a jungle all are not equal but all are vulnerable. Freedom and liberty are neither gained nor retained without cost."

Behind the scenes, Trudeau was as implacable. Angrily, he chewed out Sharp for being "weak" after Sharp had personally authorized the reading of the FLQ Manifesto over the networks. "If we give in on this, we give in on everything," he told Sharp.

In an interview they gave afterwards, Liberation Cell members admitted they "underestimated" Trudeau. They ought not to have. Two years earlier, like all Canadians, they had watched him sitting rocklike in the reviewing stand at the St. Jean Baptiste parade amid the flying Coke bottles; perhaps they had hurled some of the bottles themselves.

Long after the crisis, we learned that there was virtually no limit to the extremes Trudeau would go to defend, as he saw it, liberty. In an extraordinary and chilling passage in *Beyond Reason*, Margaret recounts that early in their marriage Trudeau warned her that if she, or their child, were abducted, there would be no deal, no bargaining, no ransom paid to release them.

"Do you understand that?" she quotes Trudeau as asking her.

"No I don't," Margaret replied. "You mean you would let them kill me rather than come to terms?"

"Yes," Trudeau replied. "Yes I would."

* * *

Was it the hero or the bully who held the upper hand? The answer is buried in Trudeau's psyche. Rather than in any factual account, some of the most telling clues to his mindset throughout the crisis are to be found in *The Revolution Script*, Brian Moore's brilliant 1971 fictional recreation of the affair. In a key passage, Moore has one of the Cross kidnappers muse out loud to himself:

How can a taxi driver like Marc Carbonneau [the actual name of a cell member] put himself inside the skull of a Trudeau, a millionaire who never had to work, a dreamer who went to see Mao . . . And how can Trudeau understand the life of a guy like Marc, the scraping up for taxi payments, losing your cab to finance companies, having a wife and four kids somewhere that you left.

Trudeau had never evinced doubts about the legitimacy of employing official violence to suppress individual violence. Back in 1958, with his customary scrupulous logic, he had written in *Vrai*: "The state must maintain the monopoly of force . . . less to use it

116

than to prevent somebody else from usurping the thunder-bolts''—even though that time the state to which he was prepared to cede the monopoly of force was the state ruled by Maurice Duplessis. (In other *Vrai* articles, he discussed with dispassion the occasions when it would be right for the oppressed to kill a tyrant, a topic of more than passing interest to anyone trained by the Jesuits.) The only way for a Carbonneau to acquire the right to exercise force, therefore, would be for him to become the state.* Trudeau had also demonstrated before the October Crisis, his awareness of the potential for violence. "Disorders in the great cities of the U.S., problems created by urbanization, problems created by racial strife," he said in Kingston, Ontario, in November 1968, "might spill across the border and lead to rebellions and large disturbances of civil order and of social stability."

In the last analysis, the gap in comprehension between Trudeau and the FLQers was probably, as Moore suggests, the most unbridgeable gap of all: *class*. The FLQers, after all, were kin to the unemployed Lapalme truck drivers whom Trudeau told to "eat shit." Late in 1969, when long-haired anti-Vietnam protestors blocked his path, Trudeau had shown the same kind of aristocratic disdain for the mob. "This is the seed of dictatorship," he said angrily. "This is the seed of totalitarianism. This is what we must attack."

Throughout the crisis—*before* Laporte's abduction let alone after it—Trudeau rejected absolutely the possibility that the ideas that the "six kids trying to make a revolution" were trying in their muddled way to espouse, might have even a grain of legitimacy.

Thus, when he explained the War Measures Act on television, Trudeau referred to the FLQ kidnappers as "violent and fanatical men [who] are attempting to destroy the unity and freedom of the country." The FLQers were indeed violent and fanatical, but they were also trying to create a new Quebec, and to create a society that would be egalitarian, and thus, in theory, freer.

* * *

This absence of empathy, a presumption that to be in authority is to be in the right, revealed itself more starkly in Trudeau's treat-

---

*In May 1975, Trudeau drew the same distinction when he praised convicted Montreal abortionist Henry Morgentaler as "a fine humanitarian," but added that he deserved to be jailed, because "he challenged the law and tested it."

ment of those detained under the War Measures Act.

Well before the Act was promulgated, Trudeau and those around him knew that many innocent people would be rounded up. Pelletier, who agreed to the Act, "with death in my soul,"* was shown as a concession the RCMP's list of suspects. Incredulous and horrified, Pelletier realized that most of the names on the list were old-line Communists, Maoists, Marxist-Leninists, even some Ukrainian nationalists. He crossed off name after name.

The incompetence of the Quebec Provincial Police and the Montreal City Police was greater. In the small hours of October 16, police descended on Pelletier's own house on Elm Avenue in Montreal and ransacked the place in search of FLQ literature for two hours, until Alex Pelletier found some official stationery with Pelletier's name and ministerial title on it, and convinced the police to leave.

No one knew how many had been picked up. The numbers kept changing, eventually reaching a guesstimate of 492. After the first day, Turner, as Justice Minister, became alarmed and phoned Choquette every morning to try to find out what was going on, but found out little. The police went about their business as they pleased, hauling in a poet, Gerald Godin, a *chansonnière*, Pauline Julien, an anglophone CBC story editor, Nick Auf der Maur. In mid-December, Turner assembled his top Justice Department officials to review what had happened; unanimously, the officials concluded that Turner had "lost control" the moment the Act was passed.

Much of the confusion was inevitable. The police forces were exhausted, demoralized by their failure to track down the FLQ, constantly feuding with one another, and contemptuous of the politicians. It would not have been easy for the federal government to intervene to enjoin moderation. In any event, no one made the attempt. When the crisis was over, no apologies, no offers of restitution were made to the War Measures Act's innocent victims.

* * *

And yet. The patronizing bully was also performing like a patrician

---

*Two other ministers, Kierans and MacEachen, questioned the need for the Act; but when Pelletier raised no objections at cabinet, neither did they.

hero. Few leaders anywhere could have done what Trudeau did.

Eric Kierans, who quit the cabinet six months after the October Crisis, and who is certainly no fan of Trudeau's, has described his performance: "Very cold, very tough, totally determined. He never lost his cool, he was always in command. It was very, very, impressive."

At the time, most Canadians recognized this. We watched him, seething yet contained, during his famous interview with Tim Ralfe of the CBC on the steps of the Parliament Buildings, snapping back when asked how far he was prepared to go to crush the FLQ: "Just watch me." We watched him, stern and implacable, explaining the War Measures Act on television. "To the kidnappers [their] victim's identity is immaterial. The kidnappers' purpose would be just as well served by having in their grip, you or me, or perhaps some child. Their purpose is to exploit the normal human feelings of Canadians, and to bend those feelings of sympathy for their own violent and revolutionary ends." And we watched him, drained and haggard, go on television again a few days later to say of Laporte's murder: "Faced by such a bloody and demented act, coolly and cruelly premeditated and executed, how can one be anything but crushed."

We did not know then the extent of the burden our Single Combat champion bore for us. In *Beyond Reason*, Margaret describes the 'phone ringing in the small hours, Trudeau answering it, listening, and then,

I heard him crying. Tears pouring down my own face, I tried to comfort him . . . I watched him grow old before my eyes. It was as if Laporte's death lay on his shoulders alone; he was the one who wouldn't negotiate, and he was the one who now would have to take on the responsibility for the murder of an innocent man. It gave him a new bitterness, and a sadness I had never seen before.

Almost everyone, literally, was leaning on Trudeau. The morning after he enacted the War Measures Act, having stayed up till well past midnight, he arrived at his office tired and tense, to spend the first half hour comforting Finance Minister Ben Benson, in a state of shock because the soldier guarding him had accidentally discharged his rifle and killed himself. For three weeks, he had to prop up Bourassa's government, frequently close to collapse, Choquette erratic and Bourassa alternately stubborn and panicked. He had to control the "hawks" around him—Lalonde, George McIlraith, responsible for the RCMP as Solicitor General; Jean Pierre Goyer, soon to succeed to the portfolio; Marchand, often wild and distraught, saying "blood will flow in the streets," in cabinet—who all had urged enactment of the War Measures Act during the crisis's first "moderate" week. He had to reassure Pelletier, who knew that by agreeing to the Act, he would corrode his credibility with his peers. Much of the time he had to make decisions without really knowing what he was doing: the RCMP could not tell him; Trudeau only began to comprehend the nature of the crisis during its third week when the secret Strategic Operations Centre began to function.

*　*　*

Like a kaleidoscope with just two patterns, the images of hero and bully kept on shifting.

In the interview with Ralfe, in hindsight, it was the voice of the bully speaking.

At first, he toyed with Ralfe:

Q: "Sir, what is it with all these men with guns around here?"

Trudeau: "Haven't you noticed?"

Q: "Yes, I've noticed them. I wondered why you people decided to have them."

Trudeau: "What's your worry?"

Q: "I'm not worried, but you seem to be."

Trudeau: "If you're not worried, I'm not worried."

Q: "I'm worried about living in a town that's full of people with guns running around."

Trudeau: "Why? Have they done anything to you? Have they pushed you around, or anything?"

For about ten minutes, Ralfe hung in, refusing to be pushed around, the two arguing about the use of troops to protect ministers and senior officials. At last, Trudeau unloaded.

"Well, there are a lot of bleeding hearts around who just don't like to see people with helmets and guns. All I can say is, go on and bleed, but it is more important to keep law and order in the society than to be worried about weak-kneed people."

On October 18, after learning of Laporte's death, he went on national television and spoke to Canadians in the voice of a hero:

"Accustomed to hate, the FLQ has recourse to violence to sow

120

hatred, to employ it and propagate it insidiously on the assumption that this is the way to spread disorder, disarray, and panic. That is its principal aim. That is the trap it has set for us: to set us, one against the other; to divide us in hatred and racism; and to accentuate the disagreement between generations to the point that they may become irreconcilable.

"Powerless to triumph in liberty, they wish to triumph in tyranny. Let us not fall into their trap.

"The only passion which should move us at this moment is a passion for justice. Through justice, we shall defend our values, our order, and our laws. Through justice, we shall rid ourselves of perversion and terrorism. Through justice, we shall recover our peace and liberty."

When he'd said the last words, Trudeau stared straight into the camera. Every listener – he was speaking in French – must have known that the natural next line, which he left unuttered, had to be "*Nous Vaincrons*" – we will win – the battle cry of the FLQ. And he did win.

8

Ceaseless Pursuit

"The Federal Government has not organized itself to deal with the problem of separatism ... in such a way as to provide a systematic attack on the problem of separatism."

— Final report to Cabinet from the
Strategic Operations Centre,
December 12, 1970, stamped SECRET*

On October 19, Trudeau assembled his full cabinet for a special session. For the first time since the Crisis had broken a fortnight earlier, the RCMP would brief ministers about the FLQ, about the "apprehended insurrection," and about the revolutionary violence in Montreal. The briefing lasted two hours. Ministers asked a few questions and went on their way. Later, the ministers described the RCMP's presentation as "pathetic," "a farce," "unbelievable."

Never before, in its 107-year history, had the RCMP been quite so humiliated. The security of the nation was being threatened; why, by whom, and within which organizations, the national police force did not have the least notion. The easy enemies of the Cold War and the Gouzenko era were gone; a strange new civil war had begun, and the RCMP could not distinguish foe from friend.

* * *

The purpose of the War Measures Act, Trudeau explained on television, was to allow the police to undertake "ceaseless pursuit" of the FLQ. Seven years passed before Canadians realized what Trudeau had really meant. On July 6, 1977, Francis Fox, then Solicitor General, rose in the Commons to correct a statement he had made just three weeks earlier in which he described as "exceptional and isolated" the admission by the RCMP that they had once broken into the offices of a left-wing news agency in

*The author has a copy.

Montreal, to steal files and property. In fact, said Fox, a number of other instances of breaches of law by the RCMP had come to his attention. All of these would be examined by a Royal Commission headed by Mr. Justice David McDonald of the Alberta Supreme Court.

Even then, the full scope of what had been going on did not become public until March 1979, when the McDonald Commission released an edited transcript of testimony given in camera the previous November by John Starnes, a former Director-General of Security and Intelligence of the RCMP. Starnes had held the post during the 1970 October Crisis.

Starnes recounted to the Commission that on the first day of the crisis, Trudeau had praised as "a damn fine piece of work" a memorandum he had written three months earlier on twenty-one Quebec organizations "likely to promote violent confrontation with authority." At the top of Starnes's list had been the Parti Québécois, a legitimate and democratic political movement. Of the RCMP's later behaviour, which included a raid on PQ offices to secure a membership list, Starnes told the commission: "The Prime Minister was well aware of our continuing interest in the separatist movement."

In his management of the October Crisis, as the Starnes testimony makes clear, Trudeau aimed at a double objective: (a) to deal with the FLQ, (b) to deal with separatism.

"They wanted to smash separatism. They wanted to give it a death blow," one cabinet minister of that era has said of Trudeau's conduct, and that of Marchand and Lalonde. Another source can be cited, and he can be quoted. Bud Drury, one of Trudeau's senior ministers and for a decade English-Quebec's cabinet representative says, of the anti-separatist role of the RCMP, "We didn't fight against it."

Late in 1970, Trudeau unleashed the RCMP on revolutionaries who threatened the security of the state. At the same time, he unleashed the policy against legitimate political opponents, who constituted, as he saw it, as serious a threat to security.

* * *

If the RCMP in October 1970 had little or no idea what was going on in Montreal, neither did anyone else – not just here, but equally as much in Paris, where two years earlier an uprising by students

123

and workers had almost toppled the government of De Gaulle, nor in London, where an immigrant Pakistani student, Tariq Ali, had become a national figure able to pack tens of thousands into Trafalgar Square. In West Germany, a pair of lovers had formed something called the Baader-Meinhof gang. In the U.S. a curiously-titled organization, the Weathermen, had just issued a "Declaration of a State of War." The remarkably literate Tupamaros guerrillas were supreme in the jungles of Uruguay; in the mountains of Bolivia, Che Guevara would soon die in a romantic, hopeless cause. Something was happening, and nobody knew what it was.

Hindsight makes everything clear. The mysterious "something" was a brew of social irresponsibility made possible by prolonged affluence, of guilt on the part of those who by doing some good to others were doing very well themselves, of frustration on the part of a generation which had missed the chance to prove its manhood during World War Two, of violence glorified through films like *If*, even more because it was really real, *The Battle of Algiers*, and of the sheer arrogance of individuals who thought themselves superior to those who worked from 9.00 to 5.00 for the sake of their mortgages and their kids. But the "something" was also something more: the product of impassioned idealism, forged out of outrage at what was being done in Vietnam in the name of democratic progress, out of disgust at the spiritual emptiness of liberal capitalism. This second "something" amounted to a quixotic quest, the well-off looking for a sense of purpose by identifying themselves with the wretched of the earth, whether in their own country, or among the colonies, political or de facto economic, of the Third World. In their muddled way, these revolutionaries were the last members of the Thou Generation, the last believers in causes other than themselves.

In his book, Pelletier numbers the hardcore FLQ members as "40 to 50 (perhaps 100)." Isolated these few could have done nothing; they accomplished as much as they did because they could swim like fish in a pool of disaffected liberal intellectuals. The last half of the 1960's and the first few years of the 1970's was the age of the Romance of Violence. The intellectuals didn't practise violence; they condoned it,* and so helped to legitimize vio-

---

*An illustrative example is the December 1970 article in *Canadian Dimension* in

124

lence to the point that even years after the October Crisis, accounts of it generally devote more space to describing the hardships of those detained under the War Measures Act (many of these, surely no coincidence, fellow-intellectuals) than to describing Laporte's terror-ridden death, or to describing the squalid discomfort, hand-cuffed and hooded, that Cross suffered for sixty days, and which left his eyesight impaired permanently.

In a prescient paper written in 1969, Quebec journalist Adele Lauzon described the armchair revolutionaries as "dandy radicals," a phrase that prefigured uncannily Tom Wolfe's later, famous "radical chic." They thrived, she wrote, "in the trade unions, the liberal professions, journalism . . . even the civil service." Essentially voyeurs of violence, dandy radicals had "more sympathy for them [terrorists] than for politicians and well-fed bourgeoisie."

Dandy radicals knew that Fanon had written, "Violence is a purifying force; it frees the native from his inferiority complex," and that Marighella had written, "to be a terrorist is a quality that ennobles." They pinned Guevara posters on their walls, lent their xerox machines to those whom they suspected were real revolutionaries; from the safety of tenure, they delighted in embarrassing the Establishment of which everyone else, the terrorists most of all, considered them a part.

Quebec dandy radicals invariably were separatist. When Trudeau said on October 16, "Canadians have always assumed that it couldn't happen here," he was only half-right. We'd become almost accustomed to violence of a kind. During the preceding seven years, about 100 bombs had exploded in Montreal, killing or maiming dozens; all had been the work of the FLQ. But, during those years, it was very hard to tell where the terrorists ended and where the separatists began. Then, early in 1970, the bombs stopped. Everyone was waiting to see whether democracy would work instead.

* * *

Perhaps the most compelling of all the many might-have-beens that encircle the core of the October Crisis like a maze is whether

---

which McGill University political scientist Daniel Latouche declared: "Violence and democracy are not incompatible."

the Crisis would have happened at all if the Liberals hadn't stolen so blatantly and so sleazily the Quebec election of April 1970. Robert Bourassa would have won anyway, but to make absolutely certain, his party cheated in every conceivable way, from electoral gerrymandering, to patronage, to the emotional blackmail of "economic terrorism," as Lévesque later called it, of which the apotheosis was the famous "Brinks Affair," in which, on election day half a dozen Brinks trucks, supposedly crammed with securities, made a well-publicized dash for the Ontario border. Despite all this the Parti Québécois, only a year and a half old and formed out of a grouping of splintered separatist movements, still won 23 per cent of the vote, although only 7 of the 108 seats.

From then on, thousands of Quebec separatists believed they had the right to do to the federalists as had been done to them. When the opportunity came, during the October Crisis, they exploited it to the full. Some provided direct assistance to the FLQ: a junior secretary in Choquette's office, her lover a militant separatist, performed as a spy. Others, such as journalists and academics, hyped up the crisis, and did their best to discomfit authority. They also did what they could as, in the so-called "provisional government plot," to shake the new and vulnerable government of Bourassa.

"I never believed it for a moment," Pelletier has said of that supposed plot, leaked to the press by someone close to Trudeau late in October, through which a group of prominent Quebecers, including Lévesque and Claude Ryan, purportedly intended either to displace the Bourassa government or to find themselves a place in it. Yet Lévesque was conspicuously slow to criticize the FLQ. And Ryan, for his part, made an odd telephone call to Lucien Saulnier, the power in the Montreal civic government, to discuss the "theoretical" possibility of reinforcing Bourassa's administration. (Saulnier said he thought the idea was crazy and there the matter ended; if Saulnier's answer had been different, it is reasonable to speculate that other calls might have been made.) Odder still, and evocative of the attitudes of many nationalist Québécois, was Ryan's October 16 editorial in *Le Devoir*: "There is more in the Cross-Laporte drama than the necessity to check the risks of insurrection at all costs. There is also, and above all, a unique opportunity to affirm at the highest level the responsibility of the Quebec State." Advancing the unspecified political aims of the state of Quebec, in other words, was more important than preventing violence in the streets.*

* * *

The conviction that their cause was just does not change the reality that Quebec nationalists, separatists, and "dandy radicals" were playing, literally, with death. "Have you ever seen a bus full of English blow up? Have you ever seen a Protestant Church burning? Be sure you soon will," declared *Victoire*, an FLQ pamphlet circulated in the CEGEPS (junior colleges).

The key man among the radicals was Pierre Vallières, in person a gentle, long-haired utopian who in 1971 renounced violence and became a community organizer (on a project funded, predictably, by Ottawa).** Vallières aimed, he told everyone, to help create a "just, free and egalitarian society." Vallières in print was something else entirely, certainly, if he was in fact the author, as the police believed, of the FLQ's strategy paper, *The Role of the Advanced Guard*. In it, echoing Lenin, Vallières (or the anonymous author) called for "escalating revolutionary violence . . . armed struggle and urban guerrilla warfare," for the purpose of "raising the creative violence of the masses." By way of moral absolution, Vallières (or the document's author) added: "It is not bombs that create oppression, but oppression that makes bombs necessary." For the document's readers – taxi-drivers, labourers, the unskilled unemployables whose lives of clamorous desperation in Montreal's east end slums Vallières himself had described memorably in *White Niggers of North America* – these words became a battle hymn. In their own lives, disconnected from the values and support systems of the rural parishes from which they had come, and unconnected to the

---

*Trudeau was so angered by Ryan's behaviour that he refused to talk to him for four years. At the time he remarked on Ryan's conduct, in a play on Acton's famous phrase, "lack of power corrupts and an absolute lack of power corrupts absolutely." (The first to think up this line in fact was the author Kildare Dobbs.)

**Vallières subsequently supported the PQ, then renounced it for failing to follow policies that were "autonomous, socialist and self-governing," and now lives on a remote farm and preaches the beauties of the simple life.

raw, competitive urban world all around them, *Felquistes* had almost nothing. So they were prepared to treat the lives of others almost as nothing. Even the "moderate" Liberation Cell discussed killing Cross, in his hearing.

* * *

Eight years later, in his testimony before the McDonald Commission, retired RCMP Commissioner W.L. Higgitt said of the force's conduct during and after the October Crisis, "They were reasonable, then. Desperate situations require desperate measures."

A number of Quebec journalists and intellectuals, including Vallières, have believed for years that these "desperate measures" went far beyond anything suggested by the public record of the events of the October Crisis. The wildest of these conspiracy theories supposes that authorities, unspecified, actually murdered Laporte in order to smear both the muddleheaded *Felquistes* and, by extension, the separatists. The commonest theory holds that Ottawa, at the very least, instigated the entire affair, RCMP agent provocateurs pulling strings within the FLQ cells they had infiltrated, in order to "smash separatism."

Examining the fine print of the Crisis would take a separate book. Here, as a prologue to what the RCMP actually *did* do on Trudeau's behalf, it's enough to record that not a scrap of evidence exists to support any conspiracy theory whatever. Except perhaps for Louis Riel's rebellion, trial, and execution, no other incident in Canadian history has been studied as exhaustively as the October Crisis: a dozen books, of which the most comprehensive is *Rumours of War*, by Ron Haggart and Aubrey Golden, and an ambitious 1975 CBC documentary, which for six months deployed a dozen experienced journalists in a six-month search for a "smoking gun." The documentary came up with important new information, such as the existence of the Strategic Operations Centre (SOC) co-chaired by Jim Davey and Bryce Mackasey's aide Arnold Masters, which co-ordinated and analysed the best available information from the RCMP, the Montreal police, the armed forces and other sources, including, the CRTC, which, in a contravention of all rules, supplied a confidential daily analysis of radio and television coverage of the crisis. Yet this unprecedented exercise in investigative journalism uncovered nothing resembling a "smoking gun."*

Far from being prepared, the RCMP and Trudeau were dismayed and confused. The final report of SOC to cabinet, for instance, declared that although "sufficient information was available to forewarn the government (of impending violence) little or no action was taken." Although it was leaked that an interdepartmental committee on Security and Intelligence had reviewed the War Measures Act as early as May 1970, months before the Crisis, a mid-July, SECRET, memo from Starnes to the committee chairman makes no reference to this, and refers only to the need to "take full advantage of the provisions of existing laws." Few ministers had heard of the Act when it was brought before cabinet. "I was struck by the fact that it gave us the power to ration sugar," Pelletier recalls.

* * *

But the "smash separatism" theory is quite another matter. The crucial difference between it and all the conspiracy theories lies in the weight of evidence.

In a speech in Saskatoon on April 19, 1977, after English Canadians had acquired almost a year's experience with the Parti Québécois in power, and through familiarity had begun to feel less tense about it, Trudeau lashed out at the separatists as "the inside enemy that wants to destroy this country." (On April 15, 1980, the day on which the date of the Quebec Referendum was announced, he repeated the phrase in the Commons.) The phrase is telling: for Trudeau, separatists were, and are, not just political opponents or misguided, if idealistic, ideologues. They are enemies. Always, when he apprehends an enemy, whether a political one of the moment, such as election opponents, or an argumentative reporter at a press conference, Trudeau's response is overkill. Enemies, for Trudeau, exist not to be defeated, but to be crushed.

"At bottom, the Separatists despair of ever being able to con-

*The author was a member of the CBC team, responsible for research in Ottawa. Material in this and the preceding chapter has been drawn from that research, although information about the SOC final report, and about Choquette's abortive attempt at compromise described in Chapter Seven was acquired as part of the research for this book.

vince the public of the rightness of their ideals," Trudeau had written in *Cité Libre* in 1964. "So they want to abolish freedom and impose a dictatorship of their minority ... And when things don't go fast enough, they take to illegality and violence."

To Trudeau, it didn't really signify that by 1970, the various separatist factions, purged of radicals like Pierre Bourgault, had merged into the Parti Québécois, a conventional, vaguely social democratic party, headed by a well-respected former cabinet minister, Lévesque, who had, so leftist separatists complained, "bourgeois-ified" the party. Trudeau's perceptions did not change. The enemy had merely put on middle-class business suits. "The climate of terror, the climate of violence [is] the real outcome of separatism," Trudeau said in November 1970, to a Quebec Liberal convention. Laporte's death he said in mid-Crisis could be "not a pointless tragedy [but] a landmark in the crusade for Canadian unity."

The men around Trudeau acted as if they too were engaged in a crusade, as much against separatism as the FLQ. "This subversion constitutes separatism, from the FLQ to the PQ," said Marchand. Even Pelletier, in his book written much later, dismissed as "dialectical" the PQ claim "that it cannot be held responsible for the crimes that some madman might commit in the name of the independence of Quebec ... [this because] the strategy of the PQ since its creation has been to convince the population that it was the *only* political movement openly and unequivocally advocating the independence of Quebec." (In fact, the FLQ committed its crimes in the name of social and economic justice, topics which interested the revolutionaries far more than independence, which they dismissed as merely a means to a revolutionary end.)

The most revealing words, always, are the ones never intended to be read – by the public. The mid-December secret report to cabinet from SOC scrupulously distinguishes between the PQ and the FLQ: "There could be no political co-existence if separation were attained ... For the FLQ, the PQ represents only a French-speaking bourgeoisie taking over from an Anglo-American bourgeoisie."

In its conclusions and recommendations, however, the SOC report treats the two movements as twins. The report calls for "Continuous attention to the basic material problems that are exploited by both the separatists and revolutionaries ... Funds for a study of the problems of separatism and revolutionaries ... Permanent organizational structures to deal with revolution and separatism ... Co-ordinated and expanded intelligence-gathering operations."

This report was submitted to the Cabinet Committee on Security and Intelligence, chaired by Trudeau, on December 16, 1970, and was discussed by the ministers, along with a parallel RCMP memorandum on the touchy question of the need by the RCMP to break the law at times so as to carry out its assigned role by, for instance "having members of the RCMP, or paid agents [informers] commit serious crimes in order to establish their legitimacy [within FLQ cells]." Cabinet reached no conclusion on either matter. Six weeks later, though, Starnes sent a memo to the RCMP's newly-formed G-section in Quebec. This memo was headed "Disruptive Tactics."

* * *

Canadians learned what "Disruptive Tactics" meant in March 1979, when the McDonald Commission released the edited text of Starnes's testimony.

Starnes makes an impressive witness for the prosecution, and for himself. He is tall, handsome, silver-haired, wealthy, educated at private schools in Canada, Switzerland, and Germany, a former Ambassador to Bonn and Cairo. Late in 1969, Trudeau named Starnes the first civilian head of the RCMP's Security and Intelligence Branch, one of the most exacting and sensitive posts in the public service. As a civilian, even though his great-uncle had been a former RCMP Commissioner, Starnes had to work hard to prove his hard-line credentials to the para-military Mounties, a proud, close-knit force; its reputation unsullied, except briefly during the "Red Scare" of the late 1940's, by any suggestion of oppression, still less of illegality.

With Trudeau, Starnes established his credentials by his July 1970 memo which ranked the PQ at the top of the list of Quebec's violence-prone organizations. Trudeau praised the memo. The next day, Starnes was felled by pneumonia; through most of the October Crisis period, he lay flat on his back in bed while his branch humiliated the force by its "pathetic" briefing to the cabinet. Back in action, Starnes despatched his "Disruptive Tactics" memo to Montreal's new G-section, later known as the "Dirty Tricks" squad. This involved, as a second memo from

Starnes explained, "Making sophisticated and well-researched plans built around existing situations, such as power struggles, love affairs, fraudulent use of funds, information on drug use, etc., to cause dissension and splintering of separatist/terrorist groups." (Again, the twins.) Harassment, in other words, the same kind the FBI had practised against Martin Luther King, not long before. Deliberate law-breaking, in other words, as an unavoidable stratagem in a crusade.

Here based on evidence given to the McDonald Commission is a list of what the RCMP then proceeded to do: *December 1970*; broke into the Toronto office of the left-wing organization, Praxis, to steal files and start a fire; *early 1971*; composed and distributed a fraudulent FLQ *communiqué* urging violence (this got a mention in *Time* magazine); *through 1971*; enrolled by "force and pressure" nine FLQ informers; *July 1971*; compiled and circulated to cabinet ministers a list of twenty-one federal civil servants who should not be employed or at the very least not promoted because they were members of "the extra-Parliamentary Opposition" (voting NDP was about as far as any of these people had ever sortied into Opposition); *June 1972*: burnt a barn north of Montreal to prevent a planned meeting between the FLQ and the Black Panthers; *October 1972*: broke into the Montreal offices of a left-wing news service, *L'Agence de Presse Libre du Québec* (APLQ) to steal some 200 files; *January 1973*: broke into the Montreal offices of the Parti Québécois to steal a six-foot stack of computerized PQ membership lists; all throughout the period, *up to July 1975*; "screened" applicants for federal jobs in a search for those with "separatist sympathies, associations and activities."*

The specific laying of blame, on the RCMP and on the Trudeau government, will be set out by the McDonald Commission in its final report due late in 1980. The general nature of the blame is already evident. The RCMP repeatedly broke the law; it did so because it believed Trudeau wanted it to. Trudeau was "well aware" of the RCMP's interest in separatists, Starnes told the McDonald Commission. In late 1969, said Starnes, the government decided "that separatism should be treated as a subversive

*The practice was halted in mid-1975 at Trudeau's order after he heard about it for the first time, he said. The information that Trudeau had stopped the surveillance was leaked to the press, specifically the *Toronto Sun* which criticized Trudeau severely for *not* treating the separatists as enemies.

movement," and while cabinet ministers were reluctant to say this in memorandums, "they had, of course, already taken the decisions in private." In a later comment, Starnes added: "The buck, of course, has to stop with the ministers."

*　*　*

When the stories of the RCMP illegalities began to break in 1977, public support for the force was so strong that the main concern of the Conservative Opposition, and equally that of the Liberal government, was to accuse the other of smearing the RCMP.

Deference to authority is perhaps the most pronounced character trait of Canadians. Our constitution, as the historian W.L. Morton was the first to point out, invokes us to establish "peace, order, and good government" rather than to seek "life, liberty, and the pursuit of happiness." In no other country is the national police force a national symbol. During the October Crisis, a Gallup Poll measured 85 per cent support for the War Measures Act; another poll, in April 1971, showed that by a margin of more than two to one, Canadians wanted the Act continued even though by then the Crisis was long over. Any time any Canadian police force is criticized, as in Toronto in 1979 after a policeman shot a twenty-one-year-old black suspect, public support for the police is massive and instantaneous.

Yet, in the kind of contradiction that is also central to the Canadian character, we may be the freest society in the world. In few other countries are so many opponents of government – from native groups to environmentalists – encouraged and funded to get on with their opposition. Out of the purse-lipped, monotone society Canada was in the 1950's, has blossomed a multi-coloured, pluralistic society in which more minorities can uninhibitedly do their own thing – be a Rastafarian, be not just a homosexual, but a militant gay rights activist in a long denim skirt and at the same time an ascendant public servant – than in probably any other country in the world. The so-called "enemies list" circulated to cabinet ministers in 1971 under the signature of Jean-Pierre Goyer, then Solicitor General, was one of the most reprehensible of the post-October Crisis acts. Equally, though, it was one of the least effective. Four of the twenty-one on the list have since risen to the rank of assistant deputy minister, and one, Robert Rabinovitch, is Secretary to the key Cabinet Committee on Planning and Priorities. Mind you, this shows only that times haven't changed in Canada. Of the 135 delegates to the 1933 CCF convention that produced the "socialistic" Regina Manifesto, seven went on to live in Rockcliffe Park in Ottawa, one of the nation's best addresses.

The avoidance of extremes, the search for compromise, is, ultimately, the governing principle of the Canadian character. It is the direct opposite of Trudeau's governing principle. When the RCMP illegalities became known, Canadians supported their national police force as if instinctively aware that the one sure way to provoke a backlash and oppression is to destroy the credibility of those employed to protect society.

Trudeau, of course, believed that he too was protecting society against revolutionaries and against separatists. But he did it his way – by extremism, and by seeking a confrontation out of which would come the chance for victory in climactic Single Combat.

In the end, by choosing to invoke those provisions of the War Measures Act that suspended *habeas corpus*, Trudeau did more than smirch his own reputation as a civil libertarian. He took advantage of our collective instinct to defer to authority, for the unspoken assumption behind this instinct is that authority will itself defer to the principles of law. As with his Imperial Prime-Ministership, Trudeau cut against the grain of the country. The root difference is that Trudeau is capable of violence; Canadians, as a people, aren't.

* * *

Yet Trudeau, than whom the earth has seldom produced a more complicated man, was also performing, throughout the October Crisis, as an idealist. He did what he did because he believed with every fibre of his being that if the separatists succeeded, they would destroy not just Canada and, as he saw it, Quebec, but also an idea – the beautiful idea of people of different races and cultures living together as a "role model" to the world.

Perhaps, in the end, the most perceptive analysis of the October Crisis is that of Jean-Luc Pépin, then Minister of Industry, Trade and Commerce. Asked in an interview for a CBC television documentary why Trudeau and the federalist francophones around him took so seriously the notion that a small band of terrorists, aided by separatist "dandy radicals" might actually bring off a revolution, Pépin replied. "I cannot swear it, but I think we were all thinking about ourselves. We ourselves were a very small group, Trudeau, Pelletier, Marchand, Lalonde, Chrétien, myself, and a few people in the civil service, say, fifty, all told . . . And we were bringing off a revolution. We held the key posts [in Ottawa]. We were making the civil service, kicking and screaming all the time, bilingual. We were a well-organized group of revolutionaries, just like them, but working in a quite different way of course."

9

Sugar Ray Robinson

"Liberalism . . . an ideology as malleable as Silly Putty."

Christina McCall Newman
Maclean's, October 1974

On Monday, October 30, 1972, Trudeau and Margaret, Davey and Head, press secretary Peter Roberts, speech-writer Rolland, Porteous and his wife Wendy – all Trudeau's top aides, except for Lalonde who was running as a candidate – gathered in the twenty-fifth floor penthouse at the Skyline Hotel to watch the returns. The refrigerator was stacked with magnums of champagne. A bank of telephone operators stood by to connect Trudeau, instantly, to each of his winning candidates.

The last Gallup Poll had narrowed Trudeau's lead to just 6 percentage points. Yet as the evening began, only Mary Macdonald looked anxious, and no one was inclined to take *her* seriously: far from being "a new guy with new ideas," Macdonald, who functioned more or less as office manager, was a holdover from the Pearson era. The early results showed just how old-womanish Macdonald was being: in the Atlantic provinces, three additional Liberals were elected. Then, an hour later the polls closed in central Canada. Soon afterwards the telephone operators were told they could go home.

The impossible had happened. By midnight, CBC reported the Liberals barely ahead, 106 to 103 for the Conservatives. Half an hour later the parties were tied. Some aides shouted, "bigots," "fools" at the television screen. Mostly, they sat silent. Off in a bedroom, Trudeau and Margaret watched the returns alone. Campaign chairman Robert Andras, flying in after being re-elected in Thunder Bay came in, put his arms around Trudeau and told him: "I blame myself. For too long I was mesmerized by Pierre Trudeau. You're a pretty hard guy to get through to." Andras braced himself for an icy blast. Instead, Trudeau's eyes turned gentle. "Is that what you really feel?" he asked, and added, "You may be right."

By 1.00 a.m., CBC reported the Conservatives ahead, 109 to 107; then the count evened once more to 108 for each. Downstairs, in the Skyline ballroom, the press waited for Trudeau to concede. He might yet squeak out ahead, but he had suffered one of the worst trouncings of any Prime Minister since the Depression.*

In the penthouse, Trudeau gave no hint of his feelings, except that sometimes, eyes glued to the television screen, his hand would reach out to hold Margaret's. He joked with the Porteouses about a climbing trip they planned to take in the Yukon the following summer. "Probably we won't qualify for the free flight, but at least we'll have lots of free time." He was, an aide remembers, "in a controlled state of shock."

Meanwhile, advice poured in. Some ministers argued that no matter whether ahead or behind, he must stay; others argued that whatever the final count, he had clearly lost and must go. Pitfield called: Trudeau had to stay on, he urged, even if he were behind. To clarify his options, Trudeau sent for Jerry Yanover, an aide to the House Leader, Allan MacEachen. If he were ahead, said Yanover, Trudeau could either quit or stay on, but he would have to face Parliament as soon as possible. In these circumstances, Yanover recommended that Trudeau stay and fight. Trudeau nodded. If he were behind, Yanover went on, Trudeau's options were identical, but he himself would recommend resigning. Trudeau shook his head, though whether in disagreement or dismay, no one around him could tell. Before Trudeau went down to face the press, Head handed him a text he had written hurriedly. Trudeau glanced at it and handed it back. "This has nothing to do with reality any more." Into the cameras and microphones, Trudeau uttered one sentence, and then spun away: "Whether or not it is clear to you, no doubt the universe is unfolding as it should." Reporters, checking hastily, discovered the quote came from *Desiderata*.

The count when all the results were in was: 109 Liberals; 107 Conservatives; 31 New Democrats; 15 Créditistes; and a couple of Independents. Since Confederation, only one government –

---

*Outside of Quebec, Trudeau's share of the vote was scarcely higher than the share Pearson held on to during the debacle of 1958, when Diefenbaker achieved the greatest electoral victory in Canadian political history.

Mackenzie King's in 1925 – had tried to govern with so small a majority. And King had only been able to hang on for less than a year.

* * *

For a week afterwards, "a deep pall," in the words of an aide, settled over Trudeau. He acted unsettled: when he called on the Governor General to say he would be staying on, he wore a fringed buckskin jacket, and thereby got the public angry with him all over again. Publicly, he said his survival would "depend on the will of the House of Commons." Privately, he sunk into something close to a depression. Trudeau had lost the first fight of his life. He'd lost it, moreover, while the entire country watched.

Many around Trudeau attributed the debacle to a backlash against bilingualism and French Power. Marchand, who predictably threatened to resign, blamed the results on "bigotry"; Donald Macdonald, on national television, blamed it on "rednecks." Not since the Khaki Election of 1917 had the country been so polarized politically on language lines. Federalist francophones felt isolated and friendless. Their own people had called them "*vendus*" for coming to Ottawa; now English Canada, in return, had told them to go home.

Although racism did contribute to the result, a post-election Gallup Poll unearthed only 8 per cent of respondents who said they had been motivated when voting by bilingualism or by "too much attention to Quebec." Far more voters said they disapproved either of specific policies, such as unemployment insurance, or, overwhelmingly – "he wasn't interested in the common man," "too arrogant" – they said they disapproved of the man himself, disapproved really, of the man Trudeau had become.

Trudeau never indulges in wishful thinking. Neither then nor later, in private or in public, has he ever attributed his near-defeat in 1972 to a bilingual stab-in-the-back. In his most extended apologia, given during an interview with Patrick Watson on December 18, 1973, he said: "I'd almost say that my faith in politics, my faith in the democratic process has changed a bit. I used to think it would be sufficient to put a reasonable proposition to a person, for the person to look at it reasonably, without passion, but that's obviously not true. Nine-tenths of politics – debate in Parliament, speeches on the hustings, commentary by the media, nine-tenths of it appeals to emotion rather than to reason. I'm a bit sorry about that, but this is the world we're living in, and therefore I've had to change."

After seven years in politics, four of them in the top job, Trudeau had realized at last that he would have to become a politician. At fifty-three, he taught himself this new role; in about three months he was performing it like Guinness and Olivier combined.

* * *

Jerry Grafstein, the Toronto communications lawyer and Liberal pooh-bah, believes that the press is quite wrong to compare Trudeau to Muhammad Ali. The real comparison, Grafstein suggests, is to Sugar Ray Robinson, perhaps the most skilled boxer – as opposed to puncher – of all time. "Most good boxers have two or three combinations of punches; Robinson had fifteen," says Grafstein. "And so does Pierre."

Supreme politicians – the kind who are praised by the press and re-elected by voters – are first to last wily, devious, and manipulative. They are also blatantly partisan, concerned exclusively with the advantage of the moment, prepared to use every tool and all the money in the public purse, to win re-election. Trudeau, the rationalist supreme, did all these things: with a flick of the magician's wand, Trudeau's imperative, post-1972, changed from doing what was right, rationally, to doing what was advantageous politically. –

So Trudeau had been criticized for ignoring the Queen; in 1973, the Queen came to Canada twice, a history-making precedent, with Trudeau at her side every step of the royal progress. So he had been accused of sloughing off the ethnics; up sprang a trebled multiculturalism program that functioned as a slush fund to buy ethnic votes. And so it went. Trudeau had been accused of caring more about balanced budgets than the poor; in 1973 and 1974, federal spending soared by more than 20 per cent each year, a rate of growth never equalled before or since, even distantly. Public service bilingualism had lost votes; the implementation date was put back to 1978, and civil servants assured they all would get the chance to learn French, at public expense. The new unemployment insurance scheme had lost votes; out went Mackasey. The west had been grumbling; it got a Western Economic Opportunities Conference. Stanfield, while Turner had ridiculed him, had won middle-class votes by promising to "index" income taxes to discount the effects of inflation; Turner's first post-election budget "indexed" income taxes. Later, when the bills started coming in, Trudeau's apologists justified this splurge as having been necessary either to sustain a minority government, or as a moral imperative undertaken in the name of national unity. Trudeau has never bothered with such sentimentalities. "I'm that particular kind of person who doesn't like being kicked out," he said in an interview. He did what he did to win, because for him, winning is the only thing.

* * *

The last temptation is the greatest treason; to do the right deed, for the wrong reason, T.S. Eliot's Becket says in *Murder in the Cathedral*. Whatever his motivation, the real magicianship involved in Trudeau's metamorphosis from philosopher king to political opportunist was that he has never, in a dozen years, been more genuinely creative. In sheer productivity, the record of his 1972-74 government is equalled only by Diefenbaker's 1957-58 minority, and Pearson's creative burst in 1963-64 following his disastrous "Sixty Days of Decision."

During his minority term, Trudeau developed a new national energy policy that in all its essentials remains unchanged today: a single, subsidized, national oil price; a national petroleum company; export taxes on oil. He initiated an ambitious "total review" of social security. His device of "indexing" made Canada's tax system unique in the world. By extending the "experimental" abolition of capital punishment for an additional five years, he ensured that the noose would disappear out of simple desuetude. He created the Foreign Investment Review Agency (FIRA) to screen take-overs through the test of "significant benefit."

Between 1972 and 1974, Trudeau also made the two most inspired appointments of his career: Bora Laskin to be Chief Justice of the Supreme Court; Justice Thomas Berger of the Supreme Court of British Columbia to head a special inquiry into a proposed gas pipeline down the Mackenzie Valley.

When Canadians handed Trudeau back his majority in July 1974, they did so for a simple reason: he had demonstrated that when he wanted to, he could be the best Prime Minister around.

And yet, to complete the conundrum, Canadians felt this way

even before Trudeau had done anything. In the first week of January 1973, just six weeks after the election, Gallup found that Canadians, by a margin of 57 to 38 per cent, believed that Trudeau had already "changed his personality." Respondents specifically judged Trudeau "less arrogant . . . easier to get on with . . . cares more about people." Quite possibly Trudeau could have won an election without doing much more than to say, "I'm sorry, I'll pay more attention to you." The poll demonstrated the nature of the bond between him and Canadians that would be confirmed time and again: Canadians saw in Trudeau exactly what they wanted to see. In 1973, they wanted the old Trudeau back, with just a dash of humility.

As Sugar Ray Robinson, Trudeau had two seconds to help him make certain he would win: the Liberal Party and Allan J. MacEachen, a minister whom, like the party, he'd spent the last four years ignoring.

* * *

The enigma of the Liberal Party has always been this: is it successful because it is the way it is?; or is it the way it is because it is successful? The formula most likely is an alchemy of both elements. There is also, on reflection, a third element: the Liberals' opponents, the Conservatives and the New Democrats, each have principles over which they consistently trip.

The Liberal Party, to get its supposed first principle out of the way, is not liberal. It's middle-of-the-road Establishment. It leans now to the left, now to the right; most frequently to the left only because that is where the votes are. (Although voters cannot be bribed with their own money, they can be bribed, and are invariably, with what they think is other people's money.) Liberal ideology, as Christina McCall Newman has said, is like "Silly Putty." Only an ideological fragment remains, preserved like a splinter of the true cross, to be paraded from time to time in public, mostly to appease the media.

The Liberal Party is also the most successful party in the western world. Between 1935 and 1980, it has held power for all but seven years. It has maintained its hegemony through every conceivable circumstance – Depression, war, post-war reconstruction, the countercultural revolution of the 1960's, the "siege economy" of the 1970's. The porous rock of Canadian Liberalism has absorbed every wave of public opinion: Quebec nationalists; Canadian nationalists; environmentalists, small c conservative tax-haters, "socialist" big spenders, flower children, urban guerrillas, feminists. The part of each wave left unabsorbed has curled back, has ebbed, and then has disappeared into the glassy sea of Canadian political normalcy.

But if the Liberal Party amounts to little in terms of ideas, it amounts to a very great deal in terms of people. Shortly after the 1972 election, Trudeau dined at 24 Sussex with a group of Ontario Liberal workers and asked them, in puzzlement: "I don't understand what motivates you guys. What's in it for you anyway?" The workers looked at their shoes, and mumbled.

First, they should have said, fun: the joy of being part of a competitive team, feeling the adrenalin coursing. Second, they should have said, jobs: not jobs *per se*, but certain special kinds of jobs unattainable elsewhere, with security or with status (everything from the lasting splendour of a judgeship or an ambassadorship, to the transitory glory of being named to something like the CBC Board of Governors or the National Capital Commission). There is also, for Liberals, the glow of being an Insider; the sensual satisfaction of being known as the guy in town whom cabinet ministers – those important guys who get on television – talk to, even call once in a while to ask your opinion. And there is, a long way down the list, the ideological fragment to nurture: national unity, economic nationalism, "being for the little guy," and all the rest of it.

Liberals, uniformly, are born aged thirty-five and never grow older than forty-five. At puberty, they learn the golden rule: the sure way to do good to oneself is to be seen doing good to others, through "public service." They grow up resolutely bilingual, out of smoking and into jogging, sophisticated and successful, in bespoke tailoring. Mostly, they are lawyers, academics (entrepreneurial ones who get lots of research contracts and who turn up on television), civil servants and journalists, socially aware clergymen. Businessmen who are Liberals work on the trendy fringes, like advertising and management consulting; they leave sombre matters like banking and insurance to the Tories. Liberal men wear gold-rimmed glasses and use blow dryers. Liberal women carry briefcases, and abandoned blow dryers in 1980 for the rolled, 1930's look. Liberal women are assertive, but not aggressive;

142

Liberal men are supportive, but not scared. They don't drink rye and ginger. They know the difference between Manet and Monet, and between Pucci and Gucchi. They know, above all, the difference between being In Power and Being Out. If the Liberal Party isn't the Natural Governing Party, Liberals are Canada's Natural Rulers. The interesting aspect of this circumstance is not so much that Liberals know this as that Canadians, the most conservative electorate in the west, know this.

Ex-Newfoundland Liberal leader Ed Roberts has made perhaps the most perceptive comment about the Liberal character. Watching Liberals stream past at a policy convention, Roberts remarked to a reporter: "These people aren't winners because they belong to the Liberal Party. They are winners in their own lives, and so they have made the Liberal Party a winner."

For the "New Trudeau," as the press soon began to call him, the Liberal Party was the ideal instrument. It was docile (Liberals prefer to say "disciplined"). For four years, Trudeau had scarcely given the party the time of day, and not one member of it had peeped. It was malleable: during 1968-72, as Trudeau changed beyond recognition most of the policies he inherited from Pearson, none but Walter Gordon had peeped. The party had, also, and perhaps this is the true source of Liberal staying power, the quality of a succubus. Liberals, as Denis Smith has written, "have appropriated the basics of Canadian political beliefs ... and smothered the alternatives."

Trudeau, though, had to work to win his party spurs. If Liberals have few opinions, they have a great many loyalties. Trudeau 1968-72 had not just ignored these blood ties, he had been completely unaware of them. He had not realized, for instance, that his high-handedness toward Pearson, taking power so fast that he denied Pearson the chance to mark his fifth anniversary as Prime Minister, and far worse, not to have consulted Pearson about his foreign policy review, had deeply offended the key Liberals of English Canada: Keith Davey, Jim Coutts, John Nichol, and their blood brothers, such as Grafstein, John Roberts, Martin O'Connell, Royce Frith. Only these people, with their cross-country contacts—to Ed Roberts, for instance—could make Trudeau a member of the Liberal family.

Trudeau went directly to the heart of the matter. Within four months of the 1972 election, he offered the command post of campaign strategist to the two core Pearsonians, Davey and Coutts. First, at the suggestion of Andras and of Pitfield he tried Coutts – then a Toronto management consultant – who said no. Trudeau then turned to Davey, on whose behalf Coutts and a ginger group of Ontario lobbied,* and who had written to Trudeau in mid-campaign to warn him he was about to blow it. Davey said yes, although the formal announcement was delayed for three months while Trudeau allayed anxieties about Davey among Quebec M.P.s.

* * *

The grudge the Quebec Liberals held against Davey was that in three tries as Pearson's campaign strategist, 1962, 1963, and 1965, he had never won him a majority. Davey's nickname "the Rainmaker" had a bittersweet twist; somehow it always showered on his parade.

Of all the aides who have exercised influence on Trudeau, Davey has the least in common with him. Indeed apart from not smoking and drinking only rarely, the two have nothing in common. Davey's passions are baseball, football, hockey, Liberal Party politics, and the media (about which he chaired a special Senate Committee). On the night in March 1973 that Trudeau called to offer him the campaign strategist post, Davey was watching a hockey game on television.

Davey dresses as if auditioning for the part of Nathan Detroit in *Guys and Dolls*; black and white stripes and checks that manage to be colourful and constantly at war with each other. He is gregarious, open, impossible to dislike although one of the most manipulative party pols around, a bit tender about his "jock" image, and except for perhaps Coutts and Dalton Camp, the fastest man with one-liners in Canadian politics. With Trudeau, most of Davey's one-liners landed on the floor in a heap. His heroes are Pearson and Walter Gordon; Trudeau has never quite made Davey's personal pantheon.

In 1973, Davey was also more than a trifle sensitive about his image, if not as a loser, then as a less-than-sensational winner. He was restive through the four years of "rational government," as much removed from the action and the glow of being on the

---

*The group first got together at Pearson's funeral on New Year's Eve, 1972, and then set out to sell Davey to Trudeau.

inside as if the Conservatives had been in power. Because Davey was also sensitive about his reputation for bragging about elections certain to be won before they had even been called, he kept a card in his wallet that read, STIFLE YOURSELF.

Davey told Trudeau that in order to win, he needed to do three things: convince Liberals that he really was a Liberal; convince Canadians he really wanted to be Prime Minister; act contritely, while not suppressing the scrappy quality that the public liked.

* * *

Trudeau followed Davey's instructions to the letter. To answer the charge that he had isolated himself, he tossed out all Supergroup members who had been seen to have isolated him. Out went Pitfield, to become deputy minister of Consumer and Corporate Affairs. Out went Jim Davey, to the Transport Department. Out went Peter Roberts, to be replaced as press secretary by a well-liked journalist, Pierre O'Neil. Out – or out of sight at least – went Ivan Head, his speechwriting chores taken over by a former *Time* editor. Back from Hong Kong came Eddie Rubin, a bright, popular former aide from the leadership race. To replace Lalonde, now a minister, as chief of staff, Trudeau brought in O'Connell, a defeated M.P. popular in the party.

For the first time at 24 Sussex, the cook worked overtime. Except for Pelletier and Marchand, scarcely a minister had crossed the threshold in four years. Now, ministers, M.P.s, and anonymous parvenu workers crowded the dining room and living room, to engage Trudeau in such newly intriguing topics as the editorial policy of the *Toronto Star*, and the merits of not abandoning railway branch lines. Each time he travelled out of town, Trudeau hunkered down with yet more party workers, each of whom afterwards told everyone who would listen, that it simply was not true that Trudeau would not listen. In September 1973, at the party's annual convention in Ottawa, Trudeau was enough of a party pol to bring workers to their feet cheering as he told them, "We don't want an election, but believe me we are not afraid . . . They'll have the fight of their lives."

All of this was fine. But, in order to have the chance to fight, Trudeau had to stay alive in Parliament. This time MacEachen was his instructor; as with Davey, Trudeau followed MacEachen's script to the last apostrophe.

Until the winter of 1979-80, when he was unmasked as the mastermind of the plot that defeated the Clark government so unexpectedly, and so returned Trudeau to power after the formality of an election he could not lose, hardly anyone in the country had heard of MacEachen. Hardly anyone, that is to say, except the entire population of Cape Breton, and those M.P.s who paid attention in Parliament, and those Commons' officials who thrived on the differences between Beauchesne and Bourinot, and all Celtic cultists.

MacEachen, by 1972, had already been on Parliament Hill, as M.P. or backroom adviser for nineteen years. Somehow, he seemed to have dissipated his promise. He had impressive credentials, as an economist who had studied at the Massachusetts Institute of Technology. He looked and sounded impressive; a great waving mane of jet black hair and a command of Parliamentary English that reminded some listeners of immortals like Charles James Fox. He was also, everyone said, very, very shrewd, although he pretended not to be by adopting a cosy, old-bear manner, which was part of his shrewdness.

Certainly, MacEachen had begun well. First elected in 1953, at thirty-three, he then moved to Pearson's office as a key adviser after a 1958 defeat. Re-elected in 1962, he became one of Pearson's youngest ministers in 1963; later, at Health and Welfare, he enacted Medicare. Then, things started to go wrong. In 1968, he ran for the leadership to make a point about left-liberalism, made the mistake of taking his chances seriously, lost badly, and finished $100,000 in debt. Thereafter, not to put too fine a point on it, MacEachen hid. An intensely private bachelor, at times melancholic, he acquired a reputation for laziness and unproductive brooding. Trudeau shuffled him sideways, to Manpower, and then downwards to the tedious job of House Leader.

MacEachen, though one of the most progressive members of cabinet, quite simply wasn't a "new guy with new ideas." He refused to take "rational government" seriously. He was skeptical about the way bilingualism was being applied. (Changing signs from English and Gaelic to English and French on the golf course in Cape Breton's National Park did not help.) Even worse, he was given to uttering heresies, as in, "There has existed a one-sided and superficial view of Mr. Trudeau's role which I have never shared. I have never believed that if he were not Prime Minister, the country would come apart." Instead of to Trudeau, MacEachen's political loyalties were to Pearson, to the Liberal Party, above all, to his native Cape Breton.

As the country discovered when MacEachen became a late-blooming media "star" in 1980, the only way to understand him is to understand Cape Breton, that tribal, private, tightly knit kingdom peopled by cynical romantics and canny innocents, peopled that is to say by Catholic Highland Scots, given to beholding the Hebrides in dreams. MacEachen is happiest in the past, which to him is part of the present. He speaks Gaelic fluently and visits Scotland regularly to revivify his roots. To his Cape Breton tribe, he is shepherd and icon combined, but also "Allan J.," the guy down the road with the real Scotch and stack of records of real, Scottish songs. He was about to quit in 1976, when Trudeau took away from him the plum of External Affairs and handed back the prune of House Leadership, but did not, because friends convinced him he would be letting down Cape Breton.

In the winter of 1972-73, MacEachen brought to his assignment a crucial asset. He'd served through four minority Parliaments: two under Diefenbaker; two under Pearson. In February 1968, when Pearson's government had blundered into an accidental defeat on a money bill, MacEachen had saved the day with a skilfully worded motion that this had not really been a vote of confidence. MacEachen knew that although on paper it always looks easy to bring down a minority government, this is extremely difficult to do in fact. Of the four minority governments since World War Two, only one – John Diefenbaker's in 1963 – had been defeated. The reason is simple: it is seldom, *simultaneously*, in the interest of all the opposition parties to force an election.

Yet MacEachen's and Trudeau's parliamentary problems were uniquely acute. The numerical difference between the Liberals and Conservatives was so slight – just two M.P.s – that by constitutional practice, early defeat in the Commons would not lead on to an election, but, horror of horrors, to the accession to power of Stanfield and the Conservatives. MacEachen thus had no stick with which to beat the smaller opposition parties into line; so he offered them carrots.

147

* * *

About his survival strategy, MacEachen was, if anything, more fiercely secretive than even about his private life. Trusting no messenger he personally delivered numbered copies of his strategy paper to key ministers, then retrieved each copy in person a few days later. His plan comprised two principles: to duck rather than fight; to rule by dividing. If the government could survive until the Easter recess, MacEachen calculated, then it could survive until fall. By then, Trudeau ought to have won the constitutional right to call an election if defeated. Thereafter, the government could change its strategy and arrange its own defeat at the most propitious moment.

MacEachen's actual tactics were very simple and very smart. All controversial legislation would be postponed until after Easter. Not all non-confidence votes would be treated as non-confidence votes. (To justify this, MacEachen dug up precedents back to John A. Macdonald.) In order to set the three opposition parties at each other's throats, as many "Opposition Days" as possible would be scheduled, in the certain knowledge that each and every time, the opposition parties would vote against one another's motions. Finally, MacEachen insisted, the Trudeau government would have to be nice as pie to the NDP.

* * *

The NDP had emerged from the election with no increase in the popular vote (18 per cent), but with 31 M.P.s, its highest number ever. The party held the balance of power: it could tilt away from Trudeau and put Stanfield into office, or it could tilt toward Trudeau and sustain him, for the short or long term. After a special caucus in mid-December, party leader David Lewis announced a "C.O.D. policy": if Trudeau increased old age pensions, took immediate steps to create jobs and to halt rises in food prices, the NDP might, temporarily, support him.

For all his apparent power, Lewis was vulnerable. His own aides and most of the younger NDP M.P.s were "hawks" who deeply mistrusted Trudeau; his "doves," veterans like Tommy Douglas and Stanley Knowles, feared a repetition of the electoral disaster that had overtaken them in 1958, when Diefenbaker transformed his minority into the largest majority ever. Thus, as Vernon Harder of Queen's University points out in his definitive master's thesis study "*House of Minorities*," of the 1973-74 tussle, "the NDP lacked the boldness necessary to bring about a formal coalition, either legislative or ministerial, which some party members advised."[*]

When, soon after the election, private talks between Lewis and MacEachen led to press speculation about a possible coalition, NDP caucus "hawks" leaked word of this conversation to the press, forcing Lewis to declare publicly that he would "refuse to have alliance with or make any deal with" either the Liberals or Conservatives. In fact, through 1973, Lewis met privately with MacEachen a half-dozen times, without either his caucus or the Liberal cabinet knowing, to negotiate such issues as the size of the pension increase to a system for monitoring, in terms of job creation, the $500 million in corporate tax cuts granted by Turner in his 1972 budget.

Even in hindsight, it is difficult to see how Lewis could have improved his strategy, as opposed to his tactics (of which the most egregious was the moment he chose to defeat Trudeau). For eighteen months, he harassed the Trudeau government into being more progressive than it has ever been, before or since. But Lewis paid a political price: Trudeau became steadily more attractive to more and more of the people who had voted NDP.

* * *

Parliament met on January 4. Trudeau, on MacEachen's instructions, immediately distinguished between strictly technical votes of non-confidence and votes which "go to the very roots of our policy." Just as quickly, he replied to Lewis's "C.O.D." offer: the Throne Speech promised action on social security, job creation, and food prices. Lewis declared he would support Trudeau, inspiring Paul Hellyer, a newly hatched Conservative, to attack the "unholy alliance." Yet the alliance was both effective and productive. In his February 19 budget, Turner unlocked the doors of the treasury, and threw away the keys: out flowed higher pensions and family allowances, the removal of the sales tax on children's clothing and shoes, personal income tax cuts, plus "indexing." "There is enough in this budget to make it our duty to support this budget," Lewis declared. Soon after, came a Parliamentary inquiry

---

[*]Harder cites Walter Pitman as an example.

into food prices, out of which came the Food Prices Review Board, and legislation on election expenses and on foreign take-overs.

By the Easter recess, pundits were praising Parliament as one of the most productive ever. Soon after Parliament reassembled, they switched to criticizing the Conservatives. In June, Trudeau's resolution to "reaffirm" the principles of bilingualism provoked sixteen Conservatives (Diefenbaker and Jack Horner among them) to vote against it, and another thirteen to abstain. Already out-manoeuvred, the Tories had been routed. By early summer, Trudeau and MacEachen had reached their point of no return: they had won the right to call an election instead of handing power over to Stanfield. All they needed to do now was to pick their moment to get themselves defeated.

*   *   *

One piece of legislation, that winter, stood out from all the others: the nearly $2 billion extra that Lalonde, as Minister of Health and Welfare, had handed out to pensioners and parents. This stood out for a simple reason: Trudeau's much-heralded Just Society had never, in his own mind, encompassed much in the way of social spending initiatives. "All social security measures," he had written long before he became Prime Minister, "must remain theoretical if the economic structure is incapable of bearing the cost." Now, push come to shove from the NDP, he changed his mind, and allowed Lalonde to bring off the only comprehensive change in social policy in his decade in office.*

Lalonde overnight became the new political star. *Time* christened him "the Happy Minister." Deftly, he dismantled the roadblock that had prevented agreement at the 1971 Constitutional Conference in Victoria, by allowing provinces to vary their family

*Mackasey's 1971 reform of unemployment insurance is an anomaly, and indeed Mackasey only got his way because the Finance Department could not bring itself to admit that the 4 per cent unemployment floor it had defined, above which Ottawa would pay all costs, was hopelessly inaccurate. Also in 1971, John Munro, then Health and Welfare Minister, had wrested a pittance of $250 million from Treasury Board, which he offered to Parliament in the guise of an imaginative Family Income Support Programme (FISP), which would have cut off family allowances to the wealthy and increased them to the poor. For no evident reason, Hellyer blocked the scheme on a technicality, but Munro confessed later that FISP probably would have died anyway; angry telephone calls from middle-class housewives were flooding in to Liberal members.

allowance payments. In the west, his unaloof directness charmed audiences. Commentators speculated he might become the next Prime Minister. Yet, Lalonde accomplished nothing else beyond 1973. As Quebec leader, in succession to Marchand, he was detested by his M.P.s. As Minister of Federal-Provincial Relations, he was detested by the provinces.

Lalonde's own personality – superficially open but inflexible at core, unpretentious but arrogant – was part of the reason. So was his ready-aye-ready willingness to do the dirty "bad cop" jobs Trudeau wanted done. But when it came to Lalonde's ultimate failure to realize his dream of a new social security system, the real problem was a stroke of irony: Lalonde became the last victim of his and Trudeau's obsession with rationalism.

In April 1973, Lalonde's Orange Paper on Social Security set out the nature of the problem. The idea, explained Lalonde was "to develop a comprehensive, logical and hopefully imaginative approach" to encompass "the whole sweep of social security." Then, for two years, with eager support from Al Johnson, moved over from Treasury Board to be his deputy minister, and scores of planners constructing models, Lalonde dragged provincial governments (only the Quebecers had the foggiest notion what he was talking about) through the incomprehensible intricacies of "income maintenance" and "income supplementation" schemes, plus a two-tiered system of guaranteed annual incomes. By early 1975, when Lalonde had at last come up with what he reckoned was the perfect scheme, the cabinet realized it could no longer afford it. A $2 billion package was slashed to $1.1 billion, then down to $350 million. By the time Lalonde was ready to offer that to the provinces, in mid-1976, they had lost interest. When social policy eventually was significantly restructured in late 1978, by the introduction of a Refundable Child Tax Credit, it was done in the old irrational way, to buy votes on the eve of an election, and by another minister, Monique Bégin.

* * *

As the fall of 1973 approached, Trudeau seemed to be politically untouchable. In August, Lewis tried and failed to convince his caucus to defeat the government in the coming fall session; as a substitute, he issued a new set of "C.O.D." demands, from 6 per cent mortgages to food subsidies. Stanfield, trying to recover from

151

his embarrassment over bilingualism, announced that his solution to inflation (then 8 per cent) would be wage and price controls. In reply, Trudeau told cheering Liberals at their September convention, he would give the Tories "the fight of their lives." Then, Trudeau, and the entire western world, turned a corner in history.

* * *

Early in the morning of October 6, 1973, Egyptian commandos stormed across the Suez Canal. When the Yom Kippur War ended eighteen days later, the Arab armies, though as usual bested, were for the first time, unbroken. On October 16, the Organization of Arab Petroleum Exporting Countries announced a 25 per cent cut in production. From $3 a barrel, the world price for oil jumped to $6; by the year's end, it had reached $10. One by one, the industrial democracies hunkered down into the "siege economies" from which most have yet to emerge.*

Most Canadians felt no immediate worry. In 1969, Energy Minister Joe Greene had declared we had "many hundreds of years" of oil supplies; to get rid of the "surplus," he proposed a continental oil deal. In 1970, within the cabinet, only Kierans, always a maverick, had opposed a huge new gas export sale. In June 1973, Donald Macdonald, by then Energy Minister, had forecast, in his *Energy Policy for Canada*, surpluses for "eighty years," and had calculated that the price might reach $5 a barrel by the year 2000. The single item of interest in his report had been a curiously brief reference to "a national petroleum corporation [that] could have as one of its key objectives the increase of Canadian knowledge" about the energy industry.

This notion had first seen the light of day in a conversation three years earlier between Trudeau and his new deputy minister of energy, Jack Austin, a hustling, ambitious former mining lawyer. Trudeau, as Austin recalls, had no specific idea of what he was looking for, only a general belief that energy, somehow, could be used as a "lever" to change the socio-economic structure of a country. With Trudeau's blessing, Austin recruited talent to his moribund department: Ian Stewart and Joel Bell, both bright civil

*Canada's ability to criticize the oil cartel was constrained, somewhat, by the fact that we, together with Britain, France, South Africa, and Australia, were operating an identical cartel to fix the international price of uranium.

servants, and Bill Hopper, an oil industry consultant, then in the U.S.*

This quartet undertook the first systematic – yes, rational – study of Canada's energy industry, which no one then knew anything about, nor cared about, since energy was cheap and the multinationals knew best. One conclusion of the group, which Macdonald quickly bought, was that Canada needed its own publicly owned oil giant, to act as a pace setter in frontier exploration and as a "window-on-the-industry," through which government could learn what was going on. A second conclusion was that if world prices rose, multi-nationals would be wallowing in windfall profits. Neither conclusion, though, was made public in *Energy Policy for Canada*; both were excised out by cabinet right-wingers – Drury, Sharp, Andras – and, more important than any mere minister, Simon Reisman, the deputy minister of finance. Only Trudeau's intervention, made because, as Austin recalls, "he enjoyed a public debate about issues," kept the reference to the national company in the final published version of the report.

By late October the Arabs had acted. So had Lewis. His latest "C.O.D." became a national oil company (he had in mind nationalizing Imperial or Gulf) and an oil price freeze. Within cabinet, the right-wingers said no. "I thought we'd hired a businessman," Drury told Austin. "It turns out that we hired a socialist." Almost alone, but with the backing of Lalonde, Macdonald fought on.

Enter MacEachen. In mid-November, NDP House Leader Stanley Knowles told MacEachen, "we can't hold David back much longer unless you come through." Already, MacEachen was on Macdonald's side ideologically; now he added the power of political persuasion.

Enter Trudeau. On November 22, with the cabinet still split, he had gone on television, at the urging of his advisers, to make what Stanfield called, "a masterful non-statement." Canada had enough oil to last the winter; an energy policy would soon be announced. Lewis' reply was to announce he would vote against the government in a non-confidence vote on December 10. Aware at last that the government had no policy, the public for the first time became

---

*Stewart, Bell, and Hopper are in 1980, respectively, deputy minister of finance, and vice-president, and chairman of Petro-Canada.

alarmed. To make matters worse, industry spokesmen declared that the public had misunderstood them all along: those estimates of supplies had been based on "potential" reserves rather than "recoverable reserves" already discovered in commercial quantities. To bring on additional supplies, industry spokesmen said, they had to have higher prices.

Trudeau, in everyone's memory of these events, was the calm eye in a hurricane. He appeared to be enjoying himself; resolving a problem, both abstract and practical, in all its multiple economic, financial, constitutional (the first shots in the war with Alberta were sounding), and political dimensions. In the space of eight days, a key group of cabinet ministers met six times. Through most of them, Trudeau stayed in the middle. Then at last, he tilted.

On December 6, Trudeau returned to the television screens of the nation to announce "a new national oil policy." He clicked off its components: an extension of the oil price freeze for three more months; extension of the western oil pipeline to Montreal; a single national oil price, with the five eastern provinces which depended on high-priced oil imports to be subsidized by a special tax on oil exported to the U.S.; a program to develop Alberta's tar sands; lastly, "a national petroleum corporation." All together these would achieve, said Trudeau, "before the end of this decade, Canadian self-sufficiency in oil."

"A victory beyond my expectations," remarked Lewis. Asked about this, Trudeau quipped: "We've gone beyond the Communist Manifesto. Next question." On December 10, he won the vote in the Commons.

In its essentials, that December 1973 policy has survived for nearly a decade. The principal change is that Trudeau's target of self-sufficiency by 1980 was first dropped, then revived by his successor Clark as "self-sufficiency by 1990," and then dropped again by Trudeau.* Also, then, as now, Trudeau said almost nothing about conservation.

* * *

Robert Stanfield has always attributed his defeat in 1974 to Tru-

---

*In a mid-campaign interview with CTV, in February 1980, Trudeau said, "Hopefully, we'll be arriving at some form of self-sufficiency before the end of the century."

deau's handling of the 1973 oil crisis—we got through the winter without any shortages, and with the world's lowest prices—rather than to campaign problems with his own policy of wage and price controls. The evidence supports Stanfield; during the campaign, he in fact gained ground. Stanfield's real problem was that, long before the election, Canadians had already decided that they needed their Single Combat champion to lead the way out of the threatening, freezing, dark.

All through that winter, the sun blazed down on Trudeau's parade. In December, a Gallup Poll put the Liberals ahead, 43 per cent to 33 per cent. In Quebec, Bourassa's Liberals swept to victory, winning 102 of the 110 seats. And on Christmas Day, the magic unbelievably worked yet again: Margaret gave him a second son, Alexandre Emmanuel, Emmanuel meaning *light*.

* * *

When Parliament reassembled on February 27, 1974, its mood was ambiguous. Publicly Trudeau said, "I want to stick around, at least until the end of my mandate." He said the same thing in private, underlining that he meant it. Still, he kept on going out of his way to taunt the NDP, as "seagulls, squawking and squealing above the ship of state, and pretending to steer it."

Day by day, reporters maintained a "death watch" on Parliament. Plainly, its days were numbered. Lewis had turned snappish, angry at press stories that the NDP were "in bed" with the Liberals and that he was "PET's pet." Lewis had come to realize he had gotten all he could out of the government—the new Throne Speech promised few new initiatives—and in exchange was paying the political price of having made Trudeau look good.

As the oil scare receded (at a meeting on March 27 Trudeau wrangled a $6.50 a barrel price out of the premiers) the inflation scare replaced it. In 1973, the rate had been 9.1 per cent—a twenty-two year record. By April 1974, it had climbed to a scary, "double-digit" peak. Across the country, audiences now were cheering Stanfield when he said that only controls could break the "inflation psychosis."

While Stanfield was out criss-crossing the nation, Liberal pollster Martin Goldfarb was feeling the public's pulse. It was beating erratically, Goldfarb found. People said they liked wage and price controls; what they actually meant, however, was that they liked

155

price controls, but wage controls only on the wages of the guy next door.

Suddenly, on April 29, Consumer and Corporate Affairs Minister Herb Gray announced a most unusual piece of legislation. He called it an Anti-Profiteering Bill. It would halt "gouging" of consumers by giving the government power to order a rollback of price increases that produced "above customary profits." Corporate offenders could be sentenced to up to two years in jail. Gray was the ideal instrument to produce such legislation: he was a stolid, solid, decent, almost morbidly serious minister; he was also, as a colleague recalls, "the only one of us who took it seriously." (The legislation was dropped out of sight the instant the election was over; and Gray was dropped from the cabinet.)

At the time, the legislation looked good. After three days of bitter debate, the NDP caucus decided it was too good to be true. Lewis denounced it as a "sham" and announced he would vote against it. The government's defeat was certain. All that was left to be decided was the occasion and the date.

Trudeau selected both. Right to the last minute, insiders remember, he did not entirely believe he would be defeated. But if it happened, he would not be worried. He had, as Davey put it, "the numbers." He had the occasion: Turner's budget, which cut taxes, opening huge loopholes for the middle class, and increased spending by 26 per cent. As for the timing, this was superb. Turner would bring down his budget on May 6, so that if defeated, the election could be called for July 8, just a few days before the next monthly Statistics Canada report on inflation was due, and as far as possible away from the agency's previous report. On May 8, on an NDP non-confidence vote, Turner became the first Finance Minister in Canada to see his budget defeated. The vote was 137 to 123. Watching from the gallery, Keith Davey heaved a sigh of relief.

* * *

Later, for all that it was so successful, Trudeau's aides preferred not to talk about the 1974 election. For Trudeau, it was both the best of all his elections and his worst.

He campaigned with a joyful panache unmatched before or since. As curtain-raiser, he sang along with a choir of pensioners, The Gadabouts from Kingston, collected in the House of Commons lobby. As finale, he and Margaret ate hot dogs and pizzas

156

with Toronto's ethnic communities at a vast open-air picnic on Toronto Island. In between, he travelled by train from Sydney, Nova Scotia, to Montreal, evoking memories of Diefenbaker's epic campaigns of the 1950's. He stepped into a hot-air balloon. He travelled with reporters in a plane without compartments, kidded around with them, joined them at lunch in cafeteria line-ups.

It was the morning of the magician, all over again. "In 1972, my campaign never really got off the ground. But this year, I've found the secret. I have a train, and I have Margaret," he said, and everyone knew it was true. He could do nothing wrong: while Stanfield fumbled his famous football, Trudeau scrambled over a six-foot wrought-iron fence and looked graceful doing it. Reporters grumbled that Trudeau's policy announcements all were issued just before their deadlines, so that they had no time to make more than headlines out of them; no matter, the headlines appeared and the rest of the time reporters had all the colour and anecdote they needed to feed the Goat.

Above all, there was Margaret. She'd made up her own mind to campaign. Davey and Coutts were appalled and urged Trudeau to stop her; he tried and luckily for him he failed. "He's a beautiful guy," she said, gauche and nervous, to a crowd of 2,500 in West Vancouver. "He taught me a lot about loving." The crowd tittered at the unintended *double-entendre*. Davey and Coutts winced, and despatched an aide, Joyce Fairbairn, to hold Margaret's hand and, if possible, to close her mouth. Reporters giggled, then discovered the next day that the whole country had fallen in love with her. Overnight, Margaret had become a magician in her own right. As always with true magicians, everyone saw in Margaret exactly what they wanted to see: flower child, emerging liberated woman, Harlequin heroine, devoted nursing mother who brought five-month old Sasha along; a princess come down from her tower to fight next to her cavalier—fragile and nervous—but oh so incredibly beautiful and young and innocent. She travelled on her own from British Columbia to Prince Edward Island, Fairbairn nervously in tow.

All the way through, from presenting Trudeau to the public as the political equivalent of a rock superstar, to media manipulation, Trudeau's 1974 campaign was an exercise in political technique not seen since John Kennedy's march to the Presidency in 1960. His strategy, in two ways, came close to political genius. First, he recognized that the prime catalyst of contemporary voting behaviour is negativism: voters will vote *against* somebody (Stanfield) and *against* something (wage and price controls) with incomparably greater zest and conviction than they will vote *for* somebody or something.* Second, he recognized – "The issue is leadership" – the primacy of charisma over content. In the late 1950's, some commentators, among them Arthur Schlesinger Jr., had argued that charisma had become obsolete in advanced democracies; then Schlesinger met JFK. Irvine Schiffer, the Toronto psychologist, has described the phenomenon best: "All leaders, including the charismatic, are to a meaningful degree creations of the people." Schiffer adds: "There is no evidence that the wheels of democracy are busily churning for the enlightenment of a society that might select leaders who transcend the glamour of the charismatic." Only in the elections of 1972 and 1979, when he tried to substitute content for the "hypnoid" (Schiffer's word) appeal of charisma, has Trudeau failed to be recreated by the public.

The dark side of the 1974 campaign – the demon inside the magician – is that Trudeau, who had it won anyway, got so carried away by his compulsive competitiveness that he fashioned, out of his triumph, his own subsequent destruction.

The single issue of the campaign was wage and price controls. Stanfield was advocating controls ploddingly, doggedly, awkwardly, and yet somehow beginning to win respect for his sheer tenaciousness. (In the leadership polls he came to outrank Trudeau on the "integrity" component.) Stanfield explained, qualified, adjusted, but he never once changed the core of his policy.

Trudeau went after controls, like a terrier after a rat. "We are going on the attack," he told Liberals early in the campaign. "I challenge any candidate to fight harder than I am going to fight." For eight weeks he kept it up. Each of his verbal onslaughts was brilliant; "Zap, you're frozen." "Stanfield's freeze has turned to slush." "The only things controls will control will be your wages.". "Controls will not work; one-third of what we consume we import, and who can control imports?" "A proven disaster look-

---

*In fact, the much-discussed "swing" voters who are said to decide each election – to the extent that each election has not been decided months in advance – are less that, than uninterested voters. Uninterested voters, who by definition have little faith in the political process, can be convinced much more easily to vote *against* something, than to vote for anything.

ing for a new place to happen." Since Trudeau then had a contingency plan for controls which he knew perfectly well he might have to apply, each of these flights of rhetoric was grossly irresponsible – as close to lying as a politician can come.*

All elections in the end amount to an exchange of trust, to a pact between the leader and the led. Few voters comprehend the intricacies of issues; they make up their mind on a gut feeling about which candidate knows most about the issues, which candidate is best able to handle those issues, and which candidate can be trusted the most.

In politics, it is the lie rather than the scandal or the blunder or the misapplied policy that defeats a politician. Once they realized that he in effect had lied to them, Canadians withdrew their trust and defeated Trudeau at the first available opportunity. Except that Trudeau, with the luck of the true magician, later found a way to get Canadians to trust him again, by convincing them that his opponent in 1980 – "broken promises" – was even less trustworthy than he.

* * *

For the present, on July 8, 1974, Canadians gave Trudeau back their trust. He won a majority, the first triple victory by any Prime Minister since King. At 43 per cent, his share of the vote was only fractionally less than his 1968 mark of 45 per cent. He won everywhere, except in the west ("Let Eastern Bastards Freeze in the Dark" had been Alberta's slogan through the 1973-74 price war), although even there, he won half a dozen extra seats.

Shortly before midnight, Trudeau arrived at the ballroom of the Chateau Laurier, where Liberals and press were assembled. With him was Keith Davey, beside himself with delight that he had done it at last, adding only the caveat, "I wish I'd been able to do this for Mr. Pearson." In the stifling heat, Trudeau bounded up to the microphones, to wave after wave of cheers. He praised Stanfield for his "courage." Then he beckoned into the spotlight the two people who had done more than anyone else to help him win so hugely. One was Margaret. The other was John Turner.

*Trudeau's set speeches on controls did in fact contain qualifiers of the "not-at-this-time" variety. Since no politician ever delivers a formal speech without building into it disclaimers which allow him later to deny that he had said anything, this bureaucratic prose, which even the audiences who heard it ignored, can be ignored as having been in a political sense, meaningless.

159

10

Le Roi Soleil

"Just when you think you have it all, it starts to fade away."

National Film Board
Labyrinth, 1967

His victory on July 8, 1974, placed Trudeau in the pantheon of Canadian political giants: Macdonald, Laurier, King. He was certain now to serve in office longer than any Prime Minister since World War Two. Trudeau now would wield more personal political power than any predecessor, except perhaps–comparisons this far back are iffy–John A. Macdonald in his later years. At home or abroad, he could do pretty well what he wanted.

Abroad, Trudeau soon became the senior statesman of the west. It was as much because of his personal reputation as because of Canada's economic importance that the annual summit meetings of the industrial democracies were enlarged from an original five members to seven. (France let us join the club on the condition that Italy joined too.)

At home, Trudeau commanded the same prestige and, more to the immediate point, unconstrained power. The opposition parties had not just been defeated in the election, they had been beheaded. Lewis, who suffered personal defeat, resigned immediately. Stanfield, a three-time loser, announced his own resignation within two months. Soon, within the cabinet, only one minister (MacEachen) would remain who outranked Trudeau in years of experience, and only one (Dan MacDonald, of Veterans Affairs) who outranked him in age. Newcomers around the oval ministerial table all were acutely aware that they owed their place there, and even their political existence, to Trudeau. The civil service mandarins who once had intimidated Trudeau were his creatures now: he had appointed all the deputy ministers and to watch over them he appointed to the top post of Clerk of the Privy Council late in 1974, his personal friend and political counsellor,

Michael Pitfield. (Gordon Robertson, who moved over to become Secretary for Federal-Provincial Relations, retained responsibility for recommending senior appointments but Pitfield, as he told a friend, acquired the "power of veto.") Of the eleven First Ministers, a term just beginning to come into general use, Trudeau was now the senior in service, except for Alex Campbell of Prince Edward Island. In Quebec, the province he cared about most, Bourassa, whom he dominated, governed with a huge majority and with the security of nearly three years of his mandate to run.

Only the Press Gallery was left to function in opposition to Trudeau. At his first post-election caucus, Trudeau warned his M.P.s that the press would arrogate to itself the role of semi-official opposition. Even so, he had humbled the press, and had demonstrated its impuissance. During the election Trudeau had exploited – as the FLQ had years before – the "competitive contradictions" of the media; reporters had had no choice but to publicize the policy announcements he had thrust at them; they grumbled about his refusal to hold press conferences, but could make nothing out of the issue* since by definition, no news is not news. Anyway, the public could not have cared less.

I am monarch of all I survey, my right there is none to dispute. From this mid-1974 pinnacle, Trudeau, shoulders back, head high, strode on, in a straight line directly into quicksand. Two years later, in September 1976, he placed lower in the Gallup Poll – 29 per cent – than any Prime Minister in Gallup's thirty-five year history. He directed his cabinet ministers to let him know if and when they wanted him to go, instead of having them plot to overthrow him behind his back, in the manner of Diefenbaker.

* * *

On October 2, 1975, Margaret bore him a third son, Michel Charles-Emile. Between July 1974, and the end of 1976, almost two-thirds of a Prime Minister's normal term, this was the single happy entry on Trudeau's record. The list of unhappy entries for the period runs as follows:
– He had to change his policy on wage and price controls,

---

*Trudeau did in fact stage a couple of deliberately hurried and cramped campaign press conferences. In mid-June 1974, when he'd wanted to make a statement about the latest increase in the inflation rate, just reported by Statistics Canada, Coutts on Davey's instructions, convinced him not to.

thereby contradicting everything he had said during the 1974 campaign. He then implemented controls ineptly, because he could not bring himself to begin with a price freeze, as Stanfield had proposed and as he had said could not work.

– He lost Turner, far and away the most popular of all his ministers. Just by being in the cabinet, Turner had served to reassure the business community and most of English Canada that at least one man in Ottawa knew what on earth he was doing. By the end of 1976, Trudeau had lost five ministers – Turner, André Ouellet, Mackasey, James Richardson, Marchand – more than any Prime Minister since Confederation.* Two other ministers, Drury and John Munro, offered their resignations after being implicated in scandals.

– His government was beset by the worst scandals since the ones which had almost scuppered Pearson's administration in 1964-65: the Sky Shops affair; the Judges affair; Harbourgate. One minister, Ouellet, was convicted on a charge of contempt-of-court; another, Marchand, for leaving the scene of an accident. Only luck – the press between 1974 and 1976 ignored evidence already abundantly available – prevented Trudeau being buffeted still further by the RCMP scandals that came to light later, in 1977-78.

– The economy came close to collapse. In the halcyon period 1973-74 – no oil shortages, no recession – commentators had been speculating that perhaps, as Laurier had promised, the twentieth century really would belong to Canada.** But in 1974 and 1975, Canada's strike record was the second worst in the western world, after Italy. In 1974, our international trade account moved into the red for the first time since 1961. Double-digit inflation became the norm. At the same time, the unemployment rate rose to about 7 per cent, so the "discomfort index" for 1975-76 (the sum of inflation and unemployment rates) actually was higher than during the Depression, when although unemployment had been massive, prices had declined.

– His bilingualism policy collapsed. Keith Spicer, the Official

*Mackasey, in September 1975, set his own post-Confederation record by resigning twice in the same day without intending to on either occasion, but only to get Trudeau to pay more attention to him.

**Laurier had actually said, "I *think*, the twentieth entury shall be filled by Canada."

Languages Commissioner declared in his 1976 report that Trudeau's policy of institutional bilingualism had "failed," because so few of the anglophone civil servants who had learned French, so painfully and so expensively, used it when back on the job. Spicer recommended, as Trudeau's critics had been recommending for years, that the money be spent instead in the schools to educate a bilingual next-generation. Meanwhile, inside Quebec, Bourassa appeared to turn his back on bilingualism by Bill 22, which made the province officially unilingual. In the summer of 1976, when air controllers and pilots went on strike to oppose an experimental program of bilingual air-traffic control, almost all of English Canada cheered with a single voice.

And so it went. The Montreal Olympics racked up a deficit of $995 million, which all English Canadians knew they would have to help pay for. Mirabel Airport, opened in 1975, became an instant white elephant that English Canadians also knew they'd have to pay for. By now, in any event, everyone had realized just how much they were having to pay for the government's extravagance. The final spending totals for 1975-76 turned out to be $32 billion, instead of the $22 billion Turner had forecast a year earlier. And Trudeau, at the same time as he was imposing wage and price controls, was implementing a 33 per cent increase in salary for M.P.s, and for himself. Late in 1975, in an attempt to convince the public he was serious about restraint, he slashed $1.5 billion from spending estimates. No one took this seriously. A year later, the skepticism was justified: "Parliament – and indeed the government – has lost or is close to losing effective control of the public purse" declared the Auditor General, James Macdonnell.

There was more. As the country gaped and Trudeau glowered, his marriage fell apart. Late in 1974, Margaret entered the Royal Victoria Hospital in Montreal for "observation." She held a press conference to admit she had suffered a nervous breakdown. From then on the marital crisis built: confessional appearances on national television to declare "I'm a pretty private person"; a botched attempt to launch a career as a "photo-journalist"; and, early in 1977, in a trip to Toronto to hear the Rolling Stones and an "ultimate freedom trip" to New York out of which came her notorious "garterbelt" interview in *People* magazine. In May, 1977, their marriage reached its inevitable end.

On November 15, 1976, had come the worst news of all. In

Quebec, the Parti Québécois swept to victory. Far from being "dead," as Trudeau had proclaimed six months earlier, separatism was alive and in power.

Trudeau by now was Murphy's Law incarnate. He had piled the quicksand right up to his neck.

Less than a year later, Trudeau was back up on top of the pinnacle. By the summer of 1977, his rating in the Gallup Poll had soared to 51 per cent; had he called a snap election, as his advisers urged, he probably would have won the largest majority of his career. This coup of Trudeau's was the most magical of his career. Like a true sorcerer, he got his opponents to serve as his apprentices: between them Lévesque and Margaret spun a double halo round his head. Alakazam, Trudeau emerged as (a) National Saviour, (b) Single Parent, non pareil. But these are stories for later chapters.

* * *

While we were watching it happen, the story of Trudeau's incredible fall from grace 1974-76, seemed as incomprehensible as Egyptian hieroglyphics: a giant, brought hapless to his knees, for reasons no one quite could put a finger on. In hindsight, one event is illustrative. This was a CBC television interview between Trudeau and Barbara Frum, on October 13, 1976, marking the first anniversary of controls. The part of the interview that matters went like this:

Frum: "It's so hard to say this, Mr. Trudeau. I don't know if anyone says this quite to your face. A lot of Canadians don't think you understand them because you are privileged yourself, you are secure yourself. That's a very isolating thing for a hard time."

Trudeau: "Well . . . I'm . . . you know, a Prime Minister is secure. He's got policemen around him and he's got a house to live in and he's got a car. In that sense, all Prime Ministers have been no less secure than me. But what you call isolated, do you know any Prime Minister who has travelled more than I in the country, and met more groups more often?"

The most revealing part of the exchange took place off camera. The interview over, Trudeau turned to Frum in puzzlement. Why on earth had she asked the question? Wasn't she wealthy herself? Did she really believe this isolated her? When Frum answered yes, she thought it did, and on the job was constantly aware of it,

Trudeau's unnerving blue eyes stared at her in blank incomprehension.

* * *

Scott Fitzgerald was right. The very rich *are* different from you and me. At fifty-seven, after a decade in politics, after more than half a decade as Prime Minister, coping with everything from the October Crisis to a minority Parliament to three election campaigns, Trudeau remained about as knowledgeable of the human condition as a Trappist monk.

Or as a spoiled child. Trudeau quite simply had not the least idea that brilliance, power, riches, and fame set him entirely apart from almost everyone else; that he existed in a quite separate space from those whose lives, if not precisely nasty, brutish, and short, were monotonous and pre-ordained.

Thus Trudeau could not understand why Canadians were furious when after telling them to "exercise discipline" and set aside baubles like electric toothbrushes, he flew off to join the Aga Khan on his yacht in the Adriatic. He couldn't understand why Margaret, at once insecure and narcissistic, came crashing out of the bell jar he had placed over her at the moment of their marriage, to try, futilely and pathetically and embarrassingly, to build an identity for herself. He could not understand that opposition to bilingualism, magnified by anti-French bigotry though it may have been, constituted at core nothing more than a defensive-aggressive reaction to protect job security by middle-aged anglophone civil servants, and by a huge if inarticulate constituency of middle-class English Canadians, who realized suddenly that it was too late for them to learn French, and that their lives and careers would be constrained because of that lack.

The "emotionalism" Trudeau had put to use in place of reason during his 1972-74 minority turned out to be ersatz as soon as he won back his majority. In the manner of a Bourbon who learned nothing and forgot nothing he went right back – the style is the man himself – to the personal ruffles and flourishes that Canadians, to a point, had rather liked. But this time, instead of the insouciant leather coat of the carelessly elegant aristocrat, he put on the shimmering gaudy robes of a Sun King.

* * *

First the royal pool. Then the chariot. Then the court.

The first step in the wrong direction was taken on the lawn of 24 Sussex within a fortnight of the election. There, Trudeau chatted with his friend William Teron, president of Central Mortgage and Housing Corporation. Wouldn't an indoor swimming pool be a great idea? It would cost, Teron reckoned, about $60,000 and could be built easily and without fuss by Public Works. It was not anyone's fault, exactly, that the pool eventually cost over $200,000 – too much rock, mostly – and had to be paid for by wealthy Liberal donors, in exchange for anonymity and a tax writeoff. Nor was the idea itself anyone's fault, exactly. What mattered about the pool was that it soon became a metaphor for breach of trust. Trudeau had persuaded Canadians to give him a second chance; he was using it as a passport to travel back to a style they had rejected in 1972.

After the pool, came the car. This was a silver-grey Cadillac, armour-plated, and weighing five tons. It cost $80,000. He needed it, Trudeau explained, because the RCMP said that he needed it. The RCMP had indeed said this; the point was that Trudeau, as did Clark in 1979, as did Trudeau himself in 1980 when he ordered the car left in storage, could have said no.

Next, for a king, a *mise en scène* fit for a king. Tom Cossitt, a zealous Conservative M. P., made it his life's work to unveil for the public each and every expenditure on renovating and refurbishing Trudeau's office on Parliament Hill and his home on Sussex Drive: $86,700 for refurbishing Trudeau's Parliament Hill office turned out to be the least of it; changes at 24 Sussex cost $250,000. More than the sum totals, it was the details that shocked Canadians: $180 for six ashtrays; $8,200 for a single sofa; $62 for a marble soap dish. Under the Diefenbakers and the Pearsons, the style at 24 Sussex had been that of a frugally managed manse. Under Trudeau in his middle period, it took on the splendour of the Peacock Throne.

* * *

Returned with the King were the courtiers. Some new faces; same old hauteur. Ivan Head, the self-styled "cutting edge of the left" who'd been blunted after 1972, passed down orders to External Affairs. Teron, a newer recruit, promulgated the Teron doctrine that any civil servant had the right to stamp any document whatsoever, CONFIDENTIAL. As Pitfield, back from exile, set up Byzantine shop in the East Block, the last of the pre-Trudeau, independent-minded mandarins folded their tents and faded away. Reisman, the deputy minister of finance, quit at the end of 1974 after he read in the newspapers that Trudeau was planning to switch him to another post. Similarly, Jake Warren, a former deputy minister who had become High Commissioner in London, discovered that he was about to be dumped to make way for the Liberal Senator, Paul Martin. As one senior cabinet minister, a loyalist who remains in cabinet today, admits, "A quality of sycophancy pervaded the civil service." The injunction, "Clear it with Michael" replaced the 1968-72 slogan, "Clear it with PCO."

Under Pitfield and, more surprisingly, under Robertson, keeper of the old civil service conscience, the dividing line between Liberal Party and public service, always fuzzy, disappeared completely. Three of Trudeau's former aides – Jim Davey, Peter Roberts, Tim Porteous – were parachuted into the civil service; later he made an old *Cité Libre* friend, Charles Lussier, head of the Canada Council. Through 1974-75, a former deputy minister, Austin, was chief of Trudeau's personal staff. Another former deputy minister, Pierre Juneau, was named to the cabinet in 1975 (but defeated in a by-election later that year) replacing a cabinet minister, Pelletier, who had just been named Ambassador to France. Pelletier, who succeeded an earlier ex-minister, Leo Cadieux, joined three other ex-Liberals in ambassadorial posts: Martin in London, Jean-Louis Gagnon with UNESCO in Paris; Lucien Lamoureux in Brussels. Another ex-Trudeau aide, Henry Lawless, was given the plum post of Consul-General in Bordeaux.

Public servants watched the politicians, and learned to break the rules. More and more public servants took advantage of the indexed pensions they had engineered for themselves to retire early. Often, they signed up immediately with their old departments, on contract, or, like Reisman, put their contacts and know-how to work as lobbyists, or "consultants" as they preferred to be called. This practice, unknown in the past, became so common that in 1976, Trudeau had to issue guidelines to enjoin retired civil servants to "ensure by their actions that the objectivity and impartiality of government service are not cast in doubt." All down the line, middle-rank and junior civil servants took their cues from the top. Out the window went the old ideals of integrity and frugality.

"The real conversational passions of your federal public service," Harry Bruce wrote in 1975 in the *Toronto Star* are

> raises, promotions, transfers, pensions, reclassifications, bureaucratic boondoggles, raw deals, sweet deals, departmental sweatshops, individual ripoffs and the injustices, extravagances, stupidities and blazing absurdities of the effort to make the public service bilingual.

As the court reassembled, one message came through loud and clear. Those courtiers who were strictly political were beginning to matter as they had never mattered before. "After 1974," says Mitchell Sharp, "Mr. Trudeau put himself in the hands of the political pros. Their influence permeated the entire government." A non-political aide of that era explains the transformation. "Trudeau never really believed he'd won the 1974 election. He'd been told so often that he didn't understand politics, that he'd come to believe it. Thereafter, he attributed the election results entirely to the wizardry of Davey and Coutts. So he turned the party over to them, and trusted their judgement completely."

In August 1975, Coutts succeeded Austin as Trudeau's chief of staff. Coutts holds the same position today, the only difference being that he's grown even closer to Trudeau. He wields the same kind of power, though in a different arena, as Pitfield.

* * *

Coutts was and is a political phenomenon such as Canada has never known before: Machiavelli masquerading as a cherub. Jack Pickersgill is the obvious comparison, for their mutual love of the Liberal Party, their mastery of the intricacies of keeping it in power, not to mention a certain streak of sentimentality under the ruthlessness. But where Pickersgill, midwife with Joey Smallwood of Newfoundland's entry into Confederation, cared about leaving his mark in the history books, Coutts does not, or not so that anyone has so far noticed. At forty-two, he has already exercised more backroom power than anyone else in modern Canadian political history; more than Tom Kent, say, under Pearson, more than Lalonde during Trudeau's first term. But he has used this power to less purpose than any, even the most briefly tenured, of his predecessors.

During Coutts's half-decade as Trudeau's most influential political adviser, no minister, or civil servant, or other Trudeau aide can recall him putting forward in debate any principle, ideology, or policy conviction other than the political advancement of Trudeau, the Liberal Party, or Coutts himself. Toward the end of Trudeau's third term, 1978-79, the adjectives that reporters used most frequently to describe him were no longer "arrogant" or "aloof" but "cynical," "opportunistic," "manipulative." In every instance – Trudeau's abrupt mid-1978 conversion to massive spending cuts; his late-1978 musings about holding referendums on contentious issues such as capital punishment – the source of the policy change could be traced to Coutts, and beyond him to the party's latest polls.

The polls in fact were the most visible of the changes Coutts initiated when he joined Trudeau. In Jim Davey's era, Trudeau's schedule for the year had been mapped in detail on wall-size flow charts, maintained in a locked "war room." Coutts replaced these with a graph of the monthly Gallup Poll, plotted out over the past ten years. Each month, the new results were matched against the 282 Commons constituencies; then, depending on whether the figures were up or down, the notations against ridings would be changed from "safe Liberal" and "Liberal-leaning" to "doubtful" or "Conservative/NDP leaning." Thus, as one staff member describes it, "we knew exactly where we stood electorally, month by month."

Coutts treasured his charts and graphs as another man might treasure photographs of his wife and children. "The Liberal Party is really Jim's family," a friend of his has said. Earlier, the party had been his ticket out of obscurity.

He was born in 1938 in Nanton, a small sad town in southern Alberta just eighteen miles from High River, where Joe Clark, his life-long opponent was born the next year. He became a politician at fourteen, working in the election of a provincial Liberal candidate. The next year, at fifteen, he became campaign manager for a federal Liberal candidate – probably the youngest in history. At the University of Alberta, he was Opposition Leader in the campus Mock Parliament to Clark's Prime Minister. From this point on, although much more on Coutts's part than Clark's, an intense rivalry developed between them. Coutts gave Clark the nickname, "the Wimp," that hung round his neck like an albatross in the 1980 campaign. He could never quite believe that Clark had actually bested Trudeau in 1979, because, as he has said, "In this game, you have to be a bit of a son-of-a-bitch. Joe just doesn't quite have it." ("I'm a son-of-a-bitch, but I'm an honest son-of-a-bitch," Coutts says of himself.)

In 1963, after Walter Gordon spotted him as a comer, Coutts came to Ottawa as appointments secretary to Pearson. Already, he had developed the mien of a merry, worldly elf–short, chubby, ginger-haired, and freckled–much sought after by hostesses; as funny and as engaging a dinner partner as anyone, male or female, could hope to find. He charmed women by recognizing their perfume and remarking on it by name. He impressed men with his riverboat gambler skill at poker. Then as now, he read a lot, collected pictures, paid off political bets in bottles of Chivas Regal. In 1966 he left for Harvard to add an MBA to his arts and law degrees, then moved to Toronto to start his own firm of consultants, The Canada Consulting Group.* He added wealth to his string of accomplishments, redecorated an old town house in the Annex with the kind of witty, adventurous taste that earns spreads in architectural magazines, developed an encyclopaedic range of contacts that reached well beyond politics into the arts, the media, business.

Coutts never stopped nurturing his Ottawa contacts. Through them, he won contracts with Central Mortgage and Housing Corporation (Teron): PCO (Pitfield), Secretary of State (a fellow ex-Liberal ministerial aide, Mike McCabe). But early in 1973, when Trudeau asked him to be campaign strategist, he said no.

At that time, Coutts did not much like Trudeau. He had been aghast at the Prime Minister's indifference to party regulars, furious about his neglect of Pearson, whom Coutts idolized. (Like Pitfield, Coutts is a hero-worshipper: first Pearson, then John Aird,** a prominent Toronto financier, then Trudeau.) In 1974, he joined the campaign as tour manager because Keith Davey asked him and out of loyalty to the party. In mid-1975 he became Trudeau's top aide.

"What happened to Jim after that is the old familiar story," says

---

*Once in Trudeau's office, Coutts was too savvy to practise the scientific management stuff he'd preached. He kept all lines of responsibility deliberately blurred, so only he knew who was supposed to be doing what, and kept his shop in such a state of confusion that it ran permanently in the red so that, to balance his books, he had to raid the office budgets of cabinet ministers.

**In June 1980, Aird was named Lieutenant-Governor of Ontario.

a friend. "He sailed off on a power trip." The first manifestation was his manipulation of the press relations during the 1974 election. But Coutts really only began to attract attention when he took over as chief of staff.

Quickly, Coutts worked as hard as he could to make himself, in the manner of Pitfield, Trudeau's indispensable man. Deliberately, he cut off access to Trudeau by all other staff members. From the beginning, he ignored the Liberal caucus. Before long, he ignored every cabinet minister, except for Lalonde, just too tough and too powerful to be ignored, and MacEachen, with whom there was a common bond of loyalty to Pearson. (MacEachen, for his part, deliberately kept his distance from Coutts, and made certain that meetings between them were held in *his* office.) Except for Pitfield and Robertson, he ignored the mandarins. During the "post-Bonn" exercise in cutting spending in 1978, Coutts functioned like the deputy minister of finance, chairing in all but name the meetings of top civil servants assembled to decide just how and where the cuts Trudeau had ordered would be made. From 1978 on, he even elbowed out his close friend, Davey. By now, almost no one trusted him; reporters swapped stories of how Coutts had misled them.

Yet if it was calculating, Coutts' devotion to Trudeau was also unstinting and wholly genuine: the single-minded devotion of a curiously vulnerable loner, who every now and then evinces a sense of regret that he's cut off his own Alberta roots and never put down new ones through wife and family. In the 1979 campaign, as he listened to Trudeau making a bad speech, tears ran down Coutts's face. He hung a portrait in oils of Trudeau by the Toronto artist, Danae Chambers, over his mantelpiece. Coutts's thick political hide conceals a vein of generosity, even of tenderness; toward artists whose careers he has advanced, toward politicians whose legs have given out, toward old friends whose luck is down, and toward Trudeau when he was a loser.

In turn, Trudeau depends on Coutts because he is totally loyal, because he's resilient and unruffled through the worst crises – a knack he picked up from Pearson – because he is well-read and can say things like "In a situation like this one, Laurier did . . ." and because – the political quality Trudeau most admires – he is *daring*. Daring enough to have co-engineered with MacEachen the

171

December 1979 coup that brought the Clark government down; daring enough, as is less well-known, to have tried to convince Trudeau to call a snap election in the *spring* of 1977, right after the PQ victory. And Trudeau has reciprocated Coutts's devotion in kind. In December 1979, when dissident Liberals on the National Executive tried to remove Coutts from his job, Trudeau let it be known that he would return as leader only if Coutts stayed at his side.

Above all, Coutts is indispensable because his own greatest strength is Trudeau's greatest weakness: the management and the manipulation of people. Coutts, particularly in recent years, has become Trudeau's talent scout and fixer, doing for him what Trudeau cannot or will not do for himself. He recruited Jack Horner, the Conservative frontbencher, a transient success that turned into stupendous failure because Horner, simply by leaving, transformed the Tory caucus into a united team. He tried to recruit Ed Schreyer to the cabinet, and almost succeeded. He recruited John Evans, the former president of the University of Toronto, a much-heralded political comet, until he was brought down in the 1978 Rosedale by-election. He recruited as a Liberal candidate Maurice Strong, former chairman of Petro-Canada, until Strong, recognizing his ineptitude for politics, withdrew. He lured three Conservative M.P.s – Claude Wagner, Jack Marshall, and Bob Muir into the Senate, thus opening up by-elections in promising constituencies.

All these were the dirty jobs of politics that Trudeau knew had to be done. He was delighted to have Coutts ready to do them. But in the process, Trudeau dirtied his own hands.

The accusations of "cynicism" and "opportunism," from which Trudeau has never escaped, did not begin in earnest until early 1977, when Horner announced he was crossing the floor to join the Prime Minister he once had compared to Adolph Hitler. Even so, quite soon after the 1974 election, Canadians began to realize, for other reasons, that Trudeau, his majority regained, was something less than the leader they imagined they had re-elected.

* * *

On July 10, two days after the election, by design of the Liberal electoral strategists, Statistics Canada reported that inflation had reached a new post-Korean war high of 11.4 per cent. That same month, the Bank of Canada hiked its prime lending rate to 9¼ per cent, double the rate a year earlier. By winter, the inflation rate was over 12 per cent. Workers who had been locked into two- and three-year contracts scrambled to catch up. Transit workers in Toronto and Montreal went on strike, as did Vancouver grain-handlers and Ottawa teachers.

On September 30, Parliament assembled to hear a Throne Speech that said inflation was "serious and urgent," but then said nothing else about it. On October 2, Trudeau gave his first speech in public since the election, except for a brief appearance in July to announce his new cabinet. (Gray went out; MacEachen, as his reward, went to External Affairs.) Trudeau spoke for one hour and twenty minutes. He talked about bilingualism, about Parliamentary reform, about the constitution. About inflation, he said exactly one word. Trudeau ended his speech with this statement: "There are other subjects I could deal with. Native rights . . . the status of women . . . um . . . inflation." Then he sat down.

Having been handed back his majority, Trudeau had simply reached down and switched the government's motor off. For a year, until late 1975, he did almost nothing. Then, he acted only because he had no choice: Turner's resignation threw Canadians into a panic-stricken conviction that their economy was about to collapse.

Trudeau's behaviour was so odd and so disastrous that it has spawned a host of explanations, and an inflexible determination on the part of Liberals not to repeat the mistake when they returned to office in 1980.

Some partial explanations are obvious. Trudeau was tired, physically and emotionally, after the eighteen-month strain of keeping a minority government going, followed by a hectic campaign. Most of his ministers were also tired, and Trudeau had brought in only a couple of activist newcomers: Roméo LeBlanc at Fisheries; Barney Danson at Urban Affairs. As a practical constraint, considerable legislation – Petro-Canada, the Election Expenses Act – had been presented in the last Parliament and now had to be ground through the legislative mill.

Margaret is another explanation. Unquestionably, from mid-1974, his disintegrating marriage drained Trudeau's energies and distracted his attention. Even so, and to a degree that's almost inhuman, Trudeau can compartmentalize his relationships with others. And if marriage was not working out for Trudeau, father-hood was. The same kind of psychological rejuvenation Trudeau always has been able to get from nature he was now getting from his sons. His relationship with Justin and Sasha, later with Michel, was one of unrestrained love, all the more unrestrained because they had come late in life. When they were with him, he was an entirely different person: tender and joyous, as if not quite believing in his luck. At home, they were always around, sometimes upstaging important visitors, like provincial premiers who, in the midst of making some point crucial to the survival of Confederation, would suddenly feel a small hand tugging at their pant-leg.

Perhaps the best answer for Trudeau's curious behaviour – or lack of behaviour – is that he decided it was his turn to do what he damn well wanted. For six years, he had given Canadians good government, even though they failed to appreciate the benefits of rationalism. By acting contrite, and providing the entertainments they seemed to want, he'd got them to vote for him again. So he deserved a rest. All his life, "freedom" had been Trudeau's holy grail: the freedom to do whatever he wanted; whether to pursue whichever intellectual goal he aspired to at the moment or to take off on vacation at the drop of a hat.

So Trudeau, post-1974, set about redefining the job of Prime Minister to one that suited him. More and more, he took pleasure in the perqs of office: in 1975, he used a Defence Department helicopter to ferry him to a political picnic. He took more and more vacations, although now, in keeping with his station, these amounted to imperial passages abroad. The trip to Mexico, Cuba, and Venezuela early in 1976, as an example. And finally, he went back to the great intellectual love of his life: the pursuit of rationality in government. He would show them he had been right.

* * *

Immediately after the election, unbeknownst to the public, Trudeau set in motion the most exhaustive, most encyclopaedic, and most determined attempt ever made by any government anytime, any-place, anywhere, to develop a logical, systematic, rational program of policy priorities. The process amounted to Management by Objectives, at a cosmic level. The government would decide its objectives, in ranked order, objectively and scientifically. Then it would spend the rest of its term implementing these objectives.

To make certain that this exercise would be done properly, unlike the botched effort of 1968-72, Trudeau appointed a top-level team from his own office and from the Privy Council Office down the hall: Mike Kirby and Hal Kroeker, respectively.* He ordered ministers to make available in their schedules all the time that Kirby and Kroeker needed for interviews. He assembled thirty deputy ministers for lunch at 24 Sussex and told them the same thing. Each deputy minister then called in his assistant deputy ministers and passed on the marching orders. So it went down the line.

For a year, Trudeau poured his best people, and their best energies, into figuring out what they ought, rationally, to be doing. Ministers were interviewed for two- and three-hour sessions. Each department prepared position papers, submitted them, got them tossed back, rewrote them, bargained with other departments for a piece of the action. "I didn't take the priorities exercise seriously," Hugh Faulkner, then Secretary of State, remembers. "But you had to or your department would be wiped out."

By late July, 1975, the exercise was over. The final document – thirty-four foolscap-size pages – would be discussed on September 17, by the full cabinet at a special all-day meeting at Meach Lake, just north of Ottawa. Here, leaked to the press by its then-proud authors, are the document's principal conclusions, in turn the distilled wisdom of a year of effort by Ottawa's best and brightest. The government's priorities for action were to be:

"A more just, tolerant Canadian society

"With a greater balance in the distribution of people, and in the creation and distribution of wealth between and within regions

"Which makes more rational use of resources and is sensitive to the natural and human environment

"Accepting new international responsibilities, particularly with regard to assisting developing countries

"With an evolving federal state, capable of effective national policies as well as responsive and competent government at all levels."

The point about this grab-bag of pieties isn't so much that a first-year political science student could have put it or a better one

---

*In 1981, respectively, Secretary for Federal-Provincial Affairs and director of planning in the Ministry of Economic Development.

together in a week. Nor is it that none of them was ever implemented (CIDA's budget, for instance, soon was cut). The point rather is that the document reflects faithfully Trudeau's political style. Left to his own devices, he dithers, and falls back on abstract generalities; only under pressure, such as the need to create an instant oil policy in 1973, does he set out, usually superbly, to "create counterweights."

Another point to be made is that the document reflects accurately also Trudeau's particular, post-1974 mindset. No one reading it would have the remotest idea that while it was being written, Canada was experiencing its worst combined inflation and unemployment since the Depression, nor have known that government spending soon was to be brought to an abrupt halt, or that Canadian manufacturing was beginning its long, sickening, slide downwards. Revenues, jobs, inflation, all were mundane matters to be moved to one side as the Sun King gazed toward the far horizon of a revised version of the Just Society.

Luckily for Trudeau, several of those close to him didn't take him seriously. Turner for one. A few days before the scheduled Meach Lake meeting, Turner reduced the year-long priorities exercise to the level of relevance of Hammurabi's Code. He quit, and by quitting gave Trudeau no choice but to snap out of his slumber and set about creating counterweights.

The other doubter was Coutts. In the summer, he'd commissioned an attitudinal survey. It showed, entirely unsurprisingly, that Canadians cared not at all for any of Trudeau's priorities, but cared deeply only about the economy, and about crime on the streets.

At the Meach Lake meeting, the priorities document was never discussed. Instead, the cabinet spent its day discussing the economy and crime in the streets. One minister, Ron Basford, won himself an instant promotion to Justice (from National Revenue) by coining the phrase, "Peace and Security" as an alternative to the popular but ominous-sounding tag, "law and order." The debate on the economy was less productive. The solution, everyone knew, was wage and price controls. But the problem to the solution, as everyone knew, but could not bring themselves to be so rude as to mention, was that just a year ago, Trudeau had said definitively, irrevocably, and repeatedly, that controls would not work.

11

Wrestling Inflation to the Ground

"Since it is no longer taken for granted that what goes up must come down, what goes up probably will continue to go up indefinitely."

Robert Heilbroner,
New Yorker, October 8, 1979

Of all the contests Trudeau has engaged in as a Single Combat champion on behalf of Canadians, the ones he has lost most clearly have always been the economic ones. None has provided him with an opposing Single Combat champion – other than Turner who, because Canadians saw in him the embodiment of economic virtue, was exactly the wrong opponent for Trudeau to pick. And, time and again, Trudeau let himself get embroiled in unwinnable contests. His comment in December 1970: "We have beaten inflation"; his June 1974 campaign promise, "We will wrestle inflation to the ground," created expectations that even a Prime Minister in whom Adam Smith, Ricardo, Marx, Keynes, and Friedman were all reincarnate could not have fulfilled.

In his book, *Paradox*, Anthony Westell makes perhaps the best and certainly the most balanced judgement of Trudeau's economic record. Discussing Trudeau's first war on inflation, 1968-70 (the judgement applies as well to his entire economic span), Westell remarks that Trudeau's policies of spending cuts and tight money, imposed in the belief that higher unemployment would produce lower inflation, "were not cruel or shocking or appalling, but simply conventional." Then Westell delivers his epitaph. "The pity was that he was not able to rise above convention to produce the unorthodox solution."

* * *

John Maynard Keynes, among his other predictions, once forecast that economists would eventually rank below dentists in social stature. In Ottawa, in the late 1960's, unluckily for Trudeau, economists were still worshipped as high priests. Ottawa's Economic

Establishment—Louis Rasminsky, Governor of the Bank of Canada, and Simon Reisman, deputy minister of finance, were unofficial co-chairmen of the club—still believed in "fine tuning," believed, that is, that government could alternately spend its way out of recession and unemployment, or slash its way out of inflation by spending cuts and tight money. They believed, essentially, in themselves.

Eric Kierans did not. From 1968 to early 1971, he fought the Ottawa Economic Establishment. In response, it smothered him. He quit in April 1971 when Trudeau told him he would never be appointed to an important economic portfolio. In his letter of resignation Kierans told—pleaded with—Trudeau: "If Canada is to be an industrial force in the 1980's, we must be prepared now to husband our resources and to select those areas in which we can be internationally competitive, and to manage and invest the resources, physical and human, that will give us a compelling position."

Today, as Canada's economy "de-industrializes" in the vogue phrase, few if any believe any longer that the economy can somehow be "fine tuned" to inflation-free health. Few if any doubt any longer that the root causes of our industrial decline, as Kierans foresaw, are either "structural" (everything from our failure to translate scientific invention into commercial products to the inexplicable circumstance that despite mass unemployment and the world's most expensive education system we're critically short of skilled workers), or are "attitudinal" (essentially, Canadians are not prepared to work as hard as, say, South Koreans, nor as hard as they did when working to acquire their first car). Few doubt that tinkering with the money supply or with tax cuts, while useful, are in the end more than that—tinkering. Few any longer are in the least surprised when, in 1980, a zero growth rate leaves inflation at the 10 per cent mark.

When Trudeau lost Kierans, he lost the one minister who was capable of original economic thought, except perhaps, though he is far less intellectual and flamboyant, Herb Gray, whom Trudeau rescued in 1980 from the six years of oblivion he had sentenced him to.*

*I should declare an interest here. From 1968 to 1970, I was Kierans' executive assistant.

In most respects, Trudeau's economic opinions are entirely conventional. Businessmen thought otherwise, imagined he was a closet socialist, all the more after the famous December 28, 1975 telecast when Trudeau mused about "a New Society" in which government would have to play a large role, because "we haven't been able to make it work – the free market system."

In fact, Trudeau admired the free market system out of which his father had done so well. Like Franklin D. Roosevelt, similarly excoriated by businessmen, Trudeau was only trying to save the free market system from itself.

Trudeau rarely wrote about economics before coming to Ottawa. Except for some sentences invariably quoted out of context from his essay in *Social Purpose for Canada*, nothing he wrote should have caused the least alarm in the boardrooms of the nation. For instance: "It is a rare state that can disregard economic or technological goals with impunity. A government trying to do so, even for excellent social motives, would so impoverish its economy that its social goals became unattainable." In another passage which bankers, whom he later called "the worst bitchers of all," ought to have regarded as the soundest of political collateral, Trudeau wrote: "What really matters is that the per-capita income be increased as quickly as possible. To achieve this, the economy of Quebec must become extremely efficient, technologically advanced, quite specialized, and capable of offering products at the best prices in all the markets of the world." Good, sound thinking, free market stuff.

Prescriptions like this are easy to write. Practising them is quite another matter. "Structural reform" is painful. What Prime Minister wants to give the order to close textile and clothing mills in Quebec, or Chrysler Canada in Windsor? Who wants to threaten the entrenched self-interest of a profession – lawyers for instance, of whom there are 25,000 in Canada and 10,000 in Japan? Who wants to risk the government's prestige on a single product, however attractive – a STOL plane, say – when it may end up, scores of millions of dollars later, like the Bricklin car?

In his first three terms, Trudeau lacked the courage, the imagination, or indeed the expert advisers – except, in the Privy Council Office, Ian Stewart – to prod him to take a dare on the unorthodox, and the necessary. So he fiddled with "fine tuning."

Yet the alarms of businessmen weren't entirely self-invented. While Trudeau believed, unquestionably, in the free market system, he also believed in the strong state, "the servant state," wise and good, of its very nature. The idea of intervening in the economy caused Trudeau no philosophic difficulty. On Stewart's advice, and as a consequence of reading for himself John Kenneth Galbraith's *Economics and the Public Purpose*, Trudeau in fact seriously considered the possibility that the solution to inflation was neither fine tuning nor temporary controls, but *permanent* controls imposed upon what Galbraith called "the planning sector" – those large corporations and unions which as a consequence of their size could plan their future by arranging their profits and wages pretty much as they wished, aware that these costs could be passed on to consumers who could not, after all, shop around the block for a competitive telephone, or whatever. But when Trudeau, in a 1975 interview, tried to raise this topic to the level of public debate, he botched it. In fact, he was bound to botch it, because by then he had destroyed his own credibility: Canadians no longer believed, and for a long time after would keep on refusing to believe, a single thing he said.

* * *

The story of Trudeau's first War on Inflation, 1968-70, can be told quickly. He won it, which was a pity. His victory wasn't so much pyrrhic as illusory. Faced by an inflation rate that had climbed above 4 per cent, Trudeau did what his Economic Establishment told him to do: froze government spending, cut the civil service by 5,000, balanced the budget in 1969 for the first time in more than a decade, imposed tight money and a Bank of Canada prime rate that soared to 7 per cent. The inevitable consequence was higher unemployment but that would produce, Trudeau was assured, lower inflation. Sure enough, the inflation rate went down – to 3.3 per cent in 1970, the lowest among the twenty-one member nations of OECD.

"We have won last year's victory, the one against inflation," Trudeau announced in December 1970. Thereupon, he turned his attention to unemployment. The flaw in this analysis was that no evidence existed that higher unemployment had in fact caused inflation to diminish. Rather, the 1968-70 bout of inflation had been caused by an economic force outside Canada; the U.S.

"guns-and-butter" policy of waging a war on poverty at home, and a war in Vietnam simultaneously. Instead, by causing unemployment in the hope (faith, really) this would cause inflation to decrease, Trudeau ensured that productivity would decline, and hence, because of industrial bottlenecks, that inflation would increase later on.

In 1974, confident as always in his own rhetoric, Trudeau declared: "We will wrestle inflation to the ground." By then, inflation had the economy in a stranglehold. Before the year ended, the annual rate hit a peak of 12.4 per cent. Yet, in contradiction to the theory of fine tuning, unemployment was also on the rise, to the tune of more than 7 per cent by March 1975. Indeed, during the last quarter of 1974, the Gross National Product showed an actual decline for the first time in a decade and inflation hit its peak.

* * *

In August, 1974, one month after the "Zap, you're frozen" election, the prestigious C.D. Howe Research Institute urged Ottawa to implement "some form of wage and price controls, regardless of election promises." Instead, Trudeau and Turner dithered for a year, hoping for a miracle to save their faces.

During that lost year, a number of things happened. Unions won record settlements, led by government employees at all levels, ranging from postal workers–"to hell with the public," said their leader, Joe Davidson–to Ottawa teachers who, much more circumspectly and far more efficiently, won themselves a 34 per cent salary hike, over *one* year. During the first half of 1975, wage settlements averaged 18 per cent, twice the rate in the U.S. To get what they wanted, workers went on strike: in the first half of 1975, more days were lost through strikes and lockouts than in the five years, 1960-65, *combined*. In both 1974 and 1975, our strike record was the worst in the western world, not counting Italy, which nobody did.

As a result, labour's share of the national income, which had dropped in 1973 and 1974 to 71.7 per cent of the total from a 73.5 per cent in 1972, recovered in 1975 to 73 per cent. In fact, by the time controls were eventually imposed, labour had recovered all its lost ground. Thus, paradoxically, controls succeeded because they placed a new floor *under* the incomes of unionized labour.

181

(Government had intended to set a "ceiling," a maximum increase of 12 per cent on controlled contracts, but as always happens, unions transformed this ceiling into a floor.)

Turner, almost as much as Trudeau, was as concerned to save his face as to save the economy. His campaign rhetoric had been nearly as intemperate. "They won't work," he had said of controls. "A cure worse than the disease." Turner, mark you, was quite right. In the sense of attacking the root causes of inflation, temporary controls never *can* work. At most, controls produce a period of stability during which governments can enact the structural reforms needed to root out inflation. The trouble was that neither Turner, nor any of his successors, had the least idea what reforms they wanted to put in place.

Even these benefits of controls have a price tag attached. Controls distort the market economy. Investment decisions are postponed; thus production and employment opportunities are lost. Corporations have to divert time and talent into dealing with bureaucracy instead of getting on with the job. Ultimately, all these costs *increase* the rate of inflation.

Trudeau believed in the private enterprise system. So did Turner, but far more strongly. "People do best at making their own decisions," he said. He also favoured private enterprise because it "decentralized" decision-making away from top-heavy centres like government. But the real difference between them wasn't so much their attitude to business as their attitude to government. Appalled by the extravagance that the auditor general would soon criticize, Turner profoundly disbelieved in government's ability to manage the economy better than businessmen. In Trudeau's case, although it took him a long time to be persuaded that controls were necessary, he never doubted that they were feasible. The "servant state," after all, could do no wrong.

For a year the charade continued. In November 1974, Turner tried exhortation: "Various groups ... are making demands on the economy which add up to more than the economy is capable of producing." By April 1975 he'd advanced to plea bargaining: "We must achieve a consensus on the necessity of exercising voluntary restraint." He invited unions to accept voluntary guidelines – 12 per cent up to a $2,400 maximum. Since this meant unions doing for government the job it lacked the willpower to do for itself, labour rejected the proposal at a Canadian Labour Congress meeting where Turner's request was debated for exactly five minutes. Turner then described the unions as "lemmings," rushing to their own destruction. This not only did not help, it showed that Turner was rattled.

* * *

Three policy choices now confronted Trudeau and Turner: to do nothing; to adopt the "old time religion" of slashing government spending and tightening the money supply then being practised by U.S. President Gerald Ford; or to impose wage and price controls, as both the U.S. and Britain had done earlier.

The do nothing approach had its advantages. Wage settlements, in fact, were contributing only marginally to inflation, (no larger a share of the total national income than during inflation-free 1973); inflation, rather, was being produced by high food prices resulting from world-wide crop failures, the hike in oil prices, and the momentum of price increases produced by the 1972-73 world-wide economic boom. Thus controls as a solution were almost irrelevant to the central economic problem. Further, controls would do nothing to affect the causes of inflation, even if these had been induced domestically; it would simply apply a poultice to the symptoms of high prices and high wage settlements. Even the slogan "checking inflationary expectations" had more resonance in the minds of politicians and academic economists than in reality: it implied that Canadians, somehow, were wrong to act, after several years of inflation, as if they expected inflation to continue. In fact, all along, the only Canadians really hurt by inflation have been those who failed to act, or who couldn't act, on the expectation inflation would continue.

This unresolved debate—controls will not work, but spending cuts and tight money will increase unemployment—continued unresolved into September 1975. Then, on September 10, Turner ended the debate. He quit. Behind him, he left a political vacuum that Trudeau had no political choice but to fill with controls, like a fist thrust inexpertly into a gaping dike.

* * *

Like a sulky Bonnie Prince Charlie to an unbudgeable George II, Turner's unique contribution to Trudeau's political career has been to ensure that just by being there – whether in cabinet or in the Toronto corporate law offices at McMillan Binch to which he retired in exile – the crown would forever rest uneasily on Trudeau's head. Throughout most of Trudeau's Prime Ministership, party polls showed that more Canadians wanted Turner as Prime Minister than wanted Trudeau. Always popular in the west, popular also in Quebec to an extent that was seldom recognized, Turner could probably have become a truly national leader, *a mari usque ad mare*, in a way that's always eluded Trudeau. Trudeau knew this. One reason he's remained in office so long is to make certain that Turner would never occupy it. Like all great men, Trudeau has little wish to be succeeded by someone more popular than he.

Much of Turner's extraordinary popularity is obvious. Begin with the physical magnetism. He has the flamboyant good looks of a matinée idol, hair now mellowed to reassuringly bankerly silver. He has the lithe physique of a onetime all-Canadian winner of the 100-yard dash. He has fierce blue eyes, not icy like Trudeau's, yet almost as unsettling in their intensity. He is gregarious and affable, a man who oozes charm from every well-scrubbed pore.

Turner's credentials have equal panache. He is a Rhodes Scholar who later put in time at the Sorbonne. He first flashed to fame in 1958 as the man Princess Margaret insisted be invited to partner her at a ball at Rideau Hall. He's a scion through his stepfather (his father, a British journalist, died when he was two) of one of British Columbia's "first families"; he married Geills Kilgour of the Winnipeg, Great-West Life, Kilgours.

Move on to Turner's record. He became an M.P. at thirty-three, in his first try. He joined the cabinet at thirty-six. At thirty-eight, he was a contender for the Liberal leadership – a possible winner until Trudeau came in to snatch away his Quebec delegates and many of his young ones. After that, he became the heir apparent, with an undiminished hold on the affections of hundreds of Liberal workers, with whom he maintained close contact through his famous card index file. (A quick instance of Turner's fabled efficiency: in 1976, when the Conservative frontbencher Jim Gillies went to hospital, his first get-well card came, not from one of his own relatives or colleagues, but from Turner.)

From 1968 to 1972, Turner refused to take Trudeau's "rational government" seriously. Nor, post-1974, did he admire the Sun

King style. In fact, Turner was an old-fashioned House of Commons man; he loved Parliament and the cut and thrust of debate, the no-hard-feelings camaraderie between M.P.s who had just done their best to crucify one another in public. He respected the old-style civil servants and was disturbed by the politicization of the civil service that Trudeau and Pitfield were perpetrating. He had a particular view of the responsibility of ministers as "fiduciaries," responsible for public money entrusted to them.

And then there was Turner's style. Everyone assumed he was a "jock," and they were right. He hero-worshipped athletes and loved having lunch with the Ottawa Rough Riders. His language was a weird, 1950's jive talk, "man's," and "broads," in alternating sentences. He didn't go in for being a workaholic; as he saw it, God created afternoons for tennis. He didn't believe in writing memos—heresy of heresies to the Trudeaucrats—and indeed never wrote one in all his years as a minister. Instead, he ankled round to see colleagues in person: "Hey man, there's this problem I need your help with," and usually emerged smiling. He leaked to reporters, which to Trudeaucrats was another heresy.

Yet behind Rock Hudson-in-cabinet, dwelt a considerably more complex character. Turner was well- and widely-read: Dickens and Thackeray, Conrad and Faulkner, and, as a devout Catholic, Graham Greene, Mordecai Richler, and Leonard Cohen. He had a rare appreciation of music, went to Tanglewood with Charles Munch, counted Mstislav Rostropovich and Maureen Forrester among his friends. In the early 1960's, as a freshman M.P., he tried to persuade fellow M.P.s and Liberal aides to read "this guy who's very interesting and who really knows Quebec. He writes in this magazine, *Cité Libre*, and his name is Trudeau."

Between Turner and Trudeau, competitiveness was inevitable. Their relationship, says an insider who knows both men well, "was curious and quixotic." It was also asymmetric. Turner admired and envied Trudeau for his intellect. Trudeau admired and envied Turner for his political skill: his deft piloting through of the Official Languages Act; the agreement he negotiated on constitutional reforms between the nine English-speaking provinces in advance of the 1971 Victoria Conference.

But what Turner really wanted Trudeau to admire him for was his intellect.

Bitterly, Turner would say to his friends, "Those guys just think of me as a jock with political charm." He was a good deal more than that. As Justice Minister, he enacted as many reforms as any predecessor including his immediate one, Trudeau: the Canadian Law Reform Commission; draft wiretap legislation; proposals for a Freedom of Information Act and a Privacy Act; the appointment of Bora Laskin to the Supreme Court. As Finance Minister, his "indexing" of income taxes in 1973 constituted one of the most important fiscal innovations of the past two decades. Simultaneously, Turner released Canadians from the burden of paying higher income taxes when their income increased by no more than the inflation rate and removed the "inflation dividend" of automatically escalating revenues out of which Ottawa had financed its headlong expansion of spending.

Yet Turner's character lacked the adamantine quality of Trudeau's. He wanted to be Prime Minister (his mother had told him it was his duty to do so); but every bit as much, Turner wanted to be well-liked. After he resigned, his wife, Geills, told a reporter: "How would you like to spend your days saying 'No' [to other ministers' spending projects]." In fact, apart from his epic 1975 battle with Lalonde over social security spending, which he won, Turner rarely said no. Instead, he unleashed his deputy, Simon Reisman, to play the "bad cop." This curious vulnerability, so at variance with his outward self-confidence, dogged Turner all his life, from Oxford, where contemporaries remarked on how hard he worked to do just the right thing, to the winter of 1975-76, when he could not bring himself to hurt his Liberal friends and plunge into the Conservative leadership race – as many Conservatives, among them Jack Horner, pleaded with him to do – and which, if he had taken the risk, may have made him Prime Minister today.

In 1979, bad luck in the form of Trudeau's return to the leadership denied Turner the crown he had sought all his life. But Turner, unlike Trudeau, and this is the flaw in the bonnie prince, had lacked the daring to create his own luck.

Month by month, from the 1974 election on, Turner grew more restive. He worried that his future was already behind him; that he was on the way to becoming another Paul Martin, too long at the next rung down from the top. He had wanted External Affairs but that plum went to MacEachen. Increasingly, he felt isolated. The Supergroup had re-assembled round Trudeau; repeatedly, Turner waged battle with Pitfield. His close friend Reisman resigned. When he found out from the newspapers that Trudeau intended to appoint his own Council of Economic Advisers, which would have undermined the authority of his Finance Department, he forced Trudeau to abandon the plan – but only by threatening to resign. More and more, he came to resent the absence of invitations to 24 Sussex; while true that no other ministers went there either, it galled that a gaggle of aides – Pitfield, Head, Coutts – went there. Ultimately by mid-1975, Turner knew that either he had to put up or shut up about controls. Unable to make up his mind, he asked Trudeau to release him from his portfolio. Trudeau said no. So Turner quit.

* * *

Afterwards, in private to aides, Trudeau admitted that he had blundered. But since Trudeau never apologizes, and never explains, the most he's ever been able to bring himself to say for the public record, was, in a tone that lacked all conviction, "I probably should have made Turner feel more wanted, more necessary, more desired." The virtue lacking in their crucial encounter was empathy.

As early as the spring of 1975, Turner had raised with Trudeau the possibility of moving to another portfolio. Distractedly, Trudeau mentioned Industry, Trade and Commerce, or Transport, both of which, in terms of status, would have meant a demotion. Through the summer, Turner stewed. In August, at the family summer place at Lake of the Woods, he reached his decision: either Trudeau granted him a new appointment commensurate with his rank as crown prince, or he would quit. One friend, with whom Turner discussed this decision remembers him describing his years as M.P., joyous battles long ago in the Commons, and then stopping abruptly in mid-sentence, because tears were running down his face.

On September 10, 1975, just after lunch, Turner arrived by appointment at Trudeau's House of Commons' office. Of what then happened, two versions exist. Turner later claimed he only made up his mind to quit during the interview, forgetting that earlier he had told friends such as Supreme Court Justice Douglas Abbott and columnist W.A. Wilson that he was going to see Trudeau to resign. Trudeau at first confessed he had bungled the affair, but later shifted the blame to Turner for copping out.

A fair guess at what actually happened is that Turner had made up his mind to leave but could have been talked out of it by a leader who understood human nature enough to read the mixed signals Turner was sending him. Certainly, when Turner said it was time for him to leave Finance, Trudeau's response, that maybe he would like to move (downwards) to Trade and Commerce, showed jarring bad judgement, although not as jarring as his offer later in the conversation to appoint Turner to the Senate. After a talk that grew progressively more bitter, Turner left, strode over to his own office, and dictated his letter of resignation.

In hindsight, two observations come easily to mind. Turner was bugging out of a critical decision he ought to have had the courage to stick around and make. Trudeau lacked the *nous* to recognize that what Turner was really asking for could scarcely have been granted more easily. Private reassurance that he played an essential role, and public recognition as heir apparent by naming Turner deputy Prime Minister—an honorific he later awarded to Mac-Eachen. Trudeau also lacked the political savvy to recognize the political consequences of Turner's departure.

By this encounter, Trudeau demonstrated that after a decade in politics, he knew hardly anything about politics: that politics is about relationships between people and about very little else. Partly, the problem was his reserve. Part was self-indulgence. Trudeau demanded that everyone measure up to his intellectual standards. It never occurred to him to live up to their standards of human relationships. During this same period, Trudeau never once asked Mitchell Sharp about his wife, who was terminally ill, or Donald Macdonald about his wife, Ruth, who had had a cancer operation. Quite apart from not wanting to bestir himself to social graces, one reason he never asked ministers round to 24 Sussex was that he did not want them on his territory: he was the Sun King; it was ministers' duty to raise their gaze up to him. Even Dan MacDonald, the veteran, one of the few ministers truly fond of Trudeau, once remarked to a colleague: "If only as a small boy he'd been spanked more often."

* * *

Turner's letter of resignation, which he dictated in his office right after leaving Trudeau, gave no reason for his departure, so that press and public speculation grew wilder and wilder. As a consequence, and as Trudeau failed to recognize, everyone held him alone responsible for the economy's success or failure. Unprepared, and a bit bewildered by what was happening to the nation's psyche, Trudeau found himself forced into Single Combat against an enemy he could not wrestle to the ground.

For a while, relations between Turner and Trudeau remained correct, if cool. Turner absented himself from the November 1975 Liberal convention where Trudeau's leadership was at issue. (Even so, 19 per cent of the delegates voted for a leadership review.) He let go by the chance to contest the Conservative leadership. In March 1976, Turner resigned his Commons seat to join McMillan Binch in Toronto. He took a couple of sideswipes at Trudeau's "New Society" musing: "The Prime Minister warns us that we must change men's motives. I doubt that we can change men's motives, including the drive for material wealth."

Through this period, despite the impressions of some observers, Trudeau, as an aide recalls, "uttered not one mean word about Turner." The mean words tended to be said by aides and supporters on both sides: Sandra Severn and John De B. Payne for Turner; Colin Kenny and Joyce Fairbairn for Trudeau.

The unspoken aggression pact ended in 1977. Commentators assumed the reason was a series of McMillan Binch "newsletters," co-signed by Turner, which criticized cabinet ministers, among them Jean Chrétien, then Finance Minister, for creating a "credibility gap" by his rosy-hued optimism.

The real reason Trudeau's coolness to Turner turned to white anger was that he became convinced that the Turners – one of Margaret's closest confidantes, Gro Southam, was also a close friend of Geills Turner – were the source of some of the wilder rumours about the Trudeau marriage then common currency in Toronto.

Relations now turned spiteful. In the early summer of 1977, when the U.S. Ambassador Tom Enders invited Trudeau to a party to which he also planned to invite Turner, he was given the message; if you invite Turner, you won't get Trudeau. (Turner wasn't invited but Trudeau didn't come anyway.) In mid-1979, as Opposition Leader, Trudeau joined a northern canoeing party. On being told that Turner had canoed the same river and having spotted a side stream that led on to murderous rapids, Trudeau told the group: "Pity he didn't head down that way."

Turner is even more bitter. All he will say for the record is, "Trudeau is the most remarkable Canadian of our generation." In private, he leaves no doubt that he considers Trudeau the least-likable Canadian since, well, John Cabot discovered the place. Turner's bitterness is closer to the surface. Understandably. From their Single Combat, he emerged the clear loser.

* * *

By leaving, Turner gave Trudeau no choice but to act. Under pressure, he sprang back to life, as he always does. Instantly, the year-long priorities exercise was scrapped. Within three weeks, he shuffled his cabinet, replacing Turner with Donald Macdonald, one of the ministers he admired most. Macdonald was also one of the few who dared stand up to Trudeau. Once, as Defence Minister, after Trudeau had criticized a policy he submitted to cabinet, Macdonald snapped back, "If you don't like it, get yourself another Defence Minister." At first, Macdonald demurred; he had been thinking of leaving politics to start a new career and to give himself more time with his family. Out of a sense of duty, he eventually agreed. He also agreed, though ideologically opposed to controls, to consider them seriously.

By now, the Finance Department had in hand a detailed implementation program, based on work done as early as 1972 by the then (voluntary) Prices and Incomes Commission. In its essentials, the scheme involved a three-month total freeze, followed by two years of comprehensive controls in wages and profit margins, these latter as an indirect way of controlling prices.

When Macdonald put this scheme to cabinet, Trudeau said no. Having pronounced, "Zap, you're frozen," he could not impose a freeze without making himself a national laughing stock. Thus, he eliminated the most effective element of any control scheme: an island of calm at the beginning which gives all participants an experience in zero inflation, and thereby an idea of what might be accomplished if everyone co-operates.

There was another factor. By now, Trudeau and the cabinet had become alarmed by the horrendous wage settlements that were becoming the norm: 25 per cent plus by groups from electricians to butchers. Economically, these settlements made no sense: officials coined the phrase "expectational inflation" to describe them. If this went on unchecked, reasoned Trudeau's advisers, the entire national wage structure would spin out of control.* Tommy Shoyama, the new deputy minister of finance, began updating the department's program.

A decision still had to be made about the program's scope. The Finance Department's scheme, as Andras later put it, "would have controlled every grocery store and barber shop in the country." Trudeau and Macdonald wanted a more limited scheme; what no one could figure out was how it could be made to work.

Early in October, Andras and Sharp attended a reception at the British High Commission. There, they chatted casually about controls theory with High Commissioner Sir John Johnston. As casually, Johnston mentioned that, by coincidence, a British expert on controls would be in Ottawa within a couple of days: perhaps they'd like to meet him. Yes, nodded Sharp and Andras, they would indeed.

At noon on Monday, October 6, 1975, the mother country — by stretching a helping hand across the sea to a troubled former colony — Edmund Dell, a junior minister to Denis Healey, then Chancellor of the Exchequer, stepped briskly into 7 Rideau Gate, the government's official guest house just outside the grounds of Rideau Hall. Assembled to meet him were Trudeau and all his top economic ministers (Sharp, Andras, Chrétien — not Macdonald, who was away), plus their top advisers (Pitfield, Stewart, Shoyama, and Coutts). Over lunch, Shoyama outlined the original departmental plan for controls. "It's a recipe for disaster," pronounced Dell, who had had direct experience with the controls program Britain had introduced a year earlier. The task of regulating virtually every firm in the country would take an army of bureaucrats. Only large companies and large unions should be regulated; their settlements would fix the pattern for everyone else.

*The cabinet's alarm was genuine, but probably was unfounded. *Private* sector wage settlements, after an initial burst of excess, are invariably brought back to reality by the market. The only serious wage problem involved the *public* sector, which government then lacked the will to control by the ordinary bargaining process. Later the Economic Council of Canada released figures that showed that provincial governments had led the spiral upwards by granting employees average settlements of 19.3 per cent followed by 14.7 per cent, in the private sector, followed lastly by Ottawa, though it took the most flak, at 13.6 per cent.

The next afternoon, October 7, the key Cabinet Committee, Planning and Priorities, matched the Finance Department's scheme against Dell's, and made its choice. Less than a week later, on Thanksgiving Day, October 13, Trudeau announced the decision to the nation: It was the "Dell" scheme.

* * *

On television, Trudeau's actual speech was anti-climactic. "We have to swallow strong medicine," he said. "We need to cool the fires of inflation." All companies with more than 500 employees – about 1,500 in all – and all government employees, would be subjected to three years of wage and price controls.* The goal would be to reduce inflation to 8 per cent in the program's first year, to 6 per cent in the second, to 4 per cent in the third and final year. An Anti-Inflation Board would be established to regulate the firms, the unions, and also professionals such as doctors and lawyers who, like all workers, would be limited to a maximum gain of up to $2,400 in the first year. The AIB chairman would be Jean-Luc Pépin, a former Liberal minister defeated in 1972.

Pépin plunged into action "like Cincinnatus brought back from private life to save the Republic," (in his own phrase); he worked six days a week, from 9.00 a.m. to midnight. Yet quickly he ran into difficulties. Without a freeze, his first priority had to be to act to roll back wage settlements. The Canadian Labour Congress went into all-out opposition. To make matters worse, the Finance Department's advance planning turned out to be inadequate: far from the staff of 200 that Trudeau had pledged, the AIB payroll grew to 1,000. Still, the board managed somehow to keep the paper burden flowing, rolling back wage settlements and also, though much less frequently, prices.

In the end, Canadians themselves made the program work. Two weeks after Trudeau's speech, a Gallup Poll measured support for the program at 62 per cent; opposition at 27 per cent. This ratio never changed substantially: 58:30 per cent in March 1976 (including 52 per cent approval in "labour" households); 46:19 per cent in April 1977; 56:25 per cent in July 1977.**

*The cabinet tacked an additional year onto the department's two-year scheme as a hedge against the political future.

**Public acceptance was made easier by the circumstance that inflation was *not* in

192

The point – a sad point in light of Trudeau's dithering – is that Canadians have always supported controls, whether out of deference to authority, or out of a common sense judgement that even the "rough justice" of controls is preferable to fighting tooth and claw in an inflationary jungle. As early as June 1970, Gallup reported a 60:31 per cent approval rating for controls. The only time in the last decade that Canadians have doubted the value of controls was in September 1974 when, after Trudeau had spent two election months ridiculing controls, he did shift public opinion to an even, 44:43 per cent, balance.

Thus Trudeau's task on Thanksgiving Day 1975, could scarcely have been easier. All he needed to do was convince Canadians to believe in something they already believed in. But because he also needed to admit that he had been wrong, he botched it.

* * *

The only important part of Trudeau's statement on October 13 was the one he did not read. For a week, his advisers had been divided as to whether, after announcing controls, he should say, in effect, "I'm sorry. Stanfield was right." One aide recalls: "He knew he ought to explain, he wanted to, but he was persuaded not to, by Coutts."

Most likely this is wishful nostalgia. For Trudeau to have apologized would have been out of character. Of all his personal possessions, the one he prides most is his *amour propre*; he will never admit a mistake. At a guess, Coutts would not have had the slightest problem persuading Trudeau to accept his advice: say nothing about the past, talk only about the present and the future, because the public, after all, has a memory span measured in months.

Quite apart from being cowardly, Trudeau's choice was crashingly bad political judgement. For years afterwards, Canadians refused to believe anything he said, whether about bilingualism in the air as a threat to national unity or about government spending restraints. Nor, in the immediate, did they believe any of the

---

fact hurting Canadians. In 1970-75, Canadian incomes, in real terms, increased 5 per cent a year, the fastest in the west, and twice as fast as in the U.S. Controls thus put a floor under the gains, and, more important, froze everyone in place to the benefit of the middle class which had begun to lose ground (the surplus of professors, for example) to the newly-in-demand skilled workers.

things Trudeau was beginning to say about the need for "new values," indeed, for a "New Society."

* * *

After his controls announcement, Trudeau talked to Canadians in ways that he had never tried to do before. He shared an economic vision with them. "Unless people's attitudes change, as soon as controls are lifted, inflation will shoot up again," he said in Hamilton in December, 1975. "All we are doing with controls is buying some time. We must use that time to get down to the roots of the evil . . . an attitude by which we judge people on the basis, not of what they are as people, as human beings, but of their wealth and possessions." A couple of days later, in a television interview: "If we don't use this period to change our social structure and values . . . then the same economic mainsprings will create inflation and unemployment all over again."

This vision had not sprung suddenly out of Trudeau's head, although it attracted attention only after he implemented controls. As early as January 1975, he had startled Liberals at a fund-raising dinner in Montreal by saying, "Violence is coming to our land. Not the kind of confrontation we knew in the sixties, but a more pervasive, less organized, less collective individual violence." In March, in the course of a remarkable television interview with Lord Chalfont of the BBC, he had sounded the same theme: he worried about "the ascendancy of materialism," and about the need "to husband our wealth a bit more carefully; we have to shift our values from values of acquisitiveness to values of sharing."

The point here is that when Trudeau made that comment, Tom Wolfe was still two years away from coining his Me Decade epitaph for the 1970's. Already, Trudeau had sensed the massive social change underway: private narcissism displacing a collective sense of purpose; the values of "the Thou Generation" being replaced by the new norm of self-interest. Trudeau was not only right, he meant what he said. But Canadians didn't believe him. The sad irony, the tragic core of the relationship between Trudeau and Canadians, is that they were right not to believe him.

* * *

From 1975 on, "sharing" has replaced "Reason over Passion" as Trudeau's personal slogan. He made it a key part of his speech in

April 1980, in reply to the Speech from the Throne. The trouble is, Trudeau is the apostle but not the disciple. He doesn't share much himself. He hoards his personal fortune like a miser. He is indifferent to material possessions but the ones he does care about – his clothes, for example – were no less resplendent and costly, post-1975, than before. In keeping with the Trudeau family tradition, he doesn't give Christmas presents.

Nor, in a deeper sense, has Trudeau used his political power to translate abstract ideals into practical reality. He has never supported with government funds, except marginally, the Conserver Society, the movement which comes closest to following the principles he says he favours. In 1975, to win newspaper headlines, he axed the Company of Young Canadians, which more than any other program embodied Trudeau's ideal of a New Society "where people would come together to share and help each other." In 1980, his election promise to keep on subsidizing oil prices actually gave consumers an incentive to keep on guzzling gasoline. So much for "husbanding our resources."

In his own person, Trudeau is "a taker," not "a giver." "He sucks in all the oxygen," according to his friend, quoted in Chapter 1. Margaret was another who early in their relationship spotted this characteristic. "He has a quality about him that makes you want to be as pleasing to him as possible," she wrote in *Beyond Reason*. "It is hard not to sink into sycophancy."

Sycophancy, which Trudeau was well aware he encouraged in others, is the inverse of sharing. From 1975 on, Trudeau talked more and more about sharing; at the same time, he turned his government into the most sycophantic in Canadian history. In the 1979 election, Canadians sent Trudeau the message that they were fed up by the contradiction between rhetoric and reality.

* * *

For all its botched beginnings, the controls program worked, or at any rate, it appeared to. The rate of wage increases dropped. So did inflation, down to 6.5 per cent in September 1976, at the end of the program's first year.

In fact, little of this decline had much to do with controls. Food prices by happenstance were falling. World-wide inflationary pressures were easing, thanks to a decline, in real terms, in the price of oil. At the same time, because of an increase in the value of the

Canadian dollar – by four cents, to $1.02 U.S. – the price of our imports declined.

On October 14, 1976, to mark the program's first anniversary, the CLC staged a Day of Protest. One million workers downed tools. But reporters were hard put to find any who were really angry. For one thing, wage settlements, at up to the ceiling of 10 per cent, were running higher than the current inflation rate. For another, inflation had not really been all that painful. Late in 1975, the Economic Council of Canada reported, to its own surprise, that inflation, "regardless of age or income," had produced no redistribution of income. And by 1976, Canada raised itself into the middle of the international table of working days lost through strikes.

From the autumn of 1976 onwards, the only real problem Trudeau had with his controls program was how to end it when the public supported it so strongly. Since controls were discouraging investment, his economic advisers, Macdonald prime among them, urged a quick dismantling. Trudeau's political advisers, led by Coutts, read the polls and urged him to leave them on. Eventually, Trudeau ended the program on April 14, 1978 but, as a political gesture, ordered the Economic Council to set up a powerless, watchdog agency. By then, no one cared any longer: inflation was rising again and controls, clearly, were irrelevant.*

* * *

All through the controls program, Trudeau had said, time and again, that controls would do nothing to treat the root causes of inflation, but would only provide "a breathing space" to allow government to search for the true remedy. On December 28, 1975, in a year-end interview with Bruce Phillips and Carole Taylor of CTV, Trudeau delivered his diagnosis and outlined his cure. This is the gist of what he said: "It's a different world, and you can't live in a different world with the same institutions and values that you had before. It [controls] is a massive intervention in the decision-making power of the economic groups, and it's telling Canadians that we haven't been able to make it work, the free market system. That means the government is going to take a

_____

*Just how irrelevant was demonstrated by a 1979 Conference Board in Canada Study which concluded that the 1975-78 controls program had had "only a modest overall effect on the price level in Canada."

196

larger role in running institutions . . . It means there is going to be more authority in our lives.

"I'm not as wise and experienced as Galbraith, but there's no doubt that his thinking has permeated my thought . . . If it's obvious at the end of three years that the planned sector of the economy as opposed to the market sector is going to go back to its old ways, then we'll have to keep the controls on in one way or another."

Almost the moment Trudeau had finished speaking, the country went crazy. Ted Burton, the president of the Toronto Board of Trade called him a "socialist." CLC president Joe Morris said he was an "Orwellian Big Brother." Toronto businessman Cliff Haughton put an ad in the newspapers: "Mr. Trudeau . . . you are not Emperor. We are not ants." Within a week, Haughton received 30,000 letters, all cheering him on. Liberal M.P.s were receiving more letters and phone calls about Trudeau's musings than any subject in their memory; all these calls and letters were angry. When Trudeau, by coincidence, travelled to Cuba in February, and by ill-luck delivered a speech that ended with the salutation, "Viva Castro," the business community treated it as proof positive that he wasn't just a socialist but an out-and-out Communist.

Collectively, everyone lost their heads. The CLC executive, having published a pamphlet that accused Trudeau of trying to remake Canada into a "corporate state," embraced corporatism itself, or at least, joint economic planning by government, industry, and labour, by passing a resolution at its May convention committing itself to "social corporatism." Delegates, evidently unaware what the phrase meant, approved the resolution but changed it to "social democracy." In the best tradition of creative Canadian muddle, this came to be interpreted to mean "tripartism": government, industry, and labour leaders meeting periodically to talk to each other in generalities.

Throughout 1976, ministers and officials frantically explained that Trudeau had only been tossing out ideas for public debate, not trying to sell a particular economic program to the country. Ironically, those who remained skeptical about Trudeau's actual intentions were quite right to be skeptical.

* * *

In January 1975, while vacationing in Jamaica, Trudeau had sat on a beach and had read Galbraith's new book, *Economics and the Public Purpose*, in which Galbraith advanced the thesis that inflation was a product of sweetheart deals between the big corporations and big unions of the "planning sector," and that only *permanent* controls would check the disease. Over a dinner with Turner, also on vacation, Trudeau asked his opinion about Galbraith's ideas. Turner told him he thought they were bunk.

Back in Ottawa, Trudeau soon discovered his own Galbraithian in the person of his PCO economic adviser Ian Stewart, a dedicated and brilliant idealist, moved over from Energy and before that from the Bank of Canada. Stewart believed fervently that the economic system had changed fundamentally, that "fine tuning" was out of date, and that to avert industrial decline, an entirely new economic course was imperative. Trudeau's "New Society" musings repeated almost verbatim memos that Stewart had written to him.

For a while, Trudeau tried to defend his diagnosis. In a speech on January 19, to a hastily organized dinner meeting of Ottawa's Canadian Club, he toned down his rhetoric but left everyone even more confused as to what he had really meant. In April, he said to a meeting of Liberals in Toronto: "We can't rely on the free market system any more. We need rules even if they mean that you and I end up being called Communist or Socialist."

But the pressure, political and economic, was too intense. Unemployment was rising; investment falling. In October 1976, Trudeau threw in the towel. He issued a document, *The Way Ahead*, that mouthed reassuring platitudes: "The role of government policy should not be to direct the economy in detail ... Governments can become too pervasive and oppressive actors in the daily lives of Canadians." The paper went on to describe the free market system as "the mainspring of economic activity." Thereafter, Trudeau did what everyone – the economists and his political advisers – told him to do. He restrained government spending, and when in mid-1978 expenditures kept on mounting, slashed at them on his return from the Bonn Economic Summit. Instead of trying to reorganize industry, he threw money at it: subsidies to the pulp and paper industry, handouts to automotive companies, tariff protection for manufacturers of "soft" products such as textiles, clothing, and shoes. Businessmen had not really been upset by government spending, it turned out. What had upset them was government spending public money on people instead of them.

* * *

Trudeau's failure to sell his vision of a "New Society" constitutes a tragedy in the classic Greek definition of the word. The reason for his failure is not to be found in some exterior circumstance, but within the hero himself: Trudeau's overweening pride, or *hubris*, as the Greeks would have it. Because he had failed to take Canadians into his confidence when he implemented controls, Canadians refused to place their own confidence in him.

The larger tragedy is that Trudeau missed his single chance to be truly creative in economic policy. There existed, during 1975 and 1976, a real sense of public panic. The public was in a mood to accept Draconian solutions. And Trudeau had got hold of the right solution.

In 1980, after another five years of intransigent inflation despite tight money and high interest rates and government spending cuts and this and that bit of fine tuning, it is much easier to recognize just how percipient Trudeau had been in 1975.* He himself, in the broad generalities, Stewart at the level of the particular, had anticipated Robert Heilbroner's now well-known diagnosis that inflation is systematic rather than aberrant: not an illness that can be cured but a "condition" of our system of liberal capitalism, in that the welfare state and the practice of government bail-outs for inefficient industries (Chrysler today, perhaps IBM tomorrow) make inflation endemic by ensuring that prices and incomes are never allowed to fall.

Since, in Heilbroner's analysis, the task is to change a condition rather than to cure an illness, the only solution is a fundamental change in our economic system, comparable to the change ef-

*In its 1977 report, the Economic Council of Canada pronounced the epitaph on "fine tuning." It stuffed all the economic numbers into a computer, applied variations from tight money to tax cuts to massive government spending and discovered that all its projections of economic output, unemployment, and inflation scarcely changed. "These traditional instruments don't really make a heck of a lot of difference any more," said the ECC vice-chairman, George Post.

fected in the 1930's by Roosevelt's New Deal. Specifically, Heilbroner proposes permanent wage and price controls, or an incomes policy.

This is what Trudeau had been talking about in 1975-76. But because he had destroyed his own credibility, no one would listen. To be kinder to Trudeau, maybe he had done no more than commit the cardinal political sin of being right ahead of his time. Just as Kierans had been right in April 1971, when it was Trudeau who would not listen.

The Trudeau of the Cité Libre era, in China in 1960, with Jacques Hébert. "The world is so full of a number of things; I'm sure we should all be as happy as kings."
(OXFORD UNIVERSITY PRESS)

The winner. Trudeau at the Liberal leadership convention, April 1968. "He would wave to the crowds looking endearingly bashful, an impish little-boy half grin on his face."
(TORONTO STAR)

Margaret dancing with Pierre in 1969. "A flower child, who then turned out to be almost as compleat a magician as he."
(CANADIAN PRESS)

Trudeau playing frisbee during the 1979 campaign. "The elusive jester who dared us to catch him and laughed as we tried."
(UNITED PRESS CANADA LIMITED)

Trudeau in 1972. "A rather carefully chosen flamboyance, the clothes he wears, the kind of blondes he dates."
(CANADIAN PRESS)

The pirouette at Buckingham Palace, May 1977. "Behind the mask of the statesman, Peter Pan sometimes peeps out."
(CANADIAN PRESS)

Trudeau in his 1979 campaign plane. "A flawed hero pulled down by his own hubris."
(UNITED PRESS CANADA LIMITED)

Trudeau leaves Rideau Hall after handing in his resignation as Prime Minister, June 4, 1979. "I'm beginning to feel my freedom."
(UNITED PRESS CANADA LIMITED)

Trudeau as opposition leader in 1979. "Above all there are the pale and predatory eyes that tell of skepticism, inquiry, ferocity."
(CANADIAN PRESS)

February 18, 1980. Trudeau Resurrectus. "Welcome to the '80's."
(UNITED PRESS CANADA LIMITED)

Trudeau with Quebec Liberal leader Claude Ryan during the 1980 referendum campaign. "History was on the turn."
(TORONTO STAR)

Trudeau and Lévesque meet in October 1977. "To their hostility is a quality of nobility."
(TORONTO STAR)

Trudeau with Jean Marchand, 1974. "Emotional, impulsive, generous."
(PHOTO FEATURES LIMITED)

*Gérard Pelletier, "a moral authority of the highest order, and my friend,"
Trudeau said of him.*
(TORONTO STAR)

John Turner. "Those guys just think of me as a jock with political charm."
(CANADIAN PRESS)

Marc Lalonde. "The mien of a Robespierre."
(TORONTO STAR)

Michael Pitfield. Clerk of the Privy Council. "Admired and feared in equal parts."

Eleven First Ministers, 1975. "A mysterious new form of national government." Standing (left to right): Premiers Ed Schreyer, Manitoba; Prime Minister Trudeau; Alec Campbell, Prince Edward Island; Gerald Regan, Nova Scotia; Frank Moores, Newfoundland; Federal Finance Minister, Donald

Macdonald; David Barrett, British Columbia; Richard Hatfield,
New Brunswick; Allan Blakeney, Saskatchewan; William
Davis, Ontario. Seated are Robert Bourassa, Quebec (left);
and Peter Lougheed, Alberta (right).
(CANADIAN PRESS)

Senator Keith Davey, 1973. "Gregarious, open, impossible to dislike although one of the most manipulative party pols around."
(TORONTO STAR)

Allan MacEachen. "The only way to understand him is to understand Cape Breton, that tribal, private, tightly knit kingdom peopled by cynical romantics and canny innocents."
(TORONTO STAR)

Jim Coutts. "Coutts is indispensable because his own greatest strength is Trudeau's greatest weakness: the management and the manipulation of people."
(CANADIAN PRESS)

Trudeau and Alberta Premier Peter Lougheed in 1980. "The sadness, on both sides, is that westerners and Trudeau are really each other's kind of people."
(CANADIAN PRESS)

Margaret and Pierre in 1971. "Despite everything that has happened since, both are still touched by the grace of that love."

Trudeau and unidentified partner in 1979. "A Victorian romantic about women and a compulsive flirt."
(CANADIAN PRESS)

Trudeau with Justin, Sacha, and Michel. "His relationship with his sons is one of unrestrained love, all the more unrestrained because they came late in life."
(CANADIAN PRESS)

Trudeau dances with Sheikh Yamani in Saudi Arabia, 1980. →
"Like all international stars, Trudeau takes care to keep his lustre sparkling."
(CANADIAN PRESS)

Trudeau in 1978. "He has poured his creativity into his personality."
(CANADIAN PRESS)

12

The Thorn in his Lapel

"I'm the woman who gave freedom a bad name."

Linda Griffiths
Maggie and Pierre

"Young sells better than old, pretty sells better than ugly, music sells better than television, television sells better than movies, and politics doesn't sell at all."

Richard Stolley, Managing Editor
People

Pierre Trudeau pulled off his most remarkable feat as a magician on March 4, 1971. He married a flower child, who then turned out to be almost as compleat a magician as he.

Margaret seemed to have been born knowing the tricks of an illusionist. For a while, she convinced feminists she was one of them—"Sisters, we must bury Dr. Spock and assert our rights"—and received as covenant of sisterhood an approving letter from Gloria Steinem. She cooked organic meals for cabinet ministers, carried a tub of clean water through the streets of Vancouver, interviewed Buckminster Fuller on television and thereby for a time persuaded ecologists, environmentalists, and futurologists that she, too, was a passenger on Spaceship Earth. She hitched a ride on a press bus—"I hear you have more fun back here"—and for a while seduced cynical Press Gallery hands into casting themselves as her cavaliers, defenders against stuffy Ottawa protocol, hard-eyed Mounties, and a cold-hearted, arrogant Trudeau. In an article in the *New York Times* magazine, Gerald Clark pronounced her "sacred"; *Le Devoir* praised her "*connaissance intellectuelle*."

Margaret also seemed to have the gifts of a seer. In 1974, her election prediction—141 Liberal seats—was closer to the actual result, 144, than those of Davey or Goldfarb or Coutts. Buried in the midst of the notorious interview she gave to *Playgirl* a few days after the 1979 election, between the horrific account of her abortion at seventeen, and the still more horrific act of allowing her interviewer to listen in on a private conversation with Trudeau, is this astonishing line: "My prediction is that Joe Clark's government will be defeated within six months . . . on the floor of the House of Commons."

But it was with Trudeau—either as loving partner or as bitter opponent—that Margaret truly came into her own as a magician. In 1974, she probably won him more votes than any minister or backroom adviser by softening his image to that of "a very loving guy." In 1977, by her scandalous departure, she spun round his head the halo of Model Single Parent (Male), two years before Dustin Hoffman mythologized the role in *Kramer vs. Kramer*, and added about five points to his standing in the polls.

Behind the scenes, during their courtship and early married life, Margaret wove another kind of spell. She convinced the country's best critical mind to take seriously what a close friend of Margaret's describes as "her revolution bullshit"—much more seriously than she ever thought of taking it herself. Insatiably curious intellectually, and quite without a sense of the ridiculous, Trudeau questioned her intently and intensely about troubled youth, Consciousness Three, peace, love, freedom, identity, organic baking, and everything else in the Whole Earth Catalogue. At one stage, having first convinced Hugh Faulkner, one of the few ministers who knew what mantra meant, Margaret convinced Trudeau that the entire cabinet ought to take a course in transcendental meditation. (Trudeau sounded out the notion with a couple of senior ministers, who managed to dissuade him.)

The last of Margaret's feats of magic is unmatchable. Among all the opponents who have engaged Trudeau in Single Combat, she alone has held him to a draw. Each has wounded the other grievously, but his wounds may be deeper because, after everything has been weighed and balanced, he, inescapably, is older. Margaret knows this. Not long ago, she got under his armour with a slash that was murderous because, as he told friends afterwards, there was simply nothing he could say in reply. "I'll win in the end," Margaret told him, "because I'm going to live longer. When the boys are grown up, I'll still be around."

* * *

Magicianship apart, the truth about Trudeau and Margaret is elusive. The Harlequin formula – beautiful innocent girl meets powerful, mysterious older man – will take you part of the way. Anna Karenina, the heroine with whom Margaret most likes to identify – "not running away with Vronsky so much as the way she feels so horribly stifled at the beginning" – will take you another few steps. There are elements of Daisy and Gatsby in their relationship, of Heathcliff and Cathy, of Professor Higgins and Eliza. In the end, though, nothing from fiction applies. Margaret and Trudeau have created their own reality, their own legend; the kind of legend – love and pain and the whole damn thing – that when everything else about the Trudeau era has been reduced to a dusty file in the archives (or to a seldom-pushed button in an information retrieval system) will still be part of Canadian folklore.* For surely the most extraordinary part of the saga is that it should have happened in so bland a country as Canada.

On reflection, it perhaps helps to cast Margaret as the first genuinely erotic Canadian heroine, the answer to the gap in our literature that Margaret Atwood has defined as "the absent Venus," the first flamboyantly sexual, fecund woman among all our repressed Hagar Shipleys.

It also helps to recall a couple of real-life precedents. One is Lady Caroline Lamb, in London in the early nineteenth century, leaving the future Prime Minister Lord Melbourne for Lord Byron, "mad, bad, and dangerous to know," and sending Byron, when his interest was flagging, a package of her pubic hairs. The other, closer to our own time, is Zelda Fitzgerald jumping into the fountain in front of the Plaza Hotel, trying desperately to find her own identity as a writer. Zelda was mad of course, while Margaret, even at her most outrageous, was only wilfully careless. The part of the comparison that obtains is that Zelda, brilliantly talented as Margaret is not, competed with Scott Fitzgerald, just as Margaret competed with Pierre for the attention of the crowds.**

"She's headstrong," Margaret's father, James Sinclair, warned

---

*The prototype is *Maggie and Pierre*, Linda Griffiths's hit of the 1980 season.

**Like Margaret, both Caroline Lamb and Zelda Fitzgerald wrote books about their marriages and subsequent affairs. Zelda's *Save Me the Waltz* and Lady Caroline's *Glenarvon* are thinly veiled fiction. In keeping with the style of her period, Margaret's *Beyond Reason* is confessional autobiography.

Trudeau before they were married. Trudeau, at fifty-one, paid no more attention than most bridegrooms do. Even if he had listened, Trudeau would have found it hard to understand anything either about Margaret or about the nature of women in general.

* * *

Trudeau sees womanhood through the prism of his mother, Grace Elliott, who "never imposed her will on us"; she who was so refined, so delicate, so lively, so feminine. Once, when an interviewer asked Trudeau the quality he looked for most in a woman, he gave the ambiguous reply: "Grace."

Trudeau makes just one demand of women: that they make no demands upon him. Therefore they must be young, and the fact that he is now over sixty makes no difference. "Thank God she's twenty-two," Marchand remarked to a colleague when informed of Trudeau's marriage. They must also be beautiful, it goes without saying, and be successful, because beautiful, successful women do not need to search for emotional sustenance from a man. "He has absolutely no capacity for intimacy," says a friend. "He can be a wonderful conversationalist about abstract topics, but anything intimate is taboo."

If there are historical precedents for Margaret that fit imperfectly, one precedent for Trudeau fits him like a glove. As remarked earlier, the figure he resembles in many ways is the turn-of-the-century Viceroy of India, later Foreign Secretary, Lord Curzon. Of Curzon, one of his mistresses, the novelist Elinor Glyn,* wrote:

> He has always been loved by women, but he has never allowed any individual woman to have the slightest influence on his life ... He likes their society for entirely leisurely moments. He likes them rather in the spirit in which other men like fine horses or good wine, or beautiful things to embellish a man's leisure, but not as equal souls worthy of being seriously considered or trusted with that scrupulous sense of honour with

*Glyn, like Margaret, made it to celebrity status. As the popular jingle went:
"Would you like to sin
With Elinor Glyn on a tiger skin?
Or would you prefer
To err with her
Upon some other fur?"

which he would deal with a man. They are on another planet altogether. He must be free and unhampered.

Glyn went on:

He never gives a woman a single command and yet each must be perfectly conscious that she must obey his slightest indication. He rules entirely, and when a woman belongs to him, he seems to prefer to give her even the raiment which touches her skin, and in every way shows absolute possession, while in words avoiding all suggestion of ownership, of all ties and all obligations. It is extremely curious.

Like Curzon, like Trudeau, except that Curzon appears to have parted with his money more easily.

Trudeau "is incapable of a relationship with a mature woman," in the words of a close friend. Beyond their first youth, women might make demands, or might refuse to "sink into sycophancy" as Margaret wrote that she had to struggle against doing. Not to mention the fact that by the time he decided he wanted children, a mature woman might not have been able to give them to him. So he discarded his constant companion and quasi-official hostess of the 1960's, the university professor Madeleine Gobeil. Lacking the courage to tell her himself, he asked Pelletier to let her know that he was flying to Vancouver to marry Margaret.

For a time during their courtship, Margaret worried about another mature woman, Barbra Streisand, whom Trudeau saw occasionally in New York, and who flew up to Ottawa for a week-end in the winter of 1970. She needn't have. Trudeau was delighted to be photographed on Streisand's arm but found her conversationally a bit of a bore. Streisand was into colour psychology, and kept on telling Trudeau that he had a blue aura, or a red one. (Another problem: Streisand's sister came along as chaperone.)

Before marrying Margaret, Trudeau had seriously contemplated marriage only twice. In his twenties, he was actually briefly engaged to a brainy contemporary. Her first name was Thérèse, and she is now a university professor in Montreal. She broke off the engagement. The problem, Trudeau explained to friends, was that she was worried about him constantly dashing off around the world. She told friends that she reckoned he would be impossible to live with and recounted how, at a tea party at 84 McCulloch, when she reached out for a slice of cake, he had said, in a loud voice: "If I had hips like yours I wouldn't eat cake."*

Not long afterwards, when working in Ottawa at the Privy Council Office, he fell deeply in love with the daughter of a Swedish diplomat. She eventually returned home. Otherwise, but for Margaret, and for one other attachment to a woman slightly younger than he, talented and attractive, who married someone else and who now lives in Ottawa, Trudeau's relationships with women have been non-committal. He adores having them around, but misses no woman in particular when she's no longer around. His allure for women – "the elusive jester who dared us to catch him and laughed as we tried" as Carole Treiser wrote in the *Sherbrooke Record* – has existed all his life and is undimmed by age. The hint of the *farouche* Peter Pan. The hint of cruelty. The hint of ambivalence. Beyond all of this, a quality Trudeau possessed even before he became Prime Minister, the aphrodisiac aura of a powerful man.

To say that Trudeau is a male chauvinist is to utter a cliché. At heart, he is a Victorian romantic about women and a compulsive flirt. Within five minutes of arriving at a party, Trudeau seeks out the prettiest girl in the room and stays with her for the rest of the party. Aboard planes, he chats up the prettiest stewardesses. And so on and so on, wherever the women are pretty and young. "It is in his nature to be charming and complimentary to women," Margaret wrote of their first date, "and away from that sort of old-fashioned gallantry for so long, I had quite forgotten how beguiling it is."

Beyond these limits, which he defines and controls, Trudeau goes no further in his relationships with women. Any further and he might become somehow in their debt and thus lose some portion of his freedom, including his freedom to find the next woman to flirt with.

* * *

From Margaret, Trudeau learned more about women than he had ever learned before. He tried to understand her, and in a couple of remarkably candid interviews tried, with his unvarying scrupulous honesty to convey what it was that he had learned. "Marriage can

*Trudeau never told Margaret of this engagement. She learned about it only in 1980, from an acquaintance.

206

be a regressive institution," he said in a BBC interview in March 1975, not long after Margaret's breakdown. "You are young, you're free, you've at least got rid of parental authority. Suddenly you get married, and authority is here again ... So it can be a regressive institution, and for all married couples it can be a traumatic experience. I think husbands, particularly when they are as busy as I was, are not as sensitive as they should be." In October 1976, six months before they separated, he told a Radio-Canada interviewer: "It was a good thing I did not marry sooner because I was very domineering and I doubtless would have wished to remake my wife – in my image – that is to say, destroy her personality. And it was only when I was able to accept that another person could be very different from myself, and that in spite of this I could love her, that I could make the gamble of getting married. But back to the point of view. Perhaps because of our institutions, society, the woman always remains a bit subjugated by marriage ... I think that women now are beginning to leave this confinement, but it takes a great deal of maturity on their part – and on that of the man."

Though Trudeau could intellectualize about his marriage, he could not – even this close to the breakup – act to save it. Even now, it is hard to find anyone who knew them together who blames Margaret for leaving him, as opposed to criticizing her, harshly, for what she did afterwards. "He was unreal, quite unreal. The only thing that surprises me is that she didn't go sooner," says a woman who is fond of Trudeau and in most respects censorious toward Margaret. "When things were falling apart, he would talk at length about his marital problems," another woman adds. "But he never talked about Margaret, as a person. He would talk about himself, or, more often, about women as an abstraction, about women's liberation and women's identity." Trying to find out what was going on in women's heads, Trudeau, on holiday in early 1975, shortly after Margaret's breakdown, read his first piece of contemporary fiction in decades: Erica Jong's *Fear of Flying*.

In hindsight, it is clear: Their marriage could not be saved. The two were incompatible; the incompatibility in their ages being the very least of it. He was solitary, and remains so. He is also self-contained, self-motivated, self-regarding, so self-disciplined that he never wastes a moment at work, nor a single paddle stroke when canoeing. He is also entirely predictable: a man who swims precisely forty-four laps a day, who once fired a maid who kept on disarranging his pristine array of toothbrush, toothpaste, and shaving gear. Margaret is impulsive, emotional, generous, spoiled, truculent, scatter-brained, and flighty. In common, they have just one single quality: both are quite extraordinarily self-centred; he an egotist, and she a narcissist.

Margaret, though, is by nature more a giver than a taker. He, with everyone but his sons, is overwhelmingly a taker. Perhaps Margaret came closest to understanding why it could never have worked when she remarked. "He never was my *friend*." In the summer of 1974, when she flew off to Paris alone, she told him in advance, hoping he would tell her not to go. He told her, instead, to do whatever she felt was right. Time and again, Margaret flailed around in search of herself, frantically trying to get him to tell her what to do and how to behave. He never did. He never gave her of himself because as she guesses now, and surely guesses right, if he had ever given her advice or instructions, he would have made himself responsible for her. For Trudeau, freedom in the end means being responsible to and for himself, and no one else.

Nor, in retrospect, was Trudeau ever really Margaret's husband. Instead, he was her Pygmalion and she his Galatea. Or, in the modern translation, he was Henry Higgins and she Eliza Doolittle. "He was going to fill her up with himself," says a close friend. Except that Trudeau, like Higgins, did not want to "let a woman in his life." She would have to learn to be like him—disciplined, rational, intellectual—by osmosis. Once again like Higgins, Trudeau had no idea that inside every flower child, there is a woman.

* * *

The first thing to understand about Margaret is that she has no fear of flying. With anyone, in any way, at any time.

Much of her mystique, it is true, is the sheer power of beauty; beauty, like an erotic equivalent to the Peter Principle, has pulled her far beyond her level of competence. But it is *not* true, as has often been suggested, that if she had not met Trudeau in Tahiti at New Year's 1968 she would have acted out a standard late-1960's scenario: middle-class girl does her love/peace/freedom/identity/revolution/organic baking number and then settles down with a stockbroker and an "interesting" little job. Even among the soul-

208

sister revolutionaries of the 1960's, an abortion at seventeen, five hours spent up a tree on a mescaline trip imagining she was a bird, six months spent with drug-drenched hippies in Morocco, suggested someone who could cut a wider swath through life.

Margaret's style amounts to a sort of insolence toward life. "She's a bandit, a wholly delightful bandit," says a close friend. "Brave, bold, funny, bright, provocative." Then the friend sketches in the other side. "She is ruthless, competitive and narcissistic. Switch the conversation away from her, and you can watch her eyes glaze over."

Margaret's ruthless/competitive streak is a legacy from her father, a Liberal cabinet minister of the St. Laurent era, who later became a successful businessman. That she dislikes him intensely is evident between the lines of *Beyond Reason*. "The dour outlook of a Presbyterian Scot . . . Five girls and a domineering father; it made for competition." Given this clue, it's easy to speculate that she has spent much of her life rebelling against her father, and against father substitutes. As another friend remarks, "Something inside her forces her to hurt strong men she is attracted to."

Intellectually, putting it politely, Margaret is unremarkable. She lives a good deal of the time in a fantasy world. Her attention span, except on the subject of herself, has been compared to that of a humming-bird. Her tastes run to "All My Children" on afternoon television and the gothic horror novels of Stephen King. Yet when it comes to observing human nature she can be unexpectedly shrewd. "They are living out their sex fantasies through me," she has said of the group of Volvo-driving, Montessori matrons who kept on being her friends in Ottawa while she committed every transgression in the book. In *Beyond Reason*, she evokes marvellously the manipulative character of life in the court of a Sun King. Of courtier Ivan Head, for instance, during the 1974 campaign: "He did his best to ease me out, creating an indefinable but unmistakable aura that I was totally redundant to the trip. He was always smiling, always whispering something in Pierre's ear, and I felt moments of pure childish jealousy." Trudeau himself, in a 1976 television interview, described Margaret well: "At bottom, she is a very earthy woman. A sensual woman with both feet on the ground. A woman who wants to be a mother, a woman who also loves cooking, domestic things, and yet at the same time can go off into the clouds."

209

Her real qualities are in her guts, not her head. She hurled herself, headlong, into the life that Trudeau studied so circumspectly. Even in the appalling *Playgirl* interview, there are comments that stand out like tattered, defiant banners: "Life isn't easy. It's easy if you don't care. If you don't take risks. If you put blinders on. If you suffocate yourself in your own boredom. Otherwise, it ain't easy." And this comment about her hopes for a daughter, if she had one. "She *will* get hurt. Everyone does. But to be hurt by *love*. Not just by being fucked around."

Margaret can be calculating. She knows how to manipulate the media. "She thinks in terms of camera angles," says a friend. Certainly, in person, she is a knowing and adroit actress. Yet she also has a quality of almost childlike innocence, a total lack of guile. "You meet her with your back up, knowing she's done all these terrible things," says a new-found friend. "And what you quickly discover is that there's no way you can possibly dislike her. She's like a being from another planet." Margaret has put it best herself. "I got into trouble at the start of this campaign for talking about love," she said at the close of the 1974 campaign, "and many people took it the wrong way. But that's all I *can* talk about."

* * *

Theirs was an extraordinary love, a high romance and a grand passion. She so young and so beautiful. "She's incredible, isn't she," Trudeau kept telling friends. "Her eyes are so extraordinary, aren't they," he kept insisting. And she *was* incredible, like Elizabeth Taylor around the time she was doing *Giant*, brimming over with the same bravura sexual energy, and with Taylor's huge, seductive lavender eyes.

Soon, so very soon, so much went wrong. Indeed, except for Justin and Sasha and Michel, just about everything went wrong. But for a few golden seasons, Margaret and Pierre were wholly and rapturously in love. She so generous and passionate. He so bold and powerful. He, an emotional neophyte at fifty, unbuckling his armour to her spontaneity and innocence and youth; she exalted and awed by his brilliance, his integrity, his discipline.

Despite everything that has happened since, both are touched still by the grace of that love. "It's unbelievable, but she still has a certain spell over him," says a close friend. "Try to imagine the humiliation of so proud a man to find, after all the terrible things she has done to him, that he still feels for her." Early in 1980, they dined together at 24 Sussex: one of the party watched fascinated as they flirted with each other across the table. Then Trudeau stood in the doorway of 24 Sussex, watching Margaret drive out of sight. She came home from the dinner party with her eyes shining, until another friend reminded her: "When he's good, he's very very good, and when he's bad, he's horrid," and Margaret sadly agreed. Since their separation, Trudeau has been seen with many women but none has mattered to him; after Trudeau, Margaret has matched the many men she has met against him, and found them all one-dimensional.

* * *

The story of their marriage and its ending has been told many times. Only a few lines between the dots need filling in. Their romance began to fade almost from the day they came back to 24 Sussex after a four-day skiing honeymoon. Tenderly, without realizing he was doing it, Trudeau set her inside a bell jar and cut her off from life. Then he set out "to fill her up with himself." A few days after their return he said to her, "I've spent a lot of time courting you and now I must give time to being Prime Minister." "You must do anything you want to do," he added. "You can do anything you want to do."

The trouble was, she could do hardly anything she wanted to do. She was in purdah. Trudeau, she came gradually to recognize, was a true solitary, complete unto himself. He left no spaces within himself for her to fill, except with sons. He hardly ever asked anyone to the house. They went almost nowhere except alone together, for hikes and canoe trips, or to the Harrington Lake retreat. Each night he came home, plunged into the pool for forty-four laps, changed into jeans and sweatshirt, dined alone with her, and then retreated into his "damned brown boxes." As early as the autumn of 1972, married less than two years, she wrote a note to herself and stuffed it into the back of a drawer, to find it nearly five years later, when she was packing up to leave. "I am so lonely. I should be happy. I am married to a man who loves me, and I have a wonderful baby. But I am terribly unhappy."

Stuffy Ottawa protocol did not help. Nor did Trudeau's own idea of wifely protocol. When Margaret proposed re-enrolling in a child psychology course at Ottawa University that she had started before

211

their marriage, Trudeau demurred: only bored wives filled their time going back to college. When a girlfriend invited Margaret to go down to Montreal for a day of shopping, he demurred again: wives should be home when their husbands got back from the office. But the real problem ran much deeper. Trudeau was self-motivated. He knew how to use his freedom creatively, down to the last second. That Margaret needed outside stimuli baffled him totally. When she complained she had nothing to do, he told her "read Plato," and was exasperated when she did not. When francophone friends came for dinner, he talked only in French, often to their acute embarrassment, knowing she understood scarcely a word. He took for granted she would apply herself to learning French. At their first post-marriage public appearance, at a sugaring-off party near Montreal, Margaret created a scene by complaining that someone in the crowd had pinched her bum; quite simply, she was terrified by understanding nothing of what was being said around her, of being there as the Prime Minister's consort but left on her own while he wandered off to do what interested him.

During the 1974 election, Margaret broke out of the bell jar on her own. Trudeau and his advisers opposed her solo appearances. But instantly, she became a star, a magician in her own right. She assumed that in Trudeau's eyes she had become her own person. Instead, she was bounced back to being wife-and-mother. The election over, no one bothered to congratulate her, or suggested how she might apply her new status in practical ways. "Something inside me broke," she has written. "I felt I had been used."

Once out of the bell jar, there was no going back. She dashed off alone to Paris, without her passport, and disappeared for a couple of weeks. Then she turned up at the Royal Victoria Hospital in Montreal, being treated for what were described later as "emotional problems." She talked about her troubles on television: "I'm a pretty private person." She went to Japan, on a $20,000 junket, to launch a supertanker, and got criticized. She next tried to become a photo-journalist, and botched it. She told the wives of Commonwealth Prime Ministers to bury Dr. Spock, then retired from the public eye to have a third son, Michel, in October 1975. Four months later, she re-emerged in Latin America, singing a serenade to the wife of the President of Venezuela at a state banquet, and wearing a Liberal T-shirt in Cuba. Later, she wore the wrong kind of dress to the White House.

Then in March 1977 came the ultimate freedom trip. Not by coincidence, she spent her sixth wedding anniversary in Toronto at a Rolling Stones' concert, to be spotted wandering the corridors of their hotel in a white bathrobe. From there to New York, where *People* published the famous interview (given in exchange for a photo assignment) in praise of Trudeau's body – "It's like that of a twenty-five year old" – and in praise of garterbelts as a "turn-on." She also discussed the effect of her nipples, as outlined through her dress, upon state visitors. When she came home to 24 Sussex, where Trudeau was entertaining James Callaghan, the British Prime Minister, Trudeau may or may not have punched her in the eye.

* * *

Trudeau, during, after, and through all the months leading up to that cataclysm, gave the nation and indeed the world, a demonstration of superhuman grace under inhuman pressure of a kind almost no one else could have brought off. He never once complained. He never once explained. He defended Margaret on every occasion. "I do not indulge in guilt by association," he said in reply to a question about Margaret's relationship to the Stones. When a reporter pushed too hard, he batted him down. "A gentleman would not ask such questions" and then took away the sting by quipping that Margaret in fact preferred the Beatles as musicians, "though I hope she doesn't start seeing the Beatles."

In hindsight, cabinet ministers and aides, looking back over the two years of unceasing tension that led up to the break, cannot recall his ever showing any sign of it at work, except for occasionally looking tired because Margaret had insisted he stay up with her to watch late movies on television. It was only right at the end, after Margaret had made him look like a cuckold in public, that the nerve ends began to show. "You could see it in his eyes," says a former aide, "a look of bewilderment. For the first time in his life something was happening that was affecting him directly and personally, and there was absolutely nothing he could do about it." Yet before 1977 was out, the aide continues, Trudeau was back in control. He'd found, somehow, an emotional compartment in which to stuff the pain. "Suddenly something must have gone click in his mind, and he bounced back." Alone, he poured out his love to his sons, and found solace in them.

On May 27, 1977, the Prime Minister's Office issued the following brief statement, that the two had composed together:

Pierre and Margaret Trudeau announce that because of Margaret's wishes, they shall begin living separate and apart. Margaret relinquishes all privileges as the wife of the Prime Minister and wishes to leave the marriage to pursue an independent career.

Pierre will have custody of their three sons, giving Margaret generous access to them. Pierre accepts Margaret's decision with regret and both pray that their separation will lead to a better relationship between themselves.

* * *

The tragedy of Margaret's "ultimate freedom trip" to Toronto and the Stones, and from there to New York and Andy Warhol and Studio 54, was that she never wanted to make it. She had wanted a friend. Instead, she found a cold, implacable stranger and she fought him ruthlessly. Once, "shaking with rage at my inability to counter his logical reasoned arguments," she tore the hand-stitched letters off his Reason over Passion quilt, and flung them in his face. The Stones and Studio 54 were only manifestations of the same kind of rage, happening out in the open.

As for incessant speculation about darker motivations for Margaret's behaviour, these can be laid to rest. None of the rumours of wild intra-marital goings on that first began to circulate in Toronto early in 1977 had the least iota of substance. Nor, back in 1974, was Margaret's much-touted romance with Teddy Kennedy the real reason for the beginning of the end of their marriage. Although at the time Margaret burbled to friends about Kennedy's "aura," she later came to regard him as a bit of a schmuck. Margaret in fact fell in love with a Canadian because he was all the things Trudeau was not: generous, funny, above all, a *friend*. Though their relationship is long since over, they remain friends.

For two years after the breakup, from May 1977 to the election of May 1979, Margaret's behaviour was unremittingly awful. She abandoned her children. She made a couple of bad movies, told the world, again through *People*, "my best feature is my bum," and got herself photographed, pantyless, by *Rustler*. In 1979, she made *Esquire*'s list of Dubious Achievement Awards twice—a feat usually accomplished only by Richard Nixon. In the middle of the

1979 election, she published *Beyond Reason*. On the night Trudeau was defeated, she was photographed kicking up her heels in disco pants at Studio 54. A few days later, she gave the interview to *Playgirl*. Rage, despair, humiliation, and, in her own words, "a regression to teenage rebellion" were the reason for most of the carry-on, along with, as she does not deny, drugs and sex. Trudeau as victim was replaced by her sons. Classmates, with the cruelty of boyhood, teased them about their mother's doings.

The *Playgirl* interview, coupled with Trudeau's defeat which devalued her own status as a celebrity, changed all that. Margaret came back to Ottawa, bought a pretty nineteenth century townhouse in New Edinburgh, and in most respects except for loneliness began to live much the same kind of life as all her Volvo-driving Montessori matron friends, putting in tulip bulbs, going to exercise classes, whizzing around in a Rabbit. At thirty-two, a bit chubbier, attractive now rather than stunningly beautiful, she looks back on everything she did with considerable remorse, most particularly about the *Playgirl* interview which she has never been able to bring herself to read. The remorse, though, is mingled with a certain pride for having stood up to Trudeau. Once she told him she would become famous by "defying" him, which he did not at all like, since it meant she'd hold him at least to a draw. At times her recollections sparkle with a bittersweet humour: the distinguished Canadian psychiatrist, for instance, who after asking about her mother and father and all the rest of it, finally got to the point: "Who do you think is going to succeed Trudeau – Turner or Macdonald?" He was one of the hundreds who used Margaret and exploited her, as she used and exploited them.

Within or between the lines, much of Margaret is contained in her autobiography, *Beyond Reason*. (In fact, the British journalist Caroline Moorehead actually wrote *Beyond Reason* while Margaret poured out her story in a suite at the Savoy.) The book infuriated Trudeau and provoked him into calling the May 1979 election a couple of months earlier than his advisers had wanted, mostly, as one of them put it, "to show Margaret." Except in summary, Trudeau has never read it. He ought to. In its entirety, it is far more perceptive about him, far more tender toward him, than anyone who has read only the newspaper excerpts would realize. "He is one of the gentlest of men and a very loving father," Margaret wrote. "But he is painfully shy, a genuinely private person who is

215

quite incapable of expressing his feelings."

What Trudeau did read, however, at the insistence of his sister, Suzette, was the *Playgirl* interview. "That finished her for him," says a friend. "She became a non-person. He stopped trusting her."

Yet paradoxically, their relationship from then on began to find a new and much more adult footing. When Trudeau taxed her with the *Playgirl* article, Margaret admitted, "I'm sick. I know now there are situations in which I just cannot control myself." At last Trudeau acknowledged her illness. For him, healthy as a horse, illness had always been a synonym for weakness. Once, after a tonsillectomy, he allowed Margaret to hemorrhage almost to death because he was sure she was exaggerating and refused to bother a doctor on a week-end until it was almost too late. Another time, when she claimed to be ill, he told her: "You're not sick. You're just covering up for your sins." In turn, Margaret did what none of the psychiatrists had been able to do for her; she began to put herself back together, by herself. She gave up drugs. She went on a treatment of lithium, which made her put on weight and kept her soporific, and which she gave up because she realized she no longer needed it.

There was also, as a force in favour of harmony, the fact that for both Trudeau and Margaret, 1979 had been a bad year. The *Playgirl* interview had coincided with his defeat. She had come down from her crystal chandeliers to find herself back in Ottawa, lonely, with the few men around afraid of her. Soon after, her publisher, Paddington Press, went bankrupt, owing her $500,000 in royalties. As for Trudeau, cut off as Opposition Leader from the escapist workload of being Prime Minister, he slumped into an aimless depression and perhaps realized for the first time how it felt to be bored. So they edged back toward each other, just a little way; not enough for Trudeau to trust her enough to tell her in advance that he intended to resign, or a month later, that he intended to come back.

During the 1980 election, she kept her profile lower than low. Once he moved back into 24 Sussex, Trudeau agreed to new joint custody arrangements: Justin, Sasha, and Michel now spend alternate weeks with each parent, their two houses only a few blocks apart.

The Single Combat between Trudeau and Margaret is over.

What remains are the scars and a contest that has settled into the more-or-less routine pattern for separated parents: rivalry for the affection of the children. Of their characters, Margaret has written: "Justin is the most like Pierre. He sees no shades of gray, only black or white. Sasha is the most knowing. Michel is a clown who fights for his life." Regarding the future of their sons, Margaret has won one decisive battle: They will not be educated by Jesuits.

* * *

Whenever they appear together, at events like Justin's First Communion, or when word appears in a gossip column that Margaret has been a guest at a 24 Sussex party, sentimentalists speculate about a possible reconciliation between Trudeau and Margaret. This will never happen. Trudeau has had a succession of dates, all beautiful, most of them young, most of them blonde. Margaret and an Ottawa lawyer have developed a permanent relationship. Only the children, and a few mutual friends, bring her and Trudeau together.

Yet the memory of Margaret and Trudeau as lovers will persist. They were not Lancelot and Guinevere, nor Heloise and Abelard, nor even Scott and Zelda, for their battle lacked the nobility of tragedy. Each, ultimately, was too self-centred to be a tragic hero. Each, moreover, for all the hurt their encounter caused, gained from it the different kinds of immortality they had been looking for: he, children; she, fame.

Yet Lancelot and Guinevere, Heloise and Abelard, even Scott and Zelda all belong to other times. The temper of the 1970's, the times on which Trudeau and Margaret have left their signatures, was closer to psychodrama than tragedy. In the 1970's, as *People* editor Stolley put it, young did sell better than old, and pretty better than ugly, and television better than the movies while politics did not sell at all.

Perhaps Margaret's most considerable, though least-intended, gift to Trudeau was to make him part of his times—not part of the heady, countercultural 1960's as he had expected when he married her, but part of the self-centred, psychodramatic 1970's. By leaving him, in the way of so many other wives and mistresses and living-together-relationships, for the sake of an independent identity and independent sex, and thus by elevating Trudeau to the modern sainthood of Single Parenthood, Margaret transformed him from hero to human being. After 1977, millions of Canadians could identify with Trudeau in a way they never had before: they had been through in their own lives, if less dramatically, what he'd been going through.

In a word, Margaret made Trudeau interesting. But for her, his story would be that of a rather dry old stick, with a computer for a brain and an accidental gift of charisma. Among the reasons Canadians re-elected Trudeau in 1980, the heavy stuff about issues aside, was that he was, well, *interesting*. Margaret could be counted on to do something notorious as Maureen McTeer, for all her bouncy worthiness, could not; Trudeau could be counted on to be photographed with a stunning blonde on his arm, as would never happen to Joe Clark.

In *Wuthering Heights*, that most resonant of all love stories, Cathy shouts with proud defiance, "I *am* Heathcliff." Margaret, in the end, has as much right to shout, "I *am* Pierre Trudeau." It is, as Elinor Glyn remarked, "extremely curious." But so is life.

13

Frog in the Throat

"I speak, therefore I am."

Albert Sorel

In 1976, for nine days in June, there were no jet trails in Canadian skies. While the 2,200 air traffic controllers and 2,700 pilots stayed off work, even the foreign airlines like BOAC, Lufthansa, Eastern, cancelled their flights. The nation spun into suspended animation. On June 23, Trudeau went on national television to appeal for an end to the strike. Nothing happened. Two days later, in the Commons, he described the strike as "the worst crisis to national unity since the Conscription Crisis (of World War One)." Nothing happened.

Instead people were buying freshly printed T-shirts from private flying clubs, or under the counter, from airline ticket offices. One said, "General Wolfe, where are you now that we need you?" Another, morbidly repulsive, showed a beaver strangling a frog. Western radio stations played an editorial that began, "Quebec, go suck a lemon" and ended, "I want a divorce. No fault. No contest." One day in the midst of the strike, Pierre Deniger, an aide to Otto Lang, the minister responsible, found a mock press release on his desk that reported a collision between two planes, caused because one pilot had spoken to the control tower in French; among the names listed as "victims" of the crash was Deniger's own.

All this came about because Trudeau, on October 17, 1968, had introduced in the Commons a piece of legislation that he described as "a conscious choice we are making about the future of Canada." Its official title was, *An Act Respecting the Official Languages of Canada*. Eight years later, by their massive support for controllers and pilots, English Canadians told Trudeau they had rejected his choice. Five months later, Quebecers elected the Parti Québécois.

Trudeau's dream, his impossible dream, of transforming a very ordinary, sub-arctic country into "a brilliant prototype for the moulding of tomorrow's civilization," as he once described it in *Cité Libre*, had turned into a nightmare.

Except that Trudeau's dream had not died. Spurred by guilt at what they had done, English Canadians, after 1976, accepted bilingualism even if they did not embrace it. Nor did Quebecers ever reject Trudeau's bilingual vision (despite the unilingualism of the PQ's Bill 101). Through bilingualism, Trudeau was able to keep alive "The Canadian option within Quebec" in the phrase of one of his ministers, Hugh Faulkner. Within Canada, he has kept alive the option of being able to speak French. In other words, he kept Canada going.

* * *

Bilingualism is the "Calais" written on Trudeau's heart. This is the passion behind his reason: the man inside the mask. When Trudeau talks and writes about bilingualism, all his inhibitions, all his defences, drop away. Sometimes he is eloquent: "Canadians are looking down at the world from a Franco-English balcony, the most favoured one there is." Sometimes he is angry: "A sin against humanity" is the way he described Quebec's possible separation; he has described Bill 101 as "A going back to the Dark Ages." Sometimes he is anguished: "The national will to exist as a country is not very strong anymore," he said six weeks after the PQ victory, in an interview with CTV.

In his implementation of bilingualism, Trudeau has made many mistakes. All of these, and some have been horrendous ones, have been mistakes of the heart. He has never made the only mistake that really matters: he has never lost faith. Nor has he ever foreshortened his vision. Bilingualism is to Trudeau as the CPR was to John A. Macdonald, his instrument for building a continent-wide country out of a huddled group of provinces.

* * *

In the beginning, Trudeau's ideal of bilingualism was quite different from the political defining principle that it became during his four terms in office. In the early 1960's, when he first wrote about the subject, his chief concern was neither to save Canada nor to affirm the French Fact, but to liberate man. Bilingualism, as he saw it, was a basic human right, no different in kind from other human rights like freedom of speech, and serving the same purpose – to free individuals to pursue excellence privately. For Trudeau, "pluralistic federalism" was simply a logical consequence of applying rationalism to government.

In his 1962 essay "The New Treason of the Intellectuals" Trudeau approvingly quotes Ernest Renan's aphorism: "Man is bound neither to his language nor to his race: he is bound only to himself, because he is a free agent, or in other words a moral being." In his 1965 essay "Quebec and the Constitutional Problem" he warned: "Excessive preoccupation with the language has made certain people forget the future of the man speaking it ... French will have value only to the extent it is spoken by progressive people."

Although he argued forcefully for linguistic equality in those days, he did so in an antiseptic way: "in terms of *realpolitik*, French and English are equal in Canada because each of these linguistic groups has the power to break up the country." Further, "historical origins" were not that important; indeed, if there were six million Ukrainians in the country, "it is likely this language would establish itself as forcefully as French." Here, Trudeau created for himself some of his future political difficulties: if equality was due French Canadians not as a right of a founding people, but only as a privilege courtesy of their numbers, then this privilege could be withdrawn if their numbers dwindled through assimilation. In Quebec, some saw Trudeau's analysis as a threat; elsewhere in the country, other minorities saw it as an opportunity.

Trudeau's ideas evolved in power. He came to comprehend that man indeed is bound, irrevocably, to his language and to his race. "Language is related to man's life in society as breathing is related to life itself ... Man is, without the means of communication, alone in this world," read his official declaration of language policy, *A National Understanding*, of June 1977.

And yet in one crucial respect, Trudeau's ideas about bilingualism have never changed. Always, he has conceived freedom of language choice as a fundamental human right. This was the reason for his outrage – advisers wished he had been more moderate – at Bill 101. This was the reason why, as many ministers recall, "bilingualism, and the mistakes we were making in implementing it, could never be broached in cabinet." For Trudeau, doubts about bilingualism policy were not so much evidence of disloyalty, as Lalonde, for instance, saw them, but as *heresies*. He would no more countenance a compromise on bilingualism for the sake of political advantage than he would have countenanced a compromise on freedom of religion or freedom of speech.

In one other respect, this one practical, Trudeau's ideas have not changed. In 1962, in one of his most frequently quoted passages, he wrote that but for Laurier, not one French-Canadian at Ottawa since Confederation, "might be considered indispensable to the history of Canada as written." Three years later, he and Marchand and Pelletier came to Ottawa to re-write history, and two years after that he became Liberal leader, for the same reason.

In power, he put his idea into practice from the start. He paid a political price. "French Power," in the phrase popularized by the columnist Charles Lynch, became an issue in the 1972 election. But he earned his reward: late in 1976, after the PQ victory, he was able to say: "The Prime Minister is French, as is the Governor General, and the Commissioner of the RCMP, and the Chief of the Defence Staff, and the head of the National Film Board." Nothing was more disconcerting to Péquistes than to find that each time they argued that there was no place for *Québécois* in Canada, they encountered a Trudeau, a Lalonde, a Chrétien, a Pépin, a Bégin, a DeBané, arguing back.

* * *

The puzzle of Trudeau's bilingualism policy is, how could something so necessary and so reasonable have caused so much trouble? The legislation itself, approved at last by Parliament on July 7, 1969 (seventeen Conservatives voted against it, on second reading) did no more than enact the main recommendations of the Report of the Royal Commission on Bilingualism and Biculturalism, though by no means all of them, and gave statutory force to a number of regulations relating to the civil service that Pearson had enacted in 1966. In effect, it amounted to "institutional bilingualism." All citizens would have the right to communicate with the federal government in the language of their choice, and all federal civil servants could work in the language of their choice. Ottawa would fund some of the cultural activities of minorities, and fund some second-language education for those minorities. Some areas across the country would be designated as "bilingual districts" and federal services there would be provided in both languages to accommodate a linguistic minority of at least 10 per cent.* But only within the federal government would English and French "possess and enjoy equality of status." The provinces need not follow suit, though Trudeau hoped they would. All of this would be accomplished, as Trudeau put it, "in a reasonable period of time."

And that was it. Yet even before 1969 was out Trudeau was driven to say: "Our policy of bilingualism has been widely misunderstood . . . It does not mean that every English Canadian must learn to speak French."

Part of the problem was that bilingualism, in the end, had to mean, well, *two equal languages*; being a little bit bilingual being as impossible to achieve as being a little bit pregnant. On the day after the Official Languages Act was passed, the *Calgary Herald* came right to the point: "For the more rewarding jobs, bilingualism is being made a practical necessity." Initially, these "rewarding" jobs meant just the top ones at Ottawa; inevitably, though, it would soon mean all the middle-rank jobs that fed the top; then jobs in the "para-government," all the way from the Canadian Manufacturers' Association to the Canadian Labour Congress, on down the line to jobs in all companies which had dealings with francophones, and to some provincial government positions. Eventually, unilingualism could mean a life sentence to job immobility.

Trudeau knew this all along. He fibbed about it as a necessary means to an end. As late as April 1977, for instance, he said in Winnipeg that bilingualism did not mean "that a lot more Canadians will have to be bilingual" nor even "most civil servants"; indeed this policy "will make it possible for the vast majority of Canadians not to have to speak a second language."

White lies like these are the acceptable tools of every politician's trade. Trudeau's difficulty was that the truth was bound to come out. Even if they were slow to comprehend what was happening, more and more English Canadians became aware they had been disadvantaged and began to react. Some expressed their feelings through hostility; others by turning away. In 1979, Dalton Camp put it shrewdly in *Points of Departure*:

The persistence and growing pervasiveness of bilingualism had alienated English Canadians from their federal government,

*Trying to define the boundaries of these "bilingual districts" caused endless difficulties, and in the end they were never established.

turning them inwards to more familiar, compatible and nearer political jurisdictions in the provinces ... The government of Canada had lost its constituency.

* * *

Without a constituency, democratic governments are just a shell: their legal authority remains, but their moral authority vanishes. During 1976, both halves of the country rejected bilingualism. A Gallup Poll that summer measured popular support for "institutional" bilingualism at an all-time low of 37 per cent. Trudeau had lost his moral authority to mobilize the national will; the centre was no longer holding.

To understand how this could have happened, and then turn out *not* to have happened irrevocably, bilingualism has to be cast in a much wider context than the kind of administrative tidying up Trudeau had said it amounted to.

Bilingualism, in truth, was nothing less than a social revolution. Like the introduction of the post-war welfare state, like the counter-cultural revolution of the 1960's, it was a development that effected fundamental changes in the character of the country. But in contrast to those transformational phenomena, no one in authority in Ottawa in the late 1960's and early 1970's let on that massive change was about to happen. Trudeau stopped talking about the subject as soon as the legislation had been passed: in those days he still believed that once he had produced a rational solution to a problem, the public would act rationally and would applaud. Once, and only once, Pelletier the minister responsible for bilingualism toured the west to explain what was going on. Ill at ease with journalists despite his own journalistic background, and ill-served by some zealots on his staff, Pelletier emerged from the tour shaken. As for the westerners, they knew no more about bilingualism than before, except that they liked it even less.

Like all revolutions, bilingualism involved fundamental changes in Canada's power structure. Unilingual Canadians – these included, as was often overlooked, the three in four francophone Québécois who spoke only French – would be disadvantaged in their lives, through no fault of their own. Bilingual Canadians would gain an advantage, as often as not by luck as by merit. There was not getting away from it: during the late 1960's and early 1970's, most *Bilingues* belonged to the same distinctive

224

breed, upper middle-class francophones and those upper middle-class anglophones, most from Montreal, who by the happenstance of their parents or their career patterns, had a chance while young to learn French. As handy examples, the first Official Languages Commissioner, Keith Spicer, learned his French in France on a scholarship, while his successor Max Yalden did so as a diplomat. Gradually, the geographic base of bilingualism broadened: by 1980, Calgary claimed proportionately more students in immersion classes than any other city. The phenomenon's socio-economic character remained unchanged. For the first time in its history, Canada was developing a distinct social elite, of young, upper middle-class, bilingual graduates.

Bilingualism thus became a synonym for elitism, more so than it need have done because Trudeau – "we do not have the time; Quebec will not wait" – rejected repeatedly the slower, populist, "schools" approach. His aim was a quick decisive victory within the federal civil service, over which he exercised direct control.

Ottawa's "bilingual revolutionaries," to use Jean-Luc Pépin's expressive phrase, were all elitist-revolutionaries, with all the characteristics of that breed. As revolutionaries, they were idealists, visionaries, and very, very few in number; perhaps a hundred or so in all: francophone federalists such as Trudeau, Pelletier, Marchand, Lalonde, Chrétien, Pépin; their anglophone allies, who included politicians like Donald Macdonald, Hugh Faulkner, John Roberts; civil servants like Pitfield, Robertson, Spicer, Yalden, and Public Service Commission Chairman John Carson; aides such as Davey and Porteous; and out on the fringes, a few academics like Paul Fox and Ramsay Cook. As elitists, they were often insufferably self-righteous; because bilingualism flowed so easily and so naturally to them, they failed to comprehend just how daunting the accomplishment seemed to most other people; because they themselves were so successful in their own careers, they failed to appreciate the fearful threat to job security that bilingualism presented to so many. Yet their strength and also their glory was their idealism; a realist would have recognized that the revolution they were engaged in had no chance of succeeding.

* * *

Of all political issues, language everywhere is far and away most

225

explosive. Basques today are prepared to kill and to die for the sake of Euskera, an arcane and quite useless language. In Russia, early in 1978, to try and preserve a language that if anything is even more arcane, five thousand Georgian students demonstrated in their capital, Tbilisi, to force Soviet authorities to include Georgian as an official language of their republic. Not since 1925, when South Africa raised Afrikaans to equal status with English, has any western country successfully bilingualized itself. Belgium, which until Canada started, had tried harder than anyone else, has failed abysmally. Walloonia and Flanders exist as unilingual ghettos inside which, by law, parents may not educate their children at public expense in the other language.

The Canadian Shield is about as unpromising a ground as anywhere exists on which to plant a bilingual flag. Looking at the troops available to him, on either side of the Ottawa River, Trudeau must at times have felt like echoing Wellington, to muse that his potential bilingual recruits terrified him more than any conceivable enemy. Québécois clung to their language as to an icon and preserved it by hardly ever venturing beyond their borders eastward or westward, only southward, to huddle together at seasonal outposts in Old Orchard Beach, Maine, or in Florida.

As for English Canadians, their governing linguistic principles, when forced even to consider languages other than their own, were smugness, stubbornness, and not to dodge the word, blind stupidity. Their ancestors, after all, had declared, Niggers begin at Calais. They viewed Quebec through a glass darkly, clouded by memories of Duplessis, of priests in foreign-looking *soutanes*, and of the noncombatant "Zombies" of World War Two. For all most English Canadians knew, the sweeping changes that the Quiet Revolution had brought to Quebec might never have happened. Even the few who had heard of Gilles Vigneault and Monique Leyrac and Marie-Claire Blais and all the other flowers of the cultural renaissance usually missed the concomitant point: that the Quebec civil service, at its top levels, was now a match for any; that in Trudeau, Lévesque, Pelletier, Lalonde, Parizeau, Claude Morin, and later, Ryan, Quebec had produced a group of intellectually acute, politically adroit politicians unequalled in Canada since Confederation. Stubbornly, English Canadians held to the old confident assumption: because everyone in North America spoke English, French Canadians would have to do so, sooner or later. At the same time, English Canadians hated being made to feel guilty about being tongue-tied. The commonest reaction to guilt is defensive-aggression.

Sooner or later, an explosion over bilingualism was bound to happen. The reason it happened in the particular way it did was because of the mistakes Trudeau made in implementing his policy.

* * *

He began in the best of all possible ways: by app.. ..ing to the ingrained Anglo-Saxon sense of fair play. He pointed out, as the B and B Commission had pointed out, that average salaries of francophone civil servants were $1,000 lower than those of anglophones; that they constituted only 10 per cent of the civil service officers against their 27 per cent share of the population.

So far, so good. Better still, in its earliest years, bilingualism was invisible. Though some civil servants bitched about "telephone book bilingualism" – a process through which a strikingly large number of candidates with Gallic surnames won promotions to high-profile positions – the civil service payroll was expanding fast enough to ensure that there were more than enough plums to go around. As for the public at large, it could not have cared less, in the late 1960's, about what was going on behind Ottawa's green baize doors.

Thus for several years the country paid little attention to bilingualism. After the west got angry when RCMP patrol cars appeared with the familiar insignia painted over and replaced by the dual purpose, POLICE, the insignia quickly came back. Some visitors got annoyed about the bilingual signs that suddenly sprouted in national parks, but let it pass. "French Power," which meant by definition less power at the centre for other Canadians, was an issue in the 1972 election, but Canadians, in that instance essentially were extending their anger at Trudeau to the people around him, just as the Texans round Lyndon Johnson, or the Georgians round Jimmy Carter, have also been surrogate straw men. Indeed, after the 1972 election, everyone felt a little guilty. Telling bilingual jokes – like the one about the lifeguard whose clients drowned because he had qualified for the job on account of his ability to conjugate the verb *nager* instead of his ability to swim – became socially unacceptable: as a substitute way to release inner hostilities, everyone took up Newfie jokes instead, including Lalonde. In 1973, everyone cheered Trudeau's resolution in Parliament to reaffirm the principles of bilingualism, and booed the sixteen Conservatives who voted against it. Everyone cheered again the next year when Stanfield, in the midst of the 1974 campaign, booted out of the party a nominated, anti-bilingual candidate, Moncton Mayor Leonard Jones.

But the truce was illusory. English Canada had not really bought bilingualism, only grudgingly accepted it on a temporary lease. Already, Quebec had begun to drift away in the other direction: in 1974, the Quebec legislature passed Bill 22, and so made French the province's sole official language.

Trudeau, by now hopping merrily in and out of his swimming pool, had hardly any idea what was going on Out There. In the fall of 1974, when Parliament opened, he talked about things he wanted to talk about – the constitution, making bilingualism "irreversible" – not at all about inflation, which was the one thing Canadians wanted him to talk about.

Bilingualism, to make matters worse, by now had become highly visible. Housewives discovered they could no longer understand one-half of the instructions on their frozen food packages and cornflakes boxes. "Turn them around" said Trudeau, on one occasion, so the story went, to his own mother-in-law. More and more English Canadians were discovering, by now, that the "rewarding" jobs indeed were going to those who were bilingual, or to francophones. At one period, all but one of the seven CRTC commissioners were bilingual Quebecers – either anglophone or francophone. The central inescapable fact of bilingualism was becoming clear: it meant a loss of power for unilingual English Canadians.

What was also becoming clear was that bilingualism in Ottawa, thanks to Trudeau, had become a gigantic boondoggle.

* * *

In his report of March 1976, Official Languages Commissioner Keith Spicer decided that the time had come to tell it like everyone knew it had become. Language training for civil servants, he pronounced, "strains both optimism and pocketbook." Among anglophone graduates of civil service language training schools, only 11 per cent attained full fluency; 80 per cent "scarcely used French at all" once back at their jobs.

228

All of this was a good intention gone haywire. In the 1972 election if there had been anywhere a "backlash" against bilingualism, it had happened in Ottawa, where the Liberals proportionately had lost more votes than elsewhere. To allay fears about job security among anglophone civil servants, Trudeau in June 1973 announced a new bilingualism policy. All posts in the public service requiring bilingualism would be identified officially as such. People holding those jobs would be given time off to learn a second language. People who won competitions to these positions, from inside or outside the public service, would also be sent off to school. The number of such positions, Trudeau suggested, would be around 25,000 – or one in ten of the total federal payroll.

Eventually, the number of bilingual positions topped out at just under 75,000. Anyone who knew anything about the nature of bureaucracy could have told Trudeau this would happen. "We knew damn well you had to be bilingual to have any hopes of promotion," one civil servant said at the time, "so we made damn sure that our own positions were classified bilingual, and for their own sake, the jobs of everyone else in sight. That way we'd all have the right to learn French." Inevitably the classification process, as Spicer's report put it, "bore distressingly little relation to job needs, except by distant and often disputable projections."

From 1974 on, more than 2,000 civil servants each day trooped off to five different language schools in Ottawa and across the river in Hull. There, they were chattered at by 600 language teachers, sometimes to be reduced to tears by petites *Québécoises* who were either separatists or feminists or both, and who delighted in their chance for revenge. Assistant deputy ministers, stolidly into their fifties, blinked and gulped their way through *Dialogue Canada*, a "structuro-global" audio visual course featuring the bilingual adventures of a portly little cartoon character called Angus MacGregor, a retired Cunard captain from Vancouver, given to expressions like "Holy Sufferin' Catfish." At the end, provided they kept their heads down and avoided nervous breakdowns, they passed their LKE (Language Knowledge Examination), a licence, as the cynical put it, "never again to have to utter a word of French." Some senior public servants got to spend a year in Quebec with their families at government expense, down to the money for summer camps for their children. Wives of senior officials, "To assist their husbands in the numerous activities required of them," as a Public Service Commission directive explained, got free French courses too. In perhaps the most astonishing scam of all, the Justice Department flew twenty-nine Quebec judges, most of them already bilingual, along with sixteen wives and twelve teachers, to spend eleven days in Vancouver, at a total cost of $18,000. "Judges are expensive," an official explained.

* * *

Spicer described his preferred alternative to this charade as "the schools option." Forcing French down the throats of bureaucrats provoked "linguistic antagonisms" and did nothing for "the parent who sees his child, like himself thirty years earlier, being crippled in the other language." Spending the money on children instead, as so many had urged – including, to Spicer's embarrassment, Mayor Leonard Jones – "would be a nice little democratic way of saying that the people are not always wrong."

Trudeau, though, would have none of it. Some francophone ministers in private called Spicer "a traitor"; Trudeau simply asked him to lunch at 24 Sussex and told him he was wrong. In public, he explained why: "We can't tell Quebec, 'Cool it fellows; in forty years we'll be able to talk to you.'" "We might save some money," he added, "But we wouldn't save the country."

So few, so pitifully few in early 1976, shared Trudeau's sense of urgency. Except for New Brunswick, which did not do that much, the provinces did nothing. In fact, the provincial contribution to bilingualism was not just a zero, but a minus. All provinces allowed their universities, in acts of conscious social irresponsibility, to drop French as an entrance requirement in order to make it easier for them to find enough "barely warm bodies," as Spicer put it, to fill up their classrooms.* Since no one needed to learn French any longer to get into university, fewer and fewer students spent time on the subject: between 1970-71 and 1977-78, enrolment in French classes outside of Quebec dropped from 56 per cent of the student body to 40 per cent. Even more irresponsibly, as *La Fédération des Francophones* pointed out in a 1977 report, only half of $36 million given to Ontario by Ottawa to further

---

*At Chrétien's urging, the cabinet considered withdrawing federal research grants from universities which failed to insist on French as an entrance requirement, then decided that political discretion was the better part of bilingual valour.

the teaching of French was used for that purpose; Manitoba expended only one-third of its $4 million allotment.

Politically, the schools option was attractive. It would have created a constituency of parents who supported bilingualism because they could see their own children benefiting from it. Whether it was politically practical is quite another matter. On the evidence, the answer is probably no. The answer to the conundrum of how on earth to make a country bilingual probably has to be pretty much the one Trudeau risked everything on: dragging his countrymen kicking and screaming behind him and, as important, making bilingualism a negotiable asset in the job market.

* * *

The debacle in Ottawa was one thing. The debacle in Quebec was quite another. Trudeau's problem, in 1976, was that his own people were abandoning him.

Trudeau, ironically, had given the first shove himself; in October 1971, he had introduced legislation to make Canada "a multicultural country within a bilingual framework." Henceforth, while only two languages were official, all cultures would be equal.

This idea had originally been floated by the B and B Commission. The point, Trudeau explained, was "to break down discriminatory attitudes and cultural jealousies." Ukrainian Canadians, Italian Canadians, Chinese Canadians and so on, need no longer feel second class citizens, because Ottawa would officially recognize their cultures, and would fund these. But while multiculturalism made bilingualism go down some throats a little easier, and bought Trudeau a lot of ethnic votes, it turned a lot of French Canadians off. The policy would "accelerate the retreat of French Canadians into Quebec," warned Guy Rocher, the vice-chairman of the Canada Council. "Outside Quebec, we now are nothing more than another ethnic minority."

Rocher put his finger directly on the problem Trudeau had created for himself. By rejecting the "two nations" concept with his customary rhetorical overkill, and by pounding Stanfield into the ground with it during the 1968 election, Trudeau had left himself with no slogan to use other than Diefenbaker's "One Canada." But for many Canadians, of either language group, "One Canada" meant, by implication, a one-language Canada.

All across Canada, francophones could look and see the demo-

231

graphic battle to make English the single language being won. Statistics Canada projections showed that from comprising 27 per cent of the total population in 1971, the proportion of francophones might drop to little more than 20 per cent by the year 2000. Still, Quebec alone really mattered. If the fight for the French Fact were lost there, then it would be lost inevitably everywhere. The point was that in Quebec, and particularly in Montreal as Quebec's nerve centre, Trudeau's policy of bilingualism was beside the point. Bilingualism made *Ottawa* bilingual; it supported French-speaking minorities *outside* Quebec. But in Montreal, bilingualism did nothing at all except to sanctify the use of English, when the real problem was that too-little French was being used.

Through the Quiet Revolution, Québécois had indeed become *maîtres chez nous*, in most respects. But in Montreal, French-speaking Québécois, as late as the early 1970's, were still the servants. Montreal's commercial and shopping core: Eaton's, Holt Renfrew, Ogilvy's, on down Ste Catherine Street to the Leghorn Barbecue and the John Bull pub were all English. So were the streets: Peel, Drummond, Sherbrooke, above all Dominion Square. The business establishment spoke English, from Sun Life to the Bank of Montreal. So did its wealthiest newspapers, the *Star* and the *Gazette*, and the majority of its radio stations. Not to mention the best university, McGill; the best hospital, the Royal Victoria; its best art gallery, the Montreal Museum of Fine Arts; and its best clubs, the Saint James and the Mount Stephen. There was also the matter of income distribution: a 1971 study showed that of head office employees earning more than $22,000, 85 per cent were anglophone. More and more it seemed that Montreal would be swamped in an anglophone tide. Four in five immigrants assimilated into English; nationalist demographers (in fact inaccurately and perhaps even fraudulently) predicted that the city by the end of the century might be 40 per cent English-speaking. Given the power of assimilation, that would amount to 100 per cent of everything that really mattered, west of St. Laurent Boulevard.

Down in Quebec City, Premier Robert Bourassa's answer was to espouse a bloodless, "profitable federalism," inside which, using a phrase he coined to get ahead of the Péquistes who were now on the rise, Quebec might exercise "cultural sovereignty." Pursuing that concept – whatever it meant – Bourassa enacted

Bill 22. At least technically, French became Quebec's only official language. Before enrolling in English-language schools, children of immigrants would have to pass a test in English "proficiency." Nationalists hated the bill because it imposed no limits on the use of English; anglophones hated it because it limited their freedoms.

No one hated Bill 22 more than Trudeau. In a speech in Quebec City, on March 3, 1976, he described it as "politically stupid." It would now be that much harder to sell bilingualism to the rest of the country, he explained. In the same speech Trudeau, inexplicably, went on to describe Bourassa as "an eater of hot dogs," and expressed doubts about his capacity to comprehend the troubled financing of the Olympics.

* * *

At the time, commentators assumed that Trudeau had somehow got up on the wrong side of bed. As it happened, he had good reasons for being angry, except that these had nothing to do with Bill 22. The morning of March 3, he had met Bourassa privately, ostensibly to talk about the constitution. What they actually talked about was the Queen.

A year earlier, Bourassa had telephoned Trudeau on behalf of Montreal Mayor Jean Drapeau, to ask him to invite the Queen to open the Olympics. Glad of the chance to send Her Majesty on a mission involving national unity, Trudeau secured royal approval. He then set up a federal-provincial task force to organize her schedule, which Bourassa approved, then got final agreement from Buckingham Palace. According to this plan, the Queen would first fly to Quebec City's l'Ancien Lorette Airport where Bourassa would greet her on behalf of the province, and proceed from there to Montreal.

He could not do it, Bourassa told Trudeau. He could not meet the Queen. It was just too politically dicey. Now, with just three months to go, Trudeau would have to invent a new schedule.* Much worse, he would have to telephone the Queen and make an excuse. Spitting fury at Bourassa's cowardice, Trudeau went straight from their meeting to deliver his public speech. But be-

---

*In the end, the Queen filled up her empty day between Halifax, where she arrived aboard the royal yacht *Britannia*, and Montreal by touring Fredericton, Chatham, and Newcastle in New Brunswick.

yond publicly humiliating Bourassa, he could say nothing in public. If English Canadians had learned of Bourassa's insult to their Queen, they might have stormed Quebec's borders with picks and halberds.

Personalities apart, Bourassa's Bill 22 dealt Trudeau's policy of bilingualism a lethal blow. At the same time as English Canadians were having French forced down their throats, those same Quebecers on whose behalf English Canadians were undergoing this indignity were spitting out English. Only a spark was needed now to turn repressed frustration into inchoate outrage. The dispute over bilingualism in the air provided it.

* * *

The bare bones of this struggle are easy to set out. After months of skirmishing over Ottawa's attempt to make French a permissible language for air traffic control under Visual Flight Rules in the control towers of all Quebec airports, to be followed later by the use of French under Instrument Flight Rules at major airports only, the patience of English-speaking controllers and pilots snapped. Claiming that planes would collide in mid-air because of confusion in the control towers, the pilots and controllers grounded the nation's planes for nine days. Eventually, they forced Transport Minister Otto Lang to accept a humiliating settlement that required safety to be proved "beyond a reasonable doubt" and be subject to a free vote in Parliament. In response to this, Marchand quit; later, a second minister, Manitoba's James Richardson also quit, convinced that the country shared his own rejection of bilingualism.

During the strike, no one in English Canada paid the slightest attention to anything Trudeau said. Instead they paid attention to their pilots, equally potent – "Daddy is going to take us flying" – father figures. Calls to hotline shows and letters to the editor ran at least 90 per cent in favour of the strike. Soon afterwards, the T-shirts blossomed, and the radio editorial "Quebec, go suck a lemon" became the rage in the west.

In the summer, Jean Cournoyer, the Quebec Natural Resources Minister, toured the country and returned to report: "Outside of Quebec, no one wants to see you any more. They don't consider you a Canadian any more."

Québécois felt the same way. French-speaking controllers and pilots had already formed *Les Gens de l'Air* and were insisting that French be the sole language of air traffic control in Quebec. Buttons reading *Il y a du français dans l'air* blossomed in lapels all over the province. Although it never became public, a comparable language crisis developed at sea, or at least, in the St. Lawrence River. Francophone river pilots printed up *Gens de la Mer* buttons and planned to go on strike to protest a new federal regulation that would have allowed captains of foreign ships to choose the language for ship-to-shore communication. (Most would have chosen English.) Quickly, the regulation, which simply followed the principles of bilingualism in federal services, was withdrawn.

In that cruel June, Canada's "Two Solitudes" as Hugh MacLennan had once described them, became, in René Lévesque's phrase, "two hostilities," each withdrawn into its own castle, and filling the moat between them with vitriol.

* * *

Through the summer, the political climate cooled – a bit. The Olympics, though far from Expo revisited, went off successfully. The Queen arrived, performed graciously, and no one had any inkling that Bourassa had snubbed her. On July 24, at a state dinner for the Queen in Montreal, Trudeau pronounced bilingualism not simply a success, but the harbinger of a new kind of integrated, homogenized Canada. "The French and English cultures are so influenced by each other, that there is really no discontinuity between them," he said. "They can be seen as a single entity."

Less than four months later, on the evening of Monday, November 15, 1976, an entirely different kind of Canadian stepped into the spotlight in Montreal's Paul Sauvé Arena. "I never thought I would be so proud to be a Quebecer," said René Lévesque, to 15,000 ecstatic, incredulous, alternately weeping and cheering supporters.

In the four years since, two things have happened. Trudeau's bilingualism policy has been born again. At the same time, a new kind of Canada has come into being.

14

This One Corner of the Earth

"A nation is a plebiscite every day."

Renan

After their first encounter, sometime in the late 1950's on a date neither can recall precisely, Lévesque said of Trudeau: "He has a natural-born talent for getting slapped in the face." They had met in the offices of *Cité Libre* where Lévesque, then Quebec's best-known television personality, had gone to offer his services as a contributor. Trudeau had discussed Lévesque's qualifications with other Cité Librists and had quipped, in his hearing, "But can he write?"

Throughout the two decades since then, the pair have fought ferociously. Yet, except for two engagements—the 1970 October Crisis and the immediate aftermath of the Parti Québécois victory in November 1976—their Single Combat has been marked by a curious quality, not of circumspection exactly, but of containment. While each wanted passionately to win, neither, down deep, wanted to destroy the other. Pelletier speaks of "a grudging respect" between them. To their hostility there is a quality of nobility.

Trudeau and Lévesque are the heroes of opposing armies. Although their means have been diametrically opposed, their ends have been identical. Each has fought for his people, the French Canadians, even though Lévesque's francophones are limited to those within Quebec while Trudeau's vision encompasses all in Canada whose mother tongue is French. By extending the French Fact across Canada, Trudeau sought to prevent it from withdrawing solely into Quebec, where he was convinced it would wither and die. Lévesque, convinced that the French Fact would wither and die if it over-extended itself, sought to consolidate it within Quebec.

Their political careers are also curiously symbiotic. Trudeau's proclamation in May 1976, "separatism is dead," benefited Lévesque in his succeeding election because if separatism indeed were no longer an issue, Quebecers need decide only whether the Liberals or the Parti Québécois could best provide "good government." Lévesque's election victory elevated Trudeau's status to that of Saviour of Canada: within a year his Gallup Poll standing went from 29 per cent to 51 per cent. Similarly, Trudeau's defeat in 1979 actually damaged Lévesque: he lost four successive by-elections soon after and trailed in the pre-referendum polls 52 to 41 per cent. As a finishing touch, Trudeau's victory in 1980, which helped reassure Quebecers they could afford to vote "oui" in the referendum, restored Lévesque's political fortunes. The first survey after Trudeau's triumph put Lévesque's yes forces ahead, 47 to 44, and his personal popularity soared to a 65 per cent approval rating. This paradox is easy to explain. Quebecers loved them both, wanted to keep them both around, wanted, above all, not to have to choose one of them exclusively. Combined, Lévesque and Trudeau encompassed the sum total of the Quebec psyche: its aspirations, its hidden fears, its hidden dreams. Trudeau, whom the polls consistently showed to be more popular, exemplified to Quebecers, like Laurier before him, the very best they could achieve: he was the bright boy from the small village who, as neighbours and peers look on in awe, goes out to conquer the metropolis and indeed the world. Lévesque, so much more obviously flawed, but so much more human, passionate, and compassionate, exemplified to Quebecers the best in their own inner lives; like Laurier's nemesis, nationalist journalist-politician Henri Bourassa, he was the bright boy who had remained in the village, and who was thus incomparably closer to its moods, its rhythms, its self-doubts.

The two, *au fond*, have much in common. Both, unusually so among democratic politicians, are daring to the point of being reckless; both are ruthless, devious, and competitive. As boys, both were street fighters. As young men, both were passionate internationalists. Both are fluently bilingual. (Almost predictably, the Parti Québécois cabinet was the most proficient in English in Quebec's history, although, significantly, most members had become bilingual at places like Harvard and the London School of Economics, rather than anywhere on the far side of the Ottawa River.)

237

As for the fundamental difference between Lévesque and Trudeau, this was not so much that they espoused different brands of nationalism – the nationalism of Quebec and in Trudeau's case, the nationalism of Canada, as his thinking evolved – as that Lévesque possessed in superhuman abundance the one great political gift that Trudeau lacks.

Trudeau can bewitch his audiences; Lévesque can make them part of himself. In his speeches, more often than not a jumbled flow of unco-ordinated sentences, Lévesque leaves spaces for his listeners to fill in by themselves; he is the personification of McLuhan's participative "cool" medium of communication. Lévesque's audiences may not understand everything he seems to be saying; they feel, though, that he understands them; they know he feels as they do.

Lévesque first demonstrated this talent as a CBC television commentator in the 1950's. On his weekly program, *Point de Mire*, he explained complex topics, principally international ones, in ways, that, as one critic remarked, "made his viewers feel intelligent themselves." As a politician he has polished his technique into a kind of broken-wing act. Pretending (though not entirely pretending) vulnerability – the sudden boyish grin, the self-deprecating shrug; the adroit exploitation of such weaknesses as his elfin stature and his addiction to cigarettes – Lévesque seduces his audiences, anglophone as much as francophone. The true theatrical triumph is that Lévesque's audiences know full well Lévesque is seducing them, and participate happily in their own seduction. "Why are we laughing," a smiling middle-aged Westmount matron once asked a reporter after one of Lévesque's English-speaking rallies. "He's insulting us."

* * *

Lévesque was born in the mostly English-speaking Gaspé hamlet of New Carlisle, the son of a country lawyer, comfortably off but distinctly small .town *bourgeois*. He studied at Laval, dropped out of law school, spent the war as correspondent for the U.S. Office of Wartime Information. Post-war, he joined Radio-Canada, and, when television came along as the new village pump of the small Quebec community, became famous. His expressive, mobile face, his curious hoarse voice, attracted the largest public affairs audiences in the history of Quebec broadcasting.

He entered politics in 1960, as a Liberal. Quickly, he became a popular hero, the point man of the Quiet Revolution, architect of the nationalization of private power companies to form Hydro-Quebec, the largest corporation Quebecers themselves had ever owned. He popularized the slogan *maîtres chez nous* which won the Liberals re-election in 1962. In June 1963, Claude Ryan wrote in *Le Devoir* of Lévesque's "extraordinary intuitions," that "help him to identify popular expectations."

Lévesque had come to comprehend those aspirations through personal experience. In 1958, CBC's French-language producers went on strike, expecting that their English-language colleagues would support them. Instead, the anglophones remained on the job. The strike was lost. Out of the realization that Quebecers in the end would have to do it for themselves, Lévesque the nationalist was born.

Lévesque has told reporters since that he became a separatist in 1963. By then, the government of Jean Lesage was constantly at war with the new federal government of Lester Pearson. The battleground was jurisdiction. Both, quintessentially, were activist governments: Walter Gordon functioning as Ottawa's answer to Lévesque, and just as staunchly nationalist as he.

It was during this period that Trudeau, then a professor at the University of Montreal, first came head to head with Lévesque. In his biography, *René*, Peter Desbarats has described brilliantly the character of these encounters. Evening after evening, Lévesque would come to Pelletier's house, to meet with a group that included Marchand, Trudeau, and Laurendeau, to test out his scheme to nationalize the private power companies, and to secure them as allies. Each and every one of Lévesque's points, Trudeau would rebut. The money involved – about $300 million – would simply buy in Quebec's name properties that already existed within Quebec. As for the symbolism, workers could not eat symbols. Time and again, writes Desbarats, "the professor would casually skim a barbed epigram at Lévesque, puncturing him in full flight and bringing him down to earth in a temper." (Years later, Lévesque must have smiled when he read that Trudeau had created Petro-Canada.)

By now, in *Cité Libre*, Trudeau was writing that nationalism would lead inevitably to "stagnation." By now, Lévesque was saying that Confederation was only "a bargain . . . and if the bargain was not very good, well it's like a couple; if you can't sleep together, you might as well have separate beds."

Pearson's answer to Quebec's incessant demands for money and jurisdiction was "co-operative federalism." Quebec could "opt out" of national programs, such as the Canada Pension Plan Continued indefinitely, as Trudeau pointed out, "opting out' would make Quebec first a "special" province different from all the others, and then, as the provincial government became for all practical purposes the only effective government for Quebec, independent in all but name. But in 1965, Marchand, Pelletier, and Trudeau went to Ottawa. Co-operative federalism went out the window. In its place came hard-line federalism; no more special deals for Quebec.

Lévesque's next move was inevitable. Briefly he embraced and then rejected – the one point of political agreement between himself and Trudeau – the option of special status for Quebec. Beyond that, only separation remained. Lévesque, even then, couched this in the form of "sovereignty-association," a cloudy concept that he said meant a fully sovereign Quebec joined in an ill-defined economic union to the rest of the country.

Lévesque has never since defined "sovereignty-association" any more precisely. But about Lévesque's feelings there never has existed the least doubt. He expressed these best in September 1967, just before quitting the provincial Liberals to form his own party. "We are Québécois," he said. "What that means first and foremost – and if need be, all that it means – is that we are attached to this one corner of the earth where we can be completely ourselves: this Quebec, the only place where we have the unmistakable feeling that 'here, we can really be at home.'"

For Trudeau, this was sentimental claptrap. Within months, he was Prime Minister. He set out to show how things should be done properly. On October 17, 1968, after the formation of the Parti Québécois, he brought down the Official Languages Act.

* * *

For the next eight years, Trudeau and Lévesque waged Single Combat only once: during the October Crisis, when Trudeau headed off the slightly-more-than-fantasy "provisional government plot" and smeared the separatists as terrorists. Nor did Trudeau need to engage Lévesque personally. His surrogate,

240

Bourassa whom Lévesque naturally called "a puppet" did it for him. In the provincial elections of 1970 and 1973, Bourassa trounced the Péquistes, and Lévesque lost personally both times. He came close to quitting politics, and probably would have re-entered journalism. Yet by the fall of 1974, Lévesque had got his bounce back. He defeated a challenge to his leadership from Péquiste leftists and sold the party his new policy of "*étapism*" (gradualism). Rather than being committed to separatism, the PQ would be committed only to holding a referendum on the subject. Only if given a mandate, would it move on to the fateful step. Since polls showed that no more than 20 per cent of Quebecers supported separatism as such, Trudeau pronounced it "dead."

Trudeau's pronouncement may have helped convince Quebecers that they could afford to vote for the PQ, much in the way that a parson, having pronounced to his parishioners that the devil is dead, has to expect them to eat, drink, and make merry. Still, it does not really matter whether the reason was Trudeau, or the bilingualism in the air crisis, or Trudeau's public ridiculing of Bourassa, or just the accumulated malaise produced by endless Liberal scandals, from rotten meat to rotten unions. All that matters is what happened, on November 15, 1976.

Of his own emotions once he realized Quebecers actually had dared to vote in the PQ, despite being told that doing so would bring about economic ruin, Roger Lemelin, publisher of *La Presse*, a staunch federalist has written: "There were tears in my eyes and I didn't quite know why."

Tears of pride is one guess, at Quebecers having conquered at last the politics of fear. Tears of joy, at the sense of oneness that overcame Quebecers that night and for weeks afterwards. As they sang and danced and embraced each other in the streets that chill November night, all Quebecers knew that their history would never again be the same.

* * *

All the hopes and expectations Canadians had invested in him for so long, Trudeau repaid during the eight or so months that followed the PQ victory. He did not "save Canada." Instead, he won for Canadians, and for Quebecers, the *time* for them to do the job themselves. Within Quebec, he kept alive the "Canadian option"; within Canada, as proved easier, he kept alive the French Fact.

From the fall of 1977 on, Trudeau had nothing more to offer. Until May, 1980.

The PQ victory disappointed Trudeau, but it by no means depressed him. "He was far less shocked by it than he had been by the failure of the 1971 Victoria Conference, where he'd really expected to succeed," says a friend. On election night, he had hoped for no more than a minority Bourassa victory, so that his comments that night, while wary, were calculated. He praised the result as a "victory for democracy" since it showed that in Canada, even a political party dedicated to the country's breakup could function peaceably and legally. Then he made his central point: "The Parti Québécois has been granted a mandate to form a provincial government, not to separate the province from the rest of Canada."

One kind of separation was inevitable though. Margaret, when she heard the news, burst into tears. She realized, as she said later, "he would never leave politics now." The next spring, they began a ninety-day trial separation. On May 27, 1977, the Trudeaus announced that henceforth they would live "separate and apart."

Bearing this inhuman double burden, Trudeau never once wavered or stumbled. Ministers and aides found him a bit more snappish, a bit less patient than before. But he was as icy cool and as precise in his analyses as ever. As is curious for someone so self-motivated in his own private life, Trudeau functions best in his public life when motivated by the pressure of outside events.

Post-November 1976, events dictated Trudeau's tactics. On the one hand, he had to arouse English Canada from the slumber into which it had lapsed as soon as it became clear, PQ or not, that the sun still rose in the morning; at the same time, he had to stop Quebecers from dancing their way right out of Confederation. A mood of extraordinary euphoria, touched off by a release from a centuries-old conviction of inferiority, set Quebecers on fire. Lévesque's popularity soared to 67 per cent, his highest ever. He seemed right then to have the chance either to declare independence unilaterally (as Rhodesia had done eleven years before) or to call a snap referendum while the provincial Liberals, with Bourassa defeated in his own riding, were both leaderless and demoralized.

The week-end immediately after the vote, Trudeau travelled to Montreal to spend two days talking privately to politicians, businessmen, academics. Then, on November 24, in a national television address he transformed what they had told him into one of the most skilful speeches of his career.

Trudeau's staging was as skilful as his content. Deliberately, he was low key and conversational. He sat in an armchair instead of behind a desk. He spoke from notes, rather than a text. But to underline the gravity of his words, he wore no rose in his lapel.

First, he exonerated Quebecers for what they had done to him. The PQ's victory, after a decade in seemingly hopeless opposition, "has few equals in the world today." Then, he ruled out the use of force to keep Quebec within Canada, an option then much speculated about: "Canada cannot, Canada must not, survive by force . . . [but as] one civil society." Next, he pledged "co-operation will be forthcoming in every way" with the government Quebecers had chosen for themselves. Concrete problems, "of language, but also in the very important areas of regional disparity and social justice," would be addressed; constitutional change would be undertaken to demonstrate, "It is possible to be at one and the same time, a good Canadian and a good Quebecer." Lastly, in the way of an understanding father reaching out to errant sons, Trudeau touched the emotional core of the issue. "There is a deeper bond than that of blood," he said. The bond of "fraternity, of hope and of charity in the scriptural sense, for if the Canadian nation is to survive, it will only survive in mutual respect and in love for one another." To fracture that bond within Canada "would be a sin against the spirit, a sin against humanity."

The tone of Trudeau's address—moderate, generous, emotional—took Lévesque by surprise. He sensed "an opening" in Trudeau's comments, he told reporters, although "it may be too little, too late." Any deal now would have to be made on the basis of "the equality of national collectivism."

By denying Lévesque a target to aim at, Trudeau gave Quebecers the room to come down, at their own pace, from their high. More than this, he had pointed the way to some new form of Confederation within which Quebecers could be at one and the same time "fraternal" Canadians and full-blooded Quebecers.

To try to recover momentum, Lévesque picked away at Cana-

243

dian pride. The offending word "province," he announced, would disappear from the next crop of licence plates. Government documents would no longer use the word "Confederation." When the National Assembly opened early in December, the Throne Speech contained not a single word in English, for the first time since 1867. But English Canada slumbered on, rousing only fitfully to notice such events as an announcement by the Royal Bank that it would soon move two hundred head-office personnel to Toronto.

Lévesque was nonplussed. He had counted on the rest of the country reacting either in outrage or in panic–either response serving his purpose equally. In mid-December, he came to Ottawa to attend a First Ministers Conference, and declared that the November 15 result was "irreversible." Yet the conference droned on like all the others of its kind, without, as Lévesque admitted to reporters at its close, "any historic confrontation" between himself and Trudeau.

In reply to Lévesque at the conference, Trudeau had smiled coolly and read off a prepared statement which few English-speaking commentators bothered to report, but which reverberated for months in the Quebec press. "When I speak of Canada," said Trudeau, "I do not have in mind an 'identity' which competes with that which a French-Canadian and a Quebecer, conscious of his or her specific history and roots, holds dear." He did not aspire to create, he said, "some higher-order Canadian 'personality' in which would be absorbed or subsumed," the distinctive cultures of any region or province. Bilingualism meant simply a "political society, the ideals of which are liberty, equality and, yes, fraternity." In brief, everyone could be a Canadian and keep on being themselves.* Only in private, afterwards, during a dinner for the premiers at 24 Sussex, did the tensions surface. All the first ministers got a bit tight, Trudeau included, for the first time in anyone's memory, and exchanged "Fuck you's" across the dining table.

---

*Up to then, at least by implication, Trudeau indeed had aspired to create a distinct "higher order" Canadian personality. Since 1968, the phrase French/English- Canadian had been banned from federal documents, and replaced by the unhyphenated, French or English speaking Canadians. In his speech at the banquet for the Queen in July 1974, he described how the French and English cultures comprised "a single entity."

During his annual end-of-year interview with CTV, Trudeau said mournfully, "I'm afraid that the national will to exist as a country isn't very strong in Canada." Still more mournfully, he went on: "If Quebecers were to vote very massively for separation, I would have failed, and I would silently go away, perhaps to fight in another field." And then, like a neap tide, the will to survive which Trudeau sought so despairingly, began flooding around him.

This resurgence of the nation's will to survive, Trudeau owed, of all people, to Lévesque. On January 25, 1977, Lévesque travelled to New York and there told the Economic Club that Quebec's separation was "natural and irreversible," in the manner of the Thirteen Colonies from Britain. This analogy charmed no one, least of all the New York bankers. More to the point, English Canadians at last took Lévesque seriously. Saying such things to his own people was one thing; saying them to New York bankers meant that he really meant them.

* * *

In the first week of February 1977, right after Lévesque's speech, Gallup discovered that the nation had woken up. For the first time in more than a year, Trudeau was ahead, 41 per cent to 37 per cent. Through February and March, readers' letters to the *Toronto Star* no longer carped about bilingualism. Their headlines expressed their contents: "Fault Ours, Not Trudeau's"; "More French in Ontario Needed"; "Canada Can do Anything"; "Vital to Keep Quebec In"; "No Canada without Quebec."

As spring led into summer, English Canadians once again fell in love with their country. The mood of Expo returned, shadowed this time by remorse, by guilt, and by a transcendent sense of impending loss. In April, when Trudeau went west to preach bilingualism, he was cheered in Winnipeg and mobbed in Saskatoon. Schools, churches, groups, service clubs, all cancelled long-planned schedules to hold seminars on national unity. Enrolment in French immersion courses shot up; people stopped bitching about bilingual cornflakes boxes.

Lévesque, for his part, could not comprehend what had got into the stolid, stubborn, and so often stupid Anglo-Saxons. Nor, really, could Trudeau. Perhaps the best answer has been provided by the University of Toronto economist and nationalist, Abe Rotstein. English Canadian nationalism, Rotstein has pointed out, lacks a cultural or economic dimension. Rather, it is "territorial" in character. Canada is a country of space, of wilderness, with a sweep *a mari usque ad mare*. Those policies of Trudeau's which have brought him closely into communion with English Canada have been his arctic environmental legislation of 1970 and his 1977 declaration of the 200-mile limit, the consequences of which Canadians could trace easily on a map. In exactly the same way, they could trace the consequences of Quebec's separation on a map. The phrases most often used to describe Quebec's separation were consistently territorial: Canada would be "torn in two"; "divided"; "split"; "fragmented."

At last, Lévesque got the message. His goal, he began to say from about the middle of 1977 on, was not "to destroy Confederation" but to arrange "a new deal"; "a new partnership of equals"; even "a true Confederation." Trudeau's problem then became that as time passed, more and more English Canadians began to believe Lévesque, and to believe that provided the lines on the map stayed the same, a country could still exist within them. Trudeau's response was to describe the Parti Québécois as "the enemy within."

* * *

For a while, Trudeau and Lévesque circled each other like opponents too far apart to score a lethal blow. On February 22, as a riposte to Lévesque's New York speech, Trudeau flew to Washington and there, in an historic first for a Canadian Prime Minister, addressed a special joint session of Congress. Quebec's separation, he said, would be "a crime against the history of mankind," Senators and Congressmen queued up to shake his hand. (Margaret, though, earned more headlines by turning up at the White House state dinner with a run in her stocking.)

Lévesque returned to the attack. His *Charter of the French Language*, published on April 11, was designed, tactically, to bait Trudeau and English Canada. Strategically, the charter's objective was to transform, irreversibly, the character of Quebec. "There will no longer be any question of a bilingual Quebec," the document declared. "The Quebec we intend to build will be essentially French." French would be the sole official language; English would continue to be used, but only as a privilege. The resulting

246

legislation brought down on April 27, as Bill 1, later changed to Bill 101, abolished the use of English in the legislature and, except for individuals, in the courts. It also required all firms with more than fifty employees to acquire "Francization" certificates as a condition of remaining in business, and required all children, other than those of native-born Anglo-Quebecers to enrol in French schools.

Trudeau reacted as the PQ had hoped he would react, as indeed, he had to react if he hoped to keep bilingualism alive. The legislation was "retrograde," he said at his weekly press conference. He would fight "absolutely" any infringement of personal rights, such as denying parents the right to educate their children in the language of their choice. Pressed by reporters, Trudeau at last lashed out: "The kind of independence the Parti Québécois is promoting is rather a going back to the Dark Ages . . . to tribalism . . . to an ethnic-centred society."

Camille Laurin, Quebec's Minister of State for Cultural Development and author of the legislation, was unperturbed. "Yes," he said, "it is ethnocentric. All nations are founded on the principle of ethnocentricity."

A fortnight later, Lévesque emerged from a cabinet meeting to tell reporters: "We have set the referendum date, but I won't tell you what it is." In August he introduced into the Assembly legislation to enable him to hold a referendum.

* * *

One of the great might-have-beens in Canadian history is what might have happened if Lévesque had held his referendum in the fall of 1977, with Bill 101 as his issue. To guess the result is impossible, but it is clear that, with feelings about language then so alive, Lévesque would have come much closer on a much harder question, than he did in May 1980.

Whether or not Lévesque in fact planned a fall referendum, Trudeau denied him the opportunity. He did this by executing the most difficult of all political manoeuvres: a retreat in full public view.

Through April, the cabinet debated testing the constitutionality of Bill 101 before the courts. Then it chose discretion over valour. The Justice Department, for one thing, doubted the certainty of success. For another, and much more importantly, Trudeau reluctantly recognized that Bill 101 was probably the most popular act of

247

any Quebec government since the nationalization of the power companies. Even Claude Ryan, who in *Le Devoir* complained of the infringement on the civil liberties of Canadians moving into the province, accepted the substance of the legislation. Unilingualism, as francophone Quebecers quickly realized, meant that anglophones would leave, and leave behind them jobs, and houses at bargain prices. It meant that Montreal at last would become truly, visibly, irrevocably French. It meant above all that Quebecers would at last be fully masters of "the one corner of the earth where we can be completely ourselves."

In his June document, *A National Understanding*, Trudeau made his retreat. The paper said all the right things about linguistic and cultural differences, quoting Northrop Frye: "A sense of unity is the opposite of a sense of uniformity." But about the key issue of educational choice, it said next to nothing. The right should exist, certainly, but "subject to circumstances which may make a deferment of application necessary." Bilingualism if necessary, in other words, but not necessarily bilingualism. On October 7, Trudeau formally announced he would not challenge Bill 101; "Frankly, I don't want to give Mr. Lévesque the choice of timing and issues," he said.

And so Lévesque had won. His vision of the future—the French Fact first withdrawing into itself before reaching out across the country—had been recognized officially by Trudeau.

Everyone else reached the same conclusion at about the same time. English Canadians no longer questioned Quebec's right to be "as French as Ontario is English";* indeed they began to question Trudeau's obduracy towards Lévesque—"the enemy within"—since the Parti Québécois government was so obviously turning into one of the best in the country: democratic, progressive, and the first to clean out the quagmire of patronage left behind by Duplessis.

* * *

The opposing champions continued to skirmish. In a speech in Montreal, Trudeau compared the new "holy mother, the nation," to the old "holy mother, the church." Lévesque offered the prov-

*In 1980, in a message to federal Liberal M.P.s campaigning in the Quebec referendum, Trudeau cited Quebec's ability to be "as French as Ontario is English" as one of the benefits to Québécois of remaining in Confederation

inces "reciprocal rights," meaning that if they provided education in French for migrating Quebecers, he would do the same thing for them. Some premiers expressed interest but changed their minds when Trudeau accused Lévesque of "using children as political hostages." At their August 1977 annual meeting, the premiers agreed to exert their "best efforts" to promote second language education "wherever numbers warrant." This, the premiers solemnly declared, amounted to "an historic achievement." Trudeau, a few months earlier, had provided a better description of the bilingual achievements of the nation. "I'm just as impatient with English Canadians as I am now with French Canadians, because if English Canadians had not been so damned obtuse, they would have understood this ten, twenty, thirty years ago."

* * *

By the autumn of 1977, the dispute over language was over. Lévesque had won the engagement, but he had lost the first referendum battle. He was beginning to encounter economic problems – 10 per cent unemployment and a steady outward flow of head office jobs from Montreal. Soon, he encountered a formidable new opponent: in January 1978, Claude Ryan announced he would contest the leadership of the Quebec Liberals. The February First Ministers Conference mirrored the change in the nation's mood. The topic was economics, and Lévesque for the first time was overshadowed by other premiers. "We're no longer scared of Lévesque," one premier said afterwards. In lockstep, Trudeau's lead in the polls began to shrink.

In December 1977, Trudeau and Lévesque met *tête-à-tête* for the first time since the PQ victory. Over lunch in Lévesque's office in Quebec City, they discussed such issues as a new pact to give Quebec an effective veto over the selection of immigrants. During the lunch, Lévesque recounted later, he raised his glass of Vosne-Romanée, 1967, to Trudeau with the toast: "To your misfortunes." Trudeau raised his own glass, and replied: "Likewise."

* * *

From this time on, language ceased to be a battle ground between Lévesque and Trudeau. Bilingualism simply began to happen. In

September 1979, when the Royal Commission appointed three years earlier to study bilingual air traffic control finally reported, and recommended that this be implemented at Quebec airports, it took the then Clark government twenty-four hours to accept the recommendation. No one wrote angry letters to Clark or to the newspapers.

The best description of what had happened was provided by the *La Presse* editorialist Lysiane Gagnon; French, she wrote, had become in Canada not "an equal" language, but "a normal" one. During the 1980 referendum campaign, the most interesting thing that happened was something that did not happen: not once did Lévesque invoke the need to protect the French language and culture as the reason Quebec had to become sovereign.

Bilingualism, though, has not come about in quite the way Trudeau hoped it would. Its final version amounts to something roughly mid-way between his vision of a truly bilingual Canada with the French Fact alive and well anywhere it happens to have implanted itself, and Lévesque's vision of an "irreversibly" French Quebec, with francophones elsewhere having to scramble as best they can to survive.

As demographer Richard Joy reported for the C.D. Howe Institute in 1978, the country is "polarizing" along language lines. More for economic than for cultural reasons, many anglophones have left Quebec (close to 100,000 in 1977-79); the exodus indeed preceded Bill 101 and the PQ victory, with the percentage of anglophones in the province declining from 13.1 per cent to 12.7 per cent between 1971 and 1976. Anglophone institutions like the Sun Life have moved, or like the *Montreal Star*, have closed for lack of an audience. By 1984, the Greater Montreal Protestant School Board expects to have to close half its schools.

In reverse, the same process continues outside Quebec. A study by *La Fédération des Francophones Hors Québec* has calculated that of 1.4 million "ethnic origin" francophones outside Quebec fewer than half speak French in their homes. Studies by the Ontario Institute for Studies in Education have concluded that so-called "bilingual" schools lead to the assimilation of francophone students into the anglophone culture that dominates the corridors and playgrounds; in a typical, defensive gesture, Acadians in Bathurst, New Brunswick, lobbied the school board into subdividing two bilingual schools into four unilingual ones; in Penetanguishene, Ontario, francophones fought for and at last won the right to run their own "parallel" unilingual school.

Canada, it seems, is on its way to becoming a kind of Belgium, divided into two unilingual ghettos with Ottawa, like Brussels, as the only bilingual meeting-ground. New Brunswick is the only province to have been declared officially bilingual, and even there, "the leisurely implementation of the Official Languages Act contrasts oddly with the stirrings of Acadian nationalism," in the phrase of Official Languages Commissioner Max Yalden. Universities still pursue "barely warm bodies" to fill their classrooms rather than insisting on French, or English, as an entrance requirement. Ontario still resists declaring itself officially bilingual, a gesture first recommended by the B and B Commission a dozen years ago.

Yet Canada is different from Belgium. Ontario, for a francophone minority that after all constitutes no more than 5 per cent of its population, does now provide most government services, including legal services, in both languages; Franco-Ontarians fill their full 5 per cent of civil service posts (against only an equivalent 2 per cent by anglophones in Quebec); TV-Ontario broadcasts one-fifth of its programs in French. Premier Davis has done as much for Franco-Ontarians as he could have accomplished through a bilingual law, and probably more, since he has managed to avoid a backlash. Also, in British Columbia and in Saskatchewan French-speaking parents can now, by provincial law, educate their children in the language of their choice.

Within Quebec, anglophones have come to terms with their condition as a minority. Symbolized by organizations such as the Positive Action Committee, attitudes have changed from condescension, through disbelief and resentment, to a sense of excitement at living out a gigantic social experiment. More and more, the phrase "Anglo-Quebecer" is used with pride. More and more, the community's catch phrase has become, *integration*.

Beyond Quebec, enrolment in French immersion schools has soared to 26,000 in 1978-79, from 17,000 two years earlier. In elementary schools, 45 per cent of students now study French compared to 28 per cent in 1970, and in secondary schools enrolment has at last stabilized at 41.5 per cent.

Middle-class parents now compete to ram French down the throats of their children, because it's chic ("bright kids take

251

French'') but even more because it's an asset in an uncertain job market.

First to last, Trudeau pursued bilingualism because it was right and just. The reason he is now in sight of his goal is because bilingualism has turned out to be commercially profitable. The Trudeau of 1968 would have grimaced with distaste at such crassness. The Trudeau of 1980 would respond with a wry smile, understanding that the profit motive is wholly rational.

* * *

The difference between Belgium and Canada may be no more than a demographic accident. As Flemish is not, both of Canada's official languages are mainstream international languages and the bearers of two of the world's richest cultures. If so, *vive la différence*.

The result of the referendum will make us less like Belgium, and more like ourselves. Yet even before May 20, 1980, the fundamental change in the character of Canada was apparent. Joe Clark said it best: ''The Canada that Mr. Lévesque wants to separate from no longer exists.''

15

European Canadian

"Canada could be called upon to serve as a mentor provided she has sense enough to conceive her own future on a grand scale."

Pierre Elliott Trudeau
Federalism and the French Canadians

From 1867 all the way to the Centennial, the *tableau vivant* image that defined the government of Canada was always the same. For *mise en scène*, the cabinet chamber in the East Block of Parliament Hill. For principals, the Prime Minister of the day, flanked by his cabinet ministers, among them powerful lieutenants like C.D. Howe or Jimmy Gardiner or Chubby Power, or, closer to our own time, Paul Martin.

During the Trudeau era, that image has changed. Except that it takes place on television, the contemporary *tableau vivant* is much closer to a flashback to pre-Confederation times: the Quebec Conference of 1864 as depicted in the famous Robert Harris painting. John A. Macdonald beating out the beginnings of the BNA Act with powerful regional warlords like Charles Tupper, George-Etienne Cartier, Alexander Galt.

Nowadays the *mise en scène* has moved a block eastward from Parliament Hill, with its marble corridors and carved stone gargoyles so redolent of history and continuity, to the bland boardroom-broadloom interior of the railway-gothic Canadian Intergovernmental Conference Centre, once Ottawa's Union Station. The principals are not the Prime Minister and his cabinet any longer, but the Prime Minister and today's regional warlords – the premiers. Together they comprise Canada's co-equal, *First Ministers*. At the First Ministers Conferences, the Prime Minister sits at the head of a horseshoe table. He gets to chair the meetings, and to say the opening and closing words. The ten provincial premiers are seated around him in order of precedence dictated by the date their province entered Confederation, Ontario (Canada West, 1867), to Newfoundland (1949). But the character of the country's new, national government is exemplified by the flags positioned on the dais behind the table. Each of the eleven banners is of equal size, except that the pole that bears the Maple Leaf stands a timorous six inches taller than the rest.

* * *

Trudeau came to power to change Canada by changing its constitution. He made two galvanic attempts, in 1968-71, and in 1976-79, and he failed, utterly. By the time he was defeated, he had won an agreement with the provinces on just one point: at a meeting in February 1979, everyone agreed to transfer Family Law from federal to provincial jurisdiction.

However, while the nation's constitution was not changed by a comma, the nation's political structures were transformed. As often as not without realizing it, Trudeau, up to 1979, presided over changes to the country's political system incomparably more important than even the most innovative of his proposed constitutional changes. Bilingualism is one example of non-constitutional, but fundamental, change. So too is unilingualism. Lévesque's Bill 101, of which only a couple of clauses breached the constitution,* constituted the most radical reform of language laws enacted by any *independent* country since World War Two, except for Belgium and Malaysia.

Federal-Provincial Conferences are another example, and here are more to the point. "Grotesque unreality, untrammelled by logic," the late political scientist R. MacGregor Dawson described these in 1947. Still true, except that no one nowadays would want to be so flip about Canada's new, and in the global context, unique, fourth level of government. By the late 1970's, federal-provincial relations had become institutionalized and formalized into a hierarchical pyramid: at the pinnacle, the First Ministers Conference held once a year at minimum; extending downwards from there through meetings (all in secret, naturally) of just plain ministers, or deputy ministers, or quite humble officials, gathered to discuss everything from the state of the nation's finances to Maritime Strawberry Crop Replacement. As the number of meetings mushroomed, from 119 in 1967 to 556 in 1976, "federal-provincial diplomacy" in the phrase of Queen's political scientist

*According to the December 13, 1979, judgement of the Supreme Court of Canada.

Richard Simeon, became the new bureaucratic growth industry. No government, it seemed, could talk to any other government without the intermediary of a domestic diplomatic corps. In Ottawa, in 1970, barely a dozen people worked at the Federal Provincial Relations Office (FPRO). By 1978, there were ninety. Alberta had FIGA (Federal and Intergovernmental Affairs); Quebec, much more stylishly, had *Affaires-Inter*. Many of these new courtiers had learned their social graces at External Affairs.

It all amounted to a mysterious new kind of *national* government through which the provinces and Ottawa ran the country jointly—out of reach of Parliament and the legislatures. From this, to Newfoundland Premier Brian Peckford's scenario of Canada as "ten separate societies" is only a short step. The point of puzzlement being that all of this had happened under the aegis of a Prime Minister who won power under the banner of "One Canada."

A parallel puzzle is that during the same decade that Trudeau was attacked unceasingly as a "rigid/inflexible/hard-line" centralist, the country underwent its most extensive decentralization of power since Confederation.

By the end of the 1970's, Canada had in fact become the world's most-decentralized country. Ottawa controlled no more than 40 per cent of total public spending;* no other central government controlled less than 50 per cent. (When Trudeau came to power in 1968, Ottawa's share had been 55 per cent.) Typical of what went on, Ottawa, in 1977, handed over to the provinces $6 billion worth of previously, shared-cost programs covering medicare, hospital insurance, and post-secondary education. Economist Thomas Courchene has described this transfer as, "a substantial devolution of power . . . a reworking, de facto, of the BNA Act."

The less Ottawa controlled, the more provincial power grew. Provinces applied their expanded power exclusively for their own sakes, naturally, but, where need arose, to the detriment of all other Canadians. By 1980, a good case could be made that more barriers to the free movement of goods, services, and labour existed between the provinces than between the sovereign member states of the European Economic Community. (For instance, doctors, nurses, notaries, architects, engineers, could move more

*Since Ottawa spent one-fifth of its outlays just on interest charges on the national debt, its share of that spending on social and economic programs was proportionately less.

easily between France and West Germany, say, than between Nova Scotia and Manitoba.) Some provinces limited land purchases to non-residents; some refused to allow non-residents to buy their industries; some refused jobs to non-residents. All, in different ways, practised discriminatory purchasing policies.

The extent of the governmental mess that Trudeau had caused to happen, or failed to prevent happening, only really became clear at the end of the 1970's. The Economic Council in its 1979 annual report concluded that Ottawa had lost so much financial control that it was becoming "increasingly powerless, to the peril of the country as a whole, and the welfare of all Canadians." Trudeau's successor, Clark, who came to power a staunch "provincialist," turned right around, and warned in December 1979, "The federal government is not as able as it should be to manage the national economy, overcome regional disparities, and conduct national policies." A C.D. Howe Research Institute Report early in 1980 diagnosed a "process of disintegration" because the provinces had abandoned the Canadian common market in pursuit of "their own balanced, self-contained little economies."

Canadians indeed re-elected Trudeau in order to repair the damage he had done to the central government, but turning back to him much in the manner of someone guided into a swamp who reckons even so that the errant guide at least ought to know the way back.

Through the 1970's, power was bound to flow to the provinces, and so to make national decision-making progressively more difficult. Small is Beautiful was the slogan of the times, a sentiment Trudeau prefigured in his 1961 essay for *Social Purpose in Canada*: "In the age of mass society, it is no small advantage to foster the creation of quasi-sovereign communities at the provincial level, where power is that much less remote from the people."

Mostly, power sharing turned out to mean squabbling over each other's share. In 1977, the four western provinces compiled a list of fifty-seven federal "intrusions" into their jurisdictions. Many of the complaints by successive Quebec governments against mother Ottawa turned out to have been justified: a task force of Trudeau's own officials, in a report kept confidential until after his defeat, concluded: "There appear to be relatively few instances in which a federal department or agency was aware of the impact of its actions on the people of Quebec."

In a backhanded way, Trudeau admitted some of these criticisms. In 1979, he scrapped his Department of Urban Affairs, which had spent the previous decade inventing things to do and blundering about in the provinces' domain. Yet, somehow, he lacked the authority to complain when the same kind of thing was done to him. Typically, in 1975, Blakeney nationalized Saskatchewan's potash industry without bothering to consult Ottawa, even though his policy affected the attitudes of foreign investors toward the whole of the country.

All the individual squabbles, pyramiding on top of one another, added up to a deeper malaise. During the 1970's, the national psyche went through a sea change, and not for the better. In his 1979 exercise in acerbity, *Points of Departure*, Dalton Camp looked at the future and cringed. Gone, he wrote, was "a communal sense of sharing in an uncommon adventure." A year earlier, in a speech to the Empire Club in Toronto, Laura Sabia, former chairperson of the Ontario Council on the Status of Women, had described things even more bleakly: "We're divided now, regionally, linguistically, ethnically, Canadian pitted against Canada, resentment piled on resentment . . . on and on into a nightmare of divisiveness."

Trudeau was responsible for some of this; 23 million Canadians were responsible for the rest of it. Partly, it was the temper of the times: the heady expansiveness of the 1960's giving way to meanspirited crabbiness as our economic expectations began to shrivel. Partly, it was the ingrown vision of the Me Generation. From St. John's to Victoria, we narrowed our sights on our own horizons, and found them lacking.

* * *

A good place to start looking for the historical causes of the decline of the pan-Canadian spirit is Heather Robertson's 1971 book, *Grass Roots*. In it, she delivers an elegy for the prairie farmer, then fast disappearing, the real family farmer who lived year round on his half section instead of wintering in a bungalow in Regina or Edmonton–or Hawaii. "His gradual disappearance," Robertson wrote, "shakes our sense of identity and makes us question the value of our history. The farmer is the guardian of the Western dream; without him, the West is just the East."

The point is that Canadians, for all our rhetoric about our

regional differences, are surprisingly all of a piece when held up collectively to the light. To any foreign visitor, the difference between a British Columbian, say, and a Nova Scotian, is almost indistinguishable; incomparably less than between a Californian and a Georgian, a Shropshire lad and one from Lancashire, a Breton and an Alsatian, a Bavarian and a Prussian, a Sicilian and a Genoese. Even the authentic regional voices among us speak with pretty much the same accent—Québécois apart, and, less markedly so, Newfoundlanders. Except for Québécois and again, less markedly, Newfoundlanders, we have all experienced too brief a history, and have been much too deeply immersed in the North American melting pot, to have developed deep-rooted, cultural differences. Always, the difference that matters between us has been not so much regional but urban/rural. The gap between a Torontonian and a Calgarian and a Haligonian, say, is considerably narrower than that between a Torontonian and an eastern Ontario scrub-farmer.

All the more because our differences are so slight, we cherish them as central to our mystique. Through the 1960's and into the 1970's, the hinterland middle class that lived outside the Golden Triangle of Toronto-Ottawa-Montreal and that, thanks to affluence and mass university education was rapidly expanding, began to realize that its own regional mystique was disappearing fast. If the family farmer of the prairies was disappearing as guardian of the western dream, so, also for instance, were the inshore fishermen of Newfoundland, keepers of another kind of dream, disappearing quickly from the bays, or being resettled out of them. Those who remained were being homogenized—if the west is the same as the east, the east is the same as the west—by affluence, by education, by highway systems, by air travel, and above all, by television. Since they no longer were different, they no longer had any reason to be where they were, and might as well all move to Toronto, Ottawa, Montreal.

So the fact that in 1980, Newfoundland Premier Brian Peckford should have emerged as the most "nationalist" of the English-speaking premiers was quite predictable. Peckford's attitudes flow directly out of Newfoundland's cultural-nationalist flowering of the mid-1970's which mirrored, on a smaller scale, the cultural renaissance that went hand in hand with Quebec's Quiet Revolution a decade earlier. Artists like Christopher Pratt and Frank

258

Lapointe, theatre troupes like Codco and the Mummers, passionate cultural spokesmen like Clyde Rose of Breakwater Press and Memorial University Art Gallery director, Edythe Goodridge, most of them products, like Peckford himself, of Newfoundland's first home-grown university generation, gave inspired and angry expression to their sense of loss and betrayal at being denied their chance to be "real Newfoundlanders," like those inshore fishermen still left in the bays, none of whom had ever had the least doubt about their identity.

Understanding Peter Lougheed's abiding suspicion of the east and his intransigence toward it is just as easy. All that needs to be said is that Alberta is the most urbanized of the western provinces, dominated by what the political scientist Larry Pratt has called "a new *arriviste bourgeoisie*" that is determined to have everything the east has, and is determined further to have it on its own turf; a new middle class that some while back grew fed up with having to knock on bankers' doors in Toronto, and at being looked at down the long noses of bureaucrats in Ottawa.

In the beginning, this new "hinterland" middle class cherished and celebrated its own folkloric past, or just muttered into its beer. Then, gathering strength and self-confidence into the 1970's, it set out to redefine its own future, on its own terms. All across the country, the new people had an identical goal: the right not to have to leave home in search of interesting, meaningful jobs that promised status and salaries not to mention, fun, but to have these jobs at home. Standing in their way were two obstacles: the cultural-communications-financial-commercial hegemony of Toronto; the political hegemony of Ottawa.

* * *

Ottawa and Toronto, place names redolent of bold men in canoes, usher in the other inexorable historical force which has shaped Canada's evolution in the 1970's, and which has reshaped us into a radically different kind of country from the "One Canada" Trudeau had in mind when he came to power. If, coast to coast, our regions are less distinct than we care to admit, we are ourselves, from sea to sea, much less Canadian than we like to suppose.

The "One Canada" ideal has lasted little longer than a decade – from 1957, when John Diefenbaker coined the phrase, to around 1970, when the memories of Expo and the Centennial

259

were still resonant enough to give weight to Trudeau's re-use of the phrase. Until the 1940's, most of us derived our identity from our membership in the British Empire; among us, only French Canadians called themselves *Canadiens*. Throughout our history, the sources of our sense of identity have either been "local in origin," in Northrop Frye's phrase, or have been pan-North American. As every local television licence holder or newspaper publisher knows, the interest of his audience is focused either upon the strictly local – themselves or their next-door neighbours – or upon *Dallas* and the (real) Big Apple – with the rest of Canada, Ottawa and Toronto only marginally less so, occupying a tenuous, fuzzily focused middle-distance.

During the hey-day of One Canada, Toronto tried hard to make itself the "one," cultural-communications-financial-commercial capital for English Canada. As for Ottawa, resting on the laurels it had won by winning the war and then presiding over the post-war boom and creating the welfare state, it took for granted it would remain the one political capital of Canada for eternity.

Toronto, in its time at the top, accomplished a great deal. Thanks to the post-war flood of immigrants, a narrow Waspish enclave metamorphosed into a true cosmopolitan metropolis, and established itself as the arbiter and market place for English-Canadian culture and commerce. Yet this sovereignty was doomed from the start. Toronto was not and could never become as London is to Britain, or Paris is to France, or as New York/Los Angeles is to the United States. All these places are natural cultural-commercial fountain-heads, acknowledged as such by their citizenry, even if detested because of it. Toronto is only a tributary of the mainstream, no matter how broad and how powerful. To an artist in Lethbridge, or Fredericton, or anywhere in Canada, the dominant cultural patterns are established in New York or, even now, in London, rather than in Toronto. (Artists go to Toronto to sell, rather than to learn.) And in commercial terms, most of the decisions a "hinterland" entrepreneur has to cope with are determined in the end, not by Toronto but by New York or Chicago or Detroit, not to mention Tokyo and Frankfurt.

Toronto reached its zenith in the late 1970's, although for a time its downtilt was masked by a sideways shift of commercial activity from Montreal. Ottawa peaked much earlier; the 1973-74 oil boycott, which freed the west from economic dependency, marks the point of transition.

* * *

It took a while for Ottawa's decline to become apparent. It was not really until 1979, and then, as much as anything because Joe Clark, as Prime Minister, happened to look weak on television that the general public became concerned that the centre could not hold, nor, therefore, could the country.

A few observers had been more prescient. As early as 1973, political scientist John Wilson described the country as "a loose collection of at least ten political systems," with Ottawa functioning "as sort of Canadian UNESCO." Again in 1973, *Maclean's* editor, Bill Cunningham, wrote:

> There's a basic difference between power and image. Image is going on TV a lot. Power is doing things. Federal politics is image. Provincial politics is power. For the last ten years, we've all been looking in the wrong place. We thought that Ottawa ran the country. They (the premiers) know better. Ottawa runs itself. They run the country.*

This analysis got right to the point. Because for reasons of network costs and because federal politics, in Donald Smiley's phrase, is "our preferred spectator sport," federal politicians were the ones who kept showing up on television, it was easy for Canadians to assume that Ottawa alone mattered, all the more because television is the arbiter of what really counts. Indeed, about the only way in which Canada became more centralized during the Trudeau years was that thanks to Pierre and Margaret acting out "Can this marriage be saved?" in sensational instalments, not to mention Otto Lang and his flying nannies, Turner and his tennis racket, Coutts hatching conspiracies in the fourth alcove on the right at the Chateau Laurier Grill, the burning question of whether or not Maureen McTeer would ever give in and call herself Clark, Ottawa, in a triumph of style over content, transformed itself into the nation's capital of gossip and entertainment, with the rest of the country waiting breathlessly for the next episode. The prov-

---

*PQ Finance Minister Jacques Parizeau claims to have realized in 1968 that Ottawa had been weakened to a point of "madness," and that, because Canada no longer was governable, Quebec, to save itself, had to separate.

inces built roads; Ottawa was the dream factory. Not Athens-on-the-Rideau now, but *Dallas North*.

The reason power passed from Ottawa in the 1970's could not have been simpler. It had run out of things to do. By then, in most of the areas of undisputed federal jurisdiction – defence, foreign affairs, trade, economic and financial management – most of the decisions that mattered were being taken not on the banks of the Rideau but on the banks of the Potomac. If Washington bailed out Chrysler, Ottawa followed suit; as U.S. interest rates rose or declined, ours locked into step. After World War Two, Ottawa, as the phrase went, had "Finlandized" Canada, selling off our resources and our industries in order to generate a cash flow to finance economic growth and the welfare state. Once these things were accomplished, Ottawa, as the historian Garth Stevenson has written in *Unfulfilled Union*, "lost most of its original reason for being and hence much of its authority and legitimacy."

* * *

If Trudeau understood the historical forces that were fragmenting the country, he seldom showed it. Strikingly, his June 1978 constitutional proposals made only a passing complaint about the most significant of all the forms of national fragmentation, that "the free circulation of goods, services and workers is not always assured," and proposed no remedies.* Only right at the end of his third term did he appear to appreciate how marginal to most Canadians the federal government had become. Late in 1978, he raised the battle-cry "Who shall speak for Canada?" On the eve of the 1979 election, in a speech in Vancouver, he warned that Canada might become so decentralized, "that we'll have a piece of geography with ten principalities with semi-sovereign status, and a federal government that can't do anything."

Trudeau, though, was describing a Canada that he had helped create. His policy of multiculturalism, for instance, had given official sanction to new hybrid identities, as in Alberta-Canadian or Newfoundlander-Canadian. His "consensual" style of decision-making emasculated his regional ministers so that, in contrast to

*The problem, which Trudeau at last addressed in his 1980 constitutional proposals, is that the BNA Act requires only that "Goods shall be admitted free" from one province to another, but imposes no restraints on non-tariff barriers, which can, even far more easily than tariffs, fragment the Canadian common market.

the Jimmy Gardiners and J.L. Illsleys of yesteryear, he had no one around him to serve his purpose by competing with the premiers as regional spokesmen.* By pulling the federal government away from daily contact with Canadians, he hastened the country's fragmentation into ten principalities. Less than a year after Ottawa's 1977 withdrawal from shared-cost health programs, Health Minister Monique Bégin was complaining bitterly about her inability to maintain national standards in the face of mass opting-out by doctors (in Ontario, 18 per cent). By the end of the decade, most Canadians encountered Ottawa only in the most cheerless of its manifestations, as a (laggard) deliverer of mail and a (prompt) collector of taxes – so that it was small wonder that in the 1979 election they paid little heed when Trudeau called for support for a stronger Ottawa.

The contradiction between Trudeau's declared reason for coming to Ottawa – "because I felt the central government was too weak" – and the reality of the frayed national fabric his first eleven years in power produced is so glaring that it almost defies analysis. Yet some explanations exist. Unlike most Prime Ministers, Trudeau came to power without any particular social or economic goals in mind, so he did not care all that much whether or not Ottawa possessed the power to achieve this or that. He came to care only when Ottawa's apparent impotence began to threaten the structure of federalism itself, which is another matter. (He also acquired, in the way of every politician and bureaucrat, a keen sense of the territorial imperative, but this was possessiveness rather than purposefulness.)

In the second place, by discouraging English-Canadian nationalism, because he feared it would provoke yet more intense Quebec nationalism, Trudeau robbed Ottawa of much of its legitimizing authority. Here and there he made certain concessions – FIRA, removing tax advantages from *Time* – as hostages to political necessity. But his heart was not in it. The truth is that unless Ottawa espouses nationalism, there is not a great deal left for it to espouse; bilingualism, as a rallying point for a pan-Canadian consciousness, just isn't enough. Revealingly, Trudeau only began to

---

*This process really began at the 1973 Western Economic Opportunities Conference, at which the four western premiers represented the west, while Trudeau's own regional ministers, such as Otto Lang, functioned more or less as his backroom aides.

espouse nationalist policies, in 1980, *after* he had reached the conclusion that the federal government no longer possessed the power to "speak for Canada."

Trudeau, third, was convinced that if Quebec acquired "special status," it would by attrition become for Quebecers *the* government, and lead on inevitably to full sovereignty. In order to give Quebec what it wanted, and at the same time keep Confederation "balanced," Trudeau gave equally to everybody. For example, because Quebec operated its own pension plan, all provinces were given exclusive control over their share of funds generated by the Canada Pension Plan. The handover of tax points to fund the Canada Assistance Plan is another example. In the process, Trudeau helped to make all provinces "special"; he also helped build up provincial bureaucracies which, predictably, turned right around and bit the hand that fed them, by demanding more. Quebec, in the meantime, lost none of its appetite for special status.

The fourth and last explanation is the most obvious. Trudeau had thought deeply about the constitution before he entered politics. He had a juridical cast of mind. He really believed in federalism as an ideal, "order based on law," as he once wrote. Which was fine, except that the system of Soviet Russia also is based on the law; its Bill of Rights is a splendid document. He missed the point that Canadian federalism is higgledy-piggledy, order in disorder, based on nothing more high-minded than political convenience leavened by common sense. So that for all their symbolic value, Trudeau's various attempts to reform the constitution had little or nothing to do with the way the country really worked. Indeed, the reason his proposal in 1980 to entrench language rights in the constitution caused so little fuss was that, by then, bilingualism had become entrenched as a political fact. Canadians by then had done for him what he had spent a decade trying to do to them.

*　*　*

Trudeau's attempts to 1979 to change the constitution accomplished so little that the task of chronicling them belongs more properly to an archivist than a reporter. But he did manage to educate Canadians about their constitution and thus, in a backhanded fashion, created a powerful momentum in favour of change. At the very least, by 1980, a decade of talk about changing the constitution had convinced everyone that it absolutely had to be changed, if not necessarily to accomplish anything in particular, then to accomplish it for its own sake as an exercise in nation-building.

In what he set out to do, Trudeau was extraordinarily bold. Not for more than a century, not since Switzerland in 1874, has any country managed to change its constitution, except when forced into it by the imperatives of war, civil war, or national liberation.

The difficulties facing Trudeau were sketched out for him eloquently at a federal-provincial conference in February 1969. The speaker was Jean-Jacques Bertrand, Daniel Johnson's Union Nationale successor as Quebec's Premier. "If there is a crisis in Canada," Bertrand said, "it is not because our country is made up of individuals who speak different languages; it is because Canada is the home of two communities, two peoples, two nations." Between this concept of Confederation and Trudeau's, there could be no compromise, and so no new constitution.

Then, in 1970, the gap between the two visions of Canada narrowed. In place of Bertrand, Quebecers elected Liberal Robert Bourassa, who preached what he described as "profitable federalism," and who ended the attempts of his bureaucrats such as Claude Morin to sneak Quebec into the sanctuary of special status by the back door route of international diplomacy.

Thereafter, Trudeau pushed ahead with his constitutional proposals, convinced that at last these would have a reasonable prospect of being accepted.

In June 1971, the Victoria Conference, which was intended to be the finale of the entire exercise, began with hail-fellow-well-met camaraderie. W.A.C. Bennett, still premier of B.C., staged a vast open-air cavalcade through the city: Trudeau in a mammoth Cadillac, in the vanguard; Prince Edward Island's Alex Campbell in a Mustang, bringing up the rear. In mid-conference everyone set off on a moonlight cruise aboard a British Columbia government ferry; those who remembered to bring along their own bottles in defiance of Bennett's equation of alcohol with sin were able to extract in exchange for a drink on the sly just about any constitutional concession from anybody.

When it came to proceedings in the legislative chamber, the fact that is remarkable in hindsight is not that Trudeau failed but that he came so close by offering so little. Distribution of powers, the holy grail of the premiers ever since, was not even on the agenda. The key point was patriation of the constitution from Westminster and an amending formula that would give Ontario and Quebec a full veto, and British Columbia a kind of half-veto. The provinces would also have a limited say in the appointment of Supreme Court judges. In return, Trudeau would get his much-cherished Bill of Rights (which did not add up to much more than pieties), official recognition of the equality of French and English, which five provinces agreed to apply within their own domains,* and recognition of the jurisdictional status quo in perpetuity.

In fact, it was John Turner, as Justice Minister, rather than Trudeau, who jollied the nine English-speaking premiers into accepting much *less*, in terms of their jurisdictional self-interest, than they would turn down at the next batch of constitutional talks, in 1978-79.

Trudeau's job, and Lalonde's as his principal adviser, was to get Bourassa to agree. They nearly did. In conversations with the pair before the meeting, Bourassa declared he was ready to sign; during the meeting, he declared he was about to do so. Afterwards, he changed his mind. Or it was changed for him. One key persuader was Claude Morin, then a top civil servant, later to become a Parti Québécois minister, who convinced Bourassa's most powerful minister, Claude Castonguay, that the federal proposals were unacceptable because they failed to concede jurisdiction over social policy. A second influence on Bourassa was Claude Ryan, then editor of *Le Devoir*, who at the time was an advocate of special status. Bourassa buckled under this double pressure, and three weeks after the conference ended announced he would not sign the charter.

Two years later, in 1973, Lalonde, by then Welfare Minister, conceded to Castonguay the jurisdiction he had wanted, quite a minor matter in fact, that gave Quebec, and all provinces, the right to vary family allowance payments. Had Lalonde made this offer in 1971, Bourassa could not have refused it, and Trudeau would have had his cherished constitution.

At the time, the collapse of the Victoria Charter was described as "a tragedy," and as "Canada's missed opportunity." Yet the charter had been drafted to conform to a country that even then

---

*Quebec, Ontario, New Brunswick, Newfoundland, Prince Edward Island.

no longer existed. It took for granted, for instance, that the federal government was *the* government of all Canadians. It also took for granted that Quebec was simply a province like all the others. If the Victoria Charter had actually been enacted, it probably would have lasted no longer than Canada's first constitution, the Royal Proclamation of 1763, superseded in 1774 by the Quebec Act. The same could be said of Trudeau's second attempt to draft a new constitution, although this time the sufferer on the Procrustean bed was no longer the provinces, but Trudeau's own embattled, bedraggled, federal government.

* * *

Four and a half years passed before Trudeau began his next attempt. This time he set off on the wrong foot. On March 5, 1976, in Quebec City for a speech, Trudeau told reporters, out of the blue, that he was prepared to patriate the constitution "unilaterally" by himself, in one fell swoop, if he could not get the premiers to agree on an amending formula. This threat amazed and discomfited his ministers and aides, none of whom could explain why he had blurted it out.

For quite different reasons, Trudeau could not explain either. That morning, as recounted in Chapter 13, Bourassa had told Trudeau privately that he could not meet the Queen when she arrived at Quebec City as prelude to opening the Olympics. Outraged by such political cowardice, Trudeau lashed out at Bourassa in any way he could, from calling him an "eater of hot dogs" to demonstrating his powerlessness by threatening to patriate the constitution unilaterally.

As it happened, nothing came of any of this, because in November, Lévesque defeated Bourassa, and immediately declared he would take no part in constitutional discussions until Quebecers had made up their minds about their future in a referendum.

For a time, Trudeau seemed to accept this impasse. Soon after the PQ victory, he warned against the "panacea of decentralization" which was fast becoming most popular of commentators' remedies to the threat to national survival posed by the PQ's accession to power. In mid-1977, he tried, and failed, to interest Lévesque in accepting a constitutional amendment which would bind all provinces into providing education in both official languages on demand; (Lévesque held out for province-to-province "reciprocal agreements," which would have bypassed Ottawa).

It was not until the autumn of 1977 that he appointed Marc Lalonde as Minister of State for Federal-Provincial Relations and, with his most trusted aide as his point man, began the work of drafting a new batch of constitutional proposals in earnest.

This year-long delay following the PQ victory — the breakup of his marriage is the most evident of the reasons for his procrastination—cost Trudeau his second and as it seemed to be at the time, last chance to redefine Canada through a revised constitution. If he had acted in the fall of 1977, he might have achieved what he by then had spent a decade trying to achieve, and so been able to proceed contentedly into retirement. Lévesque, no question, would have thrown up every roadblock possible. But the prevailing mood of English Canada—patriotic fervour spurred on by panic—might well have been powerful enough to propel the nine English-speaking premiers into giving Trudeau most of what he wanted, which he then could have deployed as a demonstration of "renewed federalism," in advance of Quebec's referendum.

By June 1978, when Trudeau published his constitutional package, first in the White Paper, *A Time for Action*, and subsequently in the detailed draft legislation, Bill C-60, the political will for change had evaporated. Ryan had become the new federalist champion in Quebec. Gratefully, English Canada drifted back into complacency. Further, by now, everyone could dismiss Trudeau's constitutional proposals as pre-election gimmickry.

After the initial flurry of dutiful editorial comment, about the only aspect of Trudeau's proposals that stirred excitement was what everyone imagined he was trying to do to the Queen. By raising the Governor General to the new status of "First Citizen" of Canada, who would open and dissolve Parliament in his own name rather than in Hers, Trudeau appeared to be trying to downgrade her. He kept on protesting his innocence. To prove it, he had to agree to scrap all the proposed new constitutional clauses that referred either to "His Excellency" or to "Her Majesty."

Then a second contrary wind blew against him. Trudeau's critical path called for agreement on patriation with an amending formula by July 1, 1979 (in the absence of which he would act unilaterally), to be followed by discussions with the provinces on the "distribution" of powers. At their annual August meeting in Regina, the premiers formed a grandiosely titled "common front." Unless Trudeau advanced distribution of powers to the top of his agenda, they would refuse to discuss *any* agenda items.

Rarely noticed in the midst of the politicking – the only Liberal Premier left was Prince Edward Island's Alex Campbell – was the imaginative sweep of some of Trudeau's proposals. He wanted to scrap the Senate and replace it with a House of the Federation, half of its members to be chosen by provincial legislatures to oversee their interests in the federal government. The new constitution would entrench minority language rights, but each province could shoulder this burden, "at once, or when they saw fit." The provinces would gain a say in appointments to the Supreme Court, and to key federal regulatory agencies.

Trudeau seemed trapped between public indifference and provincial opposition. As always, when his back is to the wall, he bounded back. On October 31, 1978, the second day of a three-day First Ministers Conference in Ottawa, he astonished the premiers by taking them at their word. Provided they moved on his agenda, he would move on theirs. To demonstrate his good intentions, he tabled a "short list" of seven items of federal jurisdiction on which he was prepared to yield ground; from limiting Ottawa's use of its emergency powers, "to instances of compelling national interest," to the handover of jurisdiction over Family Law, and a share in communications regulations. "Something is happening at last," Lévesque declared.

"I've almost given away the store myself," Trudeau admitted at his closing press conference. By agreeing to concede federal jurisdiction, he secured no more than a provincial agreement to *consider* his own proposed constitutional changes, of which most, such as the new House of the Federation, involved still further concessions to provincial expansion. A committee of ministers and officials eventually reached unanimity on just one point – to transfer jurisdiction over Family Law. Even though, at the next First Ministers Conference, in February 1979, he won an ally in Ontario's Bill Davis, who proposed, that if all else failed, "we at least bring the constitution to Canada," Trudeau lacked the political authority, by now even the energy, to cajole all of the premiers to his side. So ended his second attempt. Soon afterwards, voters ended his political career.

This time, no one called Trudeau's failure a tragedy. Rather, in prototypical paradox, that label would have been more apt had he

269

succeeded. In 1977-79, bargaining from weakness, he almost did "give up the shop" to the provinces. Had the premiers then signed on the dotted line, they would have given Trudeau his cherished Bill of Rights and patriation and have won for themselves expanded powers; in the process, Ottawa would have been emasculated, "unable to cope with increasing regional fragmentation and a deteriorating international competitiveness," as the C. D. Howe Institute study of 1980 put it. By their obduracy then, the premiers saved Trudeau from himself. By June, 1980, when he began his next attempt, his own re-election and the referendum result gave Trudeau the strength to bargain hard. He found it "depressing and distressing," he said at a July Liberal convention in Winnipeg, that the provinces should try to barter increased powers for themselves in return for a Bill of Rights for all Canadians. To his own list of demands he added, as he dared not do in 1977-79, "economic freedoms," to prevent the provinces from turning into "garrison states," into which Canadians from other provinces could not move, in search of jobs, or land. And in exchange for powers to be ceded to the provinces, in communications for instance, he now wanted expanded federal power to manage the economy.

The effect of the referendum result upon Trudeau's fortunes embodies yet one more paradox. For years, the motive force of his almost frantic attempts to change the constitution was his conviction that unless he demonstrated that federalism could be "renewed," the referendum would be lost. Instead, it was only once the referendum was won that Canadians gave Trudeau a mandate to renew federalism by changing the constitution, partly to end the endless palaver, more so to fulfil the implicit contract Quebecers signed by the way they chose to mark their ballots on May 20, 1980.

* * *

In the meantime the blows to Trudeau's pride were not all over. In February 1979, the Task Force on Canadian Unity, appointed by him in 1977, and co-chaired by the former Liberal minister Jean-Luc Pépin* and former Ontario Premier John Robarts issued its report. Mostly, the Task Force concluded, Canada had gone

---

*Pépin returned to the cabinet in 1980.

from bad to worse because of things Trudeau had done or had not done, from implementing "costly and relatively ineffective" institutional bilingualism, to failing to recognize that Canada's defining characteristics were "duality and regionalism." As token of duality, the Task Force proposed, Quebec should be granted a "distinctive" though not a special status. In token of regionalism, all provinces should get more powers, from responsibility for their residents' "cultural and social well being," and on down the line to authority to negotiate treaties in areas of their own jurisdiction.

Lévesque praised the Task Force report, for "recognizing the duality of the two people of Canada." Lalonde, when he met the commissioners, seethed with fury. Trudeau, though, was equable, and praised the group for a good job well done.

Still to come, in January 1980, and moving Trudeau yet one step further away from his "One Canada" goal, was Ryan's constitutional document, *A New Canadian Federation*, also known as the Beige Paper. As Ryan saw it, Quebec possessed "all the characteristics of a distinct national community." All provinces should acquire expanded powers (jurisdiction over manpower and unemployment insurance, for instance). Through a new Federal Council composed exclusively of provincial representatives, provinces should exercise a veto over major initiatives by the federal government. Not long afterwards, Peckford described the federal government as "an agency of the provinces, something we have created for our common welfare."

By 1980, the statement repeated, to the point of stupefaction, "The status quo is unacceptable" had become the national byword that "Participatory Democracy" had been a decade earlier. Nor did it make the least difference that the "status quo" had not been static for two decades, adding Pearson's term to Trudeau's. Constitutional change became a self-defining goal, no longer as a means to change the country, which already had changed radically and irrevocably, but as a cathartic demonstration of national harmony to be undertaken for its own sake. Once the referendum result restored national harmony, Canadians granted Trudeau a licence to make the cathartic, constitutional gesture.

* * *

A postscript. The late Saskatchewan Premier Ross Thatcher once

271

remarked that if he ranked his province's top 100 problems in their proper order, "the constitution would rank 101st." Most Canadians share this view. Yet Trudeau has put constitutional reform at the top of his priorities all his years in power.

Joe Clark, in a perceptive comment that revealed an unexpected literary sense – "Mr. Trudeau is a European Canadian rather than a North American Canadian" – has explained this conundrum better than anyone else.*

In his attachment to the rule of law rather than to the common sense of creative muddle, Trudeau is indeed more European than Canadian. He is equally European in his temperament, his preference for precision instead of compromise, his unyielding quest for excellence instead of settling for the good-enough.

The romantic sweep of his imagination harks back to an earlier time and place, not so much European as British Victorian. It harks back in particular to George Nathaniel Curzon, whom in so many uncanny ways he resembles. As Trudeau saw it, this small, tentative country on the margin of the western world might actually serve as "mentor" if she had sense enough "to conceive of her own future on a grand scale." As Curzon saw it, imperialism was not domination but a partnership, "under Providence, the greatest instrument for the good that the world has seen." The intellectual link between them was Lord Acton, whom Trudeau so often quoted so approvingly, but always a fraction out of context since Acton's case for federalism amounted to a case for lesser breeds gathered contentedly beneath the imperial diadem.

Watching Trudeau dominate the premiers at First Ministers Conferences, immobile, sphinx-like, but puissant, at the head of the horseshoe table, evokes James Morris's marvellous description of Curzon among the Indian princes and British generals, "slightly sneering . . . dominating the room with an astringency, a sheathed cleverness, that inhibited all but the most self-confident."

In 1980, Trudeau won his magical second chance to dominate. And he seized it as no one else could have. Had he not done this, the credits of his accomplishments in the cause of national unity would have been at least balanced by the debits. On one side of the scale, bilingualism and French Power. On the other, the withering

---

*The Liberals, predictably, tried to imply that Clark had mortally insulted all immigrants, all Canadians indeed except for Inuit and Indians.

away of Ottawa's legitimacy and authority, the escalation of regional self-centredness, the splintering of the Canadian consciousness into a myriad of hyphens.

The enigma has one last variation. In character and intellect, Trudeau is the least Canadian of all our Prime Ministers. Because he so little understood the nature of the country he governed, he made mistakes no other leader would have. Yet Canadians understood, viscerally, that Trudeau's vision of Canada exceeded that of Laurier, that of even John A. Macdonald. So they allowed him to dominate their consciousness in a way that no other leader, Macdonald included, has ever done. And so, when the opportunity came, Canadians granted him a second chance, knowing that without a vision, a people, even if they do not perish, diminish.

16

Westward Ho!

> "It is not the prairie dweller who invented the indifferent universe
> of the impotent men. Puny you may feel there, and vulnerable, but
> not unnoticed. This is a land to mark a sparrow's fall."
>
> Wallace Stegner
> *Wolf Willow*

He never came right out and said, in Edmonton, or Winnipeg, or Regina, "This is the way we do things back in the East." Otherwise, it is difficult to think of much more Trudeau could have done to rub western sensibilities the wrong way. From "Why should I sell your wheat?", to removing the familiar insignia from RCMP cars in the land where the Mountie is king, to describing British Columbia Premier W.A.C. Bennett as a "bigot," he behaved time and again as a Brahmin among the Untouchables.

In private, Trudeau's behaviour toward westerners was repeatedly as careless. A trio of backstage incidents demonstrates the way in which Trudeau's relationship with the west, once begun badly, went to the worse.

—Early in 1974, searching for a candidate to contest a by-election caused by the death of an Alberta Conservative, Keith Davey phoned former Liberal M.P. Hu Harries, a well-known Edmonton management consultant and rancher; Harries said he was interested, but that he would run only if he were named immediately to the cabinet, a promotion he was sure to win automatically if he won the by-election, as Alberta's only government member. A few days later, Davey called back: the Prime Minister made it an inflexible rule never to appoint non-elected persons to his cabinet, he said. Harries stayed on his ranch; the by-election in any event was cancelled by the July election. Then, a year later, Harries read in the *Edmonton Journal* that Communications Minister Gérard Pelletier had just retired to become Ambassador in Paris; as his successor, Trudeau had named CRTC Chairman Pierre Juneau, who would try to become

an M.P. at a by-election that fall. (As it turned out, Juneau lost.)
–In 1976 Trudeau flew to Vancouver to attend a commemorative dinner organized by B.C. Liberals to honour one of their most popular members, Senator Arthur Laing, a retired cabinet minister, who everyone knew was dying of cancer. Luminaries like Ray Perrault and Diefenbaker delivered tributes that were funny and tender. Trudeau, when his turn came, said not a word about Laing; instead he read a prepared text about "sharing." Afterwards, in a hotel elevator, while an aide tried to pretend he was not there, Margaret turned on Trudeau and screamed at him: "That was a fine, idiotic, Ivan Head speech you just made." Trudeau blushed, looked at the floor, and said nothing.
–Early in 1977, during a Liberal policy convention in Toronto, Trudeau dined with a group of prairie Liberals to hear out their complaints and suggestions. One suggestion was that he visit the west more often. But he went there regularly, Trudeau protested. "You haven't been out there for *two years*," one western Liberal went on. There was a pause while everyone thought back; an even longer pause as they came to realize, not so much that Trudeau indeed had not been to the prairies in two years, as that he had no *idea* that he had not.

He went rarely to the West, explains an aide, because he felt himself "surrounded by a hostile sea." Not too much should be made of this, though, for outside of Quebec and the northern wilderness, Trudeau really felt fully at home only in New Brunswick, the province that comes closest to living up to his ideal of bilingualism. He found Toronto too edgy, and southern Ontario too bland. Even more so than in the west, he felt uncomfortable in Newfoundland; the trouble there being that Newfoundlanders were too saucy: "He never knew when they were being serious and when they were sending him up," another aide says. But the west mattered, as Newfoundland did not.

* * *

"They cheered for me, but they didn't vote for me," Wilfrid Laurier remarked at the end of a triumphal trip across the west in 1917. White plumes have always found it hard to win approval from white stetsons. In that election, Laurier won just two western seats; except in 1968, Trudeau, proportionally did little better. By 1980, his western vote was down to 22 per cent, not much higher than that of the Conservatives in Quebec. Yet, as they had for Laurier, westerners often cheered for him, particularly those who lived in small towns, like Allan, Saskatchewan, and Camrose, Alberta, where crowds applauded his French. In Edson, Alberta, in 1972, he passed the most difficult test for an outsider by cracking a joke and getting a laugh: "You say you aren't loved in Ottawa. At least, we don't love you in your own language."

Such instances, though, were flashes of small town courtesy; gratitude for so distinguished a personage having dropped by. On neither side was there any empathy or ease, still less a sense of shared experience. Blame some of this on Trudeau, for being aloof. Blame some of it on westerners, for being truculent. Blame a good deal of it on the inanimate villain of geography, of which, as Mackenzie King once remarked, we have "too much." In a country stretched from sea to sea like a string of beads, there are bound to be gaps, somewhere. Trudeau closed the fault-line in the east, but some of the means he used to do this opened a new one in the west. French Power, after all, has to mean less power for everyone else: by 1980, just one of Ottawa's thirty-three departmental deputy-ministers came from west of Winnipeg. Bilingualism changed Ottawa from a city where westerners never had felt at ease (less so than Quebecers had, even during the days when it had been a dumpy WASP town), into a distant, foreign capital where they felt out of place and inadequate.

The West's practical problems, Trudeau could understand easily enough. In October 1970, for instance, in an interview with *Le Monde* he explained his new policy of taking an interest in the Pacific Rim by saying, "If we want to prevent a certain alienation in the west of the country, our policy to respond to the nations of the Pacific must be more vigorous." He did not labour under the handicap (in western eyes) of being an economic nationalist. In 1973 he got his Western Economic Opportunity Conference off to a fast start by saying that John A. Macdonald's old "National Policy" of high tariffs should not apply in the west.

But he could not understand the western psyche. He had about as much rapport with it as Diefenbaker had with Quebec's, and for the same reasons: nothing, in the experience of either, prepared him for the challenge to Confederation he had to deal with once in power, Quebec nationalism to the one, western regionalism to the other. Before he came to office, Trudeau knew few English Canadians, and those he did were too much like him for the range of his comprehension to be extended. (Several later aides, Head, Coutts, Fairbairn, Tom Axworthy, were westerners, but transplanted ones who had put down roots in the east.) He viewed English Canadians through the prism of a French Canadian intellectual, which is to say he viewed them as being all the same. So he was as much taken by surprise by the west's challenge to his concept of One Canada as Diefenbaker was by Quebec's to his concept of "unhyphenated Canadians."

The challenge itself was inevitable, so that the nation's fabric was bound to be strained. But Trudeau intensified the strain in ways no other leader, Stanfield, Turner, Clark, would have done. By his unapproachability. By his sheer combativeness. Even by the flower in his button-hole, which made him, to westerners, the personification of the suave, superior easterner. He was the least Canadian of all our Prime Ministers. To Quebecers, this did not matter because he was one of them; to westerners, he was like a being from another world, one to which they didn't want to belong.

The sadness here, on both sides, is that westerners and Trudeau are, *au fond*, each other's kind of people: self-reliant, individualistic, energetic, and enthusiastic. A deeper sadness is that westerners, in many ways, represent Trudeau's kind of Canadians. During all the long decades when most people in the east (and in British Columbia) thought of themselves as British Canadians, only Quebecers and prairie people thought of themselves as Canadians. Except that westerners couldn't articulate this, and even if they had been able to, nobody would have listened.

* * *

The difference between the west of the prairies and everywhere else in the country is that the prairies created themselves. The old Canada of the Empire of the St. Lawrence colonized its own hinterland of northern Ontario and *Nouveau Quebec*, and established outposts on the edge of the Pacific. But the vast stretch of territory between the Lakehead and the Rockies was *sui generis*. The east provided a railway, some bank loans, some salt fish during the Depression: everything else, the prairie pioneers did themselves.

In the beginning, isolated in that incredible expanse of near-desert, those pioneers, many of them exiles from eastern Europe, others drifted northwards from south of the border, created a marginal society upon the artefacts of ox carts and sod huts. Later, as the tractors and combines came, and the drought and the Depression passed by, they created their own distinct civilization; one that was narrow and unsophisticated certainly, because land and climate were so harsh and nothing could be done about that, just as nothing could be done to make wheat grow when the rain did not come or to sell wheat in the face of world gluts; but a civilization, nonetheless, with its own substantial cities from Winnipeg to Edmonton, and its own universities, and its own expanding middle class.

What the west began to want, around the 1950's, was exactly the same thing that Quebec had begun to want around the same time: respect, understanding, a sense of belonging. For six magic years, Diefenbaker made westerners believe that the national government was their national government. Then Dief was downed, the Liberals came back in, and everyone, whether in the Commons or on the national television news, began talking about nothing but Quebec. Still, in 1967-68, westerners were as much turned on by Expo and Trudeau as anyone else. Then, Trudeau, without intending to, turned them into outsiders again.

He had some bad luck. His Western Economic Opportunities Conference of July 1973 began to repair the breach, but then was blown apart itself by the oil price war of that fall. Of all his prairie ministers, only Otto Lang commanded respect back home.

Strikingly, though, Trudeau made no attempt to recruit a western equivalent of Pearson's Three Wise Men from Quebec; not counting Jack Horner in 1977, who doesn't need to be counted, and who anyway came far too late. So westerners became outsiders, turning inward toward their own provincial governments, for the most natural of reasons: whenever they turned toward Ottawa, they saw there no one like themselves. Instead, coming from Ottawa, they heard the censorious voice of their Prime Minister.

Trudeau's "bigot" crack at British Columbia's Bennett is a prime example. Through it, he lent the legitimacy of his office to the east's conviction that rednecks began at the Lakehead. Certainly there were rednecks, although in fundamentalist rural areas the target of suspicion tended to be Popishness rather than

Frenchness.* More profoundly, hostility toward bilingualism on the prairies was motivated by westerners' own sense of loss. To become Canadians, many had given up their ancestral languages, from Ukrainian to German; now they were being told that in order to become *real* Canadians they would have to learn the language of a people they had never met and who had played no part in building their western civilization. Not until April 1977 did Trudeau talk to westerners about bilingualism in a context they could relate to. "Quebecers, like westerners, feel they are not sharing fully in Canadian society," he said then in Winnipeg. "Think about it, as many Quebecers speak only French as the combined total population of the three Prairie provinces."

His "Why should I sell your wheat?" crack, made in Winnipeg in the summer of 1969, is an even better case in point.** Prairie farmers knew perfectly well that he could not, personally, sell their wheat in the midst of a world-wide glut. But what Trudeau appeared to be telling them by his flippancy was that their own Prime Minister neither understood nor cared what they were going through. For what westerners were going through, in the early years of his stewardship, was a regression to a marginal society.

* * *

In the late 1960's, while Montreal, Toronto, and Ottawa were sowing skyscrapers and blossoming with boutiques, prairie society was crumbling. Saskatchewan was losing population, a trauma suffered by no other province since Confederation, except Manitoba, briefly. The price of wheat was less than $2 a bushel; farm net income, in 1969, dropped to its level of 1942. Oil was stuck at $2.50 a barrel; worse, it was running out. No new large fields had

---

*These "bigots" invariably lived in a region far removed from that of whoever was commenting about them. While in Ottawa as Official Languages Commissioner, Keith Spicer, for instance, had had a lot to say about bigots. But once he moved to Vancouver, his columns contained no accounts of first-hand encounters with bigots.

**In an attempt to repair the damage, Head published the full text of Trudeau's speech in his 1972 book, *Conversations with Canadians*. If anything, this makes it even easier to understand why the prairie farmers got so angry, because Trudeau, in his best Socratic style, went on to ask them whether they would like the government to "step in, own the farms, and hire the farmers?"

been discovered in half a decade. The 1968 strike at Prudhoe Bay pulled the exploration industry north. Between 1969 and 1971, the number of wildcats drilled in Alberta dropped from 421 to 256; at the same time, the multi-nationals began pulling their white-collar workers back from Calgary to Houston.

The dimensions of this were lost on Trudeau. He knew, intellectually, what was happening. But he had no feeling for the frustration and bruised pride of westerners at their impotence in the face of the random forces of international economics and of climate.

Only those who live on the frontier can understand such feelings. Trudeau, then head down into "rational government," gave no sign of trying to understand them. Like most in the east, he accepted as a given that Canada was composed of two economic nations, an industrialized, urban heartland in Quebec and Ontario and appended to its east and west, a resource-dependent periphery. This dichotomy was immutable: the two economic nations, after all, had occupied the same relative positions for more than a hundred years. Government policy – Trudeau's new policy of regional economic expansion, for instance – might make things a bit better for the hinterland, but nothing could change geography.

However, when Alberta Premier Peter Lougheed told his legislature in 1974, "The '70's are Alberta's time in Confederation. Our dream of the New West will be realized," no one anywhere doubted that everything he said would come true. For by then, OPEC had changed beyond recall the relationship between the western industrialized heartland democracies and the hinterland Third World, and between Canada's own heartland and hinterland.

* * *

All the west, except for Manitoba, has been transformed since the mid-1970's. Among the four provinces, Alberta is the natural one to pick as paradigm for the others. It is the most powerful, the most glamorous, because of oil, and the most different, and always has been: when the Edmonton Eskimos came to Toronto in 1952 to represent the west in the Grey Cup for the first time, the team brought with it Alberta steaks, Alberta bread, and Alberta water in special containers.

Until the 1947 oil strike at Leduc, Alberta had been much like the other prairie provinces, except for the romantic tradition of ranching in its spectacularly beautiful southwest corner. Alberta, in a word, was boring. It produced grain, about which there is not much to be said. Its history, like that of the rest of the prairies, had been too brief and too peaceable to attract the attention of outsiders.

But even then, Alberta was distinctive. Unlike Manitoba, linked to the east through Winnipeg, which was where the two cultures met, and unlike Saskatchewan, infected by the British notion of socialism, Alberta was unto itself. Its Social Credit politics were rooted in U.S. mid-western populism. Its universities were modelled on U.S. land-grant colleges. Its early beef trade ran north and south. Americans, flocking north as ranchers or as oil men, had infused the province with a unique entrepreneurial spirit. Its real resource, in super-abundant surplus, was human energy.

Albertans, like everyone else on the prairies, compensated for the physical hardness of their lives by hating the east. "God damn the CPR," local farmers were reported to say when it hailed. They bitched on and on about discriminatory freight rates and punitive tariffs which forced them to purchase high-priced Quebec and Ontario products when they could have bought low-priced American or Asian ones.

In fact, Albertans were cursing the wrong target. "The basic problem lies in being small and isolated, rather than in being the target of discrimination by the [railway] carriers, or the central government," University of Alberta economist Kenneth Norrie concluded in a study published in 1976 in *Canadian Public Policy*.

Rather, the centralization against which Albertans railed was primarily financial: all the bank head offices were in Montreal and Toronto; Albertans had to fly east, red-eyed, to bang on their doors, in search of loans. Cultural centralization mattered too: news, and therefore trends and styles, travelled only from east to west.

The political centralization, about which Albertans complained the most, may have affected them the least. True, Ontario and Quebec dominated successive federal governments. But about those things that mattered most to the west, international commodity prices and the condition of the harvest, Ottawa could do little. Only in the 1980-81 oil price war, (the earlier, 1973-75 war was more apparent than real), did the centre really tip the political scales against the west by the weight of its population.

Once OPEC doubled the price of oil, none of these centralizing forces could hold the hinterland in thrall any longer. Statistics tell the story—between 1970 and 1980, the economic output of the west advanced from 60 per cent of Ontario's output to 85 per cent, and should exceed it before the century is out. In 1977 the west's population came to exceed Quebec's for the first time since Confederation. Through the 1980's, close to half a million people may move from east to west. In 1979, Calgary accounted for $1.3 billion worth of new construction, twice as much as Metropolitan Toronto, a city six times its size. Saskatoon, spurred on by potash and uranium, currently has as much new office space under construction as has been built in its entire history. Calgary has displaced Montreal and Vancouver to become the nation's second financial centre; its population, and also Edmonton's are racing toward the one million mark.

As early as 1975, the Economic Council calculated Alberta per capita incomes as being $2,000 higher than in Sweden or West Germany, let alone Ontario. Each year since then, Alberta has experienced the country's fastest growth, lowest unemployment, lowest taxes. In 1981, the province's Heritage Fund passed the $9 billion mark, while Saskatchewan's similar fund reached past $1 billion.

In counterpoint, the east is regressing. Montreal, as the C.D. Howe Research Institute has suggested, may end up as "a big Milwaukee." Between 1976 and 1978, average incomes in Ontario dropped from $13,518 to $12,916; technically Ontario now is a "have-not" province. In 1979, Ontario lost an estimated 30,000 people and a guesstimated $3 billion in business investment to the west. Some head offices, Imperial Oil for instance, shifted units to Calgary and the Bank of Montreal moved its chairman there.

Oil and natural gas accounted for much, though far from all, of the change. From $500 million in 1973, Alberta's yearly take from its hydrocarbons soared to $1.5 billion in 1974, and on up to $4 billion by the end of the decade. Add tar sands, coal, uranium, potash, wheat at $5 a bushel, beef, and the minerals and timber in British Columbia. Add, to heighten the contrast, "de-industrialization" in the east.

Now that it had suddenly come to have it all, it became harder and harder to put a finger on what the west really wanted. The oil-revenue-sharing battle of 1980-81 was easy to understand. So also was

Alberta's concern that its dwindling supplies of conventional crude oil were being sold off at fire sale prices. But the most the east at its most devious and Trudeau at his most insensitive might accomplish, it was clear, was the difference between allowing the west to become rich as Croesus, instead of rich as Midas.

Saskatchewan Premier Allan Blakeney explained the nature of the problem best. "Western alienation is real, it is profound, it is growing," he said at a First Ministers Conference on oil pricing in January, 1974. "We have felt neglected. We don't intend to be taken for granted any longer."

Trudeau heard out Blakeney and replied that western alienation has indeed become "a more serious threat to Confederation than Quebec." Then he showed that he had heard, but not listened. In his first, post-election speech at Parliament's opening that fall, Trudeau said not a word about western alienation, nor indeed about anything except bilingualism and the constitution.

* * *

Contemporary Canadian history might have turned out differently if Saskatchewan and not Alberta produced 90 per cent of the country's oil. Saskatchewanians don't love the east exactly, but they do understand it more easily. The NDP is one link. Several Saskatchewan politicians – Jimmy Gardiner, John Diefenbaker, Tommy Douglas – have become major national figures, but until Joe Clark, no Albertans have done so.

Geology being immovable, a more plausible might-have-been is to try to guess what might have happened if Blakeney, instead of transplanting himself from his native Nova Scotia to Regina had gone on to Edmonton, turned right politically instead of left, and wound up as Conservative leader instead of Peter Lougheed.

Blakeney infuriated Lougheed, and not without reason. He fought as hard for Saskatchewan's interests as Lougheed did for Alberta's, to the point of once accusing the Supreme Court of bias, yet was praised by the national press as a pan-Canadian. One difference between them was that unlike the recalcitrant Lougheed, Blakeney was almost as quick in debate as Trudeau, and so enlivened First Ministers Conferences. The real difference: Blakeney, at heart, truly was a pan-Canadian, a characteristic that came to him naturally as a New Democrat and transplanted Maritimer.

Cerebral cool is the impression Blakeney leaves with everyone he meets: mod but modest clothes, a loud laugh that comes not from the belly but from the chest, a taste for late night poker combined with the round-faced, short hairstyle of a banker; a readiness to answer any question posed, but a wariness in answering. Beneath the cool, Blakeney's driving quality is not passion, he's far too cautious for that, but caring. When he diagnosed Confederation's ills, Blakeney applied both coolness and caring. "The fact that we have not had any Canadian myths and symbols to which we could rally some sense of Canadian identity has left the field wide open for French-Canadian regional identity to flourish," he said in September 1977. "All signs point to a retreat from the premise that in order to develop a stronger Canadian identity, we need to control our own economy," he told a seminar on Confederation organized by the Canada West Foundation in March 1978. "How naive and short-sighted we have become," he added. "How can we expect a Canadian identity to emerge and to flourish when Canadians own so little of their own economy?"

Blakeney reinforced his rhetoric with specific proposals. "A new kind of Confederation can be built," he proposed in 1974, on a speaking tour of Toronto, Montreal, and Halifax, provided Canadians developed their own sources of energy, "as part of a national strategy that could apply later to other sections of the economy, such as iron, steel, financial institutions and other resource industries." At the succeeding First Ministers Conference, he called for a "national energy fund" into which all governments would recycle some of their windfall oil revenues, using these to develop new supplies of energy through Canadian-owned, public-private ventures.

Everyone listened politely, and then went on to the problem of the moment: setting a new oil price. "It just wasn't practical," Donald Macdonald, who was Energy Minister at the time, has said since. "Lougheed would never have allowed the federal government in on Alberta's oil industry."

Maybe not. In 1979, Lougheed rejected the plea of Prime Minister Clark, a fellow-Conservative and a fellow-Albertan, that he join in a national energy bank. But Clark, unlike Trudeau in earlier easier times, at least invited Lougheed to join. Either way, neither Albertans nor westerners as a whole were challenged to take part in a nation-building resource enterprise.

So instead, each province went ahead on its own. Blakeney

nationalized his potash industry in 1975, and through the new Saskatchewan Potash Corporation repatriated managerial and research jobs from the U.S. Lougheed, through provincial instruments such as the Alberta Energy Corporation, similarly developed his own resources, by and for his own people.

One after the other, the provinces moved into the vacuum created by Ottawa's failure to develop a national industrial strategy, a national sense of economic purposefulness. In April, 1980, the C.D. Howe Research Institute found Canada's economy "in a process of disintegration," because "all the strong provinces are turning their back on nation building and [are] trying to create their own balanced, self-contained, little economies." The best description of the price Canada has paid for Trudeau's failure to make westerners feel full partners in Confederation was provided by Energy Minister Lalonde in 1980 when he warned that Canada was becoming, "ten economic sovereignties in a political association."

Much of this process of fragmentation would have happened anyway. But not all of it. All that is certain is that when Blakeney posited a nation-building solution to Trudeau, in January 1974, he received in reply an uncomprehending stare, as uncomprehending, in its own way, as the B and B Commission received in 1965 when it warned that Canada was "passing through the greatest crisis in its history."

Mind you, no matter what Blakeney proposed and Trudeau agreed to, only Lougheed could dispose of the matter.

* * *

Every now and then, as a kind of ritual incantation, Peter Lougheed declares he is "a Canadian first." Then he goes back to talking about what he really wants to talk about. In 1976, he said of the PQ victory: "Quebecers have a desire to be master in their own houses. I have an empathy with that feeling." And on May 21, 1980, the day after the Quebec referendum, he said, "We should not be stampeded into constitutional discussions based on some euphoria of Canadianism that arose out of the decision yesterday."

As Lougheed sees it, his battle is not *against* Canada (although he is against what he describes as "the Toronto-Ottawa Establishment") but *for* a different kind of Canada. His 1978 constitutional document *Harmony in Diversity* spells out his ideas. These amount – the point Lalonde was making – to ten economic sovereignties joined into a loose political association, or the reverse of Levesque's scenario. Within this new Confederation, each provincial government would represent its own citizens at the national level. To underscore his point, Lougheed in 1978 withheld Alberta's participation from a joint federal-provincial-industry-labour series of industry "sectoral" studies, on the grounds that Alberta alone should represent its industries in national economic planning. At the November 1978 First Ministers Conference, he rejected Trudeau's proposal to limit Ottawa's use of its declaratory power to occasions of "compelling national interest" and insisted Ottawa should act only in instances of "extreme national emergency," leaving Ottawa powerless to intervene on the nation's behalf in the oil and gas industry except when just about all Canadians outside Alberta were freezing, in the dark.

Despite their public differences, Trudeau and Lougheed get along in private. In Trudeau's presence, Lougheed acts awed; for his part, Trudeau is impressed by Lougheed's dogged single-mindedness. Other premiers have noticed that at the private get-togethers at 24 Sussex, the two seldom take each other on across the dining table.

Lougheed, mind you, isn't easy to take on. Romantics say his truculence goes back to the childhood memory of watching the magnificent mansion, *Beaulieu*, which his grand-father, Sir James Lougheed, another premier of Alberta had built, being sold for next to nothing in 1938, after his father had drunk away the family fortune; even more, they trace it to his being determined to restore the family to its past patrician glories of maids, fine silver, cut crystal, and the Prince of Wales coming to stay. Pragmatists attribute it to Ottawa's 1974 decision to give the go-ahead to the Petrosar plant in Sarnia that uses Alberta crude oil to compete with Alberta's own petrochemical products. Lougheed, who is every bit as private a person as Trudeau, once attributed it all to his mother. "She taught us to enjoy competition, to compete against ourselves."

Lougheed overcame a physical handicap (he is short) to make it, just, as a professional football player. At the University of Alberta, he nosed out Ivan Head, so much more articulate, in a race for the student presidency. Later, he became a lawyer for the rough and tough Mannix construction company. After that, he took over the almost extinct Conservative Party in Alberta, and made it into the country's most solidly entrenched party, except for the federal Liberals in Quebec. He turned a moribund civil service into the most efficient in Canada, if also the most humourless. The debit against all of these credits is that Lougheed is his own worst enemy. There is a cumbersome heaviness to his persona, a brooding morbid suspicion of all opponents, especially easterners, and a sullen hyper-sensitivity to criticism. His own aides, by an unwritten rule, are forbidden to mention his small stature.

For all his lack of grace, Lougheed has a quality of caring that parallels Blakeney's, though the breadth of his concern is much more limited.

"If you want to see what happens when the oil industry moves on, go to Tulsa. It's a dead city," he once told a *Toronto Star* reporter. His goal for Alberta has been simple, and he has pursued it single-mindedly. "This province's economy is too vulnerable, too deeply-dependent upon the depleting resources of oil and gas for its continued prosperity," he told the legislature in January 1974. "How long can it last; perhaps a decade at the most, unless we're able to put in place a more balanced economy for that inevitable day ... when production begins to decline and resource revenues fall off," he said, again in the legislature, in October 1976. The economic goal, he continued, had to be "a fundamental shift in the economy of Canada, a shift in the decision-making westward, and particularly to Alberta." By the end of the 1970's, Lougheed had achieved this goal, as the statistics make manifest, not to mention Calgary soaring out of the prairie like a mini-Manhattan. Only his second, 1980-81, battle with Trudeau over oil revenue sharing keeps him from retirement.

* * *

For all the sound and fury that Lougheed has helped foment over the past seven years – threats to break off discussions and act unilaterally; overlapping taxes imposed by both federal and provincial governments until the industry forced both to compromise by pulling its rigs south; the Alberta bumper stickers that read, "Let the Eastern Bastards Freeze in the Dark," not to mention counter-denunciations of Albertans as "greedy" and "un-Canadian" – many of the battles between Edmonton and Ottawa have been phoney ones. For one thing, it was Macdonald, concerned about windfall profits tumbling into the treasuries of the multi-nationals, who urged his Alberta counterparts to increase their royalty fees late in 1973. For another, Lougheed owes the idea of the Heritage Fund to, of all people, Trudeau. By early 1974, Trudeau had become aware of just how much Alberta's soaring revenues were threatening the financial base of Ottawa's scheme of equalization payments to the provinces; he suggested to Lougheed that he hive off a portion of his revenues (eventually, this amounted to one-third) into a capital account and so shelter these sums from the equalization payments formula.

The only aspect of the 1973-75 oil war that really matters now is that Lougheed won and Trudeau lost. This outcome – buried at the time beneath tax and accounting jargon – only became clear in 1979. Canadians owe this discovery to Ayatollah Khomeini. In January 1979 when the Shah fell, world oil prices soared, eventually doubling to $35 a barrel. If Canadian oil prices (then $13.50) were brought even within reasonable reach of world prices, Alberta's Heritage Fund would balloon to an estimated $100 billion by the end of the century, and Confederation would be transformed from an agglomeration of haves and have-nots into a hierarchy of two unimaginably wealthy provinces, Alberta and Saskatchewan, and eight indigent cousins. As for Ottawa, it would have long since collapsed beneath its multiple financial burdens, such as having to equalize the cost of oil imported in the five eastern provinces.

The essentials of the deal that Trudeau negotiated in 1975 after two years of battling with Lougheed are as follows: of all new oil revenues, 45 per cent go to Alberta, and 45 per cent to the industry, which has used this largesse to double its assets, to $30 billion since 1973. On behalf of the nine in ten Canadians living outside Alberta, Ottawa gets just 10 per cent of the take. The point about this deal is that Ottawa, at the time, believed it had done just fine. The 1976 federal report, *Energy Strategy for Canadians*, for instance, declares that without the 1975 deal, Ottawa's share of oil revenues would have dropped "from an anticipated 18 per cent to 9 per cent." Ottawa ended this far down the barrel anyway, though, because of a series of "tax expenditures," or subsidies to oil companies, which, for example, in 1979 accounted for $750 million of the $850 million spent by the industry on exploration and development. Indeed, in 1980, Energy Department officials calculated that even a price hike to $20 a barrel would earn Ottawa no additional revenues since companies could apply their extra taxes due to expanding their activities.*

So Lougheed won the best possible, of both worlds. He acquired all the revenues, and more, that he could handle, $6 billion in the Heritage Fund, and another $2 billion stashed away in other accounts. At the same time, the artificially low level of oil prices allowed Lougheed to claim he had made a major contribution to Confederation, through $20 billion worth of forgone revenues during the period 1973-79. (As Albertans like to point out, they would cheerfully sell oil to Ontario at its 1973 price, provided Ontario sold them its gold at $35 an ounce.)

Trudeau, for his part, had lost coming and going. He recognized this only in 1979, and, after the 1980 election, set out to cut his losses. Low oil prices both encouraged consumption of a dwindling resource, and left Ottawa with no revenues to pay for its program to subsidize the cost of oil imported into the five eastern provinces, which in 1980 soared, as did world prices, to $3.7 billion. To push Ottawa even deeper into the red, the federal government had to subsidize the oil industry, through tax expenditures, as a substitute for higher prices at the pump. In exchange for all of this, Trudeau managed to make all Albertans mad at him, and, to complete the polarization, many Canadians mad at Albertans.

* * *

In February 1980, Clark's oil policy cost him the election. The irony here is that Clark's policy amounted to an improved version of Trudeau's oil policy of the past half-decade. This policy more than any other illustrates one of the cardinal contradictions of Trudeau's record as Prime Minister: in style and in word he is so often so tough; in his actions, he is often so timid. About no issue of public policy has he been more timid than about energy.

The foundation of Trudeau's energy policy pre-1980 was subsidized consumption. Canadians, at the equivalent of 64 barrels of oil per capita, compared to 61 barrels in the U.S., and to half these amounts in the countries of western Europe, are the world's most profligate consumers of energy. We subsidize our consumption

---

*Between 1974 and 1978, despite record profits, the oil industry halved its effective tax rate, from 37 per cent to 18 per cent. Gulf Canada, in 1978, managed to pay not one cent in taxes.

through low prices: when Trudeau left office in 1979, the gap between the Canadian per barrel price and the world price was wider than when he pledged to move Canadian prices toward "world levels" in mid-1976. At the pump, gasoline prices were lower in real terms, discounting inflation, than in the 1950's and 1960's. As one consequence, Canadian consumption of gasoline in 1979 increased by 4 per cent, while in the U.S. it declined by 7 per cent. As another, beginning in the winter of 1980, American motorists began crossing the border to fill up with cheap Canadian gasoline, and foreign planes touched down at Canadian airports to fill up with low-priced aviation fuel.

Meanwhile, as our consumption was increasing, our supplies were diminishing. From a "producability" rate (i.e., maximum output) of two million barrels a day in the mid-1970's, Alberta's field output of conventional crude oil declined to 1.2 million barrels a day by 1980, and was forecast to drop to 500,000 barrels by 1990. In lockstep, our dependence upon imports is forecast to increase from 300,000 barrels a day in 1980 to an estimated 650,000 by 1985. From the target of oil sufficiency "by the end of the decade (1980)" that Trudeau first set in 1973, he shifted, in the 1980 election, to a goal of self-sufficiency, "hopefully ... before the end of the century."

Through his fixation on the *price* of oil, rather than its *supply*, Trudeau managed to delay both the industrial and lifestyle adjustment that most western countries already have gone through, and has delayed the development of a major new Canadian energy industry. At the same time, because his price fixing threatened their control of their resource, he managed to get westerners ferociously angry at him, even though his revenue sharing formula had helped make them rich.

After the 1980 election, Trudeau named the toughest guy on his team, Marc Lalonde, to do battle for him as Energy Minister. "Albertans will have to give more," Lalonde declared. "We will not accept any reduction in net benefits," Lougheed shot back. He went on to warn, "Ottawa had better not move unilaterally on our resources, or the backlash will be extreme. People in Ottawa are not aware of the depth of feeling of people in Western Canada." As witness to this feeling, after the 1980 election two Saskatchewan provincial members formed a new western separatist party, while in Alberta, separatist rallies attracted crowds of 10,000 and

"Republic of Alberta" T-shirts and caps sold as fast as they could be printed. As for what the west thought about Trudeau personally, it gave him as its parting gift in the 1980 election, just 22 per cent of its votes, and 2 of its 77 M.P.s.

* * *

The fault-line between west and east now is almost as wide as it once was between Quebec and the rest. Before the west can fully re-enter Confederation's mainstream, another Prime Minister, unfreighted by the burden of past misunderstandings, will have to be in office, and another Alberta premier.

Those around Trudeau blame much that has happened on the circumstance that the Liberal Party he inherited in the four western provinces had decayed into a rump of patronage lawyers and portly old bodies in the Vancouver Club. So that Trudeau had little material with which to build the western wing of his successive cabinets, and even fewer people – Coutts, Lang, his ex-aide Gordon Gibson, his friend Arthur Erickson – whom he could talk to about the west in language both understood.

All of this is true, and it is true as well that the management of human talent is the least-developed of Trudeau's managerial skills. But it is beside the point. The real truth is that Trudeau never applied himself to the west. He saw it as a problem to be coped with, rather than as a challenge to rise to. So he never came to comprehend that to "Tomorrow Country," as the west calls itself, resources, which are its one chance to become Today Country, are as central to its defining identity as is language to Quebec. Nor did Trudeau recognize that he needed to apply himself to the west. So he missed his chance to attach "the building end of Canada," in Joe Clark's description, to the rest of the country in a new, nation-building co-adventure.

In a speech in 1978, Blakeney, who is a man with a sense both of irony and of history, reached into his memory bank for a quotation that described the kind of self-reliant, purposeful kind of Canada, *the west*'s kind of Canada, that he had once asked Trudeau to help him build. "English Canadians should build a country and then maybe we would want to be part of it," Blakeney quoted his source as having said. "Be creative, believe in yourselves, and maybe then we'll believe in you too."

Blakeney then revealed that he had taken his text from Pierre Bourgault, the pioneer of Quebec separatism.

17

Priceless Asset

"The last thing we Canadians should do is to shut ourselves up in our provinces, in our own country, or our own continent. If we are to be of service to the world, and to ourselves and our own destiny, if we are to find our right place in the sun, we must look beyond our own national or local limits."

Lester Pearson
Words and Occasions, 1970

The test of a first-rate intelligence, F. Scott Fitzgerald once wrote, is the ability to entertain two opposed ideas at the same time, and still retain the ability to function. Trudeau has never demonstrated this ability more skilfully than in the field of foreign affairs. It helped, mind you, that during his stewardship, Canadians as a people quietly switched off the world. All that has really mattered to most of us is that our Prime Ministers look good to outsiders. And Trudeau, not so much in the style of a magician as of a Canadian who does not *look* like a Canadian, has looked splendid.

The two opposed ideas at play in Trudeau's foreign policy have been "national self-interest" and the "global ethic of sharing." The first presupposed that the purpose of foreign policy was to promote and enhance Canadian "sovereignty." The second presupposed a new international economic order that would subordinate, to some degree or other, the sovereign economic interests of all wealthy nations, Canada included.

Through his first term in office, 1968 to 1972, Trudeau pursued both these contradictory objectives at once. During this period, his official foreign policy, as laid out in his 1970 White Paper, was "national self-interest," as opposed to what the document described as the "helpful fixer" policy of Lester Pearson. This rupture with tradition upset a lot of people, including Pearson. Even so, it catalyzed Canada's most creative diplomatic initiatives of the last two decades.

Simultaneously, Trudeau acted selflessly toward the poor of the world. Each year, he increased our foreign aid program. In 1971, he initiated Canada World Youth, an idealistic organization headed by his old friend Jacques Hébert, which has since arranged getting-to-know-you exchanges between seven thousand young people from Canada and from Third World countries.

Around 1972, Trudeau stopped using the phrase, "national self-interest." By 1974, he was telling an audience at Duke University, "If I were to identify any single criterion by which I hope Canada's presence in the world would be judged, it would be by its humanism." In 1975, in a much-quoted speech at London's Mansion House, he proclaimed the new doctrine of "global sharing." Trudeau's own character and mindset cast him in this direction. Equally, Trudeau got caught up in a myth. Just as many Irishmen, say, behave in the way they imagine Irishmen are supposed to, Trudeau, when it came to foreign policy, came to behave in the way that as he came to recognize, Canadians are *supposed* to behave: the Pearsonian way.

* * *

Pearsonian diplomacy, a blend of burgeoning post-war identity and son-of-the-manse missionary zeal, produced, in the 1940's and 1950's, a new element in international politics: middle power as mediator; Canada as creative compromiser. By 1968, when Trudeau came to power, this style had outlived its usefulness by more than a decade. Europe had recovered; the de-colonized countries of Asia and Africa had come into their own. The Vietnam war made Quiet Diplomacy look sadly ineffectual; with all the one-on-one eyeballing going on, there were no parts left for honest brokers to play. Pearsonianism degenerated into a kind of "pseudo-Pearsonianism," as we searched frantically for peace forces we could join, or for initiatives we could invent at the UN, all to prove, to ourselves, that the world still needed us. "Sure as the Dutch made cheese, and the Danes made teak furniture, Canadians were supposed to make peace," in the words of a senior External Affairs official.

Yet myths, once they take hold, never die. Just as it doesn't matter if King Arthur and the Round Table existed to the power of the tale to excite our imagination, so the memory of the golden age of Pearsonian diplomacy – the bow tie, the self-deprecating wit, the Nobel Peace Prize – has become part of our sustaining myth. No matter that the world had changed, we still wanted to be praised as "helpful fixers." Little by little, the myth worked on Trudeau. He became as optimistic a helpful fixer as Pearson had ever been; the difference being that his compass was fixed on a north-south axis rather than Pearson's east-west one.*

The real difference was that although Trudeau's ideal – international sharing as the successor to international security – was every bit as noble as Pearson's, he was never able to get Canadians to share it. He never communicated to his own public a sense of commitment and excitement in the way that Flora Mac-Donald did during her brief term as External Affairs Minister by her stagy but effective invocation on behalf of human rights at the United Nations in September 1979 and her impassioned pleas on behalf of Cambodian refugees, earlier that summer. Trudeau, in foreign policy, failed to create a new myth to pass on to his successor.

Most of the blame belongs to Canadians. By the end of the 1970's, we had become perhaps the most isolationist country in the world, endlessly fascinated by our own problems, indifferent to the problems of everyone else. Only a dwindling and aging corps of retired diplomats and academics kept institutions like the Canadian Institute for International Affairs alive. Universities cancelled course after course on international affairs. Newspapers packed up their foreign bureaus: Canadian Press trimmed its staff in London from ten to one. In December 1977, when the Commons debated foreign policy, it was for the first time in *seventeen* years.

Some blame has to be laid at Trudeau's door. In 1972, in his book, *Canada's Search for New Roles*, Peter Dobell remarked shrewdly that Trudeau "takes an interest in international affairs normally only when he is out of the country." Or when he personally is performing on the stage.

As the years passed, and his knowledge increased, so in fact did Trudeau's interest in foreign affairs. However crowded his schedule, he makes space for virtually any visitor to Ottawa who wields significant international influence, and has dazzled callers from Sheik Yamani to "Sonny" Rampal, the Secretary-General of

*Near the end of his life, in his 1969 study for the World Bank, Pearson's own interests shifted to the north-south, rich-poor dichotomy.

the Commonwealth, with his detailed expertise. Yet his expression of that expertise has been oddly erratic. In 1979, for instance, as Opposition Leader, he criticized Clark for "weakness and indifference" in not enrolling our "economic summit" partners into a joint declaration to pressure Iran to free the U.S. hostages; yet once Prime Minister again, he took no action himself. Predominantly, his style is *personal*, as in flipping up to Lapland after the 1980 Venice Summit so that he and Justin could see the midnight sun, or pouring soft loans and grants into Jamaica because he and Michael Manley get on so well together.

Similarly, while Trudeau has preached the doctrine of "global sharing," instances of his putting it into practice are hard to find. We have imposed quotas on imports of clothing, textiles, and shoes from developing countries. During the 1977-79 General Agreement on Tariffs and Trade (GATT) negotiations, we let pass by the chance to champion the cause of trade liberalization on behalf of Third World countries. At conferences on the Law of the Sea, our stance is as self-interested as that of anyone else. More self-interested, arguably, because our claim involves not just the 200-mile resource zone, or even the Continental Shelf beyond, but the still wider sweep of the Continental Margin.*

Except for a small band of idealists, clustered in church groups and organizations like CUSO, few Canadians demand that Trudeau do more. Just by being what he is—"a priceless asset to the industrialized world," as U.S. Vice-President Walter Mondale has put it—he does all that his public asks. Trudeau is the admired friend of almost everybody who is anybody internationally: from Fidel Castro on the left to King Hussein of Jordan on the right; from Helmut Schmidt among the rich to Nyerere of Tanzania and Manley among the poor. In an age of international mediocrities, he and Castro and Anwar Sadat, and in a manic kind of way, Ayatollah Khomeini are among the few who cast a shadow, beyond their own borders.

By casting a shadow when he goes abroad, Trudeau reinforces our self-esteem, which, in the manner of the Japanese, we measure by the way others esteem us. Trudeau's real foreign policy—style over substance—is exactly the foreign policy that

---

*The coincidence that we are major producers of minerals like nickel puts us on the side of the underdeveloped angels on the issue of controlling deep-sea mining.

most Canadians want. The pity is that he had it in him to do more – and so did we.

* * *

From the inside of a jail cell in Belgrade – in his "Citizen of the World" phase in 1948, he had arrived there defiantly without a visa – to the fine points of transporting rice in Bengal, Trudeau came to office knowing more about other countries than any Canadian Prime Minister before him, more probably, than any other contemporary western leader. He had backpacked his way around the world, following Marco Polo's route, but with an incomparably more inquisitive eye. "He's the total traveller, insatiably interested in people, customs, buildings, monuments, history," says Hébert.* He had been to Russia. He had been to China, twice, his second visit resulting in *Two Innocents in China*, co-authored with Hébert, published first in 1961, a zestful travelogue crammed with anecdotal detail, such as gearing up to swallow the delicacy of sea slugs, "a fat brownish worm covered with bumps," also containing some monumental naiveties, as in, that in contrast to the new order, "pre-Communist China was excessively bureaucratic."

One other characteristic made Trudeau unusual among leaders: he quite genuinely does not recognize differences either of colour, or of race, or of culture. No student of Père Bernier's can have accepted his dictum, "all men are brothers" more wholeheartedly. No one who knows Trudeau can recall him ever indulging in even the mildest of cultural stereotyping – as in, "all Germans are efficient" or, "the Chinese are inscrutable" – let alone recounting an ethnic joke. In a fundamental sense, Trudeau really *is* a Citizen of the World.

The trouble was, all this knowledge was personal and random, gleaned around the fringes. When it came to the *realpolitik* of international affairs, Trudeau knew next to nothing. What with Quebec, bilingualism, and the constitution, he'd had no inclination to pay attention before he came to power. Early on, foreign reporters noticed when they interviewed him that although he was well mugged up on whatever country he was visiting, he steered

---

*Hébert and Trudeau compete to see who has visited the most countries. Hébert, who recently visited Mauritius where Trudeau has yet to go, reckons he is currently ahead.

the conversation away from the generalities of foreign affairs.

As with so many other matters in those early years, Trudeau masked his uncertainty with flippancy. During the 1969 Commonwealth Conference, he slid down the banisters. He blurted out, "Where's Biafra?" and pronounced, "We have no foreign policy of importance except that which flows from NATO."

For this reason, an unacknowledged purpose of both the 1968-70 foreign policy review, and of the year-long review of NATO policy held concurrently was to give Trudeau time to bone up on subjects that most Prime Ministers come to office reasonably acquainted with. Tarted up in the jargon of the era – "conceptual framework," "parameters" – and having explored every conceivable option policy including such inconceivable ones as a unilateral declaration of Canadian neutrality, both these reviews arrived in the end with conclusions predictable from the start.

But because such intellectual head-games were new, they stirred up a great deal of *Sturm und Drang*. Defence Minister Leo Cadieux, for instance, came to believe that "the object of the (NATO review) exercise . . . was to get out of NATO," as he told Peter Stursberg for his book, *Lester Pearson and the American Dilemma*. Cadieux quit six months later to become Ambassador in Paris; Paul Hellyer, who quit around the same time, though not on a foreign policy issue, became convinced the country was being run by closet fellow-travellers at best.

Pearson himself got even more upset, though for quite different reasons. The foreign policy White Paper of June 1970 declared ringingly, "Canada must in future develop its external policies in a coherent way." This managed to imply that all previous Pearsonian policies had been incoherent. (Which they had been, in a way, though that way had been singularly creative.) Pearsonian diplomacy was dismissed by the contemptuous phrase "helpful fixer." Pearson dashed off an angry, twenty-page memo, then realized there was nowhere to send it. It reappeared, toned down, as a chapter "Sovereignty is Not Enough" in his memoirs.*

Nor did the brouhaha end there. As its first priority, the foreign

---

*After the foreign policy review was published, Pearson met Trudeau once, to discuss it, at a meeting arranged by Mitchell Sharp. The encounter was entirely unproductive, because Trudeau kept arguing on the basis of facts (as he saw them) without recognizing that Pearson's argument was based on feeling and intuition.

policy review listed "Fostering Economic Growth." NDP foreign affairs critic Andrew Brewin described this as "a withdrawal from idealistically-inspired worldwide involvement." Hastily, government spokesmen explained that all the six priorities listed, including "Working for Peace and Security" were co-equal, although they were not able to explain, when pressed, how six priorities could be equal and be priorities at the same time. To sort things out, Head, in an article for the prestigious *Foreign Affairs Quarterly*, pronounced Canada's passionate concern for "the quality of life."

In the end, all the critics, Pearson included, came to realize that when the jargon and the trendy policy options and priority had been stripped away, little had changed. The essentials of Canadian foreign policy – membership in NATO and in the Atlantic alliance – remained exactly as before.

The NATO review is a prime case in point. At the time, it stirred up a good deal of hostile comment, including an accusation by the British Defence Minister, Denis Healey, that "Canada is passing the buck to the rest of us," by recommending a cut in half of our European contingent of 10,000 troops. In fact, the financially strapped Defence Department had come up with this recommendation itself. The single substantive policy change produced by the review was to "denuclearize" our interceptors in Europe; this came about after Trudeau's personal international affairs adviser, Ivan Head, in a brilliant policy analysis paper, demonstrated that our interceptors could be used only in a first-strike *offensive* role since, if the Russians actually attacked, their missiles would land on our runways in West Germany before our planes could take off.

As for the foreign policy White Paper of 1970, the most interesting thing about it was that it said nothing that was new. As Bruce Thordarson outlined in *Trudeau and Foreign Policy*, Trudeau had made all its supposedly new "realistic" points two years earlier, and was already acting on them.

* * *

Because it was delivered between kisses in the midst of the "Trudeau-mania" campaign, Trudeau's foreign policy statement of May 29, 1968, (the only extended one he has ever made) attracted little attention. Yet it represents the quintessential Trudeau. From it, he emerges unmistakably, not so much as the internationalist he's always thought to be, as a *nationalist* internationalist.

Canada's "paramount interest" in foreign affairs, Trudeau declared, had to be to "ensure the survival of Canada as a federal and bilingual state." We should "exercise realism in how we see ourselves." Rather than "crusading abroad," we should "mobilize our aspirations, energies and resources at home."

No more Mr. Nice Guy, in other words. Canada first, instead. In France, Japan, or Britain say, as an argument that charity in foreign policy begins anywhere but at home, this would have amounted to an utterance of the obvious. But in Canada, it was a decisive departure from the tradition of international altruism established and implemented so successfully by St. Laurent and Pearson, and then, much less successfully because the world had changed, by Howard Green and Paul Martin.

Trudeau recognized just how much the world had changed. "We shouldn't be trying to run the world," he said, "we should be trying to make our own country a good place." And; "I am less worried about what is happening over the Berlin wall, than about what might happen in our great cities in Canada."

Insights are one thing. The practical policies needed to implement them are something else entirely. In 1968, when he came to office Trudeau found these policies beginning to burgeon in the place he had least expected to find them: the Department of External Affairs.

* * *

External Affairs, in the late 1960's, was not just one more department of government. It was *the* Department, or just "External," beside which all other departments ranked as an uncouth crowd below the salt. External was redolent of deliberately shabby offices behind green baize doors; matters of high policy decided over tuna fish sandwiches in the basement cafeteria of the Chateau Laurier; memories of baseball games with the State Department and drinks with Scotty Reston of the *New York Times*. For External had been created in Lester Pearson's image and it meant, as Charles Ritchie once put it, "a handful of unusually gifted men, who shared the belief that Canada had its own role in the world and a conception of what the role should be." For an entire generation of our best and our brightest, the prospect of getting into External had shone like the holy grail. "It was a bit like joining the church," one recruit of the mid-1950's has recalled.

Yet like pseudo-Pearsonian diplomacy, External's time had passed. There simply was not enough work any longer to occupy all the bright people it had attracted; in the early 1970's so many moved out that at one point one in three of all the deputy ministers in Ottawa were ex-diplomats. Those who remained were like custodians of a stately, but decaying, old mansion, as they knew only too well. To make matters worse, Trudeau kept rubbing it in, through statements like "the whole concept of diplomacy today is pretty outmoded," adding that he could find more of what he wanted to know "in a good newspaper" than in all the despatches of his diplomats.*

If the main stem was withering, however, new shoots were springing up. By the late 1960's, a younger, post-Pearson generation had begun to rise through the ranks, convinced that the time had come to break with the past through a new policy of enlightened self-interest. Its leader was Allan Gotlieb, then head of the legal division, a brilliant renaissance figure possessed of an exceptional critical mind, who, after spending eight years outside first as deputy minister of Communications and later as deputy minister of Manpower, returned in 1977 as under-secretary.

Trudeau, while Justice Minister, had encountered Gotlieb as a member of the group of civil servants assembled to advise him on constitutional matters. When he asked Gotlieb for his ideas on foreign policy, he got in reply a long note that served as a catalyst for his 1968 statement of policy.

Later, Trudeau's ideas would change. But for about four years, he preached and practised the doctrine of national self-interest. As always, he pursued the idea to its logical limit: If we put our own interests first, then we had to respect the self-interests of others. In May 1971, while flying back from a state visit to the Soviet Union, Trudeau made no bones about his approach. Asked by reporters whether he had pressed the Soviet leaders to free imprisoned Ukrainian nationalists, he replied: "Anyone who breaks the law to assert his nationalism doesn't get much sympathy from me. I didn't feel like bringing up any case which would have

---

*One of these, Bruce Rankin, told Trudeau at a memorable private meeting with senior External officials: "You've fucked up the morale of the finest diplomatic service in the world." But Trudeau never held this against Rankin, who went on to become Ambassador to Japan.

caused Mr. Kosygin or Mr. Brezhnev to say, 'Why should you put your revolutionaries in jail, and we not put ours.'"

In its hey-day, national self-interest as the engine of foreign policy was out of phase with the mood of the times; a kind of countervailing force to the generous expansive spirit of the 1960's that still held sway. Later, when Trudeau switched to the doctrine of "sharing," he was countervailing once more; Canadians had turned in upon themselves. The irony is that as self-interested nationalists, we accomplished more internationally than at any other time in the past two decades.

In October 1970, for instance, we established diplomatic relations with China, the second important western country to do so, after France, since China's civil war. The year before, we had appointed our first ambassador to the Vatican, "the cheapest listening post in the world," as Trudeau explained. In Europe, we cut our contribution to NATO to fit our financial cloth. In the Pacific, we declared ourselves to be a power there for the first time, as Trudeau toured from Japan through Malaysia to Australia in 1970, showing the Maple Leaf flag.

On the one occasion when our own sovereignty was actually threatened, we reacted promptly and adroitly. The provocation was the 1969 traverse of Arctic waters, permission unasked, by the U.S. supertanker *Manhattan*; our answer was to extend our territorial sea zone from three to twelve miles and also to enact a 100-mile pollution control zone. In both instances, because the U.S. denied our claim to sovereignty, we announced we would not abide by the jurisdiction of the International Court of Justice at The Hague. (Canada's 1977 unilateral declaration of a 200-mile fishing and resource zone represented the logical consequence of these policies.)

Beyond all of this, we spoke to the world with a new voice, one that spoke French. We extended our diplomatic representation throughout French-speaking West Africa. A small aid scheme to these countries blossomed into an $100 million program, and won Ottawa allies overseas in its endless, elbows-in-the-corridor battles with France over Quebec's aspirations to international status. In the same spirit, we joined every French-language international organization on the go, and became a founding member, and indeed one of the principal architects of *La Francophonie*, the

French-speaking equivalent of the Commonwealth.*

But early in 1972, all this activity slackened. From then on, Trudeau's preoccupation became the election, and after the election, survival. The next time Trudeau turned his attention to foreign affairs, he had a new idea in mind. Its path was rocky.

* * *

The new idea was called the Third Option. Canadians learned of it by way of an article in the autumn 1972 issue of the magazine *International Perspectives*, signed by External Affairs Minister Mitchell Sharp. Sharp had hoped to put it out as a White Paper with the government's imprimatur, but had been blocked by his cabinet colleagues in Finance and Trade and Commerce. So he went ahead on his own.** In the article, Sharp advanced the case for a Third Option "to lessen the vulnerability of the Canadian economy to external factors, including, in particular, the impact of the U.S.† . . . (to) develop a more confident sense of national identity." (The other options, as defined by Sharp, were to do nothing, or to "move deliberately towards closer integration.")

At the time, this sounded like pre-election fodder for restive nationalists. But in December 1974, with his majority regained, Trudeau pressed on, pledging to reduce our economic ties with the U.S. "by more trade with other countries." By February 1975, he had accorded the Third Option his personal, philosophical sanction by saying that its purpose was "to create counterweights."

In pursuit of more trade, Trudeau that month travelled to Europe to negotiate what he described as a "contractual link" with the European Economic Community. Stanfield described this as a "big bag of fog"; one of Trudeau's aides confessed it sounded to him like "some kind of German sausage." On the evidence, both

---

*At one time two Canadians, Jean-Marc Léger and Arnold Smith, served as Secretaries-General of the two organizations.

**The article was actually written by Klaus Goldschlag, an exceptionally gifted senior official, appointed Ambassador to West Germany in 1980. Goldschlag also authored Trudeau's much-praised speech on disarmament at the United Nations in 1978.

†Our vulnerability *vis-à-vis* the U.S. had been demonstrated vividly in June 1971, when President Nixon, without consulting Ottawa, imposed a 10 per cent surcharge on manufactured imports that threatened an estimated forty to one hundred thousand Canadian jobs. The surcharge was lifted the following December as part of an international package, underlining the point that our famed "special relationship" with the U.S. had earned us no special favours.

may have been kind. Post-1975, our trade with the U.S., at 70 per cent of the total, remained unchanged. At the 1977-79 GATT talks, our single substantive accomplishment was a deal with the U.S. to cut cross-border tariffs to zero on 80 per cent of our trade with each other.

In his attempts to develop new ties to Europe as a counterweight to those which bound us too tightly to the U.S., Trudeau several times stumbled into his own footprints, some old, some new. He discovered, for example, that Europe hadn't forgiven him for cutting back our NATO contingent back in 1969. When India exploded a "nuclear device" using plutonium from a Canadian reactor, he imposed controls on our uranium exports, the one commodity Europe was most interested in. Even so, some important new trade and political ties were forged, particularly with West Germany, while Canada-France relations improved markedly.

The trouble for the "Europeanists" in Ottawa was, Trudeau's attention had shifted. By the late 1970's, he had exorcised "The Third Option" from his vocabulary, just as he had dropped "national self-interest" years before. So, in 1978-79, when a crunch decision presented itself, Europeanists were unable to persuade the government to insist that Air Canada buy – a $3 billion order – the European Air Bus rather than Boeing 767s, and so make the Third Option manifest.

As to why Trudeau's attention shifted, the best guess is that he was no more attached to the Third Option than to any other of the big ideas he enjoyed lobbing up, from "Participatory Democracy" to the "New Society." Meanwhile, on the home front, other aspects of the policy, such as the Foreign Investment Review Agency and the withdrawal of tax privileges from *Time*, not to mention Trudeau's 1976 "Viva Castro"* and Saskatchewan's nationalization of potash, managed to get the U.S. angry with us. In 1975, *Barron's*, the influential financial weekly warned its readers to be on guard against "anti-Americanism, or fervent nationalism" on the rampage north of the border. In December that year, departing U.S. Ambassador William Porter astonished a group of journalists he had invited over for cocktails by recounting a list of "unfriendly acts" by Canada toward the U.S.

Still, the tiff did not last. By 1977, the new U.S. Ambassador,

*The salutation was quite routine, and actually was added to Trudeau's original text by a departmental Latin affairs expert.

Thomas Enders, could talk publicly about the "convergence" of the two North American economies being a good idea, without drawing a boo. As for FIRA, it approved so many take-overs that *Barron's* was able to report to its readers approvingly, "The only foreign company that wouldn't be welcomed in Canada is Murder Inc." Continentalism rather than the contractual link became the new chic, with all the command posts in cabinet held by its apostles: Jamieson at External Affairs; Chrétien at Finance; Jack Horner at Trade and Commerce. Reluctantly, Trudeau's critics gave up calling him "anti-American." By February 1980, the most striking thing about Trudeau's emergence late in the election campaign as a tyro economic nationalist was that this time, everyone took for granted that his objective was no more devious than being pro-Canadian. Not that anyone took his new doctrine particularly seriously. More than a decade ago, Trudeau defined his policy of not having any Canada-U.S. policy. "I think that the problem of [U.S.] economic domination is somewhat inevitable," he told the *New York Times* in an interview in November 1968. "These are facts of life and don't worry me."

* * *

One of the reasons Trudeau was tagged for a time as being "anti-American" is that for a much longer time, he was tagged as "soft on Communism."

Early on, Trudeau made it clear he was convinced that Russia was no longer a military threat in Europe. His reaction to the 1968 Soviet invasion of Czechoslovakia was cool: "We are not led to the immediate conclusion . . . that we should necessarily escalate in NATO." A dozen years later, in response to the Soviet invasion of Afghanistan, he said as coolly. "We won't twist the Soviet bear's tail with the Olympic Games."

Trudeau's coolness extended to all things military. His interest in the Armed Forces was about as considerable as his interest in the Post Office. Indeed, one of the finest of his foreign policy speeches dealt with the subject of disarmament. On May 26, 1978, in his first and only visit to the UN as Prime Minister, he flew to New York to propose to a special session a policy of "suffocation" of the arms race, by ending all future weapons research, and by stopping nuclear testing and the production of fissionable materials.

304

Yet, four days after his UN speech, he was in Washington to take part in a NATO decision on a program of re-armament, which has involved us since in our largest weapons purchases ever; after the 1980 election, we not only boycotted the Moscow Olympics but to show that we were really serious, cancelled the Canada-Russia hockey series.

The facts fit the profile of a pragmatist. The only slightly pinkish thing that can be said of Trudeau is that as a legacy of all those LSE lectures long ago, he probably does accept the premise that for underdeveloped countries, socialism may be the best route to take, though naturally, he is far too pragmatic ever to say so in public. Plainly, he has a particular affinity for socialist leaders: Nyerere, Manley, and Castro (although, in prototypical paradox, he is fascinated by Saudi Arabia). China's appeal to him, after four visits, is well-known. And Russia itself appears to exercise an out-of-the-ordinary appeal, though in its image as Holy Mother Russia. He can quote extensive passages from Dostoevsky and Tolstoy, and came back from his 1971 visit bewitched by the country's geographic sweep.

Instead of Communism, what Trudeau is really soft on is *sharing*.

* * *

Since the late 1970's, Trudeau has tried to make the ethic of "sharing" the successor to bilingualism as the glue that holds Confederation together. He applies the same concept to the world, in the hope of preventing it from blowing itself apart.

"Never before in history has the disparity between the rich and the poor, the comfortable and the starving, been so extreme," Trudeau said in a speech at the University of Alberta on May 13, 1968, where he had gone to pick up an honorary degree. Conventional stuff, except that the solution Trudeau proposed, a good half decade ahead of its time, was entirely unconventional. The "sweet philanthropy" of foreign aid, he pronounced, had to "take on a new form . . . of preferential trade agreements."

Trudeau's problem was to be ahead of his time. The handshake of trade deals instead of the handout of aid meant, as he said at the time, "competition." And competition was exactly what neither Canadian manufacturers nor Trudeau as a pragmatic politician could afford.

As a substitute for implementing his own remedy, Trudeau sweetened our philanthropic pot. Year by year, our foreign program increased, until in 1976 it topped $1 billion, to rank as the world's fifth largest in absolute amount and also as the fifth ranked proportionately, (just under 0.6 per cent of our Gross National Product, compared to the 0.75 per cent suggested by Pearson in his 1969 report for the World Bank). Post-1976, because of restraint, the program went on hold, and in 1978, actually was cut.

By this time, the nature of the world's trade had changed anyway. First, in 1973, there was the oil boycott. From then on, the Middle East began sucking petrodollars out of the west. After that, at the fall session of the UN in 1974, came the cry, raised by Algeria, for a "New International Economic Order." In reply, while western politicians and bankers tried to figure out how to get those petrodollars back in circulation again, there came nothing.

Trudeau's own reply, through a speech delivered at the Mansion House in London on March 13, 1975, was one of the most eloquent of his career. It constituted the first attempt by a western leader to come to terms with the suddenly strident, suddenly self-confident demands of the Third World for a new deal. It delineates Trudeau's transition from nationalist internationalist to north-south interlocutor. It's the reason why he is on the short-list of candidates to succeed Robert McNamara as President of the World Bank.

The "positive freedoms" of free speech and free assembly, had been pretty much won, Trudeau said. "We now find ourselves in a struggle to establish with equal sanctity the negative freedoms, the freedoms 'from': hunger, from disease, from nuclear holocaust, from environmental degradation."

Waging this new battle would require "an acceptance of the inter-relationship of all countries and the inter-connection of all phenomena. The acceptance in brief that we are all brothers." To do this, Trudeau went on, "calls for more than tinkering with the present system. The processes required must be global in scope, and universal in application . . . We must aim for nothing less than an acceptable distribution of the world's wealth."

Since 1975, Trudeau has been no better placed to apply this remedy to the world's ills than he was earlier on to substitute trade for aid. If anything, he is worse positioned. Soon afterwards came the economic crunch. We imposed quotas on imports of textiles, clothing, and footwear. We cut and ran with everything we could from the GATT talks. We took all we could at Law of the Sea Conferences. And Canadians applauded, because now that we were suffering a bit ourselves, we did not much care whether others on the other side of the world were suffering much more, nor did we want to know.

No avenue exists to discover just how much Trudeau believed *personally* in his ideal of "global sharing" as opposed to believing in it intellectually, as intellectuals do. Years earlier, he gave Claude Ryan a dusty answer when the two met in Rome and Ryan suggested that the way for him to become truly committed was to dispose of his fortune. At the time he gave his Mansion House speech, he was reaching his own zenith as Sun King; indeed, the swimming pool was nearing completion.

The evidence is mixed. His adviser, Head, who wrote both the Mansion House speech and the trade-not-aid one in 1968, was unquestionably a true idealist about solving international poverty. At cabinet meetings, although Trudeau in time grew resigned to hearing arguments advanced for particular policies on the grounds these were "politically necessary," he always insisted that arguments about north-south policy be couched in terms of "the right," even if these high-minded discussions ended up with decisions indistinguishable from the politically necessary. Lastly, after the 1980 election, he used the licence Canadians granted him to make North-South relations his third priority after the constitution and oil; he convinced his economic "summit" partners to make the topic a priority on the agenda for the July, 1981 conference in Ottawa that he chaired; and in search of ideas to suggest, he toured the third world, from Saudi Arabia to Senegal to Brazil.

Yet Trudeau made few attempts to enlist Canadians in his cause of "sharing." Post-Mansion House, he didn't even make that many more speeches on the subject. Rather, he became a solitary in international affairs. A bravura performer who like all stars, shines best when alone.

* * *

Except for Castro and Sadat and Khomeini, no one in international politics can match Trudeau's star quality. When he went to Cuba, the crowds that Castro turned out for him stood five deep at the curbs, larger than for any other foreign visitor except Leonid Brezhnev, who after all pays Castro's bills. The Europeans sometimes seem to be a bit skeptical about him, and the prestigious British weekly, *The Economist*, can at times be quite cutting. Richard Nixon once described him as "that asshole," an inventive turn of phrase he thought he was uttering only to his Oval Office microphones, which he said subsequently he had not meant.

Otherwise, Trudeau receives only accolades. "Priceless asset," as Mondale has said. "Perhaps the world's most gifted leader," according to U.S. columnist, Joseph Kraft. "Saviour of the Commonwealth" (Singapore, 1971, for settling a row between Britain and the black African countries over Britain's resumption of arms sales to South Africa). "North-South Interlocutor" (post-Mansion House). "Star of the Summit" (Bonn, 1978, for proposing the resolution that committed the seven to take joint action against plane hijackers).

Like all stars, Trudeau takes care to keep his lustre sparkling. He prepares for international occasions such as economic summits with more care than he applies to most domestic events, except for First Ministers Conferences. He grants interviews to foreign reporters far more readily than to Canadian ones. Shrewdly, he limits most of his many international friendships to the personal rather than the practical: he has never tried, for instance, to risk his first-name relationship with Castro by trying to pressure him to limit his military activities in Africa.

Only Pearson among Canadian Prime Ministers has brought home more applause for his own country from the leaders of other countries. But there has been a difference in the quality of that applause. Pearson won it for what he did; Trudeau wins it for what he is. Perhaps though, this difference is no more than the difference between the high-minded style of international relations in the 1940's and 1950's and the showy, slightly tawdry international stage of the 1970's and 1980's. Perhaps the deeper point is that Trudeau understands this difference.

18

Decline and . . .

"After you have once ridden behind a motorcycle escort, you are never the same again."

U.S. Senator Herbert Lehman,
explaining why he sought re-election.

Trudeau accomplished less during the last eighteen months of his third term in office than any post-war Prime Minister during a comparable period, except perhaps Louis St. Laurent during his slide toward senescence in 1955-57. From the autumn of 1977 to his defeat in May 1979, much of the little he did do was positively destructive. While the crisis of national unity festered and the economy foundered, Trudeau expended his waning energies upon a single, obsessive goal – winning the next election. Winning literally became everything: a substitute for policy or political purpose; a justification for emptying the Opposition benches of half a dozen M.P.s by appointing them to the Senate or to soft civil service posts; or for breaking faith with his own best past by declaring that capital punishment, supported so strongly by the public, might yet be restored through the device of holding a national referendum.

Think of the captain of a liner buffeted by a hurricane who instead of commanding from the bridge is down in his cabin worrying about docking the ship when he reaches harbour. Think also of Captain Queeg, the hint of paranoia: "What is this hostility out here that seems to presume that anything the government does must be wrong?" he plaintively asked Toronto Liberals in November 1978. Then he identified the media as one of the "enemies" of the government, along with the Opposition.

There was also a Queeg-like hint of megalomania, though this was a development the public did not see. On Sunday, July 30, 1978, Trudeau assembled his top aides for a policy session at 24 Sussex. He greeted them in a shimmering, ankle-length *djellabah* made of pure white silk flecked with gold; as the sun set over the

Ottawa River he stood against the window, "looking just like T.E. Lawrence and knowing perfectly well that he did," as one aide put it after. Later, on trips abroad, he would wear the *djellabah* at bizarre breakfast briefing sessions in his hotel suite; he alone tucking into scrambled eggs and toast while ministers and officials, who were expected to have risen earlier and breakfasted separately, sat around the room backgrounding him on this or that agenda item – but quickly, because anyone who rambled was not invited back.

Power is an aphrodisiac, Henry Kissinger has said. What Kissinger did not say but Lord Acton did is that power affects most deeply its possessor. Modern, imperial power does not so much corrupt a ruler as coarsen him. Trudeau had come to revel in the tangible perqs of his office: the daily pro-consular procession to and fro from 24 Sussex to Parliament Hill in his vast Cadillac flanked by RCMP patrol cars; the trips overseas or within Canada by JetStar and Boeing 707; the huge personal staff catering to his every need and whim. Having governed for a decade, it was easy for him to believe that only he could govern the country; easier still for him to believe, having been told it so fawningly, so often, that only he could save the country.

More profoundly, Trudeau had become dependent on power. His addiction – the end product of so many minute compromises here, small conveniences accepted there – had come upon him so gradually that Trudeau did not realize that allowing himself to be narcotized had cost him his most cherished possession: his personal freedom. All his life, he had guarded this freedom against every enemy, from liquor to tobacco to the lure of material possessions. Power, by 1978, had conquered him. It enveloped him as totally as the *djellabah*; tenderly, seductively, osmotically, a soft translucent spider's web.

His magic allure had not departed entirely. In the spring of 1978, for a tenth-anniversary-in-office spread in *Weekend* magazine, Trudeau, against the advice of his own staff, picked out the most dramatic photo of himself: standing shirt-sleeved in his office, legs apart, thumbs tucked into his belt. At a later Liberal policy convention in Ottawa, in February 1978, he reworked this into his "gunslinger" stance, thumbs hooked in belt, standing alone at the microphone without podium or notes, the thinking man's John Wayne, the lone existential hero hanging in there to save the country from itself. He remained the only politician central to the national consciousness; Canadians hated him now rather than loved him, yet still they talked about him, argued about him, wondered what he did when he was away from their television screens.

Yet his platform tricks had become over-practised, and worse, familiar. No longer could he hold the crowd's attention by manipulating a few coins or cards or billiard balls; he now needed much too visible mechanical devices, like the free-standing microphone and the stylized, symbolic Maple Leaf flag that were trucked around with him, from platform to platform. Or else he relied on bombast: in Vancouver, just before the 1979 election, he described Lougheed and Blakeney as "enemies of Confederation" because of their demands for expanded jurisdiction. Then, since the voters in these provinces naturally gathered defensively round their own, he had to say he had not meant to say it.

Among Canadians, familiarity had bred boredom, if not contempt. In Trudeau, it had bred exhaustion. The physical exhaustion showed in the deepening lines on his face and the puffy bags beneath his eyes; all of a sudden, he looked his age. His intellectual exhaustion showed in his verbal carelessness. Heckled by Toronto students about their job prospects, Trudeau suggested they "go to another country." During the election campaign, he committed the irreparable blunder of musing to a couple of reporters aboard the campaign plane that even if he emerged with fewer seats than the Tories, he might try to stay in power by making a deal with the NDP. Gleefully, Clark accused him of "clinging to power"; and more Canadians made up their minds to remove him from it.

* * *

"We were stale," says Donald Macdonald, who left Ottawa in September 1977. "We had run out of ideas. Decisions were being made with which I was not in accord." (Macdonald, specifically, had wanted controls ended a full year earlier than was the case. The decision to maintain them had been purely political – Canadians liked controls – at a heavy cost in lost investment and economic growth.) Another senior ex-minister, a Trudeau loyalist defeated in 1979 says, "For the last couple of years, Trudeau and the government were out of control."

Robert Andras gives the most graphic description: "To paraphrase Woodward and Bernstein, a kind of cancer was growing around the Prime Minister. There was no evil intent on anybody's part, and indeed it was a benign kind of growth. The problem is that in that impossible job, in which you spend your days submerged in paper, it becomes progressively easier and easier to reach out to the familiar, to your aides and civil servants, who speak the same kind of decision-making language as you, and whom you know that when you say, 'give me a paper on such and such' will produce the kind of paper that meets your decision-making needs. As a result, you reach out less and less to the unfamiliar, to the real outside world, to people."

Yet of Trudeau, even during this late, decadent period, Andras says, "He's the most exciting, the most intelligent, the strongest person I have ever met."

The trouble was, Trudeau's strength was his weakness. Even at his worst, he was still so easily, and so evidently, the best around. He starred at the Bonn Economic Summit in July 1978. He dazzled the bankers and businessmen of New York's Economic Club when he went there in the spring. He dominated the November 1978 constitutional conference, chivying along the suspicious Conservative premiers and extracting from Lévesque the admission, "something is happening" – even if it really was not. Head to head against Clark in the "leadership" polls, his margins scarcely changed, although the overall Liberal lead narrowed month by month from late 1977 on. "What Canadians really want," said Clark shrewdly and sadly, "is Pierre Trudeau without his warts."

The weakness was, Trudeau had become the Liberal Party, the government, the state. When a Liberal backbencher, Hal Herbert, described the 1977 cabinet as "the weakest since World War Two," he was simply stating the obvious. In 1979, a former Liberal National Director, Blair Williams, described the ministers as "irrelevant," and, in an unprecedented breach of party solidarity, blamed this on Trudeau's "aloofness, insensitivity and lack of judgement." Cabinet meetings had become a charade, as had caucus sessions. In August 1978, Trudeau changed the government's entire economic policy 180 degrees without consulting any minister other than Andras of the Treasury Board who had to be involved because the new policy involved a slash in spending. Cabinet ministers first learned about the projected new policy of holding referendums on contentious issues like capital punishment by reading about it in the newspapers – all ministers that is to say, but Otto Lang who had invented the new approach in tandem with Coutts, to assuage his own Saskatoon voters.

One cabinet minister, seen standing on the Rideau Club portico overlooking Parliament Hill, and asked why he was staring so hard, remarked: "I can see the window of the Prime Minister's Office, and I'm trying to lip-read what Coutts and Pitfield are saying so I can figure out what our policies will be."

Pitfield, in fact, had begun to put a certain distance between himself and Trudeau. He was now, as one minister puts it, "less Trudeau's personal representative to the civil service than its representative to the Prime Minister." Pitfield had gained confidence in the job, and wanted to make his own mark. He also wanted to survive the transition to a Conservative government. Yet few recognized the change in Pitfield, and anyway the centralized PCO decision-making system he had created remained as Trudeau's personal bureaucratic fiefdom.

"Don't allow yourself to believe for an instant that Trudeau isn't as bright, as lucid and as resilient as he ever was," an aide remarked to a reporter. "But my God, is he isolated."

Within Trudeau's personal staff, Coutts had cut all lines of personal communication to him, except his own. In late 1977, he even elbowed out his closest political friend, Keith Davey, who from then on said anything he had to say to the Prime Minister to Coutts. Tireless, inventive, scrappy, totally loyal, as much to the point, totally dependent upon Trudeau for his own political existence, Coutts had made himself into the ideal, irreplaceable *alter ego* of a great man: the prompter, bright eyes gleaming in the wings; the apprentice who made certain there was a rabbit in the sorcerer's hat, and who embarrassed the crowd into applause by beginning it himself. As for Trudeau's other personal aides, they liked to think of themselves "as a Praetorian Guard," as one put it, a self-sacrificing elite defending the bunker to the last.

Among his ministers, Lalonde, Lang, MacEachen, now Deputy Prime Minister, and among his advisers, Coutts, Pitfield, and Robertson, were the only people Trudeau saw, or cared to see, or cared about. The old faithful warhorses, Drury and Sharp, were gone. Pelletier was in Paris. "I would have stayed if he'd asked me," he told a friend. Marchand was gone to the Senate and growing increasingly bitter about having been shuffled sideways. "Trudeau is all I ever believed he would be, but less generous than I thought he would be," he says now. Margaret was gone. When she did come back, flighty and careless, she upset the children, leaving them, and Trudeau, hurt and confused.

He was isolated from people. He was isolated from life. And he was isolated, now, even from ideas. As Kissinger has remarked, political leaders are so pressured by daily events and by paper burden that they have to get by on whatever intellectual capital they stored up before taking office. During his first two terms, right on up to his "New Society" musings of 1976, Trudeau had delighted in new ideas, tossing them out in public for the sheer joy of seeing where they would fall. But toward the end, he stopped reading, except for clips of articles and briefing notes all couched in bloodless administrative prose. After his mother's death, he moved all his books from Montreal to 24 Sussex; they stayed there, in unopened cardboard cartons, until the time came, after the 1979 election, to move them to Stornoway.

Beyond the gift of his international reputation as a buttress for Canadian self-esteem, Trudeau had nothing left to contribute. When it came to the crisis of national unity, his own cause of causes, he had become as much the cause of the problem as a possible solution to it, because of his personal rivalry with Lévesque and his lack of empathy for the west. About the country's worsening economic problems, he could think of absolutely nothing to do. A group of top economic advisers, the "DMs-Ten" (ten deputy ministers) met weekly for six months through 1976 and came up with not a single practical suggestion. "Re-privatization," or selling off hunks of government to the private sector, became a vogue word; no one, however, could think what to sell or to whom. "De-regulation," or government staying out of the nation's boardrooms, became popular too, the trouble being that the public immediately affected might not prefer more pollution to more jobs; so the Economic Council was instructed to make a three-year study of the subject.

Nobody believed in fine tuning anymore. Anyway, there was no money left with which to do it. The budget ran permanently at $10 billion or so a year in deficit; one tax dollar in five went right out again on paying charges on the national debt. Late in 1978, the dollar went down to a post-Depression 83.89 cent low; inflation went up to 9 per cent that year. Meanwhile, unemployment stayed stuck at 7 per cent, our balance of payments deficit ballooned to $6 billion, while our deficit of imports over exports of manufactured goods grew to an horrendous $12 billion.

Our entire post-war economic policy had run out of steam. "Through the structure of the branch-plant economy," wrote James and Robert Laxer, in *The Liberal Idea of Canada*, "Canada achieved economic growth without development." A Science Council study calculated that pervasive foreign ownership had cost us 200,000 jobs, particularly in high income managerial, administrative, scientific, engineering, and technical occupations. (Comparable manufacturing plants in the U.S. employed twice as many technicians and professionals.) Worse, these branch-plants were either pulling up stakes and moving back home, or were closing the doors entirely in face of the competition from newly industrialized countries, like South Korea and Taiwan.

Chrysler was still to happen. Still, everyone knew that it or something like it was bound to happen. The problem – "a truncated economy," in the Science Council's vivid phrase: plenty of bureaucrats on top, plenty of resources underneath, but no competitive industrial sector in between – was easy to describe. No one, though, could think of what to do, nor could anyone face the wrenching socio-economic changes (closing out textile mills and therefore, entire towns in Quebec) of doing anything. Some suggested protectionism. Others, like the Science Council, suggested concentrating on selected world-scale technologies, such as communications and nuclear power. Some suggested free trade with the U.S., and nobody anymore booed U.S. Ambassador Thomas Enders when he suggested a policy of "convergence" between the two economies.

Trudeau himself suggested nothing and took little action. Almost in desperation, he set up twenty-three industry "sector" business-labour-government study groups, most of which recommended that government spend more money on them. (So much for business opposition to government spending.) To save "soft" industries like textiles, clothing, shoes, he imposed import quotas and so fed inflation. To help others save themselves, he threw money at them: $68 million to Ford, $235 million to the pulp and paper industry. In November 1978, Finance Minister Chrétien lopped $1 billion off industry taxes. Right afterwards a study in the *Canadian Tax Foundation Journal* concluded that "it is not at all apparent" that any of the tax incentives to industry since 1963 had had the slightest effect.

More serious than the decline of our economy was the decline of our spirit. Trudeau's own malaise was a symptom of what was happening all across the country. We had lost or else were losing fast the attribute that Daniel Bell has called "the sense of civitas," the belief in public duty and public compassion.

* * *

At the end of a year, or of a decade, or of a century, most pundits hedge their bets by describing it as "the best of times and worst of times" at once. But when the 1970's ended, everyone agreed they had been the pits.

Critics disagreed about causes – television, affluence, permissiveness, feminism, resentment that the expectations of the heady 1960's had not been fulfilled, an unvoiced conviction that another Depression was inevitable – but they agreed unanimously: the consequences had been uniformly rotten.

In our public life, commentators outbid one another's gloom. Bell aside, Daniel Yankelovich wrote of a "crisis of moral legitimacy." In the *New Yorker*, William Pfaff suggested "the American Idea of unlimited possibilities and the transformation of humanity is no longer tenable." The Trilateral Commission concluded that democracies had become ungovernable, largely because elected governments could not make the painful economic choices that had to be made, because their voters would heave them out. Over-arching all of these was an unvoiced fear that Oswald Spengler had been right; the west was played out, and was due to be overtaken by hardier races from beyond the Urals, or the Middle East, or the rim of Asia.

Everyone, not without reason, dumped on liberalism. The "nanny state," in Barbara Amiel's splendid phrase, was producing out of mass higher education a race of languid illiterates; what was worse, it was also producing just as many poor people as ever.*

---

*Between 1959 and 1979, the distribution of income remained unchanged, at 4 per cent of the total for the bottom one-fifth, and 40 per cent for the top one-fifth. True, the poor got larger social security payments, but the rich got larger tax loopholes, and did not do at all badly out of social security: almost one-quarter of UIC payments went to families with average incomes of $30,000.

316

Everyone, therefore, stopped feeling guilty, about the young, the old, the poor, women, native peoples, French Canadians, and liberalism lost its driving force. In its place – Ayn Rand as an idea whose time had come at last – neo-conservatism came honking and trumpeting.

Our private lives were as bleak. The vogue phrase was "the new Narcissism." Narcissism meant branch-plant Régine's, the Cuisinarting of Canada, designer jeans, Gucci shoes, the hot tub instead of the cold shower, male cosmetics as the new growth industry, and psychiatrists getting asked on talk shows about sexual anorexia instead of about frigidity (1950's) or impotence (early 1970's).

Titles of best-sellers told the story: *Winning Through Intimidation; Be Your Own Best Friend.* Replacing the organization man, who at least cared about his corporation and delayed his personal gratification for its advancement, came the bureaucratic gamesman, skilled in manipulating meetings and relationships, not giving a damn about anything except his or her next job.

And so it went. In *The Culture of Narcissism* Christopher Lasch wrote about our "protective shallowness in emotional relations," and quoted Fromm's "flight from feeling." Childlessness as the new chic, divorce as the new social contract because, in both cases, he or she travels fastest who travels alone. Couples did not "break up" anymore; they "distanced," like dancing partners searching over one another's heads for their next partner.

It could not continue forever. Self-assertiveness and self-actualization and self-awareness and self-fulfilment as the imperatives of personal behaviour had to lead, in the end, to self-despair. As the family, the last social bulwark against private demons, began to fragment, there began within our own society, and elsewhere in the west, a mysterious return to balance, an unorganized yet spontaneous recognition that enough was enough. But before the pendulum began to right itself we covered a lot of ground; through punk rock and the Jonestown massacre, to S&M as the new fashion accessory.

* * *

Amid this public and private emotional and intellectual squalor,

---

Only Medicare, and to a lesser extent, subsidized housing altered the distribution of income significantly.

Trudeau functioned both as lightning rod and mirror. He, as much as Narcissus, loved the cult of himself: for Narcissus, a reflecting pool; for Trudeau, his swimming pool. His own family, as Margaret danced at Studio 54, was in even worse shape than anyone else's. His government had become the Me Government, the entire gigantic machinery taken apart and reassembled to serve a single end – his re-election.

To a degree ridiculous at the time and ludicrous in hindsight, Trudeau had also become the scapegoat for everyone's private hostilities against uncontrollable forces. He was responsible for the dollar going down and inflation going up, for too many or not enough abortions. Not to mention bilingual cornflakes boxes, separatism gaining ground in Quebec, and the noose disappearing. Even the weather was Trudeau's fault: he had discombobulated Canadians by turning Fahrenheit into Celsius and miles into kilometers. Insult piled on injury; he was even going to take nineteenth century fowling pieces and seventeenth century flintlocks away from gun collectors.

If the Me Decade had any defining characteristic, it was the denial of private responsibility. The press made matters worse, not by reporting all the bad news which indeed was crying out to be covered, but, in the disco style of contemporary journalism, putting style ahead of substance, substituting gossip for investigation and, above all, personalizing everything. Quite reasonably, anyone watching television or reading the newspapers in the late 1970's was bound to conclude that everything that was happening was happening somehow, because of Trudeau.

* * *

In the way of all beleaguered political leaders, Trudeau fired fusillades at the media messengers who brought him the bad news. "The overwhelming majority of employees in Radio-Canada are of separatist leaning," he said in February 1977, and pressured the CRTC into an inquiry, which predictably got nowhere. Justice Minister Ron Basford launched a suit against the *Toronto Sun* for a breach of the Official Secrets Act after the paper printed extracts from an RCMP report on Soviet espionage. Trudeau called the media "enemies" and treated them as such, slapping down reporters at press conferences and indulging in such arbitrary acts as ordering principal secretary Jack Austin not to go to an off-the-record breakfast with reporters, then going himself in Austin's place, to be grumpy and incommunicative,* as always in the early morning.

Not that much of this was new. In 1968, in his introduction to *Federalism and the French Canadians*, Trudeau had called the press "instruments for oppression" because they got everything wrong; in 1969, he had called reporters who accompanied him to London "crummy" because they interviewed a talkative blonde whom he had taken to lunch. Near the end of his term, he told aides, "The press tried to destroy me in '72 and in '74 and they failed. They'll try again."

Trudeau had always considered most reporters "crummy," collectively and individually. Except for some women reporters whom he admired for other reasons, among the few journalists to whom he referred favourably in private were George Radwanski, his biographer, CTV's Bruce Phillips, whose annual year-end interviews he enjoyed, and Jim Munson, a radio reporter with whom he once scuffled in a Commons corridor, but whom he afterwards described as "a gutsy little guy." With a handful of serious-minded television commentators he could be uncommonly candid and responsive: CBC's Pat Watson and its occasional contributor from London, Robert Mackenzie (a personal friend from LSE days); Global's Peter Desbarats; Radio-Canada's Alain Stanké, and, above all, the BBC's Lord Chalfont. He seldom gave interviews to print journalists, other than foreign ones, because he knew he was so good on television. (His "box-score" of interviews 1976-78, was: electronic fifty-three; print thirteen; foreign fifteen.)

But he hated the herd. "I know I've given you a hard time," he told a departing press secretary, "but I just can't stand those guys." In China in 1973, following a state banquet during which Chou En-lai told him a meeting with Mao had been arranged, Trudeau told his aides to cancel a planned news conference, "so we'll be able to fuck the press." Since courtiers always follow signals,

---

*In his advanced *L'état c'est moi* period, Trudeau refused to allow any aide to talk to anyone. He also refused to allow Pitfield to appear before a Parliament Committee—not that Pitfield was chomping at the bit to go—on the grounds it would be "unconstitutional." When Clark, in 1979 appeared before the same committee, with his Privy Council Clerk, Marcel Massé, the Liberal M.P.s could not think what to ask: no one, in any event, claimed that the constitution had been violated.

ministers, aides, and officials did as they knew Trudeau wanted them to do. His government's attitude towards information was proprietary and obsessive – for Canada to get a Freedom of Information Act, the Conservatives had to win power.

Reporters, and Trudeau's own press secretaries, concocted all kinds of explanations for Trudeau's attitude; the most popular ran to the effect that he had never forgiven the press for its complaisance during the Duplessis years. But, in fact, even then he rarely read the newspapers and so had little idea how low the Fourth Estate had fallen.*

The real explanation is much simpler. Trudeau dislikes being criticized. The press criticized him constantly, as it does all Prime Ministers, partly out of a conviction that this is the duty of the Fourth Estate, partly because critical articles are so much easier to write. Not knowing the rules of the game, Trudeau took his media battles seriously. Anyone who criticized slipped instantly and irrevocably beyond the pale. Desbarats, for instance, though he had conducted several first-rate interviews with Trudeau, criticized him severely during the 1979 campaign; thereafter, Trudeau spoke as harshly of Desbarats as he did of newspaper columnists, a breed he uniformly loathed, and during the 1980 campaign had to be persuaded with great difficulty to grant him an interview.** Another factor in Trudeau's attitude *vis-à-vis* the media was his unrelenting competitiveness. He rather enjoyed jousting at press conferences and easily won each encounter. "They amuse me in the sense that it's a good game," he said in a 1972 interview. "They try to corner me, and I try to get out of the corner." While Opposition Leader, he missed his weekly press conferences, and asked his aides to arrange more of them; gently, they had to explain that he no longer had very much to say. But he was infuriated by the fact that the press always got the last word. "He couldn't control the press, and he could never accept that this should be so," says a top aide.

---

*As Prime Minister, he enjoyed declaring that he never read newspapers. In fact, although he had far too much self-esteem to read newspapers in the anxious way that politicians do, measuring their importance by the number of their column-inches, he did read a daily file of press clippings prepared for him by his aide Joyce Fairbairn.

**It hardly needs to be said that when Trudeau himself was a columnist, for *Cité Libre*, he dealt as roughly with the politicians of the day – Pearson as "the defrocked priest of peace" – as any columnist ever dealt with him.

Much of the time, in truth, Trudeau controlled the press without the least difficulty. In 1968, it fawned on him; in 1974 he made it dance to his tunes. A myth of "media power" blossomed out of the 1979 result, which the 1980 outcome quickly punctured. All that had happened in 1979, it became clear, was that the bias of the media and of the public had chanced to coincide; when the two diverged in 1980, the public and Trudeau won in a walk.

Only beleaguered politicians and a few academics take the notion of media power seriously. As a handy illustration of media impotence, during the 1970's, most editorialists and almost all reporters have favoured abolition of capital punishment; Canadians, by a margin of five to one, consistently have wanted the noose back. Instead of influencing opinion, the media influences *the agenda of public discussion.* Unless they can get on television, politicians and political issues just about cease to exist. Television's agenda gives priority to issues which are dramatic, emotional, and anecdotal; priority to politicians who are quick-witted, physically compelling, and adroit actors. Politicians like Trudeau, in other words. Magical ones.

Trudeau did much better by the press than did his opponents: Clark ("too bland"); Stanfield ("he speaks in 30-second pauses"); Diefenbaker ("too hot"); Broadbent ("too shrill"). Reporters didn't like him personally (if Clark was "the Wimp," he was "the Prick"), but were grateful to him for giving them the diet of anecdote and gossip they needed to feed "the Goat." Only during his 1977-79 decline and fall did commentary begin to acquire a censorious harshness; as in "cynical," "opportunistic," "manipulative." Other than in the earliest years, though, the praise given to Trudeau always was given grudgingly.

An outsider has provided the best insight into how and why the Trudeau-media love affair soured.* In her play, *Maggie and Pierre*, Linda Griffiths has her reporter, "Henry," engage in a shouting match with Trudeau, which Henry ends by screaming: "You betrayed us. You made us into idealists. You actually made us believe that some change was going to happen in the system, and then you shattered it. That's why we're out to get you. Because you personally betrayed us." Trudeau saw things the same way, but with one difference: he was the idealist; reporters who cri-

---

*A CBC television documentary on Trudeau and the press was sub-titled "The Story of an Unrequited Love Affair."

ticized him were the "enemies."

Contrary to conventional wisdom among Trudeau loyalists, the harshest media comment about Trudeau, and also one of the shrewdest, was made not by a Canadian reporter but by an Englishman. "He's a totally unprincipled man in the ordinary sense of the word," said Malcolm Muggeridge in an interview with *Weekend* magazine. "He's seen that in modern government you don't really need to do anything and you don't need to have any views. All you need is a Persona, which is immediately graspable."

Muggeridge said that in 1974, when Trudeau was riding high. If Muggeridge had observed Trudeau in 1977-79, he might well have been speechless.

19

. . . Fall

Fortune, good night . . .

William Shakespeare
King Lear

No Prime Minister before him, except perhaps Mackenzie King, devoted himself for longer or with more single-minded determination to winning an election than did Trudeau. The motives of the two were not all that different: like King, Trudeau was convinced the choice was him or chaos.

The election fever began as early as late 1976, right after the PQ victory. Coutts and Davey urged Trudeau to go to the polls the following spring, arguing that he could extend his term beyond Lévesque's by capitalizing on the public's impulse to rally round its leader in a time of national crisis. But the breakup of his marriage left him in no condition to face the ordeal of a campaign.

Similarly, Trudeau's post-separation depression influenced him to let go by the next election "window" in the fall of 1977. Again, Coutts and Davey, armed with a private poll which put him at an incredible 56 per cent, higher even than Diefenbaker at his peak, urged him to go. The Quebec caucus pleaded with him to call his election during the same week in late August that Lévesque brought down his referendum legislation and to use this as his issue. In the end, Trudeau accepted the advice of Party President Al Graham that most party workers in English Canada would consider an election premature and "opportunistic." Insiders reckon, though, that Trudeau simply seized on Graham's advice to justify a decision he had already taken.

Everyone now assumed Trudeau would go to the polls in June or July of 1978, completing a normal four year term. He went through all the familiar warm-up exercises—unveiling his new "gunslinger" style at a Liberal policy convention in February, and travelling to New York in March to dazzle the Economic Club (the

323

same group of bankers Lévesque had addressed the year before). An April Gallup Poll put him ahead by a comfortable 11 percentage points. But on May 11, Trudeau told the Commons: "I have reached the conclusion . . . we should stay in this House."

A week earlier, the Cabinet's Political Committee had reached that conclusion for Trudeau. Assembled to confirm the long-planned July election, the group had spent a morning staring bleakly at the latest Gallup figures: Liberals 41 per cent; Conservatives 41 per cent. Since the party would waste so many votes in Quebec piling up huge majorities there, these figures presaged a stunning national defeat. Davey summed up the committee's recommendations: "We've just avoided losing an election we didn't call."

At that meeting, two aides, Coutts and Colin Kenny, had argued that the Gallup results had to be wrong. As it turned out, they were right. In June, Gallup put Trudeau back ahead by 4 percentage points, and by 6 in July. Had he gone ahead with his election plans, he probably would have won at least a minority. At the time, Trudeau's failure to accept Coutts's advice to call elections when he could have won them, certainly in 1977, probably so in the spring of 1978, seemed no more than one of the many might-have-beens of any political leader's career. But the details remained stored in his computer-like memory, to come clicking out two years later when, in quite different circumstances, Coutts urged him first to defeat the government, and second to gamble everything on coming back to lead the party in an election.

Trudeau's indecision in May 1978 left him off-balance. Clark mocked him for being "afraid to face the people." The press began to speculate gleefully that he might try to hang on to the end of his five year term, like R.B. Bennett during the Depression, and suffer the same fate, or try to escape it by quitting. For once the press turned out to be right—on both counts.

* * *

Voters were looking not so much for someone who could save Canada but for someone who could save the economy, and save it, for starters, from Trudeau. Through the spring of 1978, the dollar had sunk, day after day, eventually to 86.93 cents in mid-April, each decimal point decline earning black headlines as a "New, Post-Depression low." More black headlines: Unemployment rose to a post-Depression high of 8.6 per cent. Experts worried about the $5 billion balance of payments deficit, even more about the $11.5 billion budget deficit, amounting to an incredible one-quarter of Ottawa's total revenues.

Then in June, Californians told Canadians what to do. They got mad as hell and voted for Proposition 13. Governor Jerry Brown said that the $7 billion tax cut would mean ruin. Then he said the voters were right; big government was ruining everything.

No one needed to be told that our own government was bigger than California's. Between 1970 and 1976, while Canada's population had grown by 8 per cent, the federal bureaucracy had expanded by 30 per cent, while the number of senior civil servants had ballooned by 127 per cent. In July, Gallup found for the first time that as many Canadians blamed big government for their troubles as blamed the perennial scapegoat, big labour.* Coutts told Trudeau. He did what he was told and on August 1, going where Brown had gone, he went on television to announce a massive program of cuts in government spending. Two weeks later, on August 16, Andras announced that these would amount to $2.5 billion.

The full story is just a shade more complicated. For months, Andras, as President of the Treasury Board had been doing what Turner only claimed to have done—saying "no" to his cabinet colleagues. The trouble was, the bills due from a decade of "yeses" were flooding in. Like a many-fingered Dutchman, Trudeau ordered his ministers to forward him suggestions for spending cuts totalling $500 million; at the deadline, in June, half the departments sent in no suggestions at all, and the value of the nicks proposed by the remainder added up to just $18 million. At long last, Trudeau realized what everyone had been saying for years: the bureaucracy, his bureaucracy, was out of control. Or rather, that his cherished "servant state" was now his master.

In July, Trudeau went to the Western Economic Summit in Bonn, where he starred in the discussions about anti-hijacking measures, and made an obscene gesture to the assembled press of

*In its report of March 1979, the Lambert Commission confirmed and legitimized everything Canadians had ever told themselves about the mess up there in Ottawa. The Commission found a "serious malaise pervading the management of government," caused by an "almost total breakdown in the chain of accountability."

the world. In private talks, Chancellor Helmut Schmidt lectured him about Canada's economic flabbiness. Afterwards, he holidayed in Morocco, bought the white silk *djellabah*, swam, and took in the sun. Then, on Thursday, July 27, came a telephone call that brought him hurrying home.

Coutts was on the other end of the line. Goldfarb's latest survey was in. The omens favoured an election. Trudeau heard out Coutts, and gave him the go-ahead. He himself would fly back on the Sunday, July 30, and make the announcement the following day.

On Saturday, July 29, the Liberal Campaign Committee assembled in a suite in Ottawa's Inn of the Provinces to plan the election campaign. They had in hand flip-charts outlining Trudeau's itinerary and strategy. But the charts were never flipped. Goldfarb's "insurance numbers" had just come in, Coutts told the group as it assembled, and the numbers were bad. Thus Canada's answer to Proposition 13, or the "post-Bonn economic exercise" as it came to be known, became the only possible substitute. On Sunday afternoon, while Trudeau posed in his *djellabah* against the setting sun, Coutts and Pitfield and other aides and officials sketched out what had to be done.

Seldom in Canadian politics have such important economic decisions been taken by so few amid such confusion. The public was totally mystified by Trudeau's sudden conversion to such neoconservative goals as spending cuts and cutbacks in the civil service payroll (5,000 person-years, eventually), "the return to the private sector of some of the functions of government," and new incentives to "ensure our continued prosperity." Trudeau's own cabinet was equally mystified. The only minister in the know was Andras, whom Coutts reached in the middle of a golf game to ask how large the cuts Trudeau would announce ought to be. (At one point in their conversation, Coutts suggested that as much as $6 billion might be needed to ease the public clamour.) Chrétien, the Finance Minister, holidaying in Shawinigan, heard the news from an aide who himself had learned what was going on the way everyone else in the country did, via his television set. He nearly resigned and would have but for the harm his going would have done to the federalist cause in Quebec. Still, the crisis atmosphere produced openings for creativity. Welfare Minister Monique Bégin seized the chance to push through an imaginative change in social policy that shifted payments from the well-off to the needy through a new $200 a year Child Tax Credit scheme. At last, the government got a measure of control over its own spending: for the first time, spending in the following year, 1979-80, was held to a "no growth" mark.

Since that year's budget deficit remained stuck at $11.8 billion, commentators for the first time began to make the point that the red ink flowed not from too much government spending (Canada's, in fact, was almost the lowest among industrial democracies) but from too little tax revenue. The point of the post-Bonn exercise had been to make Trudeau appear as an economic Iron Chancellor, a trans-Atlantic Helmut Schmidt. He emerged instead with the image of a political opportunist. Ministers like Chrétien staged hasty press conferences to explain what was going on, to little avail, since they themselves didn't know what was going on. (In one instance, officials were arguing about the dollar amounts to be attached to new programs to within an hour of these being announced to reporters.) In any event, since Trudeau just two years before had said, "the government is going to have to do more," no one took him seriously when he said, or seemed to say, that the government now had to do less.

From the exercise, he also walked straight into a political trap. By actually practising a measure of restraint, he angered all the voters affected, a lesson in *realpolitik* the Conservatives would learn even more painfully a year later. As the election approached and as Liberals frantically urged him to trot out the usual pre-election spending promises, Trudeau could afford neither to be seen to be changing his mind yet again, nor to break a promise he had made to Chrétien. As his price for not resigning, Chrétien had won from Trudeau the power of veto over all new spending programs; to restore his credibility as Finance Minister, Chrétien vetoed each and every proposal, including a "shelter" allowance for home owners with which the Liberal campaign strategists had hoped to offset the Conservatives' highly popular mortgage tax deductibility promise.

So, in an act of self-abnegation unequalled in Canadian politics, if entirely unintended, Trudeau went through the 1979 campaign without making a single spending promise. Right after the defeat, the Liberal National Executive identified Trudeau's failure to woo voters by buying them as the principal cause of the unseemly position in which the party found itself, of being out of power. Trudeau listened, understood, and acted. In Opposition, he leaned the party to the left. In the 1980 election, he attacked the Conservatives for trying to cut back government spending, and adopted as his slogan, "not less, but more efficient government." The interesting aspect of the 1979 campaign is that this and the one in 1972 are the only elections Trudeau has gone through without performing any tricks; each time, he was booed off the stage.

* * *

The immediate penalty Trudeau had to pay for the post-Bonn bungling was that he had to let yet another election "window" go by. Instead, he now faced fifteen by-elections, accumulated during the past year and a half, all of them called for October 16. In the most severe between-elections drubbing suffered by any Prime Minister since Confederation, Trudeau lost them all except for a pair in Quebec, which nobody counted. In a breach of precedent, he campaigned personally and had to listen while Canadians told him his time was past. "I respect you and I know you are my Prime Minister . . . but I think it is time you stepped down and gave someone else a chance," an Italian Canadian, trembling at his own temerity, said to him at a rally in York-Scarborough. "I have so many questions, but I've lost confidence in you as a leader," a teen-ager stammered into the floor microphone at the same rally.

Canadians wanted Trudeau to go. But they wanted him to go with dignity, to choose the time for his going himself, not to have to kick him out themselves.

Trudeau heard the message. In public, as always, he conceded nothing. "Considering the alternatives, I think I'm the best man," he said at a press conference in December. In private, when aides told him the trouble was, Canadians no longer wanted to hear about national unity, he replied sadly, "I understand what you are saying, but my God, what does it say about this country." (Mostly, it said only that Canadians no longer feared Quebec's separation, now that Ryan had become Liberal leader, but instead feared deeply they were headed toward economic bankruptcy.)

So he decided to go. Almost decided. He would make up his mind, he told his staff, during Parliament's Christmas recess. All those who knew him best were certain he would leave. Yet early in January, back from Jamaica, Trudeau gave the word to insiders that he would stay on to the end. If he had to go down, he told them, he would go down trying to get Canadians to understand the kind of country they had to create. He called in his National Executive and told them that if any of them wanted him to go, they should leave: none did. His own condition for remaining, he went on, would be that he be allowed to talk about national unity during the campaign, no matter how many polls showed that he lost votes each and every time he uttered the phrase. The executive agreed, and then set to preparing for a campaign that most of them knew was lost.

* * *

Early in 1979, things actually got a little better. The dollar stopped sinking. Clark went round the world and lost his luggage. Trudeau inched ahead in the polls. Davey, among other campaign advisers, urged him to hang on to the very end, right up to July 8, the fifth anniversary of his last election. (In fact, as reporters discovered, once they had consulted the constitutional oracle, Senator Eugene Forsey, Trudeau could technically have delayed the election until 1980, although if he had done so, Canadians would have marched on Ottawa and levelled it stone by stone.)

Instead, on March 26, Trudeau startled everybody by calling the election for May 22. Governor General Schreyer, who had to cancel an out-of-town engagement to be at Rideau Hall to receive him, was as startled as anybody. Trudeau had picked the date more by impulse than by analysis. Margaret's *Beyond Reason* was due on the stands in April; from then on she would be blabbing away on the talk shows and would be bound to blurt out new indiscretions as she did, concerning her affair with Ted Kennedy.* Trudeau chose May 22 for his election, one of his top aides is convinced, "just to show Margaret." He would deal with all his *Gotterdammerungs* at once. It's reasonable to speculate also that Trudeau understood how legends are made.

* * *

*In fact, by now, Margaret's own gifts as a magician had failed her. For Canadians, she had become a "dingbat," "a dimwit." Since "the Margaret factor" was the only reason visiting U.S. television crews had bothered to cover the Canadian election, they were chagrined to discover that hardly anyone was interested in her enough to want to talk about her, on or off camera.

The 1979 election unfolded like a tragedy along classic Aristotelian lines: Trudeau as King Lear; a flawed hero pulled down by his own hubris, yet going down in style.

In hindsight, the election scenario reads more like a melodrama; the public acting like a landlord who evicts a tenant who has messed up his property, but then feels guilty over what he has done. Canadians, as events proved, did not really want to reject Trudeau; they just wanted to tell him to stop acting like the kind of Trudeau he had become; also, they had been seized by their decennial urge to "punish" Liberals for their arrogance. Certainly the election outcome did not result in the much-feared "Doomsday scenario," in which Quebecers, watching their own flesh and blood defeated and replaced by an "English" Conservative government, would react by defeating the federalists in the referendum. Quite the contrary happened: Lévesque, denied a target in Ottawa to attack lost momentum; he lost four successive by-elections; surveys in the early winter of 1980 put the federalists into a comfortable pre-referendum lead for the first time.

Yet the fact that what Trudeau feared would happen did not happen, does not mean that he didn't believe in, and feel deeply about, everything he said. Always, his temperament has extended his reason into passionate, Manichean extremes, in pronouncing separatism as "dead," and Confederation as facing "its last chance." In effect, in the 1979 campaign, he generalized his own personal problems, as nearly all political leaders do when in trouble. Yet by exaggerating the perils facing national unity he forced Canadians, if not to vote for him, then to start thinking about "One Canada" again, and to move away from the parochial rivalries and tensions tugging the country apart.

During the campaign, none of this really became clear. Clark deliberately said as little as possible. Only once, in a speech in his native High River did he introduce, eloquently, his own vision of Canada as "a community of communities" and his own solution for putting "a fresh face on federalism" by ending the endless bickering between Ottawa and the provinces.

Trudeau, doing as always what he does best, spent a good deal of time attacking his opponent. Clark, for his promises, became a "Seven Billion Dollar Man," and a "puppet of the premiers" for indulging their whims. Much of the rest of the time he spent to much less effect attacking Canadians: a Toronto caller to a hotline show became "almost treasonable" for not taking the problem of national unity seriously enough; a farmer who heckled him at Ste Anne-de-la-Pocatière became a "professional complainer"; Lougheed and Blakeney became "enemies of Confederation" because they were out to "weaken the federal government."

Only in the campaign's last fortnight, did Trudeau find his voice. He did it by rejecting all of the speeches and by withdrawing himself from his staff, cutting off even Coutts, whom he restricted to hurried, five-minute strategy sessions at the end of the day or to morose discussions over breakfast. He sensed he was going down. He wanted, before he did, "to say things that would survive," as an aide puts it.

Much that he said, a year and a bit into history, does not wear well. Often, like a magician past his prime, he depended much too visibly on props: a stylized Maple Leaf as backdrop, Trudeau standing in front of it alone, a lone misunderstood hero pleading for sympathy, but pleading too stagily. But he coined phrases that linger in the memory. "Although I've lost some of my illusions, I've lost none of my ideals for Canada," he said at his nominating meeting in Mount Royal on April 2. "There is a spirit of selfishness that can destroy our country," he told party workers in British Columbia on April 24.

During the last fortnight when, except for the televised leaders' debate in which he knocked Clark against ropes but did not knock him out, Trudeau, to the dismay of all his advisers, talked about nothing but the subject by which he wanted to be remembered. Before his single most important speech, to a mammoth rally of 20,000 in Toronto's Maple Leaf Gardens, Trudeau refused to show to his aides the text he had laboured over alone. Up on the stage – for backdrop this time, the largest Maple Leaf flag in the country, forty feet by twenty feet – Trudeau told the nation how he would save it: an immediate recall of Parliament to approve a resolution to patriate the constitution, a year of meetings with the premiers to draft a new constitution and, if this process failed, "we will consult the people of Canada in a national referendum. We will have a Canadian constitution, made by Canadians for Canadians, and we will do it together." The Maple Leaf audience gave him less applause when he finished than when he had first bounded to the stage.

Nothing deterred him. Next day in Montreal, he said the same thing. He said it again in Hamilton, on May 19. "Either we will have one strong united country, or we will have a country of ten independent principalities. Let us all bring it all together in one gigantic act of national will."

His finest speech was his last. On May 20, he spoke softly, and without notes, to a crowd of a thousand at a high school in Guelph. The text of the sermon he heard that morning at mass had been "Love ye, one another," taken from St. John. If Canada were to survive, he told his audience, "that's what it's all about."

On the evidence of the surveys, none of Trudeau's speeches changed a single vote. What *did* change, subliminally, were people's feelings about why they were voting against him. Soon after the election, people began to feel guilty, and when their chance came, projected their feelings of guilt onto their chosen instrument for destroying Trudeau: Clark. Like an audience unresponsive to a magician whose tricks they had seen often, they realized once the show was over that all they'd really accomplished had been to spoil the show for themselves.*

* * *

As usual, Ontario decided who would become the next Prime Minister. There, all but five of Trudeau's ministers went down to defeat. Still, through the evening of May 22, up to midnight, as Trudeau watched the returns at 24 Sussex with a small group of friends and aides, Coutts and Kenny, ever the hawks, urged him not to concede until the last returns were in. They hoped, as Trudeau so unwisely had speculated to reporters, that he might be able to hang on with NDP support, even if behind Clark. Then the polls closed in British Columbia and quickly, all was over. Clark won 19 of British Columbia's 28 seats, and his count rose to 136, almost two dozen more than Trudeau, much too wide a margin for even the most expedient of political advisers to deny.

In the ballroom of the Chateau Laurier Hotel, Liberals were

---

*Perhaps the most eloquent expression of this collective sense of sorrow at Trudeau's downfall came from an opponent: the Péquiste member, Pierre de Bellefeuille. "He's been told to go home, the trip is over," de Bellefeuille wrote in an open letter in the Montreal *Gazette*. "I'd like to say to him, if he'd listen: Come on home, to Quebec."

weeping. "Don't give up. Don't go," they shouted, as Trudeau mounted the stage. He had a smile on his face, and a rose in his lapel. "With all its sham, drudgery and broken dreams, it's still a beautiful world," he said, finding in 1979, as in 1972, the words he wanted to say, in *Desiderata*. He would call on Schreyer immediately and ask him to invite Clark to become Canada's sixteenth Prime Minister.

Trudeau had been beaten. But he had not been crushed. He did relatively better (40 per cent of the popular vote compared to Clark's 36 per cent) than in 1972, and he won more seats than he won then (114 to 109).* He denied Clark the majority that should have been his for the taking and he also denied him, since just two Conservatives had been elected in Quebec, the title of national leader.

* * *

Statistics are for historians. Clark, at thirty-nine, would soon become the youngest Prime Minister in Canadian history. Trudeau, at fifty-nine, was finished. He was also trapped, both by events – although an albatross to his party, he would have to hang on as leader until Quebec's referendum – and by Margaret, who spent election night at Studio 54, dancing in tight white disco pants and who, now that her celebrity status was devalued, would soon have to come back to him in Ottawa, or at least to his children.

On Monday, June 4, 1979, a flawless early summer day, Trudeau drove over to Rideau Hall in his silver-grey 1959 Mercedes 300SL to lunch with the Governor General, to hand over to him the eight and one-half pound Great Seal of Canada, and to say good-bye. "I have no regrets and no remorse," he told Schreyer. When he came out, a crowd of reporters and tourists had gathered round the portico. He pushed through the crowd saying nothing, but with a smile on his face and a spring in his stride. He strode over to the Mercedes, started it with a single flick of the ignition key, turned to shout, "I feel free," and then gunned the car down the driveway with a flourish, passing on his way Conservative M.P.s arriving to be sworn in as members of the new cabinet.

Really, though, the Trudeau era had ended a week earlier, in

---

*Trudeau did well in Quebec, of course. He also did well among women, as many of whom (43 per cent according to Gallup) voted for him as had in 1974. The voters who brought him down were Anglo-Saxon, male, and over thirty.

the rain. The setting, appropriate for a departing pro-consul, was Ottawa's last imperial occasion: Alice, the daughter of U.S. Ambassador Thomas Enders and his wife Gaetana, was marrying Peter Cronyn, scion of one of Canada's old families. At Notre-Dame Cathedral, later at the Ambassador's residence, everyone who was anyone was there: half the outgoing cabinet; some of the incoming one. Trudeau, as much as the bride, was the star of the show. He toasted his defeated ministers with champagne; he danced with all the bridesmaids. Then, his duty done, with the insolent grace of a twenty-year-old, he danced the night away with a stunning blonde who had arrived with someone else. A mandarin's wife watched him, and then remarked astutely in the way that mandarins' wives do. "He is sending us a message. He is saying, *You're going to be sorry.*"

20

Resurrection

"Fortune is a woman, and you must, if you want to subjugate her, beat her and strike her . . ."

Niccolo Machiavelli
The Prince

When Trudeau tooled his Mercedes down the drive at Rideau Hall, he was vanishing into history. Officially, at high noon on June 4, 1979 he became Opposition Leader; in political reality, he became a lost leader.

Canada is harder on its politicians than are most countries; the gulf between ins and outs is almost absolute. A party that loses power vanishes into oblivion. Perqs, privileges, researchers, speechwriters, serried ranks of properly deferential civil service advisers, all disappear instantly. Former cabinet ministers endure a double culture shock: their own telephones no longer ring; when they call others, the words they hear are non-committal.* Those ex-ministers unlucky enough not to have been defeated personally and thereby forced to start new careers, hang around Parliament Hill like Banquo's ghost, hoping someone will pay heed to them. Ex-Prime Ministers almost never come back: none had since King in 1935. Instead, in the manner of Diefenbaker, these deposed titans become objects of interest to tourists; eventually, if historians are kind, they become statesmen. Mostly, they become irrelevant, forgotten but not gone.

Five and a half months after his defeat, trapped for the first time in his life in a job he detested, the same way most people are most of their lives, Trudeau quit. Less than a month later, fortune smiled at him, and he wrestled her to the ground. He was never bolder; even the great Houdini never escaped from so impossible a situation as the one from which Trudeau clambered back onto

*Of the thirteen defeated Liberal ministers, only Lang, as executive vice-president of Pioneer Grain in Winnipeg, secured a position comparable to his former station.

centre stage. And he was never luckier; it was as if Napoleon had arrived at Waterloo from Elba to find that Wellington had lined up his thin red lines in the wrong direction.

* * *

Because of all that has happened since, it is difficult now to recreate the mood of the summer and early autumn of 1979, when Trudeau's return seemed not just improbable but inconceivable. Even Coutts, the professional optimist, went no further than suggesting to Trudeau there was an outside chance that Clark's government might be defeated in the spring of 1980. The conventional wisdom was Trudeau would stay on for a year or so until the Quebec referendum was safely past, so that the separatists would not use his departure as proof that Quebecers belong no place else except at home, and then leave, but only a few paces ahead of being invited to go. The single uncertainty was whether Liberal dissidents might force him out earlier by insisting on an early 1980 policy convention, as required by the party's constitution, at which his leadership could be "reviewed" by secret ballot.

Soon after Trudeau became an out, he slumped into a deep depression. For all that he put on the airs of a reluctant politician, his decompression symptoms were little different from those of either of those life-long political groupies, Diefenbaker and Mackenzie King. He depended on the reassuring busy work of power: chairing committees, making decisions, poring over his "damned brown boxes." Without them, he no longer knew how to structure his days.

The daily practicalities of his new existence did not help. His new official residence, Stornoway, was gloomy and ramshackle. He lost Harrington Lake, where he had so often revived his spirits, hiking through the woods or canoeing. He had to cut his personal staff in half, which involved some painful choices, such as letting go Colin Kenny, one of his most devoted and zealous aides. He had to fly commercial, carrying his own luggage and flagging down taxis. (In Toronto, he took one $6.00 ride and then offered the driver a quarter tip, asking "Is this enough?" Recognizing him, the driver said nothing.)

Nor had he gained the benefits of anonymity. Press and public still treated him as their property. When he played hooky from a convention of British Columbia Liberals in Vancouver and was photographed in a New York disco with an airline stewardess called Linda, the B.C. Liberals got even more furious with him than they already were·

Above all, he felt he had no future. "I just don't want to be Prime Minister again," he told people close to him, a confession they interpreted to mean not so much that the pleasure of being Prime Minister had turned to ashes, than that he was convinced he could never be re-elected.

As much as by the defeat itself, Trudeau was depressed by what he saw as the indifference of Canadians to what was happening to their country: its progressive fragmentation into self-centred regions as much as the prospect of Quebec's separation. He was depressed equally by the political polarization into left and right which he believed meant that years would have to pass before the public would again trust his type of centrist, activist government. Last, he was frustrated that as Opposition Leader he would have no defined role to play in the coming referendum. He was angered and hurt by suggestions that began to leak out from the Quebec Liberal camp (one former provincial minister, Claude Forget, voiced doubts in public) that perhaps the best role Trudeau could play in the referendum would be to stay out of it·

* * *

Bored and unhappy with his situation, bored also with himself, Trudeau went through the motions of being Opposition Leader. He did the necessaries, such as appointing "shadow cabinet" critics, among whom the most interesting was Herb Gray, plucked from six years of obscurity to be given the plum post of finance critic, a clear sign that Trudeau had acted on the advice of his National Executive and had decided to tilt the party to the left, the posture it invariably adopts in Opposition.

Mostly, he hid. It was MacEachen, not Trudeau, who emerged from a mid-June caucus of M.P.s and defeated candidates to declare that Clark deserved "a fair and reasonable chance to govern." Trudeau delayed his first post-defeat press conference until July 19, and then said little except to say of Clark, "the man should be given a fair chance," and of himself, "I'm staying on. In my judgement, I'm the best man."

In August he took his sons on holiday to Quebec and to Nova Scotia. Then he joined a canoeing party, down the Hanbury and

337

Thelon rivers in the Northwest Territories.* In September he joined Arthur Erickson and a fellow-architect on a trip to China and Tibet. By way of hoisting a flag of defiance, he grew a beard, then shaved it off as much because it turned out silver as because it turned out straggly.

The surcease revived his spirits. A fellow canoeist describes Trudeau's reaction to the wilderness as "almost religious." He found out that he still could smell the flowers. Back in Ottawa in mid-September, he delighted colleagues by plunging enthusiastically into discussions of new policy ideas, such as economic nationalism At his first post-election public appearance in Chatham, New Brunswick, he attacked Clark for "the abdication of all that has made Canada strong." (Clark had ceded jurisdiction over Loto-Canada and over offshore resources to the provinces.) On October 10, he turned his first speech after Parliament's opening into a bravura performance, mocking Clark's new system of inner and outer cabinets, and commiserating with him over the burdens of office, of which, "We will do our best to see that both the burden and the office pass quickly from him."

This reborn enthusiasm faded fast. Before long his own M.P.s realized that Trudeau was only truly animated in the Commons when he was required to defend his own old policies. During Question Period, his questions about current issues were soft and uninspired. He gave up wearing a rose in his lapel. Through the autumn, more and more Liberals began worrying. Pundits had begun to speculate that if the rejuvenated and redoubled NDP kept on grabbing all the headlines it might displace the Liberals and thus restructure Canadian politics along natural ideological lines: itself on the left, the Conservatives on the right, and the Liberals, like their British cousins, nowhere.

Frustrated by Trudeau's lack of leadership, a group of young idealistic Liberals organized an unofficial "thinkers conference" in Winnipeg early in November. It took place without any unseemly talk about leadership the fretful, unspoken thought was, no new leader, no new policies—except for a delegate who burst out. "Who is going to bell the cat?" Despite the best efforts of Trudeau loyalists, the National Executive had insisted on going ahead with its plans for a mid-March policy convention at which the

*His first wilderness trip since 1966 when he canoed 400 miles down the Coppermine River

338

Liberal rank and file would, in secret ballot, pronounce their opinion on his leadership. No doubt Liberal discipline would be sufficient to sustain him, particularly so close to the Quebec referendum, but at the very least, the magnitude of the dissident vote would be a severe embarrassment.

On October 30, in a routine speech to the annual meeting of the Ottawa West Liberal Association, Trudeau allowed his frustrations to show: "We've got to throw the government out as soon as we can," he said, "and get back in again." The Liberal caucus was startled since it had given no thought to, let alone decided upon such a strategy. Word was passed out that the leader was a bit out of sorts, and had not meant what he said.

* * *

Nor had he. In private, he was telling confidants, "I just don't want to be Prime Minister again." Two of those he said this to were Coutts and Davey in October, after they had commissioned Goldfarb to conduct a mini-survey in four swing ridings, which showed the Liberals well ahead. This meant, they told Trudeau, that he could win an election. "Even if what you say is right," he replied, "it just makes it easier for me to leave."

With his typical if unpredictable candour, Trudeau himself provided the best explanation of why he decided to quit. The day after he resigned, he told CTV's *Canada A.M.* he was certain he could win an early election, "but realistically, if this were possible for us, the NDP and Social Credit would not support us in defeating the government. So there's no way we could guarantee an election." In other words, with no election in prospect, no reason remained for him to linger on as leader.

Some time late in October 1979, Trudeau made up his mind to resign. He decided also to break the news shortly after Christmas, when his going would attract the least attention.

Appearances, though, still had to be maintained. On the weekend of November 17-19, Trudeau attended a Liberal convention in Toronto and gave three speeches; one of these an odd but oddly moving address to the Young Liberals, during which he rambled on at length about long-ago issues like wage and price controls, justifying these by saying, "circumstances change, and times change, and therefore policies have to change," and ended almost pleadingly, "I don't care if the media don't understand, but I care very much that you should understand." During a break, Trudeau slipped out to see Macdonald, by now more than two years away from Ottawa, to tell him he planned to step down in December and to ask him to "think over again" his long-standing decision not to seek the leadership. Two days later, Macdonald's phone rang ceaselessly as reporters demanded to know whether, now that Trudeau had quit, he would be a leadership candidate. Macdonald replied that he was thinking about it. (In fact, Trudeau first started Macdonald thinking along these lines the previous August, when he let him know he might not stay on for another election.)

* * *

Exactly why Trudeau advanced his retirement schedule by five weeks is a mystery Not a scrap of evidence exists to confirm the "conspiracy" theory, that he did this to lull the government into doing what it proceeded to do—to bring down a budget tough enough to allow the Liberals to convince themselves and the public that they had to defeat it.

More likely Trudeau decided impulsively, simply because he felt rotten, in considerable pain following root canal surgery All his life, Trudeau has had a low threshold of pain, a physiological condition that makes his physical discipline all the more remarkable. He telephoned one close colleague, and said, "I can't stand it any longer I just can't stand having made up my mind to go and having to keep on pretending I'm still leader "*

Whatever the reason, he left in a manner that made Canadians feel, suddenly, a lesser people.

* * *

"It's all over," he told the caucus on the morning of Wednesday, November 21 Then, not so much sobbing as breaking off every now and then to take great gulps of air, he read out his official statement. "You've always known I'm an old softie," he said to explain the tears in his eyes. M.P.s and Senators stood as one to applaud, quite a number weeping openly At the press conference

---

*One person Trudeau did not confide in was Margaret. Taken by surprise by reporters knocking at her door, she blurted out, "No comment" and then telephoned Trudeau's secretary to ask what she should do. Gently, the secretary suggested she join him at Stornoway for lunch. Afterwards, as if to underline a point, Trudeau walked his sons back to Rockcliffe Public School by himself

340

an hour later, Trudeau, entirely composed, read the same statement, explaining that he was leaving "to have more time with my family," but would still be active in the referendum "as a private citizen." He ended with a personal message to reporters: "to turn an old phrase around, I'm sorry I won't have you to kick around any more." The reporters, many of them his old enemies, broke their long-standing rule and clapped.

In all but temporary title, he became a private citizen again. He used his freedom to toss out fresh ideas, such as, in a farewell speech to his riding association, the possibility of proportional representation. He went house hunting in Montreal and bought a fifty-year-old Art Deco monument on Pine Avenue, built by the Quebec architect Ernest Cormier who had also designed Ottawa's Supreme Court; friends wondered how he imagined three rambunctious kids could grow up in such a forbidding mausoleum.* Margaret told friends she would move to Montreal, to buy a house on the same street. Her friends wondered how on earth she could survive there without French

* * *

Trudeau's most considerable political gift, his magical allure aside, is that he lives wholly in the now. It is the reason why he has been able to re-write the rule that intellectuals make lousy politicians. In the way of all successful executives, he wastes no time and energy either in sentimental wishful thinking about the past as it might have been, or about the future as it might be. He is an existential politician. Post-retirement, he became, for once, an introspective one. Perhaps only because he had time on his hands, he indulged in the luxury of second-guessing a decision he had made. "So that's what they think of me," he said crossly to an aide, after he had spent a morning reading an inch-thick folder of farewell editorials and articles that he called "my obituaries."

Except for the Quebec commentators who were kind to their own, the editorialists and pundits, in a rough preview of what the history books would say, gave Trudeau more minuses than pluses. "History will not be lenient to Mr. Trudeau," said the *Ottawa Citizen*. "Any enduring Trudeau mark on either his party or the country remains strangely obscure," said the *Ottawa Journal*. "He

*Trudeau completed the purchase in December, then rented the house for three years.

controlled the political system absolutely," pronounced Geoffrey Stevens of the *Globe and Mail*, "but he could not make it work " As Douglas Fisher of the *Toronto Sun* saw it, he had "deprived us of a rising national confidence and feeling, and left us in constitutional and economic disarray " Almost everyone said he left the country in worse shape than he had found it.

Ordinary Canadians felt quite differently Each day hundreds of letters, telegrams, and calls flooded into his office. When he travelled, groups who spotted him burst into applause spontaneously. "Pierre Trudeau did this one magnificent thing," wrote a Robin Carlsen to the *Victoria Times*. "He created passion where there was dullness, elegance where there was drabness, spontaneity where there was artifice, mystique where there was ordinariness." Indeed, Trudeau's mystique had worked its magic from the beginning: a Gallup Poll taken in July, one month after he left office, but unreported at the time for technical reasons, showed him 10 percentage points ahead, just as his popularity had soared right after his near-defeat in 1972.

Nor were Canadians near as defeatist about what Trudeau had done to the country as were the pundits. During the summer, polls taken both in Canada and in the United States, showed deep pessimism, south of the border, about government's ability to do anything, but in Canada, a widespread conviction that government was failing to live up to people's expectations of themselves.

Contrary to Trudeau's pessimistic analysis, the public already was prepared to have government do things for it. In November, a Gallup Poll found that two out of three Canadians supported the government's present size, or were demanding that it do more, even if taxes had to be increased. Although Clark did not realize it, the Canadian flirtation with neo-conservatism and its kissing cousin, monetarism, had run its course. In telling Canadians that to cure inflation he would cut back government, Clark was telling Canadians what they no longer wanted to hear. The middle class, in particular, was beginning to worry less about inflation than about the job prospects for its university-educated sons and daughters.

As a further boost to reborn confidence, the news from Quebec could not have been better. In December, after Lévesque at last had made public the referendum question, polls put the federalist, *non* side into a comfortable 47:37 lead. (Trudeau faced the humiliating prospect that the referendum would be won while he watched from the sidelines.)

All these circumstances made Canadians more and more puzzled as to why, in Ottawa, Clark seemed to be so determined to create a vacuum. Few doubted that Canada already was the world's most decentralized nation. Newfoundland's action in refusing jobs on oil rigs to non-Newfoundlanders, and Alberta's demand for an oil agreement that would double the petrodollars flowing to it from pockets of eastern Canadians, reinforced the growing public conviction that without strength at the centre, the country could not hold.

All of which was interesting to mull over, but beside the immediate point. With Trudeau gone, Clark's minority government was safe probably to late 1980, while the Liberals elected a new leader, and Quebec went through its referendum.

* * *

On election night, February 18, 1980, Trudeau praised Clark's "courage in the face of adversity." He deserves more mention than that.

The differences between Clark and Trudeau in power were mostly refreshing. To the office of Prime Minister, Clark brought qualities of personal courtesy and kindliness that had been lacking for a decade. Astonished officials let it out that there was now a man at the top who actually sent thank-you notes for work well done, and who remembered to ask about ailing wives and errant children. He restored to Parliament a sense of purposefulness, and to government, a quality of anti-bureaucratic openness. Unexpectedly, and perhaps only because he was new, Ottawa under Clark bubbled with innovative ideas about everything from social policy to financial management, in a way it had not done in years. Lastly, contrary to his public image, Clark in some ways was far bolder than Trudeau. The budget that brought him down was the first in a decade actually to raise taxes, as part of the first serious attempt to set Ottawa's finances in order.

Among the many miscalculations that probably have consigned Clark to a place in the history books as an asterisk, a couple are relevant here. As a life-long backroom political groupie, he over-compensated by trying to act like a statesman – "We will govern as though we have a majority," he said – and so forgot that the first duty of a politician is to get re-elected. Not until far too late did he recognize – his staff was too shy to tell him – just how lethal politically his television image of awkwardness was. Last, in a lapse that is incomprehensible, Clark underestimated Trudeau and the Liberals. He allowed himself to doubt that, given any opening, Trudeau and the Liberals would do anything other than risk everything on regaining power.

But Trudeau is "lucky Pierre." And Clark was too polite to treat fortune like a woman.

* * *

On Thursday, November 22, the *Toronto Star* in its headline story on Trudeau's resignation expressed what everyone was thinking: 'TORIES OFF THE HOOK." Instead, less than three weeks later, the Tories were defeated in the Commons and were plunged into an election they had lost before the campaign started. Nothing like it has happened before in Canadian politics, nor probably, in the modern political history of any democracy.

Two interpretations of how the events happened exist: a "sentimental" one, put out at the time by Trudeau's aides, which has him being taken by surprise at the government's defeat, and then deciding, reluctantly, to respond to the "overwhelming" draft of his M.P.s; a "conspiratorial" one, which has him plotting each step of his return. Neither version is true. Instead, both are true. Here is the story, bizarre, flukey, absurdist, as it unfolded day by day

* * *

Monday, *December 3*: Gallup reports its monthly poll: Liberals 47, Conservatives 28. Reporters downplay the story. The figures are so absurd that they have to be wrong; in any event, no election is in prospect.

Tuesday, *December 4*: In his office in Toronto, Martin Goldfarb, the Liberal pollster, receives an unusual call. Allan MacEachen, for the first time in Goldfarb's memory, is at the other end of the line. As Goldfarb is to polls, so is MacEachen to Parliament. He understands its moods and rhythms, which are so much more important than its rules, better than anyone in Ottawa. Further by his resilient, ruthless partisanship, MacEachen commands the unquestioning loyalty of the Liberal caucus.

What do the Gallup figures mean? MacEachen asks. They mean that if an election were held now, the Liberals would win in a walk, Goldfarb replies. Really? MacEachen presses. Absolutely, Goldfarb replies. MacEachen thanks him

MacEachen's motives, like those of everyone else involved in the coming coup, are mixed. Trudeau's successor as Liberal leader has to be an anglophone, by tradition, which means that MacEachen, as an anglophone himself, may lose his number two rank But should the government be defeated and Trudeau not come back to lead the Liberals the party might turn to MacEachen and make him Interim Leader. Later, in mid-crisis a friend remarks to MacEachen, "Why Allan J., I do believe you're trying to crown yourself." MacEachen gives him an enigmatic smile.

Monday, *December 10*: Turner surprises everyone by announcing, in Toronto, he will not be a candidate at the leadership convention scheduled to be held in Winnipeg on March 28. Publicly Turner gives no reasons. Privately, he is well aware that the three-month run to the convention leaves much too much time for rivals to savage him unmercifully for past disloyalties; Turner is also aware that he is on the short list to become head of one of Canada's largest corporations.

As of today, Macdonald becomes the overwhelming favourite. He says he will announce his decision shortly In fact, Macdonald has made up his mind to run; already he is drafting a series of policy position papers.

Tuesday, *December 11*: At 8.00 p.m., Finance Minister John Crosbie delivers in the Commons the first Conservative budget in seventeen years. To halve the budget deficit over four years, taxes will go up by $3 7 billion, including a hike of 18 cents a gallon in the gasoline excise tax. Later, Trudeau tells reporters, "We are going to have to vote against the budget." The press treats the comment as ritualistic, Opposition chest-thumping.

Wednesday, *December 12*: In the morning, as the Liberals assemble for their weekly caucus, MacEachen is the key figure. He tells the assembled members the time has come to hurl themselves against the barricades. The government has lost control of the Commons, MacEachen says; if the Liberals fail to vote against the budget, they will give the government time to recover, and in the meantime be rendered politically impotent.

Trudeau says little, other than describing the budget "socially regressive," to approving nods. As for him returning as leader should the government go down, "The Sovereign would have to ask me on bended knees, three times." The M.P.s, of whom a majority are either themselves potential leadership candidates (almost a dozen in this category) or are supporters of various candidates, haven't the foggiest notion what Trudeau means. They assume he means he is gone for good. Thus reassured, caucus agrees to vote against the budget on a routine NDP non-confidence motion due to be called on Thursday evening. Walking back from caucus, MacEachen remarks to a Liberal M.P. Ed Lumley, "It's over. The government is going down. What you're watching now is history "

To give history a nudge, MacEachen, the previous Friday, had sought out the Liberal Deputy Whip, Charlie Turner, to tell him to make certain that all M.P.s would be on hand for the vote. Also, to cancel all pairs. The press, naturally, knows none of this, so it reports the caucus decision dutifully, but skeptically Behind the scenes, the pace keeps quickening. After the caucus meeting, Coutts commissions Goldfarb to conduct a quickie, ten-riding poll to test voter preferences, and, as important, to test voter preferences between Trudeau and alternate Liberal leaders. Lalonde likewise makes calls, to two Quebec M.P.s who are in hospital; in sickness or in health, they must get themselves to the Commons on Thursday evening.

Trudeau, (contrary to the later "sentimental" account) begins now to consider his own future. "I believe the government will be defeated tomorrow," MacEachen tells him as they sit side by side in the Commons during Question Period. "If that happens, there will be an election, and you'd better figure out what you're going to do."

"What does one do?" Trudeau replies. "One does one's duty, of course." He gives MacEachen an enigmatic smile. From this point on, MacEachen is convinced Trudeau already has made up his mind to return. A day later, Trudeau confirms his conviction. As the actual vote is being taken, and as the government is going down, Trudeau turns to him and says, "I see my duty "

Later, at their annual Christmas party in the Confederation Room in the West Block, Liberal M.P.s and party workers present

346

Trudeau with a chainsaw "to cut the Tories down." As the drinks flow, the affair takes on the boisterous air of a pre-nuptial stag. M.P.s seek out reporters to tell them, "You don't believe us, but watch us tomorrow night." Bryce Mackasey, dislodged from his nest at Air Canada, wanders about saying, "Defeat the government. Defeat the government."

Thursday, *December 13*: On the early morning news broadcasts, the press begin to speculate that the government may actually be defeated this evening. By now, the five Créditistes M.P.s upon whose support the Clark government has so far depended, have issued a press release saying they may abstain on the vote because of the punitive effect of the gasoline excise tax on their constituents.

At 9.00 a.m., in the Conservative camp, Clark's key advisers assemble for their daily meeting. The principal topics of discussion are (a) next week's First Ministers Conference on the economy, (b) the tiresome behaviour of a maverick Tory, Paul Yewchuck, who had already abstained on an earlier confidence vote and who now was demanding a cabinet post as the price of voting with the government on the budget.

Nancy Jamieson, Clark's legislative assistant, interrupts this conversation. "I think we're going to be defeated," she tells the group. "I don't think we've got the numbers." Jamieson's handicap in getting anyone to pay attention is to be young and pretty. The group listens politely as Jamieson spells out the numbers. At full strength, the Conservatives muster 136. With the 5 Créditistes, this makes 141, compared to the Liberal-NDP tally of 140. Three Conservatives are away, though: Lloyd Crouse on holiday in the South Pacific; Alvin Hamilton in hospital but unbreakably paired with Liberal Serge Joyal; External Affairs Minister Flora MacDonald, in Europe on her first solo trip abroad.

MacDonald now is the key Present, she and the Créditistes would bring the government's tally to 139, equal to the NDP plus the Liberals minus Joyal. If the vote is tied, Speaker James Jérome, although an ex-Liberal, has made up his mind to support the government, on the basis of precedents which show that Speakers support the government automatically on motions, such as the budget, about which the House will have other opportunities to pronounce its opinion

The group agrees that Jamieson should phone MacDonald and tell her to hurry home. Then they go back to real business. (Even at the time, let alone in hindsight, the group's confidence seems puzzling since the Conservatives had done no polling since August. Yet, throughout the day, only Transport Minister Don Mazankowski was alarmed enough by the party's election prospects to urge Clark to do everything he could to avoid defeat.)

MacDonald could have made it back, but the night before, in Paris, she received a telex from Clark's office: "WE HAVE NO/RPT NO INTENTION OF ASKING FM TO RETURN STOP DESPITE BOLD TALK WE BELIEVE DIPLOMATIC FLU WILL HIT LIBERAL BENCHES." By the time Jamieson reaches MacDonald, all westward flights across the Atlantic have already left.

Without MacDonald, the government is defeated, no matter what the Créditistes do – provided some Liberals don't come down with "diplomatic flu." Some almost do.

All morning, from Montreal where he has gone on business, Donald Macdonald has been calling his caucus supporters to urge them to halt the party's lemming-like surge to suicide. These supporters flail around trying to unmake the decision they played a part in making. Andras, one of the most senior of the ex-ministers spends the morning trying to reach Trudeau by phone; none of his calls are returned. In the afternoon, Andras and two other ex-ministers, Buchanan and Pépin, discuss abstaining, but decide they cannot split the party. In late afternoon, Andras wins from a Trudeau aide the promise that the ex-leader will see him at 9 00 p.m., an hour before the vote is due, to hear out his argument.

The government could still save itself by delaying the vote for a day to give Flora MacDonald time to get back. But the person with the power to do so – House Leader Walter Baker – has no idea there is any need to do it. So Baker, a rumpled, universally liked Ottawa Valley lawyer who in six months has done more for Parliament by way of planned committee reforms and a draft Freedom of Information Act than MacEachen had done in six years, spends the morning scheduling next week's business. After Question Period, when MacEachen casually asks him the business for the day, Baker replies that naturally the budget debate, and vote, will go ahead as scheduled. Later, when reporters corner Baker to tell him that the Créditistes have now declared definitely they will not vote for the government, his face turns ashen. "Well then gentlemen," he says, "welcome to an interesting evening.""*

At 9.00 p.m., Andras turns up for his appointment with Trudeau. He waits for twenty minutes, then leaves. Trudeau arrives five minutes later, but does not send an aide to fetch Andras back

On her way into the Commons to vote, the former minister Jeanne Sauvé tells a reporter, "I don't know why we're doing this." Lloyd Axworthy, a rising Liberal star, describes the vote as "a game of Parliamentary chicken." As Winston Churchill said in the same chamber almost forty years earlier: "some chicken, some neck." At 10.21 p.m., by a vote of 139-133, the neck of the Clark government is wrung. Trudeau hurries from the Commons Chamber without talking to reporters. At 4.30 a.m. Brussels time, when an aide comes in to tell her the news, Flora MacDonald breaks down and weeps. "It's over," she says.

* * *

Friday, *December 14*: At 10.30 a.m., Liberal M.P.s and Senators assemble for a special caucus. Their agenda item, now that Clark has set the election date for February 18, is to decide what on earth to do with themselves. They have no leader, no policy, no candidates. Quickly the meeting divides into regional caucuses. At noon, the national caucus reassembles, and the regional chairmen report.

By a narrow margin, the Ontario caucus declares for a leadership convention which everyone assumes Macdonald would win. Overwhelmingly the westerners hold the same opinion, and make it plain that by this they mean anyone but Trudeau. Most astonishing of all, the Quebecers declare that while they are wholly behind Trudeau, they will support as strongly any successor. Only the Maritimers, MacEachen at their head, declare that Trudeau must return.

Implicitly, Trudeau's own M.P.s have told him they do not want him back – although, to mitigate this rejection, Trudeau has not indicated yet whether he wants to come back.

Trudeau's own mind is hard to read. He talks to the caucus in a low, almost inaudible voice. He lists all the reasons why he should

---

*After the election, ribbed unmercifully about his inability to count, Baker protested that he had mentioned to Clark the option of delaying the vote. He did this, at a mid-day meeting, but he did not recommend the action, and indeed advised Clark that he believed the Liberals and Créditistes were bluffing.

not be asked to come back as leader, from the election defeat to the accusation of opportunism that will be made against him if he changes his mind. Then he takes a new tack, and begins what Jeanne Sauvé later describes as "the rape of the caucus," although skilful seduction of a willing victim would be a better description. Should the caucus demand him back by an "overwhelming vote," he would respond to the call of duty and give everything he had to the campaign. Then, without a backward glance, Trudeau strides out of the room, gets into his car, and heads for Montreal.

Re-enter Allan MacEachen. Later, one M.P. compares his speech to Eugene McCarthy's famous invocation on behalf of Adlai Stevenson – "Do not forsake this man who made us all proud to be Democrats" – at the 1960 Democratic convention. The crucial difference between the two flights of rhetoric is that MacEachen, unlike McCarthy, knows his audience. He begins with a ritual denunciation of the "socially regressive budget." He proceeds from there to bash the Tories. Then, with the caucus's dander up, he turns to serious matters. "When, following the decision of caucus, I voted against the budget, it never occurred to me that it could occur to anyone that, if we defeated the government, we would be led in the election by anyone but the leader who led us against the government," MacEachen says. From now on, dissidents are hard put to explain how any other thought could have occurred to them. The alternative of a mid-campaign leadership convention is unthinkable, MacEachen goes on, because rival candidates would be tearing each other apart while voters were wondering and watching. Dissidents wonder how they ever could have thought such a thing. By the time MacEachen is done, the deed is done. Almost by osmosis the caucus reaches the conclusion that Trudeau must be asked back. Still, a number of leadership aspirants and Macdonald supporters argue for four more hours against Trudeau and the draft is not exactly overwhelming: no vote is taken.

Saturday, *December 15*, Trudeau, incommunicado, is at his sister's house in Montreal. The thirty-six member National Liberal Executive meets in Ottawa. Its members are far from pleased at the week's events. Caucus representatives present are informed they have been "reckless" and "irresponsible" to have forced an unnecessary election, while leaderless and unprepared.

Executive members demand that Coutts be dismissed from his post. (Trudeau, later, refuses the request, but as a conciliatory gesture to dissidents downgrades Davey's role in the campaign.) Still, faced with the decision of the caucus, the executive has no choice but to go along and add its voice to the "overwhelming" draft.

Sunday, *December 16*: Early in the evening, Trudeau returns to Stornoway. A procession of senior Liberals, led by MacEachen, Coutts, and National President Al Graham drive out through a blizzard to inform him officially that he is wanted back. Trudeau insists on a detailed and accurate report. The group has something equally important to report. Goldfarb's survey is done. He has detected wide and deep anti-Clark feeling. The Liberals are far in the lead; Trudeau, as leader would put them further ahead.

Trudeau is also told how difficult it would be, if he does not come back, for the Liberals to organize a mid-campaign leadership convention to pick a successor. Those who tell him—chiefly MacEachen and Coutts—have a vested interest in convincing him that this is so. Only cursorily is Trudeau informed of an alternative scheme Graham has concocted for a series of cross-country "regional" conventions, candidates flying from city to city to make their speeches, after which delegates would cast their votes in sealed ballot boxes, to be opened at a culminating convention in Ottawa on January 18.

He receives a number of contrary opinions, however. Through Sunday and Monday, a succession of ex-ministers call or meet personally with Trudeau to urge him not to return as leader: Andras, Buchanan, Reid, Ouellet, Chrétien, and, most remarkably of all, Lalonde. Some believe Trudeau cannot win an election (and that they can); others (Lalonde, for instance, also Jean Marchand), fear that Trudeau will lose and so do irreparable harm to the federalists in the coming referendum. The one key voice urging him to return is Pelletier, whom Trudeau phones in Paris.

Monday, *December 17*: Trudeau spends the day in the Opposition Leader's office, just across Wellington Street from Parliament Hill. He asks all his staff members, down to the secretaries, what they think he should do. He lunches with his former top civil service adviser, Gordon Robertson, at the Chateau Laurier Grill; later, he joins Coutts, Davey, and MacEachen at their table across the room. He asks them what he should do. He goes on to talk about how he is beginning to enjoy life as a private citizen, about how he wants to spend more time with his children. He muses aloud about the equivocal nature of the caucus's "overwhelming" draft. "Think of the effect on the referendum when you win," one of the trio tells him. "But think of the opposite," Trudeau replies. He goes back to office, and again wanders about asking people what he should do.

An interpretative note: at this point, the "conspiratorial" and 'sentimental" versions merge, into a surrealistic symbiosis. Beyond much doubt, Trudeau had made up his mind to return as leader before defeating the government, and play-acted with his caucus at its Wednesday and Friday meetings in order to inspire a 'spontaneous" draft that would make his return a clean one. As much beyond doubt, however, is that Trudeau by Monday no longer knew what he wanted to do. The counsel of so many ex-ministers had softened his resolution; uncertain whether he really was wanted back, he talked more and more of the pleasures of private life. By the time Trudeau left the office, even aides as close to him as Coutts had no idea what he would do.

One conversation now becomes crucial. At 5.00 p.m., two M.P.s, Don Johnston, a personal friend and Ed Lumley, by no means close to him and indeed a supporter of Turner, come to Stornoway to see him. For close to an hour, they tell him why, for the sake of the party and the country, he must return. Johnston and Lumley are attractive and persuasive individuals. Most persuasively, probably, they tell Trudeau that the election is his chance for "vindication." Trudeau thanks them, but gives them no indication what he will do.

Yet the pair have helped to convince Trudeau he really was wanted back. The irony is that had Trudeau stayed out, Johnston and Lumley had already made up their minds to head a draft Turner movement, which about two dozen Quebec M.P.s, led by Sauvé and Ouellet, had begun to muster, and the two western M.P.s, Axworthy and Art Phillips, were ready to join. As ironic, Turner, who said later, "I would have given it very serious consideration,"-which is a politician's way of saying he would have run, would most probably have won the convention (he had polls showing him three times as popular in the country as Macdonald), and have won the election more easily than Trudeau did. Indeed, because he would have picked up seats in the west,

Turner would have emerged as Canada's first *national* leader since Trudeau himself in 1968. The last irony is that, although Turner would have run, this prospect played no part in Trudeau's decision. When it was raised as a reason he should stay, Trudeau dismissed it. As always, he made up his own mind, for his own sake.

Alone now at Stornoway, Trudeau makes several key calls. To Macdonald: if he himself did not return as leader, would Macdonald run? Yes, Macdonald replies and, assuming that Trudeau is out, makes plans to announce his candidacy the next afternoon. To Pitfield, now in exile at Harvard. if he ran, would Pitfield return as Clerk of the Privy Council? Yes he would, Pitfield replies. Trudeau now knows that he doesn't need to run because Macdonald will replace him, but that if he does, Pitfield will be back at his side.

Some time late in the evening, Trudeau makes up his mind. He tells no one, and instead goes off on a long walk through the snow. Several key insiders, such as MacEachen and Graham, are certain Trudeau will return, Coutts, though, is less sure. He drafts out two statements, one to justify Trudeau's return as leader, the other to justify his resignation.

Tuesday, *December 18* Shortly before 9.00 a.m. Coutts goes by taxi from his new condominium across from the Inn of the Provinces Hotel to Stornoway. Trudeau greets him, and tells him his decision. "I'm not coming back." His manner is relaxed, almost off-hand.

Alone, for two hours, Coutts and Trudeau go over the familiar ground, the evidence of Goldfarb's poll, the difficulty of holding a mid-election leadership convention, the effect of his victory on the referendum. After this, Coutts recalls, "There was no moment of Eureka." Instead, the pair suddenly realizes it is close to 11.00 a.m., the time of the already announced press conference at which Trudeau will announce his decision. Coutts mentions this to Trudeau, and he replies, "Okay, I'll do it."

Before leaving Stornoway, he calls Pelletier and he calls Macdonald.* The first outsider to learn of Trudeau's decision is an Italian-Canadian woman who happens to be walking by the National Press Building just as his car pulls up. "Mr. Trudeau—" she

---

*Though Macdonald says now he was "immensely relieved" to learn Trudeau's decision, he continues, through faithful attendance at party meetings, to conduct himself like a candidate in waiting.

says, "please tell me you will run." "Sì signora," he replies, and ducks into the building.

Inside, Trudeau tells reporters, "It is my duty to accept the draft of the party." He adds that this will be his last campaign, and that he will resign "well before" the next election.

* * *

The reasons why Trudeau made up his mind the way he did after almost deciding the other way, just as in 1968, probably never will be known for certain. A genuine sense of duty to the party; love of a fight; an urge to be vindicated. One Liberal insider provides an explanation as good as any of these: "What Clark forgot is that Trudeau, and MacEachen and Coutts are all high-stakes gamblers; or, to switch the metaphor, each of them would rather risk trying for a touchdown bomb than go for a surefire, six-yard gain." Which is another way of saying that when fortune looked Trudeau's way, it never occurred to him to do anything other than treat her like a woman.

* * *

The campaign was over before it began. In December, the Conservatives' own polls, as well as those taken by Carleton University and by Gallup, confirmed the earlier Gallup finding that the Liberals were 20 percentage points ahead:* Clark fought doggedly and in the end shaved his deficit in half. But he did not have a hope. Against him were the Clark jokes, the nickname "the Wimp" that Coutts had coined, and, most of all, his image of awkwardness on television, with his too long, too thin hands, and his receding chin. Perhaps also, in a darker sense, Clark became a mirror-image to voters. They saw in him all the things they liked least about themselves.

As a magician, Trudeau has seldom had less to do. Most of the time, he said nothing. When he did, he practised his familiar rhetorical overkill, attacking the excise tax as "unfair" and "punitive," and so making certain that one of his government's main post-election preoccupations would be to find different ways to do the same thing.

*The Gallup Poll, taken in the first week of December when the Liberals were leaderless, but showing the party as far ahead as when Trudeau led it, suggests that any Liberal could have beaten Clark

Boredom with his own campaign was almost the only real problem Trudeau had to contend with. A couple of times he broke away from his handlers to give impromptu "scrum" press conferences, not because he had anything to say, just for the hell of saying something. He ducked a television debate with Clark because Coutts urged him to, but had the networks called his bluff and removed reporters from the format (Trudeau's pretext for his refusal), he would probably have gone along.

To avoid losing the election in the only way he could—by reminding voters why they had heaved him out nine months earlier—he did as little as possible. "We 'low-bridged' him," Senator Keith Davey explained later, adding a new word to the political lexicon. No hotline shows. Just one formal press conference, during which his answers were deliberately convoluted and prolonged. The gunslinger stance of 1979 gave way to being one of the boys, with as many Liberal luminaries as possible crammed onto each platform with him. As if the nation's most capacious memory had suddenly surrendered to hardening of the arteries, he read out the texts prepared for him, laboriously line for line, at about the speed of six-year-old Sasha.

Around the middle of January, a few signals flickered that some voters were beginning to wonder what the hell was going on. The Liberals (who polled every day of the campaign) detected some softness in their surveys. Clark, by then, had begun to counter-attack with Trudeau jokes, of which the best was, "Trudeau's campaign slogan is, Elect Me and I'll Quit," and the press kept on mocking Trudeau's "Peekaboo" campaign. Liberal strategists began to worry that voters might switch, not to voting for Clark from voting against him, but to voting against Trudeau.

Whether or not such difficulties were real, the Russians rescued him by sending their tanks into Afghanistan. Anti-Russian hawkishness swept north across the border. Seizing the chance to project himself as a tough leader, Clark switched from Trudeau-bashing to Red-baiting. On January 29, when, thanks to the "Canadian Caper," six American diplomats slipped out of Tehran, Clark for an instant seemed to have Trudeau on the run. But it turned out that all Clark was really doing was running on the spot. Liberal surveys showed that Canadians did not for an instant doubt Trudeau's superior competence in international matters. All Clark achieved by his foray into foreign affairs was to divert everyone's attention from Trudeau. By the time Clark switched back to attacking Trudeau in early February, time had run out on him. Trudeau spent the last fortnight enjoying himself. He actually said something to his audiences now, about national unity and about "sharing"; he engaged in a "poetry war" with accompanying reporters, they trying to stump him with stanzas remembered from their schooldays, and he, naturally, clicking out the correct authors and sources.

All that lingers in the memory about the 1980 campaign are its television commercials. These were the sleaziest and nastiest in Canadian political history. The style was "negative," in the sense of bashing the opponent over the head with a club, instead of promoting the candidate. It had been the Conservatives, in 1979, who first imported the technique from the U.S.* In 1980, both Liberals and Conservatives used "negative" ads; the difference being that under protests from the public, party workers, and the press, the Conservatives abandoned theirs in the last ten days for "positive," Clark-and-his-team ones, while the Liberals remained "negative" to the last. (Mostly, the Liberal ads focused on Clark's recessive chin and awkward hands.) A further difference was that Trudeau insisted on screening all of the Liberal commercials, and on approving each and every one.

*   *   *

On February 18, the evening was over as soon as the results came in from Ontario. Eventually, Trudeau's count reached 147, his best performance since 1968. In Quebec, where he won all but one of the seventy-five seats, he did better than anyone since Mackenzie King in 1921, who won the lot. He swept Ontario. He gained seats in each of the Atlantic provinces. Only the west, as ever, remained obdurate: it allowed him just two M.P.s, one fewer than the year before.

In one way, Trudeau's triumph was far less dramatic than it appeared to be. For any Liberal leader actually to lose an election requires, like Trudeau in 1979, exceptional maladroitness. In Ca-

---

*Since political TV commercials are aimed primarily at "uninterested" voters rather than at "undecided" ones, negative commercials are incomparably more effective than positive ones, because voters in this category are much more easily persuaded to vote *against* something or somebody than to vote in favour.

nadian politics, Liberals are General Motors; the NDP, American Motors; and Conservatives, Chrysler. Canadian politics has evolved into a "one and a half" party system that is unique in the world. In contrast both to conventional, two-party systems, as in the U.S. and Britain, and also to one-party systems, as in Mexico, while the Liberals are almost permanently in power (thirty-eight of the past forty-five years), and so have acquired a lease on the irreplaceable political asset of managerial credibility, voters periodically "punish" the Liberals for "arrogance" by reducing them to a minority, and occasionally, in error since one voter does not know what his or her neighbours will do, defeat them. Each time the unthinkable happens and the Liberals lose power, voters rethink their recklessness.

In another way, Trudeau's triumph was more many-splendoured even than it seemed to be. He had come back, as only Macdonald and King before him had done, and they in easier, less-edgy, pre-TV times. He had come back, further, as he had first come in. At 44 per cent, Trudeau's share of the vote was scarcely changed from the 45 per cent he had won as a philosopher-prince back in 1968. Among the young, he had done as well now as he did then. Indeed, but for a low turnout in Quebec where the certitude of Liberal victories made voters lazy, his share of the vote might have been as high as a dozen years earlier. So munificent a victory won by so little effort established Trudeau as the most skilled electoral politician among all his rivals in all post-war democracies.

* * *

In the ballroom of the Chateau Laurier, where Liberals nine months earlier had been sobbing and keening their loss, the same people were stomping and shouting and hugging and kissing. Even the anticipation of power is aphrodisiac enough. Trudeau might have chosen to sweep in solemnly, like an elder statesman, ancient of days and throned in glory. Instead, with a red rose back in his lapel, he bounded up to the platform wearing his six decades as lightly as a magician's cloak. He spread his arms and grinned at the crowd. "Welcome to the '80's," he said.

357

21

Manifest Destiny

"Father, is it true you are not a real king, but only a magician?" The king smiled, and rolled up his sleeve. "Yes my son. I am only a magician."

"I must know the truth, the truth beyond magic."

"There is no truth beyond magic," said the king.

John Fowles
The Magus

Trudeau is still making history, his and ours. He has re-established the Liberals as the permanent governing party. He has won the referendum. He is within reach of his self-defined apotheosis, a new constitution. He has presided over a reorganization of the oil industry that constitutes the most ambitious economic policy attempted by any government since World War Two. At the same time, the fault-line between east and west has never been wider. Relations between the federal and provincial governments have never been less co-operative, more corrosive. And the bills for a decade's worth of economic dilettantism keep piling up, all of them invoiced in bright red ink.

The story of Trudeau's post-election stewardship is too recent and too tentative to be cast into an historical perspective because no one, perhaps not even Trudeau himself, knows when he will retire. The single event that stands apart, because nothing that happens now can change the result, is the Quebec referendum.

Yet one central truth has become self-evident. Trudeau is different now. His fourth term as Prime Minister has already taken shape as a term unlike the others. From 1968 to 1979, with the crucial exception of bilingualism, he behaved often as a dilettante. Time and again, the pattern repeated itself: he would take up grandiose ideas – "The Just Society"; "Participatory Democracy"; "The New Society"; "The Third Option" – lob them around for a year or so, and then move onto something else as if he hadn't really believed in what he was saying and had simply enjoyed the fun of startling everyone by saying it.

No one has ever doubted Trudeau's physical courage. * Nor has anyone doubted his political courage as demonstrated, for instance, during the October Crisis, the morality of his actions at that time aside. Conspicuously, though, he has lacked the knack of persistence, the ability to apply consistently his awesome mastery of political means, and his ferocious combativeness, to defined political ends.

Since winning the election in February 1980, more precisely, since winning the referendum on May 20, 1980, Trudeau seems suddenly to have acquired this knack. The point is not that any of the political ends he is aiming at are new. The constitutional thrust of 1980-81, for instance, has its antecedents in his argument in the 1965 essay, "Quebec and the Constitutional Problem," that a bill of rights would "limit the powers that legal authorities have over human rights," and so free everyone to pursue excellence equally. The counter-attack on provincial power, encompassing both the constitution and the planned renegotiation of federal-provincial financial arrangements is based on his often-articulated "counterweight" theory of federalism. As for the economic nationalism of the National Energy Policy, and other forthcoming policies such as a national industrial strategy, these are prefigured in the phrase he coined years ago, "the servant state," meaning a benign government doing for citizens those things they want done, but cannot do for themselves. Instead, what is new is the fixity of purpose, a relentless quest for self-vindication reminiscent of De Gaulle, if only because he's just about the only other modern democratic leader to have regained power.

In 1978, at a time when Trudeau appeared so obviously to have been a failure, and would soon suffer the ultimate failure of losing an election, his biographer George Radwanski described him as an "unfulfilled" as opposed to a "failed" Prime Minister. The judgement now seems extraordinarily prescient. Trudeau still may fail: on

---

*The most vivid illustration of Trudeau's adamantine refusal to act like a sixty year old, and also of his almost reckless physical courage, happened in the summer of 1979, when he was on holiday in Nova Scotia. With friends, he had gone with his children and theirs to an isolated waterhole. Three toughs in black leather jackets, swigging beer and Bright's sherry straight out of the bottle, spotted him and began to taunt. One of them, peacocking in front of his friends, bawled out to Trudeau: "What would they do if I slugged you?" Trudeau strode up to the punk, banged his finger on the man's chest and said, "If you touch me, I'll kill you." The punk turned away.

energy policy, on economic nationalism, on federal-provincial relations. Even the constitution–if the Supreme Court confirms its legality–may prove unworkable in the face of the adamant opposition of the provinces. Yet Trudeau is closer to fulfilling himself than he has ever been. At the tag end of his political career, he is doing many of the things that Canadians took for granted he would do when he first arrived.

It would seem that two events have combined to change, not so much Trudeau himself, as the way he operates. The first was his defeat in 1979. During nine months out of power, he probably learned more about politics than in eleven years as Prime Minister. He found out that politics is mostly about people, and about the relationships between them. He learned how to trust people; back in power, he delegated authority as never before. Mostly, this happened by osmosis. As Opposition Leader, he had been ineffectual. Yet, a core of MPs, party workers, and aides had somehow kept the show going, harrying the Clark government in the Commons, feeding lines to the press and developing a series of policy proposals that, if they didn't quite add up to Camelot, had fulfilled their vote-winning function during the sudden election campaign every bit as effectively as the platforms Trudeau had concocted to suit his own fancy for all previous campaigns. Nor was Trudeau unaware that the election hadn't been so much won by him as lost by Clark and that almost any Liberal could have won.

The decisive event was the referendum. It liberated him, once and for all, from the spectre of Quebec's separation. For the whole of the previous decade, Official Ottawa had been living on its nerve ends, in much the same atmosphere of apprehension and tension that marked Washington on the eve of the Civil War. Trudeau and those closest to him, Lalonde and Pitfield in particular, had functioned as if listening for the first shot at Fort Sumter; the possibility of Quebec separating functioned as the organizing principle and overarching imperative of everything they did. The referendum freed Trudeau and the others to apply their energies and talents to all the other things they'd put aside.

* * *

The sweep of the power Canadians ceded to Trudeau on February 18, 1980, has few equals in the post-war political history of any Western democracy. He was in absolute command of his cabinet and government and, thanks to his majority, in untrammelled command of Parliament. Within Ottawa, all opposition collapsed. Both the Conservatives and the New Democrats were unhinged by a sense of their own impotence, and by the disheartening knowledge that even when Canadians cooled towards Trudeau – as the polls showed during the fractious winter of 1980-81 – there was no other leader they warmed towards. As for the press, the election result had demolished the myth of its power. Most reporters and columnists had fired their best shots at Trudeau and had ended up with their own credibility riddled. Post-election, commentary about Trudeau turned joky, flip, and insubstantial, albeit with an undertone of rueful admiration.

The Conservatives, by getting themselves heaved out so swiftly, had added an overlay of clownishness to their reputation for fractiousness. Their mood swivelled between sullen despair and self-destructive bitterness – the half-dozen Conservatives who screamed and shook their fists at the Speaker during the constitutional debate, as a case in point. In the fall of 1980, there was a brief Tory upsurge as Clark, demonstrating once again his unsung capacity for stubborn resilience, gave his party some of its spirit back by his courageous opposition to Trudeau's constitutional proposals. Yet Clark's success didn't last; his personal popularity fell, according to Gallup, into the low thirties. In February 1981, the Conservatives reconfirmed Clark's leadership at a policy convention, but the size of the "No" vote, at 34 per cent, confirmed his tenure for no more than a year. By mid-1981, most conversations in Conservative circles centred on the identity of the most effective messenger for telling Clark it was time for him to go.

The condition of the New Democrats was scarcely better. The party had lost its balance-of-power bargaining role and had lost, perhaps forever, its chance to replace the Liberals as a major party. True, the NDP had elected a cluster of able and aggressive western MPs, but in Ontario, as the provincial election of March 1981 confirmed, its core vote was eroding. Reinventing reasons why Canadians should vote New Democrat would not be easy now that the Liberals had been born again as economic nationalists, and it would be made no easier by Broadbent's idealistic decision to support Trudeau on the constitution.

For all practical purposes, Trudeau's only effective post-election opponents were the provincial premiers, who lobbied together against him to form an extra-Parliamentary opposition unique in Canadian political experience. Still, there was only so much the premiers could do. They were out in the wings; he was at centre-stage, with direct access to the national media. Their script had ten parts; his, just one.

Ultimately, Trudeau was powerful because, quite literally, he was unaccountable. Thanks to Machiavelli's *Fortuna*, he could do what he wanted and get away with it, because Canadians could not get at him in another election. He no longer needed to prove anything. He could quit whenever he wanted, and still quit ahead. Trudeau alone would decide how he would use his magical second life.

* * *

Often, people living a second life after surviving a plane crash, or a supposedly terminal illness, or some murderous engagement during a war, behave quite differently the second time around. They become more detached, more philosophical, and less fretful when things go wrong.

Trudeau has never been particularly introspective. "I don't waste much time speculating on historical might-be's," he has said. A friend applies to him the French phrase, *Il se jouait de la comedie*, meaning that he deals with life's comedy by play-acting, from behind a mask. Yet, post-election and at first almost imperceptibly, he began to act out a second-life scenario.

For a start, he stopped performing as if he were his own deputy minister. Instead of three briefcases, he took home only one. He began to take days off, after trips abroad or important conferences. He spent some of this extra spare time supervising renovations at his art deco mansion in Montreal, and choosing furniture and *objêts d'art* for it. He delegated authority over broad administrative areas that didn't interest him, from defence and agriculture to transportation, and freed his ministers to make their own mistakes.

"Rational government," hand in glove with all its flow-charts and decision-making trees and paper burden, was trundled off to the archives. The nature of cabinet meetings underwent a change. For a decade these had been structured like tutorials, as Trudeau quizzed each minister about his or her policy proposals, in the manner of a professor picking holes in a thesis. Now, most decisions were taken by cabinet committees, often in Trudeau's absence. Meetings of full cabinet turned into free-wheeling affairs, starting out with a discussion about "communications" (*i.e.*, propaganda), continuing on to a discussion of politics, and ending with any minister free to raise without notice any subject he or she chose. He kept his personal staff at the lean dimension it had shrunk to during Opposition. As for Pitfield, back as Privy Council Clerk, he became an apostle of the new, hang-loose creed, opining aloud that no doubt in the past decision-making *had* been too centralized, his own beloved PCO too obtrusive. Still more difficult to believe, Pitfield had become positively chatty, even with reporters.

Yet while it was refreshing, the new casualness was also calculating. If on some matters Trudeau decentralized authority, when it came to things that touched his own core, he gathered decision-making unto himself as not even during his heyday as a Sun King. To deal with the constitution, federal-provincial relations, major economic matters such as energy, and in foreign-policy, the "North-South dialogue," Trudeau created a government within a government. This comprised just five people: Trudeau himself, Finance Minister Allan MacEachen, Energy Minister Marc Lalonde, Pitfield, and Coutts. In September, 1980, for instance, this quintet made all the decisions (three to two against a recommendation to nationalize an oil multinational outright) that resulted in the National Energy Policy. Just outside the magic inner circle stood Justice Minister Jean Chrétien, point-man on the constitution and the minister with the largest popular following; Tom Axworthy, the Prime Minister's top policy aide, due to become Coutts's successor as principal secretary in July, 1981; and Michael Kirby, Robertson's successor as secretary for federal-provincial relations and a former political aide to Trudeau. Clustered at the fringe of the inner circle were Fisheries Minister Romeo Leblanc, a former press secretary upon whom Trudeau relied to learn what real people really thought; Treasury Board Secretary Don Johnston, a personal friend; Ian Stewart, the deputy minister of finance, and his former economic adviser; the Undersecretary of State for External Affairs, Allan Gotlieb; and the top officials in the Department of Energy, Mickey Cohen and Ed Clark. Half of these key players were ministers, half advisers; most were Trudeau's protégés and thus were dependent on him, though MacEachen and Chrétien, for reasons distinct unto themselves, were not.

With the same air of slightly deceptive insouciance, Trudeau reorganized his personal affairs. As if Margaret's interview with

Playgirl had served as exorcist, he no longer froze when her name was mentioned, but joked about her in the way of a fond, but detached, uncle. Soon, he and she, seizing once again upon a societal trend and writing their names on it, reached an agreement to share custody of the children, week on, week off. (Much to Trudeau's annoyance, Margaret allowed the boys to watch television *.)

In 1981, Margaret developed a live-in relationship with a young, wealthy Ottawa lawyer and furniture dealer, Jim Johnson. To recoup her financial losses (the bankruptcy of her first publisher; a robbery) she gave lessons in Japanese cooking, became host for a local Ottawa morning television program, and imported her British ghost-writer, Caroline Moorehead, to produce a second volume of autobiography, *Consequences*, to be published early in 1982.**

As for Trudeau, now that Justin, Sacha, and Michel weren't always around, he was free to be a sexagenarian Peter Pan. His companions were always around, if always changing, always gorgeous, always young. Somehow – beyond *Beyond Reason*, what did it matter – it no longer seemed to upset him if his ladies kissed and told: a journalist who'd recounted to her colleagues how she'd spent most of their date at 24 Sussex watching him bounce up and down on a trampoline was invited back; similarly, a Quebec craftswoman who had been overlooked for months, was invited round again only *after* she had cropped up, anonymously but identifiably, in a *Toronto Star* survey of his social life.

Mellowed is one way of describing Trudeau's style and mindset post-election. Emancipated is probably a better word. In some ways, he reverted to the style of his earliest years, saying and doing whatever he felt like without giving a damn for the consequences. In June, 1980, he described the performance of the premiers on constitutional negotiations as "distressful and depressing" even before

---

*For all practical purposes, Trudeau never watches television, even though his staff installed a Betamax video-recorder, and regularly sent over tapes in the hope he would screen them, and thereby get a feel for the tastes of his constituents. One of the few tapes he has ever commented on was a television profile of his personal friend, Paul Desmarais, a poor boy from Sudbury turned tycoon, from the series, "The Canadian Establishment." Trudeau's observation was, "Too soft on Desmarais."

**To help Margaret out when her luck was down, Trudeau took over the mortgage on her house. Typically, he ordered her to tell no one of his out-of-character outburst of generosity. She, just as typically, told *People*.

any talks had begun. Exactly a year later, tense because of the Supreme Court's delay in ruling on the constitution, he called Opposition MPs "jerks." He could be as insufferable as ever. In June, 1981, he dismissed as unimportant a strike by CBC technicians on the ground that he himself never watched TV or listened to radio. He abandoned any last vestiges of squeamishness about how press and public might react to patronage appointments, or displays of personal vanity. In July, 1981, he booted a wealthy, forty-six-year-old MP into the Senate to create a Commons vacancy for Coutts.* A few months earlier, when he attended a gala Metropolitan Opera performance in New York shortly after the assassination attempt on President Reagan, U.S. secret service agents pleaded with him to enter anonymously, by a side door; Trudeau instead made a bravura entrance through the main door, with a dazzling blonde Texan on his arm.

Mostly, he was equable. He teased reporters at press conferences, and astonished the Press Gallery by inviting it over for drinks on the lawn at 24 Sussex. At parties, he now beguiled his hosts and fellow guests; instead of taking for granted that it was others' duty to entertain him, he bounced in, devil-may-care, making comments like, "Now, what shall we do to have some fun?" On trips abroad, he took logistical-foul-ups in stride, even the combination of lousy weather and lousy local planning that aborted the first half of his January 1981 global tour. And in an interview in June, 1980, he came as close as he has ever come to apologizing for the War Measures Act. "Legislators don't always see the full implications of their laws. When they do, it is not always beyond them to invoke their highest devotion to the *raison d'état* to snuff out a little bit of freedom here and a little bit of freedom there. It's a temptation every government, and I should know, has."

The style of the late-period Trudeau took a while to become apparent. Just a few days after the election, he prefigured his *que sera sera* mood to a friend who telephoned to congratulate him. "It must be destiny," he said in reply, and then sent down the telephone wire the equivalent of a verbal shrug, so that his friend couldn't tell whether Trudeau really believed he had been singled out from on high, or whether he regarded his political second life as a cosmic joke.

*Spadina voters defeated Coutts in a by-election on August 17, 1981.

As telling as the change in Trudeau himself was the change in the nature of the relationship between him and Canadians. In the way of other superstars whose careers have faltered and then sprung back to life–Judy Garland, Frank Sinatra, Richard Burton, Muhammed Ali–Pierre E. Reincarnation, in Allan Fotheringham's quip, had become part of his own audience. We marvelled at his resilience; we marvelled just as much at our own prescience and power in giving him a licence to be resilient. As with Sinatra-cum-toupee, and Ali cum-paunch, and Burton reviving *Camelot* with nothing left but the ruined splendour of his voice, we no longer wanted to judge the man for what he did but to enjoy him for what he was and for what he had been along with the rest of us–a part of our youth in the golden summer of Expo; a part of our painful loss of innocence as a people through the brutal October of 1970; and a part of our economic change-of-life in the later 1970's, as the easy affluent years slipped past us forever. If Trudeau got needlessly combative with the premiers, and if he ignored such mundane matters as interest rates and inflation (which we knew perfectly well had always bored him), well–no matter–he was as sassy and as sexy and as stylish as ever, and he did us proud in front of strangers, as in walking-the-dog with a yo-yo for the European television cameras after the 1980 Venice summit or, as in March 1981, drawing cheers from a crowd of anti-acid rain demonstrators gathered on Parliament Hill to boo visiting U.S. President, Ronald Reagan, by telling them, "Come off it you guys. They never do this to me in Washington."

Perhaps the deeper difference, after 1980, involved not so much how Canadians looked at Trudeau as how they had begun to look at themselves. It was as if his defeat in 1979 had cauterized a national wound, as if the spectacle of watching so extraordinary a leader being defeated had shocked us into wondering just what it was that we were doing to ourselves, and to compare our own lot with those of other people. The winning of the referendum in May 1980 produced a national wave, if not of youthful euphoria, then at least of middle-aged equability, a sense of quiet self-confidence, hard to measure, but palpable, at having weathered the worst. So that a number of national alarums and excursions–a flight of oil-drilling rigs across the border; interest rates that soared to 20 per cent–were treated by the public with astonishing equanimity, in sharp contrast to the reaction to similar setbacks in the 1970's. The west, true enough, was mad as hell, but Quebec was amicable in a way it hadn't been in a generation. The sense of national self-confidence was made visible in the massive public support for "Canadianization" of the foreign-owned oil and gas industry; never before had economic nationalism appealed to more than a handful of academics and journalists, and to Walter Gordon. As revealing was the massive support for Trudeau's Charter of Human Rights. Earlier, Trudeau had won only grudging approval for his various proposed charters, and even that approval only by shielding human rights inside the unassailable armour of patriation. Now, according to the polls, more than 70 per cent of Canadians wanted a Charter of Rights for its own sake, with patriation simply taken for granted.

It wasn't that Canadians had suddenly become more libertarian than before – if anything, witness the back-to-the-basics movement in the schools, they'd become more conservative – but that they'd become more *Canadian*. Instinctively, they seemed to recognize that a coast-to-coast Charter of Rights would become part of the national fibre binding them together, instead of subsisting in clumps as Quebecois or Albertans or Nova Scotians or whatever, in a large block on the globe marked Canada.

Thus, in the first third of his fourth term, most of the things that Trudeau happened to be doing were in fact the things Canadians wanted him to be doing, even though, frequently, they didn't at all care for the way he was going about doing them. Westerners felt differently, as scarcely needs to be said. And yet, setting oil and gas aside, even westerners didn't feel all *that* differently: a 1981 poll by the Canada West Foundation found that the same proportion of westerners as of all other Canadians gave their "first loyalty" to their country rather than to their province.*

* * *

The formalities of the transition were accomplished quickly, without fanfare, and except in one instance were done gracefully. Before moving back, Trudeau toured 24 Sussex with Maureen McTeer as guide. Each time he spotted a change in decor he didn't like, he rolled his eyes heavenwards and said, "Oh, my God." (Once re-installed, Trudeau in fact made few changes and even learned to appreciate one of Clark's innovations, a black and white parquet floor installed in the foyer for guests to dance on.)

*58 per cent to 26 per cent for westerners; 62 per cent to 28 per cent for all other Canadians.

Early in the afternoon of March 3, 1980, when he and his thirty-two-member cabinet were sworn in by Governor-General Schreyer at Rideau Hall, Trudeau once again became Canada's fifteenth Prime Minister, * in succession to the sixteenth.

As Trudeau's aides swarmed back into their old offices in the Langevin Building, their watchword was, "No more '74." Then, as they all remembered only too well, Trudeau had interpreted a majority victory as a mandate to goof off, and had never recovered from this lassitude. The new administration was determined to be active, rather than re-active, and to go down, if it had to, for sins of commission, not omission. As a signal of the new order, Trudeau himself turned up at his office before 8.00 a.m. the day before the swearing-in and had to be let in by a commissionaire. At the first cabinet meeting, he laid down the law: to prevent a recurrence of the post-1974 cynicism that had corroded Canadian politics, all election promises had to be kept, and fast. He assembled Parliament in just two months, in contrast to the five months Clark had waited. The Throne Speech, on April 14, read like a replay of his campaign speeches: "A new national development policy. . . [to] increase Canadian ownership and control"; "immediate relief for elderly people on low incomes"; and a "made in Canada [oil] price."

None of this, in the early weeks, curbed the prevailing cynicism about Trudeau's intentions. Some of the resemblances between his present political circumstances, and those of 1974, were uncanny. Once again, he was interested in the constitution while the public was interested in, indeed was acutely anxious about, the economy. Once again, with the promise of cheap oil as 1980's successor to 1974's promise of no wage and price controls, he had saddled himself with an election commitment he could not fulfill. Once again – some things never change – the west was angry with him.

In fact, the west was angrier than it had ever been. Just as Diefenbaker had won the 1957 election by ignoring Quebec, so Trudeau had won in 1980 by ignoring the west, indeed by implicitly running against it on behalf of Ontario consumers. Yet in order to come even close to fulfilling his election promise of cheap oil, he had to convince the west to pay the bill for him, or compel it to pay. Lougheed promptly declared he would accept "no reduction in net benefits" from the oil-revenue sharing deal he and Clark claimed to

*Like football quarterbacks, Prime Ministers keep the number they were first assigned.

have struck just before Clark's defeat the previous December.* For Ottawa to underestimate the "deep feelings" in the west, Lougheed warned, would be a "tragic miscalculation." At the Western Premiers' Conference in April, Blakeney of Saskatchewan upped the stakes. "A significant number of people . . . would be in favour of some sort of western separation."

During his first few weeks back in office, a sense of uncertainty about the circumstances in which he found himself seemed to unsettle Trudeau. Some colleagues found him subdued, almost passive. Once the rhetoric of the Throne Speech had been decided, he took little part in the early decision-making. Although deputy ministers are appointed personally by the Prime Minister, Trudeau had Pitfield tell Grant Reuber, the deputy minister of finance appointed by Clark, that he was out of a job to make way for Ian Stewart. Early on, one of those closest to him remarked, "I'm not sure if he's really got it anymore."

Trudeau's problem, as so often in the past, was that before he could perform with grace, he needed pressure. On April 15, like a second smile from fortune, the pressure came. Lévesque, back tanned and relaxed from a week in Bermuda, announced that May 20 would be the "historic day" on which Quebecers would declare at last, "if they are satisfied with their position as a permanent minority in the present regime, or if they want a new deal."

There is a saying that when fate allows someone given up for dead the gift of a second life, it is because he has something to finish. The nature of Trudeau's unfinished task was now manifest. It remained only for him to decide how to undertake it.

* * *

No means exist now to uncover from surveys, still less to tug out from the hearts and minds of Quebecers, the evidence that would say for certain how much difference Trudeau actually made to the final result of the referendum. Plainly, the eventual federalist margin, 60 per cent to 40 per cent, was too large to be accounted

*As Jeffrey Simpson pointed out in his book, *Discipline of Power*, this agreement, despite Clark and Lougheed's later claims of accord, was a long way off from being signed. Lougheed didn't treat his fellow-Conservative, fellow-Albertan, Clark, all that differently from the way he later treated Trudeau, including a threat to cut back oil production if Clark didn't give him what he wanted.

for by any individual, whether Trudeau, Ryan, or even "Yvette."* All the polls, including Goldfarb's private surveys for Trudeau, underestimated the magnitude of the silent no vote: Liberal organizers realized its existence only when, after streets had been canvassed, householders would call the party's local office to blurt out that although they had told the canvassers they were undecided so as not to offend their neighbours, they intended all the while to vote no.

Numbers are one thing: the ardour behind them quite another. Here, the difference that Trudeau made, made all the difference. As no one else could have done, he changed the meaning of the way Quebecers voted, and almost certainly would have voted anyway, from a no to sovereignty-association into a yes for Confederation. He took a decision Quebecers were impelled toward for dollars and cents reasons and invested it with pride and dignity, above all with the quality of finality.

In mid-March, when Trudeau first began to address himself to what he should do, all of this seemed like an impossible dream. Lévesque had triumphed over Ryan during the televised debate in Quebec's National Assembly to approve formally the 109-word question, which asked Quebecers to grant to their government only a "mandate" to negotiate sovereignty-association and then hedged even this with a promise of "no political change" until a second referendum. While Ryan had debated the question's actual wording aridly and dialectically, Lévesque had talked about its meaning, appealing to the pride of Quebecers, appealing also to the "continuity of history" and to "equality." Abruptly, public opinion shifted. In mid-February, a Radio-Canada poll had shown the no side ahead comfortably, 52 per cent to 41 per cent. On March 16, a *Dimanche-Matin* survey put the yes in the lead, by 47 per cent to 44 per cent. To this lead had to be added the "momentum" Lévesque had gained during the legislative debate.

As April approached, the mood of those around Trudeau grew more and more uneasy. Some, reckoning all was lost, urged Trudeau to do what Clark had said he would do: stay out of the battle

---

*Yvette is the name of a docile, female character in Quebec textbooks. In an interview, PQ Minister Lise Payette referred patronizingly to Claude Ryan's wife as "an Yvette," thereby catalyzing federalist women into staging a number of highly successful "Yvette" rallies.

entirely and so preserve his authority for the morning after R-Day. One top adviser even urged Trudeau to declare that he himself would vote yes because the question was so fuzzy, and thereby to reduce the referendum to a farce. Others, although just as pessimistic, reached a directly opposite conclusion. Several Quebec ministers, notably Monique Bégin and Pierre DeBané, pleaded with Trudeau to hurl himself into the battle full tilt, appearing on the platform with Ryan at each and every rally.

In making up his mind, Trudeau applied a political asset that is one of the most considerable he possesses, but which is often the most overlooked. He knew his way around. He had been a politician for a decade and a half. He had fought five elections. He had basked in the sunny warmth of public opinion and had felt its icy blast, and he knew how quickly the climate could change. Such a blend of political savvy and magical guile is practically unbeatable. It was more than enough to beat Lévesque.

* * *

Perhaps the most perceptive comment that has ever been made about what Quebecers really want belongs to the comedian, Yvon Deschamps, who used to crack up his audiences by describing as their holy grail, "*un Québec indépendant dans un Canada uni.*" In their different ways, Lévesque and Trudeau set out to convince Quebecers that this schizophrenic symbiosis could be theirs.

A yes vote, Lévesque told his audiences, "will put our weight on the bargaining table as a people." English Canada's response to a no vote would be to tell Quebecers, "get back in your hole." Long before the referendum, Lévesque had expunged from his vocabulary all threatening phrases like "separation" and "independence." Now, even "sovereignty-association" joined the list of unmentionables. In its place emerged, "equality as a people," the one emotional ground upon which Lévesque dared take a stand, since his own polls told him that almost half of even committed yes supporters intended to vote this way, not to achieve sovereignty, but simply to improve Quebec's bargaining position with the rest of the country. In the end, Lévesque's case collapsed under the weight of its own internal contradictions. Even so, it was, politically, a brilliant case: in effect, Lévesque persuaded 40 per cent of Quebecers to trust him, even though only 25 to 30 per cent actually wanted what *he* wanted for them.

371

Lévesque's problem was that Quebecers trusted Trudeau more.

The first big surprise of the campaign was the discovery that street by street, and hamlet by hamlet, the federalists were as well organized as the Péquistes. Two years of tireless organizing by Ryan suddenly demonstrated its worth. As important was the crash campaign, on Trudeau's behalf, by Justice Minister Jean Chrétien, the "street fighter" from Shawinigan. To the no forces, Chrétien brought money (some $3 million worth of federal advertising) and people (the awesome federal Liberal political machine). More decisively, Chrétien brought to the campaign the ultimate weapon of passion. For four years, the Péquistes had appropriated to themselves each and every one of Quebec's symbols, from the blue and white *fleur de lys* flag adopted in Duplessis's day, to Gilles Vigneault's celebratory ballad, *Les Gens du Pays*. Now, in abrupt emotional counterpoint, the federalists led by Chrétien marched out with the white and scarlet Maple Leaf as their standard, singing *O Canada* as their battle hymn.

The second surprise was Trudeau himself. In a way that Canadians hadn't seen since 1974, he fought as a happy warrior: cerebral and impassioned, serious and joyous, magical and political.

He spoke first on April 15, during the Throne Speech debate in the Commons, a few hours after Lévesque set the referendum date. His manner was professional and clinical. Dispassionately and logically, he explained why Lévesque could not give to Quebecers what he had promised them, the satisfaction of sovereignty combined with the assurance of association. These goals, Trudeau said, were twinned: Lévesque himself had said they could not be "disassociated." Yet association was beyond Lévesque's reach, because all nine English-speaking premiers had said they would never grant it. Without association, no sovereignty-association. If, on the other hand, Lévesque came to Ottawa to negotiate sovereignty alone, he, Trudeau could not grant it because Quebecers had just given him and his Liberal M.P.s "a massive mandate to exercise sovereignty over Quebec and the rest of the country." Thus all that a yes vote would accomplish would be an "impasse." For many English Canadians, this dialectic seemed abstract. For many Quebecers, it went straight to the heart of the matter. After Trudeau's speech, for the first time, Péquiste spokesmen on hotline shows found themselves having to explain to callers why a yes vote would lead anywhere except deadlock.

Next, Trudeau switched to the offensive. His first target was his opponents' honour. The early separatists like Marcel Chaput and Pierre Bourgault had "deserved respect," he told the Montreal Chamber of Commerce on May 2, because they had the "courage to say what they believed in, independence." Their successors in the Parti Québécois, however, dared only to put to Quebecers "a conditional and ambiguous question." They risked humiliating Quebec, just as Irish patriots in 1916 would have humiliated Ireland had they said to Britain, "We will be independent on condition you have an economic association with us."

A week later, he attacked Péquiste pride. "It takes more courage to stay in Canada and fight it out, than to withdraw into our walls," he told a rally of 6,000 in Quebec City on May 9. "Pride and honour are not on their side with their ambiguity and their equivocation. They are on our side, *chez nous.*"

These sallies struck home to Quebecers, and to Lévesque. By early May, his jaunty self-confidence had evaporated. He was fighting, no longer to win but only to lose in the right way, with a majority of francophones at least on his side, so that he might fight again another day. "It is French Quebec that will make the decision, nobody else can make it for us," he said at Montmagny on May 11, drawing a racial dividing line down the province. A day later, in the manner of a boxer turning reckless because he knows he is behind, he swung at his tormentor: Trudeau "naturally is for the no," he told an audience that for once did not applaud one of his lines, because "his middle name is English."

* * *

On Thursday, May 15, Trudeau carried the war into the heart of the enemy's country. He stepped onto the stage of the Paul Sauvé Arena in Montreal's east end. Here, Lévesque had stood weeping for joy on the night of November 15, 1976.

For five, six, seven incredible moments, Trudeau could not speak. Above him, a dozen huge Maple Leaf flags hung from the rafters: in front of him, around him and behind him, a massive crowd of more than 10,000 refused to let him begin. Each time he started out, "*Monsieur le Président, Mesdames et Messieurs . . .*," a rhythmic roar swept through the crowd. In a coda to this climactic cultural confrontation, the crowd was shouting, not, "Tru-deau, Tru-deau, Tru-deau" as at all his political rallies, but a new war cry: "Ell-i-ott, Ell-i-ott, Ell-i-ott."

History, as the chant died, was on the turn. Each of his previous referendum speeches and this one, Trudeau had rehearsed for hours, in his hotel room, once on a plane winging from Vancouver to Quebec City, and then delivered word-for-word perfect, without notes. But this night, as if aware it was a night destiny had marked out for him, he changed his script in the midst of delivering it.

First, as he had planned, he challenged Lévesque directly. "Of course my name is Pierre Elliott Trudeau. Yes, Elliott was my mother's name. It was borne by the Elliotts who came to Canada two hundred years ago . . . My name is a Quebec name, but my name is a Canadian name also." No less Canadian, he went on, were the names of Péquiste ministers: Pierre-Marc Johnson, Louis O'Neill, Robert Burns. "That is the kind of division we are saying no to."

Then, improvising as he went, he challenged English Canada. A no vote, he said, "will be interpreted as a mandate to change the constitution, to renew federalism." He and his Quebec M.P.s were "willing to lay our seats in the House of Commons on the line to have change." He was making a "solemn declaration to all Canadians in the other provinces . . . that we will not agree to your interpreting a no vote as an indication that everything is fine and can remain as it was before."

With those phrases, Trudeau changed the meaning of the referendum result. More than just a no to sovereignty-association, it now meant a yes for a Confederation of which, through a new constitution, Quebecers could feel truly a part. He had promised constitutional change earlier, in the Throne Speech debate. Now he had transformed the quest for constitutional agreement into a contract that bound English Canadians, which was the point, as much as Quebec.

* * *

"I have never been so proud to be a Quebecer and a Canadian," said Trudeau on the evening of May 20, after the no vote had climbed to within a decimal fraction of 60 per cent, and after Lévesque had conceded defeat, his face crumpled and suddenly old, standing alone with his wife, Corinne, on the same stage at the Paul Sauvé arena where Trudeau had stood five days earlier.

Quite probably, the referendum would have been won without Trudeau. Yet the ultimate credit is his. Quebecers steeled themselves to trust English Canada because of all that Trudeau had done to English Canada in the decade before the referendum was held, beginning in October 1968 when he introduced the Official Languages Act into the Commons. It was Joe Clark who gave Trudeau the accolade he deserved when he said, in a referendum campaign speech in Shawinigan, "The Canada that Mr. Lévesque wants to separate from no longer exists." In supreme irony, Lévesque deserves part of the credit too. His unilingual language legislation, introduced in 1977, ended Quebecers' fears of cultural and linguistic subjugation. By this same legislation Lévesque had also demonstrated, unwittingly, that Confederation could be renewed, radically and decisively, without being disrupted. Never in Canadian history have two opponents been so much in each other's debt. As a last convolution in this dependency relationship, Lévesque won his election in April 1981 at least in part because Quebecers, having sent one Single Combat Champion back to Ottawa, were determined to keep the other in place back home.

The implications of what had happened on May 20 took a while to sink in. Lévesque described the result as a "reprieve" for federalism. Quebec commentators sympathetic to Lévesque argued that because the young had so overwhelmingly voted separatist, a second referendum might win at least a Francophone majority for Lévesque.

Yet within a few months, the realization dawned that, as *Le Soleil* editor Marcel Pepin put it, "It's over." Not only separatism, it turned out, but nationalism as well. "The idea itself, its concept, is bankrupt," wrote the author, Michel Morin. With astonishing speed, but as always happens when people make up their minds that a painful subject is closed, the divisions within Quebec families – Lévesque's brother had voted no; Monique Begin's sister had voted yes – began to heal. None of the predicted, post-referendum bitterness emerged.* Instead, Quebecers accepted the result and turned

---

A study by British political scientist Anthony King shows that only once in the history of 160 referendums in democracies has a decision later been reversed: in 1913, the Swiss voted no to a proposal to extend universal suffrage to women, and then in 1917 voted yes to the same proposition.

their minds to other pursuits, prime among them economic. Much as the intelligentsia had switched off organized religion for nationalist politics in the early 1960's, it switched now to commerce. Businessmen like Alfred Hamel of Nordair, Paul Desmarais of Power Corp., Michel Belanger of the National Bank and Pierre Laurin, director of the University of Montreal's Business School, became the new Quebec media heroes; more young Quebecers enrolled in business courses than in any other province.

Through the winter of 1980-81, Lévesque's government seemed headed towards defeat. He was unable to muster an effective counter-attack to Trudeau's constitutional blitz, not least because, as successive polls kept showing, Quebecers no longer took the issue of provincial sovereignty seriously, or because they accepted that Trudeau would get for them as much as anyone could. Lévesque lost a dozen successive by-elections, and lost also some of his most powerful and popular ministers, such as Robert Burns and Lise Payette.

Then, on April 13, 1981, Lévesque triumphed. He won 80 of the 122 seats in the National Assembly, and more than 50 per cent of the vote. Even so, the contrast with November 15, 1976, could scarcely have been more absolute. Canadians in the nine other provinces glanced at the next day's headlines – "PQ TRIUMPH" – and went about their business. Quebecers did the same. Everyone knew that Lévesque had won because he had promised "good government." (something he had already demonstrated he could deliver) and because he had also promised not to hold a second referendum during his second term. They also knew – the decisive factor in any election – that Lévesque, whatever his foibles, was impossible to dislike while Ryan, a grand-seigneur in a hair-shirt, was very difficult indeed to like. And deep down, Quebecers, and everyone else, knew instinctively that separatism was done with at least for a generation, and that if and when its time came again it would be the responsibility of everyone's sons and daughters to cope with a challenge that, just by jolting Canadians out of their complacency, shapes and defines and inspires this country.

* * *

After the referendum, Trudeau could have lapsed into lassitude. He could have set his sights on modest, and essentially symbolic, constitutional goals. Just to have patriated the constitution from

Britain would have earned him a chapter in the history books. He could then have stepped off-stage in the autumn of 1980, accompanied by the plaudits owed him as the Victor of the Referendum, the Architect of Patriation, the Electoral Invincible.

Instead, without even a pause, Trudeau set out to reorder history. Within a fortnight of the referendum, he had cajoled the premiers – "Everything is negotiable" – into coming to Ottawa to start negotiations to revise the constitution.

He hasn't stopped making headlines since: a new constitution, after "Fifty-four years of failure"; an attempt to renegotiate $17 billion of federal financial transfers to the provinces; a national energy policy, one that, in its economic sweep and scale, is equalled only by the reorganization of the grain trade undertaken in the 1930's, and by the creation of the railways in the nineteenth century; reform of national institutions, such as the Senate, and perhaps the Commons by way of proportional representation, to make them more representative of the regions; a national economic development strategy, coupled with an industrial strategy aimed at channelling federal money into potential "winners."* None of these new scenarios has as yet unfolded much beyond its first chapter; not even the constitution because, despite Trudeau's easy assurance that opposition to it will die away in the manner of opposition to the Maple Leaf flag after 1965, the "dissident" provincial premiers command power, legitimacy, and access to the media unlike those who opposed the flag. Also, again unlike the flag, which is symbolic, the constitution is substantive: Quebec, for instance, claims that 50 per cent of its statutes will be rendered invalid in whole or in part by the Charter of Rights.

So that all that can be usefully attempted here is to try to provide a context, personal and historical, which the three most important of Trudeau's policy thrusts – the rule of law that will be brought about through his Charter of Rights; his quest for a new balance in federal-provincial arrangements; his conversion, or reconversion, to economic interventionism – can be seen in some perspective. And to follow, a summary chronicle of his two great battles – against the West, and for the constitution.

THE RULE OF LAW. Although Trudeau is often presumed to be a

---

*In fact, Herb Gray, the minister responsible, had to spend his entire first year feeding the "losers" – bailing out Chrysler and Massey-Ferguson and extending import quotas on textiles and clothing for another five years.

social democrat (having fought the good fight against Duplessis and all the rest of it), and sometimes is seen as a "closet socialist," his true mindset is that of a juridical democrat. He believes, and has always believed, that the rule of law, by protecting the weak from the strong, can set everyone free to pursue excellence. His Charter of Rights, as chopped and changed through the Joint Senate-Commons Committee's two months of hearings, and as amended down to the final wire, as through the inclusion of a "God" clause, can stand up to Ed Broadbent's hyperbolic description, "probably the best Bill of Rights in the world." Thus, by definition, it will also be the most intrusive Charter in the world, intruding the rule of law as administered by the courts into relations between individuals (men and women; the handicapped and the able; native and non-native), and between individuals and their governments. Trudeau, the constitutional scholar, knows this full well. But most Canadians, accustomed to solving social problems through common law and common sense, have yet to realize that, except for the entrenched conservatism of Canadian courts, they face the prospect of becoming a nation of litigants, like Americans. All that can be said for sure is that by allowing Canadians to believe that his real goal was patriation, which all but a lunatic fringe of monarchists support, he has persuaded us to allow him to build his juridical New Jerusalem.

ECONOMIC INTERVENTIONISM. Once again, Trudeau baited his hook; in this case, with "Canadianization" of the oil and gas industry. Since multinationals are about as popular as real-estate developers used to be during the 1960's, Canadians overwhelmingly support this policy, according to the polls. By the middle of 1981, the slogan among Trudeau's economic insiders had become, "Who can we NEP next?" In other words, to which other industries could the principles of the National Energy Policy be applied? The genealogy of Trudeau's interventionism can be traced back to his "New Society" musings of 1976, and back still further to his professorial thesis of "the servant state." Other antecedents are more recent, and are more pragmatic.

Defeat in 1979 had thrown the Liberals into a funk; they realized they had nothing left to offer Canadians. The first to come up with some answers were Lalonde, Gray, and Tom Axworthy, Trudeau's policy chief. Together with a handful of policy groupies, such as University of Toronto sociologist Lorna Marsden, they tilted the party back to the left, and towards economic nationalism. Axworthy, not by coincidence a former aide to the godfather of Canadian economic nationalism, Walter Gordon, produced most of the new ideas. He was fortunate enough to have access to Trudeau as well as being responsible for writing his speeches for the 1980 campaign. And so, towards the end of the campaign, Trudeau talked about Canadianizing the oil industry, scrutinizing foreign take-overs more carefully, and developing an industrial strategy based on an "activist" role by government. That Trudeau had spent much of his life quoting Acton and Kedourie against nationalism no longer mattered.

Trudeau converted, outwardly at least, to economic nationalism because he appreciated that it would win Ottawa allies for its confrontations with the provinces – "Canadianization" as a trump card to place on top of regionalism. Interventionism also came naturally to Trudeau because he has scant respect for the entrepreneurial ability of Canadian businessmen, and a great deal of respect for the ability of his government and of himself.

As this is being written, the success of Trudeau's policies of interventionism are difficult to judge because so many of these are yet to come. Trudeau himself, as always when he adopts an idea, exhibits no self-doubts. In March, 1981, President Reagan came to Ottawa and described his "revolutionary" supply-side economic policies of cutting spending, cutting taxes, and generally getting government the hell off businessmen's backs. Trudeau in reply raised the banner of the servant state. "Here in Canada," he said, "our own realities have sometimes made it necessary for governments to intervene to further enterprise. Those realities, and that necessity, are still with us."

BALANCED FEDERALISM. Trudeau has always envisioned federalism as his mentor, Lord Acton, envisioned it: "The coexistence of several nations under the same state" constituting "the best security of freedom." By the end of the 1970's, as Trudeau saw it, Canadian federalism was out of sync. More barriers to the free movement of goods, services, and trade existed between the provinces than between the member, sovereign countries of the European Economic Community. At the same time, the provinces accounted for 60 per cent of the total public spending – the highest proportion by far in any federation. In Trudeau's perspective, federalism had mutated into the textbook definition of confederalism, that is, into a collection of autonomous societies, each striving to be self-sufficient, with the central government reduced, in Newfoundland Premier Brian Peckford's phrase, to "an agency of the provinces." Confederalism, Trudeau was certain, would limit freedom because citizens, in almost all matters, would be under the suzerainty of just one state – the province.

An entirely different view of contemporary Canadian federalism exists, and is held to as genuinely: That Ottawa, through its powers of taxation, of control of the money supply and of international agreements, holds all the levers of power that really matter; that the country can be strong only when all its regions are strong; that small is not just beautiful, but is inherently more creative.

The constitutional debate brought both these points of view into focus. As Trudeau pronounced it, Canada is "an association of people" who, as individuals, have ceded part of their sovereignty to two orders of government. As the premiers saw it, Canada is "an association of provinces." In this scenario, Canadians are not so much individuals within a country called Canada, as citizens of sovereign provinces which, much like the southern states before the Civil War, had united to form a federation, and had voluntarily ceded a portion of their sovereignty to a central government.

Since Canada is a flesh-and-blood body politic and not a political laboratory for theorists to experiment in, personality mattered more than philosophy through most of the debates between Trudeau and the premiers. They thought he put them down; he thought they had delusions of empire. Sterling Lyon of Manitoba regarded Trudeau as something close to a malevolent force, a closet republican at best, while Bill Bennett of B.C. went through meetings in a more or less constant condition of agitation, to the point that at a key session at 24 Sussex during the First Ministers Conference in September 1980, he kept on jumping up to say he could "bear it no longer" and had to leave. (He stayed.) For his part, Trudeau viewed Peckford as an uncouth upstart, and Blakeney as a ditherer who pretended to walk both sides of the street, but who always in the end came down on the provincial side, where his polls told him his votes were.

A decade, even longer perhaps, may have to pass before it becomes clear whether Trudeau's way of doing things will "tear the country apart," as Clark has said, or whether, as Trudeau has said, Clark's style of giving away offshore resources and Loto Canada, and giving up on a National Energy Bank, amounts to "giving away the shop." By mid-1981, the indicators conflicted. On the one hand, there were signs of a new sense of one-ness in the country, as demonstrated by the massive crowd that gathered on Parliament Hill on July 1 to wave Maple Leaf flags in the rain and celebrate an unepochal 114th birthday. On the other, there were signs of a new alienation. On July 5, the NDP, the country's one truly ideological political party, was almost split apart by regionalism, as one third of the delegates to the biennial convention, almost all of them westerners, voted to censure Broadbent's policy of supporting Trudeau's constitutional resolutions.

All that is certain is that Trudeau has never for an instant set his sights on anything other than his version of "balanced federalism." For certain also is that when Canadians re-elected Trudeau in February 1980, they knew who it was they were voting for.

* * *

Or *most* Canadians knew. To westerners, the result of the February 1980 election came like a kick in the groin. They switched on their sets, to hear the CBC's Knowlton Nash announcing that central Canada had already elected Trudeau and the Liberals with a *majority*, before a single western vote had been counted.

For a while, westerners simply acted disoriented. In Saskatchewan, the former Conservative leader Dick Collver and one other member formed a separatist party; no one took this seriously since Collver's platform, union with the United States, would have deprived Saskatchewanians of medicare and jurisdiction over resources, at the price of being eligible for a possible military draft. Lougheed, having warned that for Ottawa to underestimate "the deep feelings" of westerners, would be a "tragic miscalculation," came to Ottawa on July 24–25 to negotiate oil prices and revenues with Trudeau, and got nowhere. Yet later in the summer, after Lougheed had said that a federal tax on gas exports would amount to a "declaration of war," a provincial poll showed that Albertans, 67 per cent to 27 per cent, thought he was overdoing it. At that time, the post-referendum mood of expansiveness hadn't evaporated. And there was still at least a prospect of progress in constitutional negotiations, then being co-chaired by a westerner, Saskatchewan Attorney-General Roy Romanow, and Chrétien, "the Uke and Tuque show" as they styled themselves, in a flush of pan-Canadian camaraderie. Trudeau threw a few token offerings westward by placing three western senators in his cabinet, though his gesture was less expansive than Clark's had been to Quebec the previous year.

Then, in October 1980, Trudeau struck two sparks that set the prairies on fire. On October 2, he told Canadians via national television the changes he intended to make to their constitution. Most of these were familiar, such as the Charter of Rights and "mobility" rights. The difference was in the amending formula. Now, definitively, Ontario and Quebec would have a veto over all further constitutional amendments. Added was a new provision for national referendums that would allow Ottawa to attempt to convince Canadians, as individuals, to over-ride the wishes of their provincial governments. In fact, these clauses contained a range of protections for the western and eastern provinces; in effect, to "win" a referendum, Ottawa would have to win both regional and national majorities. But in the hinterland these were perceived as patronizing put-downs. Brilliantly, Lougheed translated these feelings into words: Alberta was being made "a second-class province" and its resources were being "put at risk."

On October 28, when Lalonde brought down his National Energy Policy (NEP), these hurt feelings escalated quickly into outright fear and soon after into blind fury. By 1990, the oil and gas industry was to be at least 50 per cent "Canadianized." Ottawa itself would take over "several large (foreign) oil companies." The revenue pie was to be resliced: Ottawa's share would expand from 10 per cent to 23 per cent, mostly at the expense of the oil companies ($4.7 billion in profits in 1979) while Alberta's would be shaved from 45 per cent to 43 per cent. To achieve these extra revenues, Ottawa, among other things, would impose a new tax on *all* gas production. No-strings tax subsidies to oil companies would be replaced by federal grants; these would be used to attract companies away from the western sedimentary basin to the "Canada Lands" of the north and the offshore, where Ottawa claimed jurisdiction. The oil industry howled and screamed and indeed, continues to do so, although its voice has become progressively fainter as a clutch of Canadian companies – most notably Dome Petroleum – have put NEP creatively to work for them.

Lougheed's response was cool, and almost surgical. Three days after Lalonde's announcement, he went on provincial television to denounce NEP as "an outright attempt to take over the resources of the province." Ottawa, he told his society of homesteaders (the sustaining myth of Albertans, never mind that many now lived in penthouses), was trying "to come into our living room." He would never accept NEP. To force Ottawa to back down, he would cut oil production by 180,000 barrels a day, in phases that would begin after a three-month period of grace to allow Ottawa to come to its senses. He would also withhold construction permits for two oil and tar sands projects upon which Lalonde depended to meet the target of "self-sufficiency" by 1990. Lougheed's most effective thrust was to appeal to Albertans to help him.

A few days later, at an oil conference in New York, Lalonde responded to the challenge. He reviewed his policies for an audience of bankers and brokers and oil executives. "We really mean it," he said.

Is Edmonton Burning?, a hastily-written paperback Gothic recounting the seduction of an innocent prairie maiden by a wily easterner, as Canadian troops sneak in to take over the oilfields, flooded western newsstands and bookstores that winter. The title reflected accurately the sentiments of Albertans. Suddenly, there were separatists everywhere: 500 in the small town of Airdrie, 1,000 at a sit-down luncheon in Calgary, 2,500 in the Jubilee Auditorium in Edmonton. They had buttons and T-shirts, bearing slogans like VIVE ALBERTA LIBRE. They had lots of money. They had a few big names, such as Carl Nickle, the grand old man of Canadian oil. Mostly, mercifully for Confederation, their leaders were zealots on the fringe, like Warren Blackman, a University of Calgary economist who used to harangue his audiences by jumping up and down in Adidas, and Elmer Knutson, a millionaire auto dealer who had developed the curious theory that the West didn't really need to separate, because it had never really joined Confederation.

The separatists generated many headlines, and much hatred. Alberta Liberals, presumably packed into the telephone booth from which they dialled, warned Trudeau not to come until at least after the New Year, for fear of violence. Nor was this fear exaggerated: in Edmonton, a service club speaker drew cheers when he said, "What happened to [John] Lennon, should happen to Trudeau."

For all their sound and fury, the separatists, ultimately, were losers fighting a lost cause. Strongest in the rural areas, they were fighting Trudeau and the NEP and the constitution less than they were fighting the late twentieth century and all that had happened to change their lives: bilingualism, feminism, metrication, legal abortions, gun control, abolition of capital punishment, multi-racial immigration. As early as January, the strength of the movement was ebbing. No more big rallies. No more donations.

Instead, Albertans, indeed most westerners, turned their anger inwards, to become more profoundly alienated. In March 1981, a poll by the Canada West Foundation showed that support for separation was still relatively insignificant compared to the previous October: 10 per cent across the west and 15 per cent in Alberta. But when it came to the next proposition, "Western Canadians get so few benefits from being part of Canada that they might as well go it on their own," support among all westerners had soared from 28 per cent to 36 per cent, and in Alberta from 30 per cent to 49 per cent. Overwhelmingly, by 79 per cent, westerners believed they were "ignored" in national politics, because "the political parties depend upon Quebec and Ontario for most of their votes."

Greed had helped fuel these attitudes; now that Albertans had their $8 billion Heritage Fund they were no more anxious to share it than are the newly-rich anywhere, all the more because joining the queue of indigents was despised Ontario. Some sentiments of racism towards French-Canadians didn't help. And in Saskatchewan as much as in Alberta, provincial civil servants and politicians had created their own private empires; for these new autocrats, the idea of being forced to share with the feds the fun of regulating and directing *their* industries was anathema.

But the core of the conflict was a clash of cultures. The west, and above all Alberta, is truly a world apart from the east. Western values are still shaped by the idea of the frontier, the idea of the land; memories of the dustbowl and of the depression linger, so that young Albertans coming of age in the affluent eighties are as much defined by the imprint of those unhappy far-off times as Quebecers are by what happened on the Plains of Abraham. In the way of professional Irishmen and professional Scots, westerners live up to their self image, as individualists (in politics, Albertans are in fact the least individualistic of all Canadians), as risk-takers, as earthy, open, unsophisticated, casual, and direct. Westerners, in other words, see themselves as everything that the east – clever, verbal, tricky, trendy – is not. Oil men, for instance, raged against NEP, not just because it would take away from their profits, but also because it would shove the clammy, limp-wristed fist of the eastern bureaucracy into an industry where deals in the millions are closed with a handshake.

Albertans felt at once a threat to their resources and a threat to their identity. Indeed, both threats were real. Setting aside the details of the oil price and revenue-sharing deal still to be negotiated between Ottawa and Alberta, the essentials of NEP – Canadianization; the shift to the Canada Lands – are already irreversible; Ottawa will progressively acquire greater and greater control over the national oil industry. Meanwhile, as cities like Calgary and Edmonton expand and soar upwards sprouting boutiques, French restaurants, wine bars, and branchplants of Toronto art galleries, they are becoming subtly more eastern; a homogenizing Hazelton Lanes lifestyle beckoning Albertans away from backyard barbecues and rodeos.

For all that Lougheed mostly used the argument of dollars and cents – i.e., Alberta's "rapidly dwindling reserves of conventional oil" – to justify his demands, he understood that the essential conflict was cultural. To keep his people behind him – often, in fact, they were ahead of him and far more demanding than he – he used phrases that spoke to Alberta pride, as in "Ottawa is trying to club us into submission...to force us to grovel." He never attacked Trudeau personally, nor Lalonde.* Instead, he spoke of "a small elite," "an Establishment" of un-named eastern bureaucrats and political operators, who had as their allies, "the eastern media."

Trudeau didn't get the message. In a speech in December 1980 in Winnipeg, he dismissed western separatism as "hysteria." Though correct enough in his analysis, Trudeau was a fool to say it out loud. Once again, it was demonstrated to westerners that their Prime Minister wasn't listening. They were crying out, in agony and anger, and he was just waiting for them to shut up so he could get back to making sure that his private view of Confederation would unfold as it should.

By mid-1981, oil itself had become irrelevent to the oil battle between Alberta and Ottawa. Already, the NEP was an accomplished fact. As a result of take-overs by Dome, the Canada Development Corporation, Petro-Canada and a dozen smaller companies that never made the headlines, more than $6 billion worth of foreign oil companies had become Maple-Leaf pure. It was true that more than a hundred drilling rigs from Alberta and B.C. had crossed the border to the U.S. (where industry "netbacks" were four times as

*Early in 1981, on a visit to Toronto, Lougheed startled his hosts at a small dinner party by saying of Lalonde, "He's the best Minister of Energy I've ever dealt with."

large). But it was also true that these rigs had been finding only natural gas, of which Canada already had more than it knew what to do with. More significantly, the lure of federal grants had more than doubled planned exploration activity from 1982 onwards in the offshore, and in the Beaufort Sea where the "elephant fields" Canada needs to achieve self-sufficiency are most likely to be found. Most significant of all, a world-wide glut had depressed international prices, nullifying the effect of Alberta's production cutbacks and relieving Canadians of the fear of being left to freeze in the dark. Even so, the loss of industrial activity and jobs, the weaker Canadian dollar and the psychic depression that affected the high-spirited entrepreneurship of Calgarians were all real costs. The greatest cost was that just as Albertans were poised to make their greatest contribution to the country, they were being told they weren't really necessary. This, much more than revenue shares and oil prices, had become the heart of the oil matter.

Restoring the east-west fault-line will take a long time, whether or not an Alberta-Ottawa oil deal is achieved this year, or is delayed until 1982. Almost as important now as the battle between east and west, is the battle taking shape within the west itself, between the big and the little westerners. Big westerners aspire to play their full role in Confederation, and are enraged that for so long they have been left out and taken for granted. Little westerners aspire only to be left alone, and are enraged at attempts to co-opt them into national enterprises.

Only another Prime Minister can bring the west back, fully, into Confederation. Between Trudeau and westerners, too much love has been lost, too much face is at stake, too many bitter memories intrude, for him to be able to vindicate himself out there. The west is beyond reach of his magic.

Late in 1980, Trudeau mused to an aide: "I saved Quebec. Someone else will have to save the west." At least, Trudeau comprehends his failure. What he has yet to comprehend fully is its extent, for which all Canadians will have to pay, probably for a decade, and perhaps for a generation. For the west, and not Quebec, is Canada's future now.

* * *

In Vancouver, late in February, 1981, reporters badgered Trudeau about all the difficulties he was having then with his constitutional resolution: the seven "dissident" premiers whom Blakeney had just joined to make an octet; the delaying tactics of the Conservatives; the opposition among British MPs. Trudeau paused an instant and then replied, "I am exhilarated by the struggle."

As this is being written, Trudeau's constitutional struggle remains unresolved. The Supreme Court has yet to rule whether his Constitution Act, 1981, is legal, in whole or in part. It's like not knowing whether the maiden slipped loose from her bonds before the train arrived. In fact, the old *Perils of Pauline* analogy is apt. It is difficult to recall a political contest in which the fortunes of the opposing sides see-sawed up and down so abruptly, so continuously, for so long.

On September 8, 1980, when he picked up the gavel at the head of the horseshoe-shaped table in Ottawa's old railway station turned Canadian Conference Centre, Trudeau looked to be irresistible. He had the polls, and his Parliamentary majority, behind him, and his referendum laurels were still fresh. Then, a leaked, federal strategy paper smudged his image, and the premiers matched him in debate more skillfully than anyone foresaw. Trudeau stormed ahead anyway, first on national TV, then at Parliament's opening on October 6. Ontario and New Brunswick joined him. Broadbent brought the NDP to his side. Only Clark, his nervous appearance masking his stubborn courage, opposed him, and seemed to have signed his political death warrant by doing so.

As so often, Trudeau, once ahead, over-reached himself. He used closure to cut off debate in the Commons, and set an impossible deadline – December 16 – for a joint Senate-Commons committee to hold public hearings and propose detailed changes to the 66-clause document. By February, Gallup found that 64 per cent of Canadians opposed the way Trudeau was doing things, although not what he was actually doing.

More trouble. At Westminster, where the 114-year-old BNA Act remains under lock and key in the records room of the Victoria Tower, British MPs turned bolshie after Trudeau told them they had to do what he wanted, "holding their noses"; as justification for not having to do what Trudeau wanted, an all-party foreign affairs committee concluded, in mid-February, that Westminster need not "accept unconditionally" Trudeau's resolution unless satisfied that the provinces were on side – which of course they weren't. In the meantime, the dissident premiers launched court challenges against the resolution. These looked to be no more than delaying tactics, until, on March 31, the Newfoundland Supreme Court ruled the resolution illegal unanimously. Sensing that their moment was at hand at last, the Conservatives brought Parliamentary debate to a halt through a remarkably effective rules filibuster. Confronted by two immovable obstacles, Trudeau wriggled between them: in exchange for an agreement by the Conservatives to end their filibuster, he agreed to wait for the Supreme Court's ruling before sending the resolution to Westminster. (As a fringe benefit, he satisfied the scruples of British MPs.) But for the Supreme Court, he was in the clear.

The public's mood mirrored these political ups and downs. At first, Canadians were mostly bemused, and indifferent. Trudeau stirred them to anger by his excessive haste. Canadians relaxed a bit when Trudeau extended the Joint Committee's televised hearings to February 9, 1981. When he accepted so many of the proposed amendments to the Charter of Rights – affecting the handicapped, women, native peoples, civil libertarians – Canadians applauded, and began to talk about "the new constitution" rather than, as always until then, of "*his* constitution." (During this period, Trudeau in fact was doing what he always criticized the premiers for trying to do – "bartering fish for rights.") A mood of exasperation took hold as the crisis went on and on and on. By June, 1981, public attitudes had shaken down into a mixture of relief and fascination: relief that the Supreme Court would either stamp the document with its imprimatur, or reject it; fascination that the opinions of nine elderly men could be so decisive – either elevating Trudeau to the pantheon of nation builders, in the company of Macdonald and Laurier, or consigning him to oblivion.

For all the twists and turns in this long, complex, at times exhilarating, at times melodramatic story, just two climactic confrontations really matter: the First Ministers Conference in Ottawa in September 1980, where Trudeau tried to negotiate with the premiers; the meeting in Ottawa in April 1981, where the premiers tried to negotiate with him. Both meetings failed. The point, though, is not to apportion the blame. The point is rather that failure, in both instances, was inevitable.

* * *

If not favourable, exactly, the portents for the September encounter seemed somewhat better than bleak. Through the summer, the federal-provincial Continuing Committee of Ministers and Officials, co-chaired by Chrétien and Romanow, had issued periodic reports of progress. Canadians wanted the matter settled. Canadians also wanted the unspoken "compact" of the referendum to be fulfilled. As for Trudeau, he was so determined to have his way that it was hard to see how he could be thwarted.

The roadblock that everyone remembers is the notorious "Kirby Memorandum," a strategy document signed by Federal-Provincial Relations Secretary Mike Kirby that advised Trudeau to pursue "divide-and-conquer" tactics with the premiers, and to accept that agreement was unlikely and therefore to stage-manage the meeting so that the premiers would come out looking like parochial ingrates. Copies of the document, which ended with a smart-aleck quote from Machiavelli, were leaked to the premiers by a (still undiscovered) "mole." Gleefully, they denounced Trudeau for "cynicism" and "manipulation." "If Machiavelli were alive today," one premier remarked, "he'd be quoting Trudeau."

In fact, the real trouble began earlier. A dinner on the eve of the conference, given by Governor-General Schreyer, at which Trudeau and the premiers were supposed to get clubby over coffee and cognac, ended abruptly when Trudeau, *lese majesté*, got up and left the table ahead of Schreyer. He was angry because, over the first course, the premiers announced they would ignore the Chrétien-Romanow proposal that on the morrow they get down to business immediately by debating those items on which agreement was closest to hand and instead insisted on making set opening speeches which were bound to emphasize the differences between them, as everyone played to his home audience. After a brief spat, Trudeau cooled down. He blew up again, and stalked out, when Bennett proposed that the conference should depart from the traditional practice of being chaired by the federal Prime Minister, and instead be co-chaired by Trudeau (as if he represented no more than one government among eleven) and by Manitoba's Sterling Lyon on behalf of the provinces.

So that in truth, from the moment they met – the Kirby memorandum was still more than a day in the offing – the two sides viewed each other with ingrained and ineradicable suspicion. Power, not persuasion, could alone decide the outcome. The debate had some high points: each with great passion and effectiveness, Trudeau and

Lyon debated the Charter of Rights, in essence arguing common sense versus the rule of law. Peckford suddenly emerged as a national figure, countering Lalonde's icy logic on offshore oil with gut feelings.

Never, though, through a week of argument, was the prospect of an agreement even close. On the next to last day, the premiers went to 24 Sussex to present Trudeau with thirteen, non-negotiable demands. Since the list included such items as Lévesque's demand for "the right of self-determination," which everyone already knew Trudeau would never negotiate, the meeting was an exercise in futility. Trudeau droned through the list: "Yes. Yes. No. Yes. No. No," and so on. But the premiers had elevated futility to high public policy by insisting that before any one of the eleven First Ministers could agree to anything, everyone had to agree to everything. "The rule of unanimity," as Trudeau put it, "has become a tyranny."

The deeper truth was that on either side, the two radically opposed views about the nature of Confederation were no longer held tentatively, but were carved into stone. This indeed had become apparent much earlier, at their brief initial meeting the previous May in the immediate after-glow of the referendum result. Trudeau had circulated a draft preamble to the constitution that began, "We the people of Canada, freely united..."

"No," said the premiers, who maintained the defining preamble of the constitution should begin, "The provinces of Canada, freely united..."

If it accomplished nothing else, the September meeting, as Trudeau said at his closing press conference, "brought into collision two views of the nature of Canada."

Neither in detail nor in nuance did these two opposing views change during the succeeding seven months. The fortunes of battle varied. The colours nailed to the masts stayed put. By April 1981, Trudeau once again seemed to be advancing as impregnably as he had before the September conference. He had on his side all the Liberals, and all but four of the federal New Democrat MPs. He had favourable decisions from two (Quebec and Manitoba) out of three provincial courts. According to the most recent news out of London, he also now had the support of most British MPs, even if considerations of *realpolitick* had swayed their decision more than of political philosophy. Debate in the Commons was due to end soon by agreement; by the same agreement Trudeau now needed only to wait for the formality – a pure formality, as most observers then took for granted – of a hearing by the Supreme Court before the judges proclaimed his constitutional resolution legal. As for the eight dissident premiers, "They," said Trudeau with a shrug, "can never agree to anything."

On April 17, 1981, the eight premiers came to Ottawa, determined to prove Trudeau wrong, and determined also to prove to Canadians that they too could do good for the country. One by one, * in front of the television cameras, they signed a piece of paper that Lyon, acting as chairman, described as "an historic document." This was titled, "Canadian Patriation Plan." Solemnly, the premiers decided that they would agree to patriate the constitution from Britain, and attach to it a modified, "Vancouver" amending formula that, effectively, would allow each province to opt out of each and every future constitutional amendment. The Plan included no Charter of Rights, no mobility rights to allow Canadians to search for work in any province, no educational language rights for minorities, and no commitment to equalization. It amounted, said Trudeau dismissively, to "incremental separatism . . . a Confederation of 500 shopping centres." The premiers left Ottawa. Within a few days, no one could remember what it was they had agreed to, or cared. Even Clark, who had for months fought Trudeau every way he knew how to ensure that the premiers could be heard, pronounced himself "disappointed."

On behalf of these premiers, MacLean of PEI explained what it was they had been after. "Canada is not an association of peoples," he said. "Canada is an association of provinces." As representatives of those provinces they could not, in their view, give away anything at all. Between this view and Trudeau's, there was no meeting ground, only a battle-ground between at best, determined opponents, and at worst, implacably suspicious enemies.

On some day in late summer or early autumn, while this book is somewhere between printer and binder, the Supreme Court will decide Trudeau's fate. If he wins, he wins everything. Yet even if he loses, he hasn't necessarily lost everything. Against that eventuality he has prepared an escalating series of counter-attacks, ranging from a snap election based upon a new, if more limited resolution, to

Lougheed of Alberta, Bennett of British Columbia, Lyon of Manitoba, Peckford of Newfoundland, John Buchanan of Nova Scotia, Angus MacLean of PEI, Lévesque of Quebec, Blakeney of Saskatchewan.

imposing the full weight of the existing BNA Act on the provinces. He will not give up until he has won. He will continue to be exhilarated by the struggle.

Trudeau's constitutional resolution, and even more his unilateral manner of imposing it, have forced Canadians to choose between opposing views about the soul and vital principle of their country. Yet, ultimately, the choice is unreal. To comprehend this, all Trudeau really needed to do was look out of his back windows at 24 Sussex, and gaze north across the Ottawa River. In the province of Quebec, support for Trudeau's constitutional resolution is overwhelming; Quebecers trust him implicitly to get the most for them, even though in fact, his resolution gives them nothing they haven't achieved already, other than the formal entrenchment of both official languages, and indeed takes from them their right to set the linguistic rules for education in their own province. Yet Quebecers also trust Lévesque implicitly, and on April 13, 1981, re-elected him overwhelmingly. Canadians, in the end don't want to choose between these two opposing views. They want each to co-exist side by side, in illogical, untidy, sometimes argumentative, sometimes peaceable union. Forcing Canadians to choose was the quintessential style of Trudeau. But Macdonald and Laurier and King and above all, Lester Pearson, could have told him, it was not the Canadian style.

* * *

The most difficult aspect of Trudeau's post-election story to pin down is when he will end it. Some readers of entrails interpreted Coutts's departure in July 1981 as the signal that he expected his master soon to follow. In fact, the opposite is more likely the case; the point being that Coutts left because he judged Trudeau would stay on long enough – a year or more – to allow him to make his reputation as an on-stage politician instead of back-room manipulator, and so qualify himself to contest the leadership.

Trudeau himself has said only that he would leave "well before" the next election. No one would be astounded if he changed his mind, yielded to a "spontaneous draft" and contested the next election. With no challenging international job in prospect, the charms of retiring to full-time single parenthood must surely be mixed. The best guess is that he will remain until at least the winter of 1982-1983, and will then retire to allow his successor to do as he did, and vault directly from convention to election. Nowadays, he likes to play cat-and-mouse with his ministers: at one cabinet meeting in the spring of 1981, he remarked of a long-term project under discussion, "Of course, most of us won't be around to see this through." Then Trudeau paused, and lifted an eyebrow. "I mean, of course, most of *you*." Increasingly, he is turning his attention to "second phase" projects, such as proportional representation and reform of such national institutions as the Senate and to economic development, which will require his attention for at least a year.

Even so, trying to guess what Trudeau will do is a fool's game. The single safe judgement is that he won't make up his mind until he has to. He lives in the now; he will leave in the now. Don't count on him not climbing back through a bedroom window, though, with an enigmatic half-smile on his face, and a rose in his lapel.

* * *

In this book I have tried to describe and to analyze Pierre Elliott Trudeau, and to catalogue and assess his record.

Neither task has been straightforward. He has "applied his creativity to his personality," in the phrase of a friend. He has made himself his life's work, so that, in contradistinction to most public personalities, Trudeau has become progressively more interesting and more complex during his years in power than during his earlier formative and unfinished years.

As for his record, Trudeau's is the hardest to score of all our sixteen Prime Ministers because his penultimate achievements – the referendum, the constitution, his status as an electoral invincible – depend so critically on a fluke. Had he remained in retirement in December 1979 as he so nearly did, some other Liberal, just about any other Liberal, would have won the laurels that have come so easily to Trudeau in 1980. Weighing Trudeau's record up to the time of his defeat in 1979, historians probably would have granted him no higher status than the equivocal one of failed hero: an exceptional political leader, but a disappointment as a Prime Minister.

Trudeau has been almost supernaturally lucky. He returned by a fluke; in 1972 he hung on to power by the skin of his teeth; in between, in 1976 and 1977, his life-long opponent, Lévesque, rescued him from the brink of oblivion. And yet, and this is the first central truth about him, from first to last he has had the flair, and the daring, and the guile to create his own luck. Luck may be a gift; it is also a talent.

The second central truth about Trudeau derives from the nature of his relationship with Canadians. The source of his appeal is his intellect and style; the source of his allure is sexual.

Partly, the relationship between Trudeau and the rest of us has been that of ill-matched partners in a long, chaotic love affair: passages of sweet serenity followed by sullen incommunicative stretches that flare into rancorous anger, that in turn dissolves into yet one more feverish reconciliation. Partly, it is an edgy *modus vivendi* between an imperious, self-willed general and his self-doubting troops. Whenever things go wrong we blame our leader and demand that he leave, but the moment he does we feel lost and demand that our Single Combat champion ride back with bugles blowing.

At core, the relationship is the bond between magician and audience. The lone figure at centre stage daring us not to believe; Canadians willing him to succeed in his sorcery.

Remarkably, for a country so often put down for being unadventurous and meagre in its imagination, we have elected three Magi in our brief history: Macdonald, Laurier, Trudeau, and we have clung onto each as long as we could. Each of them, Diefenbaker too in his wayward way, was larger than life; each made us feel different because he was there.

Two of these Northern Magi truly made a difference. Macdonald, by Confederation and by his railway, laid the foundation of our National Dream. A century later, Trudeau added bilingualism as a keystone arch. These two, alone among sixteen, have reinvented history in their own image.

Yet Trudeau's talismanic talents are different from those of Macdonald and Laurier. Their magic could be summed up in a single defining phrase: Laurier's "sunny ways," Macdonald's "ugly charm." Trudeau's magic is quicksilver. He is a litany of contradictions. A shy egocentric. "A solitary sort of fellow," in his own words, who yearns for the spotlight. A populist aristocrat. A Philosopher King who in 1974 and 1980 conducted two of the most intellectually barren campaigns of recent times. An apostle of the "global ethic of sharing" who hoards his own fortune and who "doesn't carry other people's burdens," in the words of a friend. An intellectual who delights in the company of artists, who as

Prime Minister has played almost no role in the cultural life of the country. Trudeau inspires love, from his friends and from the crowd, yet in his person he is far from easy to like. He is a Peter Pan, "co-terminous with each new generation," yet his attitude toward women is that of a Victorian. A wit without a sense of humour. Of all our leaders, he is the boldest, not to say the most reckless, but when it comes to the hardest issues, those involving the economy and energy, he has been strikingly timid and conventional. He is the civil libertarian who will soon give us a Bill of Rights, almost exactly a decade after, through the War Measures Act, he suspended the most basic right of all, *habeas corpus*. His record, like his character, does not scan.

Trying to find a key to all these riddles, at the same time, trying to cast Trudeau into an historical perspective, the image from the past that has kept on intruding is that *fin de siècle* British pro-consul, George Nathaniel Curzon. One difference is that never in a thousand years would Trudeau have allowed a woman as clever as Elinor Glyn to get under his skin. What the two had in common, beyond travel as religion, beyond federalism as a first principle, was the quality of being at once a romantic and a ruthless pragmatist, a duality that kept on confounding opponents who expected them to fit into one or the other pigeon hole. They were both the kind of men who despised sycophancy yet induced it, almost playfully, in others; egocentrics who sculptured their own personas into works of art. Each gave the impression of living on the outermost edge of his own time and place, and wishing he was somewhere else. Just as Curzon, in James Morris's phrase, "was less at home with the British bourgeoisie than he was with a delicate Maharajah, an entertaining Kurd or the wild chieftains of the Northwest Frontier," so Trudeau is less at home with Canadians than with John Lennon, or Fidel Castro, or among Tibetan monks. "He seems impatient being a Canadian," a European journalist remarked shrewdly after the Venice Summit in June 1980. Perhaps the crucial difference between Curzon and Trudeau is the difference between Canadian-ness and British-ness. Even if we occasionally turn on Trudeau for it, we cherish him for not seeming Canadian; the British never forgave Curzon for being different, and denied him the Prime Ministership.

As the least Canadian of all our Prime Ministers, Trudeau's greatest failure, beyond doubt, has been not to understand the nature of the country that he governed. He never comprehended that Canada's true identity lies neither in "diversity" nor in "pluralistic federalism" nor in any of these kinds of declamatory phrases, but in *civility*. If our record of civil liberties is better than that of most countries, and if our immigration policy is respectably liberal, the reason lies in an ingrained if inarticulate sense of civility, a feeling for the fitness of things, a social habit of amiability, and an attitude, if not quite of acceptance, then of tolerance. Of all our leaders, Trudeau has been the least civil. Much of the backlash against bilingualism, many of the tensions between Quebec and the rest of the country, western alienation as a running sore, federal-provincial bickering, the malaise that soured Canadian politics from 1975 to 1979, could have been avoided by a Prime Minister whose ways were our ways. Instead, Trudeau delighted in fomenting confrontations, because he knew he could nearly always win them. He turned opponents into "enemies." He used rhetorical overkill as a primary instrument of communication. Like the boy at Brébeuf, he has never played fair.

His greatest accomplishment, beyond a doubt, is to have inspired Canadians to reach beyond ourselves, toward excellence. In a nation of life-insurers, he is a risk taker. He has challenged us, intimidated us, tantalized us, in part because we know he has "lived his dream" as all of us would like to do, in part because we know he personifies that least Canadian of all endeavours: the pursuit of excellence as an end in itself. He plays for keeps, with his mind, with his body, with his political power, with us. This, in the end, is the quality in the man that persists. This, in the end, is the magic.

Index

412

413

414